Nasarvanji Framji Bilimoria

Zoroastrianism in the light of theosophy

Nasarvanji Framji Bilimoria
Zoroastrianism in the light of theosophy
ISBN/EAN: 9783743335646
Manufactured in Europe, USA, Canada, Australia, Japa
Cover: Foto ©Lupo / pixelio.de

Manufactured and distributed by brebook publishing software (www.brebook.com)

Nasarvanji Framji Bilimoria

Zoroastrianism in the light of theosophy

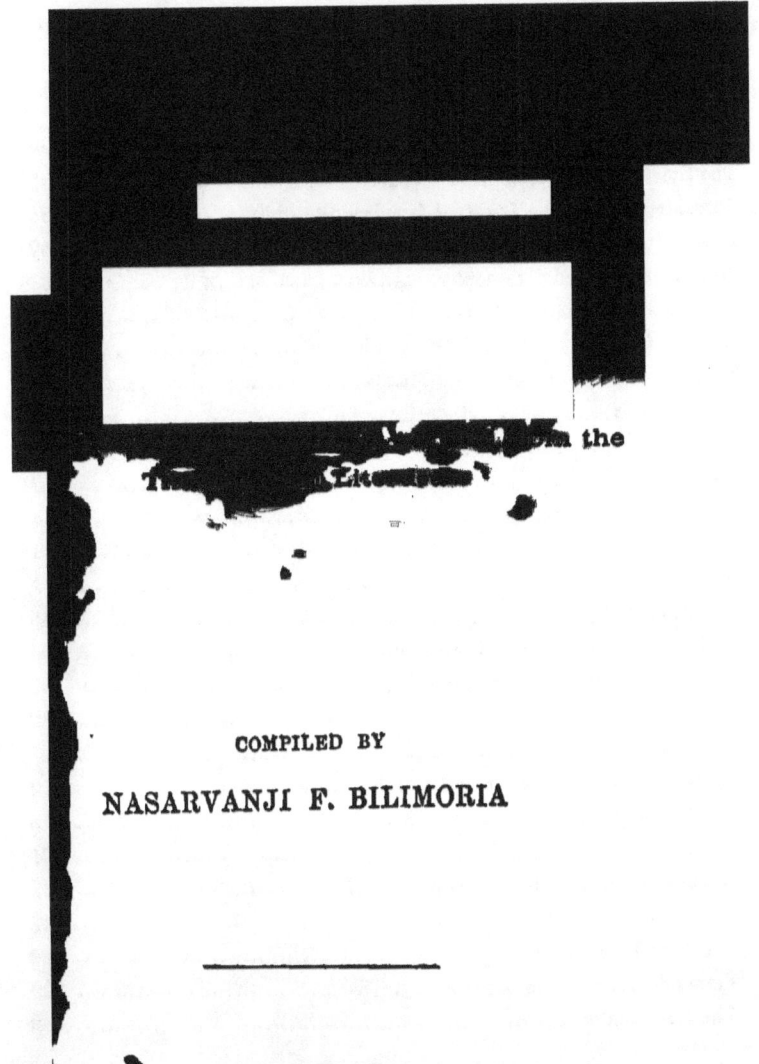

COMPILED BY

NASARVANJI F. BILIMORIA

BOMBAY:
"BLAVATSKY LODGE," THEOSOPHICAL SOCIETY.
MADRAS:
HEAD-QUARTERS, THEOSOPHICAL SOCIETY, ADYAR.
LONDON AGENTS:
THE THEOSOPHICAL PUBLISHING SOCIETY,

CONTENTS.

	PAGE.
The Spirit of the Zoroastrian Religion	1
Zoroastrianism in the Light of Occult Philosophy	35
The Scriptures	52
Zoroastrianism and Theosophy	63
The Septenary Nature of Man	71
Zravâné Akerne and Zravâné Daregokhadâté	76
The Sun as a Symbol of Ahura-Mazda	79
Ahunavairya	84
The Lunar Orb	88
The Iranian Oannës	90
Gayomard and Zarathushtra	94
The Sacred Haoma Tree	98
Evolution	109
The Philosophy	145
Philosophy and Ethics of Zoroasters	154
The Ethical System of Zoroaster	169
God, Man and Mediator	182
An Afterword	208
Zoroastrianism—Chaldean and Greek	212
The Sun-worship	228
The Fire-worship	254
Manashni—Gavashni—Kunashni	281
The Mahatmas or Adepts	312
The Last Parsi Adep	322
Transmigration in the Avesta	329
The Ceremonies	332

INTRODUCTION.

THE history of the world's religions is contained to a very insignificant extent, we may believe, in the various scriptures that have come down to our days from antiquity. Such writings are few in number, and often comprise but fragments of the primitive cults. A much larger proportion is to be found in mural pictures and inscriptions, architectural carvings and symbolical embellishments and crumbling ruins. Of some of the old religions we were quite ignorant at the beginning of this century, but are now learning much from the results of excavations, the discovery of tile libraries, the decipherment of hieroglyphs. Sometimes a new 'find' shocks our fixed ideas to their bases, or compels us to recast our chronologies and alter our beliefs. At this moment, for example, M. Le Plongeon, the French archæologist, proclaims that he has found by deciphering the inscriptions in Yucatan that all the ancient schools of the Mysteries, including those of Eleusis, Samothrace, even Egypt, were derived from the mother-school and fountain head in Mayax and the Quichi country: he even discovers in the simple Greek alphabet a distinct narrative of the destruction of Atlantis. Early in this century, books were written to prove the derivation of the Sanskrit from the Hebrew; Huc and Gabet saw in the ritualistic observances of Tibetan Buddhism a travesty of those of the Roman Catholic Church; Western orientalists have steadfastly laboured to minimize the dates of Indian civilisation and literature. Sometimes they have done this in the interest of Biblical chronology, sometimes, perhaps, to save the West from the mortification of having its own brief historical cycle made to seem still briefer and less impressive by comparison with those of the ancient peoples. A certain class among them, devoid of reverence for antiquity and for the ancient teachers of mankind, seem bent upon modernising everything, so far as possible, and by sharply contrasting the practical discoveries of our time with the supposed practical ignorance of our ancestors, to flood our sky with a blaze of glory. The close of the 19th century finds us, as it were, standing open-mouthed amid a host of dissolving views, wherein hereditary misconceptions of human evolution and dogmatic aspects of exoteric religions, born of more recent ancestral ignorance, are melting away, and the long veiled truth is bursting forth into view. We shall enter the new century with vastly broader conceptions of things and much greater capabilities for reading nature's riddles.

In no department of knowledge is this process more strongly exhibited than in that of religion. A new light is shining into the old temple crypts, making clear much that was hidden, putting life into decrepit carcases, giving a master-key to open all masked doors. Christianity has already developed its school of the Higher Criticism, and is casting into a burial trench, one by one, the horrid exotericisms which made it revolting, alike to the free-thinker and the spiritual-minded aspirant after truth. The Christianity of 1950 will be as little like that of 1850 as the ocean travel of to-day is unlike that of a century ago. A clearer, nobler, more reasonable and impregnable cult will evolve itself and it will hold its own with the best of the world-faiths. If Mahomedanism has its dreary exoteric dogmas, it has also its school of transcendental exegesis, its rules for spiritual development, its adepts and chelâs. If Judaism has its grossly materialistic side, so also has it the other and grander in its Holy Kabbalah. Hinduism, twenty years ago scorned and denounced as a body of crass idolatry, brutifying its worshippers, a mere cumberer of the earth that must be swept away by Western effort in the best interests of the race, has now —thanks largely to the work of the Theosophical Society and its enlightened individual members—taken in new life and fresh beauty; its literature is found to be incomparably rich and inspirating, and thousands of Western students are reverently sitting at the feet of the Rishis and their pupils.

INTRODUCTION.

Of all the grand old religions, Zoroastrianism, or Mazdianism, is until now in worst case. To this deplorable fact various causes have contributed. Among these, the destruction of the Persian Empire and the upheaval of its social order by military conquerors; wholesale conversions under compulsion; the ruthless destruction of temples, religious books and libraries; the driving into exile of their most pious families, who took with them bare scraps and fragments of once copious scriptures; the degradation of the terrorized remnant of the nation who stopped at home but did not abjure their faith; and the deadening effect on the exiles of a policy of eager money-getting, with neglect of spiritual teachers and teachings, the loss of understanding of their fragmentary sacred books and of the language in which they are written, and the placing of worldly success and worldly honours above all other subjects of endeavour,—are to be borne in mind.

The time has come when every pious Zoroastrian must choose between seeing his noble religion dying out of the sight of men, or doing something to prevent this catastrophe. For a catastrophe it is, when the human family loses a form of religious belief and practice which is all sufficient in itself to ensure human happiness, promote enlightenment, abate crime, foster virtue, establish the law of justice among men, and develope the higher, nobler nature, which allies us to the gods and places us at the pinacle of the scheme of evolution.

For nearly twenty years now, I have been on intimate terms with enlightened Indian Parsis and the sincere friend and well-wisher of their religion. It has been very sad to find that the community, as a whole, has not advanced within that time, that, with noble exceptions, they are still eager after money, grand houses, luxuries, fine equipages and government titles; but, at the same time, it rejoices my heart to see—as any one may in the essays which comprise the present volume—that some of the best Parsi thinkers have begun to apply to their religion the key of Theosophy, and found that it lets them into various obscure chambers of their temple. It is not for an outsider like myself to say how far the interpretations and inferences thus suggested are warranted by the facts, but most certainly a good beginning has been made, one which I trust may be pushed forward by the wide circulation of this book of my dear colleague and friend, Mr. Bilimoria. It is quite possible that, since the exiled Persians settled in India, the primitive religion has become more or less infiltrated by ceremonials and beliefs quite foreign to its spirit, and that our contemporary Theosophical students, unconscious of that fact, may have wasted time in trying to understand the incongruous, and adopted unwarranted views respecting the old religion. The use of *Nirang*, I just cite as an instance. But if this surmise be correct, the mistakes will all be eliminated in time with the progress of research ; the important thing is not to relax their present efforts, but to persevere with courage and persistence until the Punchayet, compelled by the whole body of an enlightened Parsi public opinion, shall organize a scheme of research that will yield the splendid results which are possible. What may be reasonably expected becomes clear when we look at what has been discovered in Palestine and Egypt by the explorers sent out by Christian capitalists in the interest of their religion. Since I first suggested archæological research to the Parsis in 1882,* sixteen precious years have been wasted, years in which they might have obtained highly important results, and closed the mouths of those critics who have been trying to rob the religion of its claim to a venerable antiquity. In view of the practically boundless means available among wealthy Parsis who since 1882 have shown their splendid generosity in gifts of enormous sums to local charities, and who, if rightly influenced, would have gladly given to this more sacred purpose, it is most saddening to think of this long blindness to duty and to opportunities. Not once, but

---

* *Vide* my lecture on "The Spirit of the Zoroastrian Religion" in this book.

many times, I have urged the subject upon the community, and now that the Panchâyet has for Secretary a scholar of European fame, Ervad Jivanji J. Modi, I have some hope that practical work may be begun.

Two years ago, on my way to Europe I had consultations with Parsi friends about the possibility of finding in some public library or private collection other portions of Mazdian scriptures than those known at Bombay, Navsari, Surat and Poona; I thought it worth their while to at least make a research. It seemed to me that as the Mahomedan armies were usually attended by learned Moulvis, who had brought home with them books and manuscripts from conquered countries, nothing would be more likely than that by searching in centres of Mahomedan civilisation the missing books and literary fragments might be found, at least in Arabic translations; just as we are now finding that some of the most precious of the old Buddhist books are gathered into the libraries of Tibetan monasteries. So I took from my friend Dr. Jivanji, letters of introduction to eminent Zend scholars like Monsieur Menant, of the Institute, and Dr. Mills, my compatriot, and that greatest of living archæologists, Professor Flinders Petrie, of University College, London. These were duly presented and the several answers of those gentlemen to my questions are now for the first time published. The awful visitation of the bubonic plague in Bombay which has ravaged the community and cast a black pall of grief over it, has prevented my sooner returning to the public discussion of our present subject. The reader will observe that all the great authorities to whom I addressed myself concur in the belief that it is scarcely worth while to hope to find, in the collections known to them, any of the missing portions of the Mazdian sacred texts. At the same time, all are agreed that there is a very good prospect of acquiring by a well planned course of excavations a good deal of what we desire. Professor Flinders Petrie expresses himself clearly upon this point, and he has certainly placed the Parsi community of Bombay under obligations by his kind offer to take under his supervision and instruction, any competent young Parsi whom the Panchâyet may select to work as their representative and agent, with a skilled English excavator, to be hereafter commissioned to enter upon this most important and promising field of research.

H. S. OLCOTT.

DOCUMENTARY ADDENDA.

[*Translation.*]

[FROM H. S. OLCOTT TO MONSIEUR MENANT, DE L'INSTITUT.]

PARIS, *29th June 1898.*

VENERABLE SIR,

The commission with which I have been honoured by some Parsis of Bombay is to consult you and other learned Zendists as to the practicability of recovering any fragments of their scriptures and other valuable information as to the origin, extent and value of the system of the religious teaching bequeathed to the world by Zoroaster, his disciples and the great Adepts of his faith. It is very important to refute, if possible, the recent published theory that Zoroastrianism is a composite system of comparatively modern origin. It is also of the greatest moment that some of the texts lost in the crisis of Persian affairs, when the invading Mussalman conquerors did their best to extirpate the religion of the country, and drove into exile the few faithful Zoroastrians, who would not give up their ancestral faith and who escaped the sword of the enemy, should be found. If, in any public library, in any part of the world, or in any private collection within your knowledge, there are ancient books, MSS. or fragmentary Gâthâs; any inscriptions, like those of Asoka, for instance, which embody the principles of the ancient religion; any reports to learned societies giving accounts of important discoveries at Bactriana or elsewhere, which can be copied and translated, I pray you to give me the facts in writing, so that they may be brought to the notice of the Parsi Punchayet. We have every reason to hope that, when these facts are made known, the generous and pious members of that body of Zoroastrians will supply the necessary funds and take the necessary steps to secure the precious information for themselves and their children. I shall feel deeply obliged by your embodying your reply in the form of sections, dealing separately with the above heads of enquiry, and thus increasing the load of obligation under which your distinguished literary labours have already placed the good Parsis of India.

INTRODUCTION.

M. Menant's Reply.

[*Translation.*]

68, Rue Madame,
Paris, *24th August 1896.*

Dear Sir,

I have received your letter of 29th June last, and thank you for the very interesting details which it embodies. Unfortunately I have nothing to add to the information that I have given you verbally, on the manuscripts which may be consulted at Paris relative to the Zoroastrian religion. All these manuscripts have been long known and the *savants* who devote themselves to the study of the Zend-Avesta have had them at their disposal. Although I may be very incompetent, yet I do not think that it is there that one could find *new proofs* of the antiquity of the Mazdian religion, which, moreover, seems to me quite sufficiently established; but if there is still something more needed, it is rather, as I have told you, verbally, in purely archæological discoveries that one might, perhaps, meet with new documents. In pursuance of this idea I have put you in relations with M. Blanc, who has a special knowledge of the Central Asian provinces where explorations might throw great light upon this important problem of Zoroastrian history. I believe that you have been able to come to a good understanding with him, and that he has given you all necessary explanations on this subject.

Accept, dear sir, assurances of my sincere regard.

MENANT.

Unfortunately the Reverend Dr. Mills was so fully occupied that he could not give me his views in writing, as I had requested, but having passed a social evening with him, I found that he concurred in the opinions of M. Menant, and, in a note of September 12 (1896), he writes, briefly:—

"As to the MSS., that matter has all been in the hands of experts for a long time. We do not think any more MSS. can be found."

In the course of my researches, I was fortunate enough to become acquainted with M. Blochet, of the Manuscripts section of the Bibliothèque Nationale, a gentleman whose reputation as a Zendist is great. To my letter of inquiry he replied as follows :—

[*Translation.*]

NATIONAL LIBRARY,
PARIS, 1st September 1896.

To COLONEL H. S. OLCOTT.

SIR,

I have received the letter which you have done me the honor to address to me, and hasten to reply. The question which you propound is very complex, but I shall try to give you, as well as I can, all possible information that may help the Parsis of Bombay, in the researches that they wish to undertake.

The manuscripts which can interest them are of two kinds: those in Zend, containing their sacred scriptures, the Avesta ; and secondly, those in Pehlvi, Pazend, and Persian, treating of the Mazdian religion.

The Zend manuscripts preserved at Paris in the Bibliothèque Nationale, as well as at Copenhagen, London and Oxford, contain no other texts than those known in Westergaard's Standard Edition, now reproduced with some improvements in the German Edition of Geldner. It is absolutely useless for the Parsis to pursue their researches in this direction, for it would be only to waste time.

The Libraries abovenamed contain quite a large number of Pehlvi, Pazend and other manuscripts which are either translations or commentaries on the Avesta or religious treatises of all sorts. I think that, with a few exceptions, the Parsis of Bombay will not find in these manuscripts facts not already known among themselves. All, in fact, have been brought from Hindustan since the middle of the last century, and certainly, in the majority of cases, the Parsis have kept the originals from which the above have been copied. There are, it is true, exceptions, as the most ancient manuscripts of the *Bundahish*, which is at Copenhagen, and known in Europe as " K 20 ."

You will understand that it is almost impossible to indicate to you in a single letter those manuscripts which might be of interest to the Parsis, I should first have to know what they actually possess to verify if there is not in the Bibliothèque Nationale some book not in India or older than their own copies.

. It will always be a serious obstacle to the progress of Mazdian study that we, Europeans, cannot know exactly what interesting documents of this religion are available to-day in India, and that the Parsis, on the other hand, do not know exactly what documents are at our disposal in Europe. Of course I have not in mind a simple list of titles, which would not help us forward in the least unless we could have in our hands the manuscripts themselves, but a catalogue scientifically prepared and in great detail. To meet this difficulty to the extent of my means and fill this gap, I have composed a catalogue of Zend manuscripts, &c., in the Bibliothèque Nationale, which, however, I do not offer as a model of the sort, but which circumstances of a very material nature oblige me to keep in manuscript.*

The Parsis are rich enough to be able to indulge themselves in the luxury of making known to the world the treasures of their libraries and private collections, and this is the sole basis on which it will ever be possible to build up an exact knowledge of the Mazdian religion. I believe that your relations with the Indians, dear Colonel, are such that you will be able to convey to them the ideas which I have now ventured to express to you.

Accept, sir, the assurance of my greatest regard.

E. BLOCHET,

Attaché at the Bibliothèque Nationale, Paris.

In another note of the 1st September M. Blochet informs me that he wishes to publish certain texts of great interest for Mazdianism, but cannot do so for lack of funds. The languid interest felt in France for these Oriental researches prevents his finding the necessary opportunities, and he asks me whether the Parsis of Bombay will not come forward to furnish the capital required, a comparatively trifling sum. I hope that the interest that will be felt in this present book may lead to his most laudable object being accomplished.

[FROM ERVAD JIVANJI J. MODI TO PROFESSOR W. M. FLINDERS PETRIE.]

OFFICE OF THE TRUSTEES OF THE PARSI PANCHÂYET
FUNDS AND PROPERTIES,

131, HORNBY ROAD,

BOMBAY, *29th April, 1898.*

TO PROFESSOR FLINDERS PETRIE,
University College, London.

SIR,

You know that the regions of Central Asia were once either inhabited by the ancient Zoroastrians or were under their direct or indirect

---

* M. Blochet explained to me that he could not afford the small cost of publication, say 300 to 350 fcs. The Panchâyet could scarcely apply so small a sum to better profit for their religion.—H. S. O.

influence. So the Parsis or the modern Zoroastrians, being the decendants of those ancient Zoroastrians, take an interest in these regions. They would welcome any information obtained in these regions that would throw some light on their ancient literature and on the manners, customs and history of their ancient Fatherland of Irân.

I was directed by the Trustees of the Parsi Panchâyet to request the different Asiatic Societies of Europe to be good enough to bring the abovementioned matter to the notice of their oriental scholars travelling through, and taking interest in, Central Asia.

Now I write this to you as a well-known Archæologist and organizer of exploration parties, to enlist your sympathy in the above matter. If you, or your brother explorers, scholars, or travellers will in the course of your explorations pay some attention to the above matter, and will put yourselves in literary communication in English with us, your contributions on these subjects will be very gratefully received. The Trustees will be glad to patronize any publications in English treating of the researches in these regions from an Irânian point of view.

This will be kindly handed to you by Colonel Olcott, who takes a great interest in our religion and in the past and present history of our community. He is of opinion that there is still a good deal to be done in Central Asia in archæological and literary researches from our Irânian point of view. We shall be glad if you will kindly exchange your views with this good-hearted gentleman on the subject and make us any definite practicable suggestion.

Yours faithfully,
ERVAD JIVANJI J. MODI.

[FROM H. S. OLCOTT TO THE SAME.]

MEMORANDUM—

The Secretary of the Parsi Central Committee [Panchâyet] of Bombay wants practical advice as to what can be done—

(a) Towards proving the antiquity of the Zoroastrian religion;
(b) Its relationship with other religions;
(c) Recovering any fragments of its lost Scriptures.

Presumably, the only available methods are:—

1. Excavations.
2. Search in old libraries of Oriental countries.
3. Search in Western libraries.

INTRODUCTION.

Professor Flinders Petrie is respectfully asked—

I. To indicate where excavations should begin.
II. Whether he can say in which countries and libraries search should be begun.
III. Whether he has reason to believe that such search would be fruitful.
IV. If he will kindly say what sums should be annually provided for each of the two departments of research.
V. Whether he can recommend any pupil of his own whom he thinks conspicuously competent to take charge of either the one or the other of the departments of research.
VI. What salary such person would expect.

Professor Petrie's own Egyptian experience fits him admirably to give the required information, and his help will be highly valued by the Secretary of the Panchâyet and his colleagues.

H. S. OLCOTT.

14, Buckingham St., Strand,
15th July 1896.

[FROM PROFESSOR W. M. FLINDERS PETRIE TO H. S. OLCOTT.]

UNIVERSITY COLLEGE,
LONDON, 25th July 1896.

DEAR SIR,

In reply to your request for the practical details of what seems most promising for research in early Persia, I would say—

(1) Excavation is certain to yield results in any country which held a great civilization, if properly carried out.

(2) The cost of the whole work of one explorer might be reasonably put at about £1,000 a year. *Everything* included £1,500 should be plenty. More than this cannot be spent by one man, with proper supervision.

(3). The localities I can say nothing about, they should be best settled by a preliminary study of Persian history and a visit to the country working on other excavations. The general considerations are to avoid places which have been occupied in late times, and to trust to extensive clearances in suitable sites. Three-fourths of my best results come from wide clearances, and not from following special clues.

(4) Whoever goes for such work should spend some months on practical excavations for antiquities first, so as to learn the methods and indications. I will gladly have such a student with me in Egypt.

The best practical course would be to get the Indian Government to move for permission from the Shah, after the country has been examined, to send out a trained Englishman who knows the East, and is practised in excavating (one student of mine might be suitable), and might well be associated with some energetic young Parsi who was trained in the literature and well known in the Indian community, and who should form a close link between Bombay and the work.

For the literary research one suitable person might be Professor Ross, who is just appointed as the best Persian scholar available for this College. He is young, active and fond of travelling; and is familiar with Persian, Arabic, Russian and with Oriental ways. He could not have leave long enough for excavation, but for literary work that can be done within a fixed time, he might do well. I do not know him personally, as he has not yet entered on his work here.

Yours truly,
W. M. FLINDERS PETRIE.

[FROM PROFESSOR W. M. FLINDERS PETRIE TO THE SECRETARY, PARSI PANCHÂYET.]

UNIVERSITY COLLEGE,
LONDON, *9th July 1898.*

SIR,

I need hardly say how gladly I should do anything I could to forward research in the Irânian regions; and what satisfaction it is to see the able descendants of so noble a race turning their attention to research in their history and origins.

My own work, however, lies so entirely in Egypt, I see in that country so very much more than I can ever hope to explore, that it is hopeless for me to think of taking an active part in the work in other lands. There is however one line in which I might perhaps assist you. If you should ever intend to excavate any ancient sites of Persian cities, it would be a great pleasure to me to receive at my work in Egypt any students who may wish to undertake such work, and to give them such training in the methods of accurate research and record in excavation, as might increase the value and certainty of any exploration that they might undertake. Beyond this I fear that my good will is all that I can offer to such research.

Yours very truly,
W. M. FLINDERS PETRIE.

THE SECRETARY,
PARSI PANCHÂYET, BOMBAY.

The best practical course would be to get the Indian Government to move for permission from the Shah, after the country has been examined, to send out a trained Englishman who knows the East, and is practised in excavating (one student of mine might be suitable), and might well be associated with some energetic young Parsi who was trained in the literature and well known in the Indian community, and who should form a close link between Bombay and the work.

For the literary research one suitable person might be Professor Ross, who is just appointed as the best Persian scholar available for this College. He is young, active and fond of travelling; and is familiar with Persian, Arabic, Russian and with Oriental ways. He could not have leave long enough for excavation, but for literary work that can be done within a fixed time, he might do well. I do not know him personally, as he has not yet entered on his work here.

I am grateful to my coadjutor, the late Mr. Pestanji M. Ghadiali, who first incited me to undertake this work, for the preface and the index which he has prepared for me.

N. F. B.

descendants of so noble a race turning their attention to research in their history and origins.

My own work, however, lies so entirely in Egypt, I see in that country so very much more than I can ever hope to explore, that it is hopeless for me to think of taking an active part in the work in other lands. There is however one line in which I might perhaps assist you. If you should ever intend to excavate any ancient sites of Persian cities, it would be a great pleasure to me to receive at my work in Egypt any students who may wish to undertake such work, and to give them such training in the methods of accurate research and record in excavation, as might increase the value and certainty of any exploration that they might undertake. Beyond this I fear that my good will is all that I can offer to such research.

Yours very truly,
W. M. FLINDERS PETRIE.

THE SECRETARY,
PARSI PANCHÂYET, BOMBAY.

PREFACE.

In placing before the public the present work the compiler's object is to collect in a convenient and accessible form, for the use of Theosophists as well as his Parsi co-religionists, the varied writings on the Zoroastrian religion, bearing on its philosophy, symbology, psychology and occultism, which have appeared from time to time in the theosophical literature since the establishment of the Theosophical Society in India in 1878. There is much prejudice among the Parsi community against Theosophy. But the prejudiced will see from the present attempt what an amount of light Theosophy has thrown on the hitherto obscure and unintelligible passages of their scriptures—passages which were alike the despair of Western savants and their Parsi followers in Western India. Many such passages of these scriptures which at first sight would appear as the "babbling of infants" or "absurdities" and "meaningless nonsense," will, when read in the light of Theosophy, be found of deepest philosophy and highest occult significance containing the greatest mysteries regarding the Universe and Man. The modern Parsis, yielding to the baneful influence of the present day materialism of the West and led away by the glamour of Western civilization, have become utterly disregardful of their own ancient and sublime faith ; and when they at all care to look at it through translations they find in it nothing but distorted ideas relating to God, nature and man. Sadder still it is to see that those who have made the study of their religion in the original language are following the interpretation of the philologists in the field of Zoroastrian literature, and refuse to rise above the too petty limits set down by them, and to claim for their own sublime faith the rightful place and dignity among the world's greatest religions. For any really original research in this line one should be a thorough master of the Sanskrit language and of the Vedic philosophy.

In addition to these he should be a student of occultism. With equipments like these there is every chance of restoring the Zoroastrian religion to its ancient grandeur and dignity. The materials collected in the present volume will give some proofs of the assertions made here. Every candid and unprejudiced reader and earnest seeker after truth outside the Theosophical Society will find in these pages much interesting and really useful knowledge, and much food for reflection and for further research on the same line. To the Theosophists they will offer many valuable hints and much raw materials as regards the occult teachings of the Avasta, which they may very profitably follow up as veritable "golden lodes" in the mines of Zoroastrian literature. We may, however, observe that in reading these pages it is to be borne in mind that the interpretations of the esoteric side of the Zoroastrian scriptures herein given are not to be regarded as final or complete. There are seven keys, according to the esoteric teachings, for unravelling the hidden spiritual truths underlying the world's scriptures, and only one or two at the most of these keys have been applied in the exposition of Zoroastrian scriptures contained in these pages.

After thus setting forth the reasons which have led to the publication of the present work, we may here give a brief resumé of Zoroastrian teachings for the information of our readers, based on the famous lecture of Mrs. Annie Besant on Zoroastrianism, forming part as one of the "Four Great Religions."

It is an acknowleged fact that the major portion of the Avasta have been destroyed, partly by the ravages attendant upon the conquest of the Persian Empire by Alexander the Great and partly by the later ravages and persecutions occasioned by the Mahomedan conquests. What fragments of the grand whole—twelve million verses according to Pliny, and twelve hundred parchments according to Abul Jaffir Attavari—which come down to us are mainly due to the restoration and collection of the scattered writings during the time of the Sassanian kings, in which collections many misinterpretations and interpolations are said to have taken place. Besides every religion in the course of time suffers from accretions due to the ignorance of its later followers and to the greed and worldliness of its priesthood. In order to distinguish and discriminate between the original or permanent and the interpolated or transitory elements—in other words, the essentials and non-essentials—in any religion, Mrs. Besant in the Introduction to her lectures above referred to gives the following tests as regards spiritual truths :—

(*a*) Is it ancient and to be found in the ancient scriptures?

(*b*) Has it the authority of the Founder of the religion, or of the sages to whom the formulation of the particular religion is due?

(*c*) Is it universal and found under some form in all religions?

The following tests are given as regards matters of rites and ceremonies, observances and customs :—

(*a*) Is it laid down or recommended in the ancient scriptures by the Founder or His immediate disciples?

(*b*) Can its usefulness be explained or verified by those in whom occult training has developed the inner faculties which make the invisible world a region they know by their own experience?

(*c*) If a custom be of modern growth, with only a century or two or three centuries behind it; if it be local, not found in any ancient scriptures, nor justified by occult knowledge, then—however helpful it may be found by any individual in his spiritual life—it should not be imposed on any member of a particular religion as binding on him as a part of that religion, nor should a man be looked at askance for non-compliance with it.

With reference to this last clause Mrs. Besant very wisely observes, "such custom, even if much valued and found useful by their adherents, should not be cohsidered as generally binding, and should fall into the class of non-essentials. It has been well said that in things essential there should be unity, in things non-essential there should be liberty, and in all things there should be charity. Were these wise rules followed by each, we should hear less of the religious antagonisms and sectarian disputes that bring shame on the very word 'religion.' That which ought to unite (as the root of the word signifies) has been the ever-springing source of division, until many have impatiently shaken off all religions as being man's worst enemy, the introducer everywhere of strife and hatred."

These facts must be clearly borne in mind when one takes the study of the Zoroastrian scriptures in hand. And it is a matter of great consolation, from information gathered from secret sources, that the vast library of Zoroastrian religion, philosophy and science, which was supposed to have been burnt down by Alexander under a feat of madness, has not been altogether lost to the world, but has been preserved in underground temples and libraries by the stewards and custodians of spiritual knowledge, and when suitable time arrives they will be restored to their proper and legitimate heirs—the modern Parsis. The fragments of the scriptures preserved by Greeks, such as the Nabathean Agriculture, the Oracles of Zoroaster, which are not however recognised by the modern Parsis (although some of the Western savants have given them their due place in their researches among the ruins of the Avasta literature), contain many of the most important teachings relating to the doctrine of the soul as regards its preëxistence and its reïncarnation in successive lives, no mention of which is to be found in the extant portions of the Avasta, a point which will be noticed further on.

Coming to the religion itself, if we were to believe in

the advanced views of the Sanskrit and Zend scholars, Zoroastrianism is the second religion in the evolution of the Aryan race, a fact which can be conclusively proved from the internal and external evidence of its scriptures, apart from the evidence forthcoming from ancient records not accessible to ordinary humanity and from the cuneiform inscriptions which have been recently discovered and are in process of translation. The assertions of some of the occidental savants, that Zoroastrianism is derived from Christianity or Judaism, is therefore simply absurd and far below the notice of every reasonable student of religious history and religious thought. The origin of the religion is lost far, far back in the mists of time, far beyond the scope of historic records. It is coëval with the religion of the Vedas, the immense antiquity of which even modern savants have been compelled to acknowledge. In fact Professor Darmsteter, in his able Introduction to the translation of the Avasta in the series of the Sacred Books of the East, has distinctly avowed that the key to the Avasta are the Vedas. Dr. Haug, in his "Essays on the Sacred Language, Writings, and Religion of the Parsis," has shown in chapter IV thereof the close relationship between the Brahminical and Zoroastrian Religions which cannot be merely accidental, but conclusively proves that these two religions—as in fact almost all great world-religions—have sprung up from the same source, *viz.*, from the same Mighty Brotherhood of high Initiates—the custodians and guardians of sacred and occult knowledge who watch over the development of the human race—that which in the theosophical literature is known as the great White Lodge of the Himalayan Brothers. The claims of Theosophy on this point are not based on mere vague assertions, but are grounded on tangible and visible documentary evidence which are carefully preserved by these Initiates and Adepts in underground temples and libraries where no human curiosity may find them nor any injury touch them. There are to be found men and women among the ranks of Theosophists who have been permitted to set eyes on many of these writings which are inscribed in ancient sacerdotal or priestly language which is now lost to humanity and which even the most ancient races, now extant on the face of the earth, are utterly ignorant of. Besides these there is the evidence of the Âkâshic records where pictures of all past events to the utmost details that have occurred on this earth—whether on the physical or mental planes—actions and writings of men—are to be found in faithful pictures to those who have developed their inner faculties by occult training, a fact which is at present very dimly, if at all, perceived by modern science and which, like many other ancient teachings and facts which it is now slowly and gradually acknowledging and verifying, will also be recognised by her in a measureable distance of time. It is on such unimpeachable though inaccessible sources to the ordinary humanity that the testimony of the antiquity of the Zoroastrian religion is based. It is also on such evidence that Theosophy is able to solve the moot and much vexed point about the date of Zoroaster, about which there is such a wide divergence of opinion among the savants themselves, their dates ranging from the absurdly modern time of 610 B. C. up to 2800 B. C., a Parsi follower of theirs pushing it a little beyond, *viz.*, 3270 B. C. According to Greek testimony it is set down at 9600 B. C. According to occult testimony, however, his date can be thrown as far back as 20,000 B. C., and aye, even beyond, a fact which will most probably be verified by the recent discoveries of cuneiform inscriptions which are now in process of translation. This date assumes, as a matter of fact, that there was not one Zoroaster only, but that a long line of prophets of that name flourished from those far off times, not necessarily as separate individuals, but as the same great soul reincarnating life after life at various periods according to the needs and exigencies of the people whose spiritual evolution he had to superintend, the same great Teacher, the same liberated Soul, the same mighty Instructor. According to occult history there were such fourteen Zoroasters. The Zoroaster of whom Aristotle wrote and whose date is put down at

9600 B. C. was the seventh of this name from the original Zoroaster, and not the first, as he supposed. The last Zoroaster, that is, the last incarnation of the same mighty Instructor, flourished about 4000 B. C. and of whom the savants speak of and who again revived the ancient faith in the land of Irân.

Coming to the teachings of the Zoroasters it will be observed by any careful student of the mere fragments of the whole of the Avasta literature which have remained in our hands, that they will appear to him as ranging from strict Monotheism to Pantheism, Polytheism, Dualism or Dwaitism, Adwaitism and—even atheism. This is inevitable in the comprehensive system of spiritual philosophy such as Zoroaster taught, a philosophy which embraced all known and unknown sciences, spiritual and profane, as will be evidenced by the mere contents of the Nasks as preserved to us in the eighth and ninth chapter of the " Dinkard."

Its doctrine of dualism about which so much has been written by the Western savants and about which so much confusion exists, is a purely philosophic and spiritual concept which, when seen in the light of Theosophy, represents the second step of God in his manifested aspect, God being in essence a Trinity. This fact of the triune nature of Ahura-Mazda is easily proved from a passage in the Khorshed Niyâyesh where Ahura-Mazda is described as *thrishchida*, that is, *threefold*, which the translators have perverted into "*three times.*" Many such mistranslations of the Avasta can be pointed out. But to come to our point, Ahura-Mazda is threefold and that from Him duality proceeded, called Spento-mainyush and Angro-mainyush, in order that a manifested universe might be brought into existence. These two principles are usually translated as "good" and "evil," but the terms are applicable in relation to man alone who has the power of choice between these two principles in Nature. Originally the duality was not as good and evil, but stood as spirit and matter—reality and non-reality, *Sat* and *Asat*, light and darkness. These are, as it were, two poles between which the universe is builded, and without which no universe can exist and no evolution can be possible. This idea is very clearly expressed in Yasna XXX, 3.—40. The very words "reality" and "non-reality" are found in these passages and they exactly convey the idea of *Sat* and *Asat* of the Hindu philosophy. The Unity evolving a Duality in order that many may come forth from It and that the universe may proceed. These two principles are variously spoken of in the Yasna. They are spoken of in Yasna LVII, 2, as the "two masters," the "two creators," whom the mighty Intelligence Saraosh himself worshipped, thus showing that he could not have worshipped evil, but that he worshipped the primal duality in the Divine Nature—Ahura-Mazda Himself. Even He Himself proclaims them as *My* two spirits in Yasna XIX, 9, and commenting on these words Dr. Haug in his "Essays on Parsis" rightly observes :—" They are the two moving causes in the universe, united from the beginning, and therefore called *yema*, Sanskrit *yaman*, meaning 'twins.' They are present everywhere in Ahura-Mazda as well as in man." He remarks that, Añro-mainyush is never mentioned in the Gâthâs as a constant opponent of Ahura-Mazda, as has been the case in the later writings, and adds that this is the original Zoroastrian notion of the two creative spirits who form only two parts of the Divine Being. This is a truly Theosophic idea, and one would be really glad to observe it, coming from one of the very savants who have made such a muddle of Avasta translations so far as they relate to philosophic and occult teachings and symbology.

Behind and beyond the triune Deity, Ahura-Mazda, is the Unknowable Existence or "Beness," the Zarvane-Akarne or Boundless Time. Although this idea is rejected by the Orientalists as being based on a grammatical misconstruction, still its antiquity is not denied by them, and their rejection of it is mainly due to their ignorance of occult teaching. But in the fragments of the Zoroastrian religion preserved to us by the Greeks, Plutarch says that Oromasdes (Ahura-Mazda) sprang up from *the purest light*, and Domascius writes that the Magi and the whole Aryan nation considered Space or Time as the universal Cause out of which the good as well as the evil spirits or light and darkness were seperated, *before these two spirits arose.* More distinctly is this idea asserted in the fragments of Theodorus preserved by the Polyhistor Photos, where he speaks of the doctrine of the Persians about Zravan whom he makes the ruler of the whole universe, and who, when offering sacrifices in order to generate Hormisdas, produced both "Hormisdas and Satan"—Spenta-Mainyush and Añro-mainyush. Nothing can be more clear and distinct to show that the idea of the Trinity of Ahura-Mazda, and also that of the Absolute or Para-brahman of the Vedantin, was not unfamiliar or alien to Zoroastrianism, as in fact it should not be, seeing the common origin from which Zoroastrianism and Hinduism arose.

The next point to be noticed is that regarding the seven Ameshaspentas and the host of Yazatas—the former variously styled in other world's scriptures as the seven Prajâpatis or Saptarishis of the Hindus, the Sephiroths of the Jews, the Builders or Cosmocrators of the Gnostics or early Christians, and the seven "Angels or Archangels of the Presence" of the post-Christians, and who are called in Theosophical terminology the Dhyan Chohans or the "Lords of Light." Strictly speaking there are six Ameshaspentas, of whom Ahura-Mazda is the synthesis or the seventh. Below and subordinate to these are the host of Yazatas or lower gods, the Devatas of the Hindus, and angels of other religions. All these higher and lower spiritual Intelligences or gods are regarded by the Orientalists, and unfortunately by their Parsi followers, as mere abstract ideas and attributes of the Deity, although in the Avasta prayers they are continually addressed and hymns are always chanted to them as distinct entities with definite powers and purpose in the Divine economy. In fact the whole of the common liturgy of the Parsis is permeated by their worship, and if their worship is to be wrenched out of it, as some of the modern Parsis are doing in servile imitation of the Western savants, then the entire fabric of the Zoroastrian religion would crumble to pieces, and the religious instinct would become soon extinct. This is not said by way of encouraging such worship, but as pointing out the existence and the legitimate place of these Intelligences in the gradation of beings from the Supreme Source of All down to man, and showing that Zoroastrianism is at one on this point also with the teachings of Theosophy and occultism.

The last but not the least important point to be noticed, nay, we may say of vital importance, is a point of Reïncarnation, or repeated rebirths of man on the earthly plane until he is purged of all the lies and lust of blood and becomes fit to stand in the presence of his God, or, as expressed in Zoroastrianism itself, he becomes fit to approach Him and be merged into Him. It must be acknowledged that there is no direct or explicit mention of this doctrine in the extant fragments of the Avasta, although indirect inferences may be drawn about it from various passages of these fragments confirmatory of this idea. But the most positive proof of it is to be found in the fragments of the scriptures preserved by the Greeks referred to above, especially in the "Oracles of Zoroaster," and in that most occult of Irânian books, the "Desatir." Apart from this legitimate, though unacknowledged, sources of information, the Zoroastrian scriptures emphatically and in a most uncompromising way proclaims the Law of Karma, of which law Reïncarnation is a corollary and logical necessity, as every reasoning person must concede. Besides Zoroastrianism having sprung from the same source as that from which Hinduism has taken its rise, in which religion this doctrine is taught as plainly, as clearly, and in as unmistakable a manner as could be, it would not be at all surprising to find it forming part and parcel of the religion which Zoroaster founded, though it has been lost to us in the apparent destruction of almost all his writings.

Besides the points noted above in the roughest outline, the sublime philosophy of Fire, the worship of the Sun, the Elements, the Ameshaspentas and Yazatas, the higher and lower gods and the ceremonials after the dead, which all occupy such a prominent position in the Zoroastrian scriptures, will be found sufficiently dealt with in these pages, not in a dogmatic, assertive manner, but in a manner which will satisfy both the head and the heart, both the intellectual as well as the religious, and we think it therefore superfluous to touch on these points here. Many more important writings from the pen of Theosophists we have been obliged to exclude from the present volume, partly on account of want of space and partly because of the higher subjects which have been treated of in them. But what portion has been here published will clearly show the claims of Theosophy in the field of religious research.

We cannot, however, do better than conclude this Preface by quoting the magnificent and soul-stirring words with which Mrs. Besant closed the lecture above referred to—an eloquence which will certainly set ablaze in its pristine purity the spiritual fire now smouldering in the hearts of every true Zoroastrian, and if this cannot awaken our Parsi brethren to the sublimity and grandeur of their ancient faith and urge them on to re-establish and resuscitate it in the form in which its original Founder left it to them, nothing else can. She reminded her hearers that this most ancient faith sprang from the Primæval Source, that its Prophet was one of the Divine Initiates; that it came down from the past millenium after millenium, and is but poorly represented by the comparatively materialized Zoroastrianism of to-day. The study of its scriptures might revive it; the old knowledge might again be breathed into it; these concessions to European criticism and European materialism might be repudiated by every Zoroastrian as no part of his ancient, of his glorious faith. "O! my Parsi Brothers!" she says, "your Prophet is not dead. He is not perished. He is watching over the religion that he founded, ever seeking to raise it from its present degradation, to give it back its lost knowledge, its lost powers. What nobler work for the Zoroastrian of to-day than to permeate his brethren with the ancient fire, to relight its blaze on the spiritual altars of their hearts? What nobler work than to study his own scriptures, and to go forth and teach the ancient learning with the authority and power that can only be wielded by a man of the same faith with those he addresses. The fire is not dead; it is only smouldering on its ancient altars; white hot are the ashes, ready to reburst into flames. And I dream of a day when the breath of the great Prophet Zarathustra shall sweep again through his temples, fanning the ashes on the altars of those ancient fanes, and every altar shall flash into fire, and again from heaven the answering flames shall fall, making the Irânian religion once more what it ought to be, a beacon-light for the souls of men, one of the greatest religions of the world."

P. M. GHADIALI.

ZOROASTRIANISM
IN THE LIGHT OF THEOSOPHY.

THE SPIRIT OF THE ZOROASTRIAN RELIGION.

[LECTURE delivered by COLONEL H. S. OLCOTT, President-Founder of the Theosophical Society, at the Town Hall, Bombay, on Tuesday, the 14th February, 1882.]

WITH great diffidence I have accepted your invitation to address the Parsis upon the theme of the present discourse. The subject is so noble, its literature so rich, its ramifications so numerous, that no living man could possibly do it full justice in a single lecture. Happy, indeed, I will be, if I succeed in communicating to one or two of the learned Parsi scholars, who honour me with their presence, some of the deep interest which I have had for years in the esoteric meaning of the Mazdiaznian faith. My hope is to attract your attention to the only line of research which can lead you towards the truth. That line was traced by Zoroaster and followed by the Magi, the Mobeds, and the Dasturs of old. Those great men have transmitted their thoughts to posterity under the safe cover of an external ritual. They have masked them under a symbolism and ceremonies, that guard their mighty secrets from the prying curiosity of the vulgar crowd, but hide nothing from those who deserve to know all. Do not misunderstand me. I am not pretending that *I* know all, or a fraction of all : at best I have had but a glimpse of the reality. But even that little is quite enough to convince me that, within the husk of your modern religion, there is the shining soul of the old faith that came to Zardusht in his Persian name, and once illuminated the whole trans-Himalayan world. You —children of Irân, heirs of the Chaldean lore ; you—who so loved your religion that neither the sword of Omar, nor the delights of home, nor the yearning of our common humanity to live among the memories of our ancestors, could make you deny that religion; you—who, for the sake of conscience, fled from your native land and erected an altar for the symbolical Sacred Fire in foreign countries, more hospitable than yours had become; you—men of intelligence, of an ancient character for probity, of enterprise in all good works—you are the only ones to lift the dark veil of this modern Parsism, and let the "Hidden Splendor" again blaze forth. Mine is but the office of the friendly wayfarer who points you to the mouth of the private road that leads through your own domain. I am not, if you please—a man, but only a VOICE. I need not even appeal to you to strip away the foreign excrescences that, during twelve centuries of residence among strangers, have fastened themselves upon primitive Zoroastrianism, nor to recite to you its simple yet all-sufficient code of morality, and ask you to live up to it more closely. This work has already been taken up by intelligent and public-spirited members of your own community. But I am to show you that your religion is in agreement with the most recent discoveries of modern science, and that the freshest graduate from Elphinstone College has no cause to blush for the "ignorance" of Zaratusht! And I am to prove to you that your faith rests upon the rock of truth, the living rock of Occult Science, upon which the initiated progenitors of mankind built every one of the religions that have since swayed the thoughts and stimulated the aspirations of a hundred generations of worshippers. Let others trace back the history of Zoroastrianism to and beyond the time of the Bactrian King Vistâsp; and reconcile the quarrels of Aristotle, Hermippus, Clement, Alexander Polyhistor, and the other ancient as well as of modern critics, as to when Zaratusht lived and where was his birthplace : these are non-essentials. It is of far less moment to know where and of what parentage a religious reformer was born, than to be sure of what he taught, and whether his teaching is calculated to bless mankind or not.

Plotinus, the philosopher, so well knew this that he would not tell, even to Prophyry, his pupil and literary biographer, what was his native country, what his real name, or his parentage. As regards Zaratusht one thing is affirmed, *viz.*, that about six centuries B. C. one man of that name lived—whether or not several others preceded him, as several highly respectable authorities affirm is the fact—and that the religion he preached, whether new or old, was of so noble a character that it indelibly stamped its impress upon the then chief school of Western philosophy, that of Greece.* It is also, as I believe, certain

---

* In the oldest Iranian book called the *Desatir*—a collection of the teachings of the fourteen oldest Iranian prophets (to make the number fifteen and include, among them, Simkendesh, or "Secander," is a grave error, as may be proved on the authority of Zarathusht himself in that book)—Zarathusht stands thirteenth in the list. The fact is significant. Respecting the period of Zoroaster the *First*, or his personality, there is no trustworthy information given by any of the Western scholars: their authorities conflicting in the most perplexing manner. Indeed among the many discordant notices, I find the earliest Greek classic writers who tell us that Zarathusht lived from 600 to 5,000 years before the Trojan war, or 6,000 years before Plato. Again, it is declared by Berosus, the Chaldean priest, that Zoroaster was a founder of Indian dynasty in Babylon 2200 B. C.; while the later native traditions inform us that he was the son of Purushaspa, and a contemporary of Gustâspa, the father of Darius, which would bring him within 600 B. C. Lastly, it is mentioned by Bunsen that he was born at Baktria before the emigration of the Baktrians to the Indus, which took place, as the learned Egyptologist shows us, 3784 B. C. Among this host of contradictions, what conclusion can one come to? Evidently, there is but one hypothesis left: and that is that they are all wrong, the reason for it being the one I find in the secret traditions of the esoteric doctrine—namely, that there were several teachers of that name. Neither Plato nor Aristotle, so accurate in their statements, is likely to have transformed 200 years into 6,000. As to the generally accepted native tradition, which makes the great prophet a contemporary of Darius' father, it is absurd and wrong on the very face of it. Though the error is too palpable to need any elaborate confutation, I may say in regard to it a few words. The latest researches show that the Persian inscriptions point out to Vistasp as the last of the line of Kaianian princes who ruled in Baktria, while the Assyrian conquest of that country took place in 1200 B, C. Now this alone would prove that Zoroaster lived twelve or thirteen hundred years B. C., instead of the 600 assigned to him; and thus that he could not have been a contemporary of Darius Hystaspes, whose father was so carelessly and for such a length of time confounded in this connection with Vistasp who flourished six centuries earlier. If we add to this the historical discrepancy between the statement of Ommianus Marcelinus—which makes

that this man was an Initiate in the sacred Mysteries, or, to put it differently—that he had, by a certain course of mystical study, penetrated all the hidden mysteries of man's nature and of the world about him. Zoroaster is by the Greek writers often called the Assyrian "Nazaret." This term comes from the word *Nazar*, or *Nazir*—set apart, separated. The Nazars were a sect of Adepts, very ancient—existing ages before Christ. They are described as "physicians, healers of the

Darius crush the Magi and introduce the worship of Ahuramazda—and the inscription on the tomb of that king which states that he was "teacher and heirophant of Magianism;" and that other no less significant and very important fact that the Zoroastrian *Avesta* shows no signs of the knowledge of its writer or writers with either the Medes, the Persians, or the Assyrians, the ancient books of the Parsis remaining silent upon, and showing no acquaintance with, any of the nations that have been known to have dwelt in or near the Western parts of Irân,—the accepted figure 600 B. C. as the period in which the prophet is alleged to have flourished becomes absolutely improbable.

It is therefore safe to come to the following conclusions:—(1.) That there were several (in all *seven*, say the Secret Records) *Ohuru-asters* or spiritual teachers of Ahuramazda, an office corrupted later into *Guru-asters* and *Zuru-asters* from "Zera-Ishtar," the title of the Chaldean or Magian priests; and (2) that the last of them was Zarathustra of the *Desatir*, the thirteenth of the prophets, and the seventh of that name. It was he who was the contemporary of Vistâsp, the last of the Kaianian princes, and the Compiler of Vendidad, the Commentaries upon which are lost, there remaining now but the dead letter. Some of the facts given in the Secret Records, though to the exact scholar merely traditional, are very interesting. They are to the effect that there exists a certain hollow rock full of tablets in a gigantic cave bearing the name of the first Zarathust under his Magian appellation, and that the tablets may yet be rescued some day. This cave with its rock and tablets and its many inscriptions on the walls is situated at the summit of one of the peaks of the Thian Shan mountains, far beyond their junction with the Belor Tagh, somewhere along their Eastern Course. One of the half-pictorial and half-written prophecies and teachings attributed to Zarathust himself, relates to that deluge which has transformed an inland sea into the dreary desert called Shamo or Gobi Desert. The esoteric key to the mysterious creeds, flippantly called at one time the Sabian or Planetary Religion, at another, the Solar or Fire-Worship, "hangs in that cave," says the legend. In it the great Prophet is represented with a golden star on his heart and as belonging to that race of Ante-diluvian giants mentioned both in the sacred books of the Chaldeans and the Jews. It matters little whether this information is accepted or rejected. Since the rejection of it would not make the other hypothesis more trustworthy, it may just as well be mentioned here.

sick by the imposition of the hands," and as initiated into the Mysteries (see treatise *Nazir* in the Talmud). The Jews, returning from the Babylonian captivity, were thoroughly imbued with Zoroastrian and Magian ideas ; their forefathers had agreed with the Sabeans in the Baktric worship, the adoration of the Sun, Moon, and Five Planets, the SABAOTH and realm of light. In Babylon they had learned to worship the Seven-Rayed God. And so we find running all throughout the Christian as well as the Jewish Scriptures, the septenary system, which culminates in the *Book of Revelation* (the final pamphlet of the Bible), in the Heptaktis, and a prophecy of the coming of the Persian Sosiant under the figure of the Christian Messiah, riding, like the former, upon a white horse. By the Jewish sect of the Pharisees, whose great teacher was Hillel, the whole angelology and symbolism of the Zoroastrians were accepted, and infused into Jewish thought ; and their Hebrew Kabalah, or secret book of Occult Wisdom, was the offspring of the Chaldean Kabalah. This deathless work is the receptacle of all the ancient lore of Chaldea, Persia, Media, Bactria, and the pre-Irânian period. The name by which its students in the secret lodges of the Jewish Pharisees (or Pharsis) were known was *Kabirim*—from Kabiri, the Mystery Gods of Assyria. Zoroastrianism and Magianism proper were, then, the chief source of both esoteric Judaism and esoteric Christianity. But not only has this subtle spirit left the latter religion, under the pressure of worldliness and skeptical enquiry ; it also long ago left Judaism. The modern Hebrews are not Kabalists but Talmudists, holding to the later interpretations of the Mosaic canon : only here and there can we now find a real Kabalist, who knows what is the true religion of his people and whence it was derived.

The real history of Zoroaster and his religion has never been written. The Parsis have lost the key, as the Jews and Christians have lost that of their respective faiths, and as I find the Southern Buddhist have lost that of theirs. Not to the living pandits or priests of either of those religions can the laity look for light. They can only quote the opinions of ancient Greek and Roman, or modern German, French, or English writers. This very day nearly all that your most enlightened scholars know about your religion is what they have collated from European sources, and that is almost exclusively about its literature and external forms. And see what ridiculous mistakes some of those authorities make at times! The Rev. Dr. Prideaux, treating of the Sad-der, says that Zaratusht preached incest!—that "nothing of this nature is unlawful, a man *may not only* marry his *sister or daughter, but even his mother!*"—(*Ancient Universal History*, iv., 206). He quotes no Zend authority, nothing written by a Parsi, but only Jewish and Christian authorities, such as Philo, Tertullian, and Clement Alexandrinus. Eutychius, a priest and archimandrite at Constantinople, writes, in the fifth century, on Zoroastrianism as follows : " Nimrod beheld a fire rising out of the earth and he worshipped it, and from that time forth the Magi worshipped fire. And he appointed a man named Andeshan to be the priest and servant of the Fire. The Devil shortly after that spoke out of the midst of the fire (as did Jehovah to Moses?) saying 'No man can serve the Fire or learn Truth in my Religion, unless first he shall commit incest with his mother, sister, and daughter'! He *did as he was commanded*, and from that time the priests of the Magians practised incest ; but Andeshan was the first inventor of that doctrine." I quote this as a sample of the wretched stuff that has always been written against the Zoroastrian religion by its enemies. The above words are simply the dead letter mistranslation of secret doctrine, of which portions are to be found in certain rare old ·MSS. possessed by the Armenians at Etchmiadzine, the oldest monastery in Russian Caucasus. They are known as the Mesrobian MSS. Should the Bombay Parsis show any real general interest in the rehabilitation of their religion, I think I may promise them the unpaid but, all the same, friendly assistance of Madame Blavatsky, whose friend of thirty-seven years standing, the Prince Dondoukoff Korsakoff, has just notified her of his appointment by His Majesty the Czar, as Viceroy of the Caucasus.

In one of such old MSS., then, it is said of the Initiate, or Magus, "He who would penetrate the secrets of (sacred) Fire, and unite with it [as the Yogi 'unites himself with the Universal Soul'] must first unite himself, soul and body, to the Earth, his *mother*, to Humanity, his *sister*, and Science, his *daughter*." Quite a different thing, you perceive, from the abhorrent precept ascribed to the Founder of your Mazdiasnian faith. And this example should serve as a warning to your so-called educated youth against turning up his classical nose at his ancestral religion as 'unscientific' and nonsensical.

A curious and sad thing, indeed, it is to see how completely the old life has gone out of Zoroastrianism. Originally a highly spiritual faith—I know of none more so—and represented by Sages and Adepts of the highest rank among Initiates, it has shrunk into a purely exoteric creed full of ritualistic practices not understood, taught by a numerous body of priests as a rule ignorant of the first elements of spiritual philosophy; represented in prayers of which not a word has a meaning to those who recite them daily: the shrivelled shell that once held a radiant soul. Yet all that Zoroastrianism ever was it might be made again. The light still shines, though in darkness, enclosed in the clay vessel of materialism. Whose shall be the holy hand to break the jar of clay and let the hidden glory be seen? Where is the Mobed who shall in our day and generation rise to the ancient dignity of his profession, and redeem it from degradation.* One so great as to oblige even a Parsi

---

* Not before he learns the true meaning of his own name, and strives once more to become worthy of it. How many among the modern priests know that their title of "Mobed" or "Mogbed" comes from *Mag*, a word used by the prophet Zeremiah to designate a Babylonian Initiate, which, in its turn, is an abbreviation of Maginsiah—the great and wise? "Maghistom" was once the title of Zoroaster's highest disciples, and the synonym of wisdom. Speaking of them Cicero says: "*Sapientium et doctorum genus magorum habebatur in Persis*" (The wise and learned class of the Magians live among the Persians).

author (Mr. Dosabhai Framji, see his able work on *The Parsis*, &c., p. 277) say they "recite parrot-like all the chapters requiring to be repeated on occasions of religious ceremonies. . . . Ignorant and unlearned as these priests are, they do not and cannot command the respect of the laity." . . . "the position of the so-called spiritual guides has fallen into contempt;" and to add that some priests 'have given up a profession which has ceased to be honourable and . . . become contractors for constructing railroads in the Bombay Presidency." Some of the present Dasturs "are intelligent and well-informed men, possessing a considerable knowledge of their religion; but the mass of the priesthood are profoundly ignorant of its first principles." (*Ibid*, 279.)

I ask you, men of practical sense, what is the certain fate of a religion that has descended so low that its priests are regarded by the Behedin (laity) as fit only to be employed in menial services, such as bringing things to you from the bazar, and doing household jobs of work? What is it? I put it to you. Do you suppose that such a dried corpse will be left long above ground by the fresh and critical minds you are educating at college? Nay, do you not see how they are already treating it; how they abstain from visiting your temples; how sullenly they "make kusti," and go through their other daily ceremonies; how they avoid as much as possible every attention to the prescribed ordinances; how they are gathering in clubs to drink pegs and play cards; how they are defiling themselves by evil associations, smoking in secret, and some even openly, and prating glibly the most skeptical sophistries they have read in European books, written by deluded modern theorists? Yes,—the cloud gathers over the fire-altar, the once fragrant wood of Truth is wet with the deadly dews of doubt, a pestilential vapour fills the Âtash-Behrâm, and unless some Regenerator is raised up among you, the name of Zaratusht may, before many generations, be known only as that of the Founder of an extinct faith. . . . .

In his Preface to the translation of the *Vendidâd*, the learned Dr. Darmesteter (vol. iv. of *The Sacred Books of the East*, edited by Professor F. Max Müller) says, " The key to the *Avestâ* is not the Pahlavi, but the Veda. The Avestâ and the Veda are two echoes of one and the same voice, the reflex of one and the same thought : the Vedas, therefore, are both the best lexicon and the best commentary to the Avestâ"—(p. xxvi.) This he defines as the extreme view of the Vedic scholars, and while personally he does not subscribe to them entirely, he yet holds that we cannot perfectly comprehend the Avestâ without utilising the discoveries of the Vedic Pandits. But neither Darmesteter, nor Anquetil Duperron, nor Haug, nor Spiegel, nor Sir William Jones, nor Rapp (whose work has been so perfectly translated into English by your eminent Parsi scholar, Mr. K. R. Kama), nor Koth, nor any philological critic whose works I have read, has named the true key to Zaratushta's doctrine. For it, we must not search among the dry bones of words. No, it hangs within the door of the *Kabalah*—the Chaldean secret volume, where, under the mask of symbols and misleading phrases, it is kept for the use of the pure searcher after arcane knowledge. The entire system of ceremonial purifications, which in itself is so perfect that a modern Parsi—a friend of mine—has remarked that Zoroaster was the best of Health Officers—is, as it seems to me, typical of the moral purification required of him who would either, while living, attain the Magian's knowledge of hidden laws of nature and his power to wield them for good purposes or, after a well ordered life, to attain by degrees to the state of spiritual beatitude, called *Moksha* by the Hindus and *Nirvâna* by the Buddhists. The defilements by touch of various objects that you are warned against, are not visible defilements, like that of the person by contact with filth, but psychic defilements, through the influence of their bad magnetic aura—a subtle influence proceeding from certain living organisms and inert substances,—which is antipathetic to development as an Adept. If you will compare your books with the Yoga Sutras of the Hindus, and the Tripitikas of the Buddhists, you will see that each exact for the student and practitioner of Occult Science, a place, an atmosphere, and surroundings that are perfectly pure. Thus the Magus (or Yozdâthraigar), the Yogi, and the Arhat all retire, either to the innermost or topmost chambers of a temple, where no stranger is permitted to enter (bringing his impure magnetism with him), to the heart of a forest, a secluded cave, or a mountain height. In the tower of Belus at Babylon, virgin seeresses gazed into magical mirrors and aërolites, to see their prophetic visions; the Yogi retires to his subterranean *gupha*, or to jungle fastnesses; and the Chinese books tell us that the "Great Nachus" of their sacred doctrine dwell in the "Snowy Range of the Himâvat." The books alleged to have been inspired by God, or by His angels delivered to man, have always, I believe, been delivered on mountains. Zarathushtra got the Avestâ on Ushidarina, a mountain by the river Daraga (Vendidâd, xlix.); Moses received the tables of the Law on Mount Sinai (Exodus, xxxiv.); Mahomed was given the Koran on Mount Hara (Am. Cyc., vol. xi, 612); and the Hindu Rishis lived in the Himâlayas. Sakya Mûni left no inspired books, but, although he received the illumination of the Buddhaship in the plains, under a Bo-tree, he had prepared himself by years of austerities in the mountains near Râjagriha. The obstructive power of foul human, animal, vegetable, and even mineral auras, or magnetisms, has always been understood by occult students, from the remotest times. This is the true reason why none but initiated and consecrated priests have ever been allowed to step within the precincts of the holiest places. The custom is not at all the offspring of any feeling of selfish exclusiveness, but based upon known psycho-physiological laws. Even the modern Spiritualists and mesmerists know this; and the latter, at least, carefully avoid "mixing magnetisms," which always hurt a sensitive subject. All nature is a compound of conflicting, hence counterbalancing and equilibrating forces. Without this there could be no such thing as stability. Is it not the contest of the centrifugal and centripetal attractions that keeps our earth and every other orb of heaven revolving in its orbit? The law of the Universe is a distinct Dualism while the creative energy is at work, and of a compound Unism when at rest. And the personification of these opposing powers by Zarathusht was but the perfectly scientific and philosophical statement of a profound truth. The secret laws of this war of forces are taught in the Chaldean Kabalah. Every neophyte who sets himself to study for initiation is taught these secrets, and he is made to prove them by his own experiments, step by step, as his powers and knowledge increase. Zoroastrianism has two sides —the open, or patent, and the concealed, or secret. Born out of the mind of a Bactrian seer, it partakes of the nature of the primitive Irânian national religion and of the new spirituality that was poured into it, from the source of all truth, through the superb lens of Zoroaster's mind.

The Parsis have been charged with being worshippers of the visible fire. This is wholly false. They face the fire, as also they do the sun and the sea, because in them they picture to themselves the hidden Light of Lights, source of all Life, to which they give the name of Ormazd. How well and how beautifully is this expressed in the writings of Robert Fludd, the English mystic of the 17th century (see Hargrave Jennings' *The Rosicrucians*, p. 69, *et seq*): "Regard Fire, then, with other eyes than with those soulless, incurious ones with which thou hast looked upon it as the most ordinary thing. Thou hast forgotten what it is—or rather thou hast never known. Chemists are silent about it . . . Philosophers talk of it as anatomists discourse of the constitution (or the parts) of the human body. . . . It is made for man and this world, and it is greatly like him—that is *mean*, they would add . . . But is this all? Is this the sum of that casketed lamp of the human body?—thine own body, thou unthinking world's machine—thou man? Or, in the fabric of this clay lamp [what a beautiful simile!] burneth there not a

Light? Describe that, ye doctors of physics! . . . Note the goings of the Fire . . . Think that this thing is bound up in matter-chains. Think that He is outside of all things; and that thou and thy world are only the *thing-between*: and that outside and inside are both identical, couldst thou understand the supernatural truths! Reverence Fire (for its meaning) and tremble at it . . . Avert the face from it, as the Magi turned, dreading, and (as the symbol) bowed askance . . . Wonder no longer then, if, rejected so long as an idolatry, the ancient Persians, and their Masters, the Magi—concluding that they saw ' All ' in this supernaturally magnificent element—fell down and worshipped it; making of it the visible representation of the very truest; but yet, in man's speculation, and in his philosophies—nay, in his commonest reason—impossible God."

And mind you, this is the language, not of a Parsi or one of your faith, but of an English scholar who followed the shining path marked out by the Chaldean Magi, and obtained, like them, the true meaning of your Mysteries. *Occult Science is the vindicator of Zoroastrianism, and there is none other.* Modern physical science is blind herself to spiritual laws and spiritual phenomena. She cannot guide, being herself in need of a helping hand—the hand of the Occultist and the Hierophant Chaldean sage.

Have you thought *why* the Fire is kept ever burning on your altars? Why is it? Why may not the priest suffer it to go out and re-kindle it again each morning? Ah! there is a great secret hidden. And why must the flames of one thousand different fires be collected—from the smithy, the burning-kiln, the funeral pyre, the goldsmith's furnace, and every other imaginable source. Why? because this spiritual element of Fire pervades all nature, is its life and soul, is the cause of the motion of its molecules which produces the phenomenon of physical heat. And the fires from all these thousand hearths are collected, like so many fragments of the universal life, into one sacrificial blaze which shall be as perfectly as possible the complete and collective type of the light of Hormazd. See the precautions taken to gather only the spirit or quintessence, as it were, of these separate flames. The priest takes not the crude coals from the various hearths and furnaces and pits; but at each flame he lights a bit of sulphur, a ball of cotton, or some other inflammable substance; from this secondary blaze he ignites a second quantity of fuel; from this a third; from the third a fourth, and so on : taking in some cases a ninth, in others a twentieth flame, until the first grossness of the defilement of the fire in the base use to which it was put has been purged, and only the purest essence remains. Then only is it fit to be placed upon the altar of Ormazd. And even then the flame is not ready to be the type of that Eternal Brightness : it is as yet but a body of earthly flame, a body which lacks its noblest soul. When your forefathers gathered at Sanjân to light the fire for the Indian exiles, the holy Dastur Nairyosang, who had come with them from Persia, gathered his people and the strangers of the country about him in the jungle. Upon a stone block the dried sandalwood was laid. Four priests stood at the four cardinal points. The Gâthâs are intoned, the priests bow their faces in reverential awe. The Dastur raises his eyes to heaven, he recites the mystical words of power : lo ! the upper world of space descends, and with its silvery tongues laps round the fragrant wood, which bursts into a blaze. This is the missing spirit evoked by the Adept Prometheus. When *this* is added to thousand other dancing flames the symbol is perfected, and the face of Ormazd shines before his worshippers. Lighted thus at Sanjân, that historic fire has been kept alive for more than seven hundred years, and until another Nairyosang appears among you to draw the flames of the ambient ether upon your altar, let it be fed continuously.

This ancient art of drawing fire from heaven was taught in the Samothracian and Kabiric Mysteries. Numa, who introduced the Vestal Mysteries into Rome, thus kindled a fire which was under the care of consecrated Vestal virgins, whose duty it was, under penalty of death for neglect, to constantly maintain it. It was, as Schweigger shows, the Hermes fire, the Elmesfire of the ancient Germans ; the lightning of Cybele ; the torch of Apollo ; the fire of Pan's altar ; the fire-flame of Pluto's helm ; the inextinguishable fire in the temple of the Grecian Athene, on the Acropolis of Athens ; and the mystical fires of many different worships and symbols. The Occult Science, of which I spoke, was shared by the Initiates of the Sacred Science all over the ancient world. The knowledge was first gained in Chaldea, and was thence spread through Greece to more Western and Northern countries. Even to-day the Fire-cult survives among the rude Indian tribes of Arizona—a far Western portion of my native America. Major Calhoun, of the U. S. Army, who commanded a surveying party sent out by our Government, told me that in that remote corner of the world, and among those rude people, he found them keeping alight their Sacred Fire in their *teocalis*, or holy enclosures. Every morning their priests go out, dressed in the sacerdotal robes of their forefathers, to salute the rising sun, in the hopes that Montezuma, their promised Redeemer and Liberator, will appear. The time of his coming is not foretold, but from generation to generation they wait, and pray, and hope.

In her *Isis Unveiled*, Madame Blavatsky has shown us that this heavenly fire, however and whenever manifested, is a correlation of the Âkâsha, and that the art of the magician and priest enables him to develope and attract it down.* But to do this he must be absolutely pure—pure in body, in thought, in deed. And these are the three pillars upon which Zarathusht erected the stately edifice of his religion. I have always considered it as a great test of the merit of any religion that its essence can be compressed into a few words that a child can understand. Buddhism, with its noble comprehensiveness,

---

* Occult sound as well as light emanate from "Âkâsha"; but the true Brahman and Buddhist Initiates make a great dinstinction between Astral *Fire* and Astral *Light*. Occult sounds and lights are heard and seen by the Yogi, and *he knows* that they proceed from his own *Mulâdharam*—the first of the six centres of force taught in Yoga philosophy—"The centre whose name means 'the chief foundation or basis is the seat of '*Astral Fire*,'" they say.

was distilled by its Founder into seven words; Zoroastrianism is reduced to three—*Humaté, Hukhté, Hvarshté.*

A Parsi gentleman, with whom I conversed the other day, explained the fact of your having no wonder-working priests at present, by saying that none living were pure enough. He was right, and until you can find such a pure celebrant, your religion will never be again ensouled. An impure man who attempts the magical ceremonies is liable to be made mad or destroyed. This is a scientific necessity. The law of nature is, you know, that action and reaction are equal. If, therefore, the operator in the Mysteries propels from himself a current of will-power directed against a certain object, and—either because of feebleness of will, or deviation caused by impure motives, he misses his mark, his current rebounds from the whole body of the Âkâsha (as the ball rebounds from the wall against which it is thrown to the thrower's hand) and reacts upon himself. Thus, we are told that they who did not know how to manage the miraculous fire in the Vestal and Kabiric Mysteries " were destroyed by it, and were punished by the Gods"—(Ennemoser, *History of Magic*, II. 32). Pliny relates (*Histor. Nat.*, xxviii., 2) that Tullus Hostilius had sought from the books of Numa, " *Jovem devocare a cœlo* "; but as he did not correctly follow the rules of Numa, he was struck by the lightning. This same rule applies equally to the attempt to use the black art unskilfully. The old English proverb says, " Curses, like fowls, come home to roost." He who would use the powers of sorcery, or black magic, is sure to be destroyed by them first or last. The old fables about sorcerers being carried off by the mocking " devils " whom, for a time, they had employed to gratify their unlawful desires, are all based upon fact. And, in Zoroastrianism, the Parsi is as carefully taught to eschew and fight against the powers of Ahriman, or the Evil Spirits of Darkness, as to cultivate intimacy with and win the protecting favour of the Ameshâspentas and Yazatas—the personified good principles of Nature. You will not find any of your European authorities speaking of these personifications with decent respect, any more than of the nature-gods of the Aryans. To their minds these are but the childish fancies of a florid Persian or Aryan imagination, begotten in the infancy of our race. For a good reason, too ; not one of these spectacled pandits has the least practical reason to believe that there are such good and evil powers warring about us. But I am not afraid to say to them all in my individual, not official, capacity, that I *do* believe in them ; nay, that I actually know they exist. And this is why you bear me, a Western man taught in a Western University and nursed on the traditions of modern civilization, say that Zarathushtra knew more about nature than Tyndall does, more about the laws of Force than Balfour Stewart, more about the origin of species than Darwin or Hackel, more about the human mind and its potentialities than Maudsley or Bain. And so did Buddha, and some other ancient proficients in Occult Science. Pshaw! Young man of the Bombay University, when you have taken your degree, and learned all your professors can teach you, go to the hermit and the recluse of the jungle and ask *him* to prove to you where to begin your real study of the world into which you have been born! Your professors can make you learned, but not wise, can teach you about the shell of Nature, but those silent and despised unravelers of the tangled web of existence can evoke for you the soul that lurks within that husk. Three centuries before Christ the united kingdom of Persia and Media exercised a dominion extending over an area of three or four millions of square miles, and had a population of serveral hundred millions of people. And do you mean to tell me that the Zoroastrian religion could have dominated the minds of this enormous mass of people—nearly twice the present population of India—and could have also swayed the religious thought of the cultured Greeks and Romans, if it had not had a spiritual life in it that its poor remnant of to-day completely lacks? I tell you that if you could put that ancient life back into it, and if you had your holy men to show this ignorant age the proof of the reality of the old Chaldean wisdom, you would spread your religion all over the world.

For the age is spiritually dying for want of a religion that can show just such signs, and for lack of them two crores of intelligent Western people have become Spiritualists and are following the lead of mediums. And not only your religion is soulless. Hinduism is so, Southern Buddhism is so, Judaism and Christianity are so likewise. We see following the Missionaries none of the "signs" that Jesus said should follow those who were really his disciples: they neither raise the dead, nor heal the sick, nor give sight to the blind, nor cast out devils, nor dare they drink any deadly thing in the faith that it will not harm them. There are a few true wonder-workers in our time, but they are among the Lamaists of Tibet, the Copts of Egypt, the Sufis and Darvishes of Arabia and other Mahomedan countries. The great body of the people, in all countries, are become so sensual, so avaricious, so materialistic and faithless, that their moral atmosphere is like a pestilential wind to the Yozdàthraigar (those Adepts whom we have made known to India under the name of BROTHERS).

The meaning of your Haoma, you doubtless know. In the IXth Yaçna of the Avestâ, Haoma is spoken of both as a god—a Yazata—and the plant, or the juice of the plant, which is under his especial protection, and so is the *Soma* of the "Aitareya Brâhmana."

> "At the time of the morning-dawn came
> Haoma to Zarathustra,
> As he was purifying the fire and reciting the Gâthâs.
> Zarathustra asked him: Who, O man, art thou?
> Thou, who appearest to me as the most beautiful in the whole corporeal world, endued with Thine own life, majestic and immortal?
> Then answered me Haoma, the pure, who is far from death.
> Ask me, thou Pure one, make me ready for food."

Thus in the same line, is Haoma spoken of in his personified form and as a plant to be prepared for food.

Farther on he is described as

"Victorious, golden, with moist stalks."

This is the sacred Soma of the Aryans—by them also clevated into a deity. This is that wondrous juice which lifted the mind of him who quaffed it to the splendours of the higher heavens, and made him commune with the gods. It was not stupefying like opium, not maddening like the Indian hemp, but exhilarating, illuminating, the begetter of divine visions. It was given to the candidate in the Mysteries, and drunk with solemn ceremony by the Hierophant. Its ancient use is still kept in your memories by the Mobeds drinking, in the Yaçna ceremony, a decoction of dried Haoma stalks, that have been pounded with bits of pomegranate root in a mortar and afterwards had water thrice poured over them.

The Baresma twigs—among you represented by a bunch of brass wires!—are a reminiscence of the divining-rods anciently used by all practitioners of ceremonial magic. The rod or staff was also given to the fabled gods of Mythology. In the fifth book of the Odyssey, Jupiter, in the Council of the Gods, bids Hermes to go upon a certain mission, and the verse says—

"Forth sped he . . . .
Then taking his staff, with which he the eyelids of mortals
Closes at will, and the sleeper, at will, re-awakens."

The rod of Hermes was a magic-staff; so was that of Æsculapius, the healing wand that had power over disease. The Bible has many references to the magic-rod, notably in the story of the contest of Moses with the Egyptian Magicians in the presence of Pharaoh, in that of the magical bidding of Aaron's rod, the laying of Elisha's staff on the face of the dead Shunamite boy, &c. The Hindu Gossein of our day carries with him a bamboo rod having seven knots or joints, that has been given to him by his Guru and contains the concentrated magnetic will-power of the Guru. All magic-rods should be hollow, that the magnetic power may be stored in them. In the Yaçna II., note that the priest, holding the Baresma rods in his hand, repeats constantly the words, "I wish"—properly, I WILL—so and so. By the ceremony of consecration of the sacred twigs a magical power had been imparted to them, and with the help of this to fortify his own will-force, the celebrant seeks the attainment of his several good desires: the heavenly Fire, the good spirits, all good influences throughout the several kingdoms of Nature, and the law or WORD. In the middle ages of Europe, divining-rods were in general use, not only to discover subterranean waters and springs, and veins of metal, but also fugitive thieves and murderers. I could devote an entire lecture to this subject and prove to you that this phenomenon is a strictly scientific one. In Baring-Gould's *Curious Myths of the Middle Ages* will be found highly interesting accounts of these trials of the mystical power of the rods which time forbids my quoting. At this day the rods are employed to discover springs, and the Cornish miners carry sprigs of hazel or other wood in their caps. The author of the work named, while ascribing the strange results he is obliged to record principally to the imagination, is yet constrained to add that "The powers of Nature are so mysterious and inscrutable that we must be cautious in limiting them, under abnormal conditions, to the ordinary laws of experience." And in this he is backed up by the experience of many generations of witnesses, in many different countries.

We have mentioned the invocation of the divine WORD or Name in the Yaçna. All the ancient authorities affirm that there is a certain Word of Power by pronouncing which the Adept subjugates all the forces of Nature to his will. It is mentioned by many authors. One of the latest is the author of a book called *Rabbi Jeshua*, who, speaking of Jesus, says, "He had perhaps endeavoured to employ magic arts, and to bewitch the council by invocation of the Name through which all incantations were rendered effective"—(p. 143). Among the Aryans the Agnihotra priest used to prepare the sacrificial wood and, upon reciting the appropriate Mantra, the heavenly fire of Agni would descend and kindle it. In the Avestâ, Zarathusht smites the fiends with the spiritual power of the Word (Darmesteter, lxxvii). It represents him as a saint-militant, repelling force by force. In Fargard XI, Zarathushtra asks Ahura-Mazda how he shall purge the house, the fire, the water, the earth, the cow, the tree, the faithful man and woman, the stars, the moon, the sun, the boundless light, and all good things. Ahura Mazda answers :—

"Thou shalt chant the *cleansing words*, and the house shall be clean, clean shall be the fire," &c. &c.

"So thou shalt say these fiend-smiting and most-healing words; thou shalt chant the Ahunavairya five times," &c.

Then are given various words to employ for different acts of cleansing. But *the* WORD, the one most potent—the Name which, so says Proclus in his treatise upon the Chaldean Oracles—" rushes into the infinite worlds," is not written there.* Nor can it be written, nor is it ever pronounced above the breath, nor, indeed, is its nature known except to the highest Initiates. The efficacy of all words used as charms and spells lies in what the Aryans call the Vâch, a certain latent power resident in Âkâsha. Physically, we may describe it as the power to set up certain measured vibrations, not in the grosser atmospheric particles whose undulations beget light, sound, heat and electricity, but in the latent spiritual principle or Force—about the nature of which modern science knows scarcely anything. No words whatever have the slightest efficacy unless uttered by one who is perfectly free from all weakening doubt or hesitancy, is for the moment wholly absorbed in the thought of uttering them, and has a cultivated power of will which makes him send out from himself a conquering impulse. Spoken prayer is, in fact, an incantation, and when spoken by the "heart," as well as by the lips, has a power to attract good and repel bad influences. But to patter off prayers so many times a day while your thoughts are roving over your landed estates, fumbling your money-bags, or straying away among any other worldly things, is but mere waste of breath. The Bible says, "the prayer of the righteous availeth much"; and so it does. There is the case of George Mueller, of Bath, England, who for thirty years has supported the entire expenses of his orphanage—now a very large institution of charity—by the

---

* Though properly—the WORD or the NAME is neither a word nor a name in the sense we give it.

voluntary gifts of unknown passers-by at the door, who drop into his charity-boxes *the exact sum he prays for* to meet the day's necessities. History does not contain a more curious or striking example than this. This man prays with such faith and fervency, his motives are so pure, his labours so beneficent, that he attracts to him all the good influences of Nature, although he knows neither the "Ahunavairya," nor the Aryan Mantras, nor the Buddhistic Pirit. Use what words you may, if the heart is clean, the thought intense, and the will concentrated, the powers of Nature will come at your bidding and be your slaves. Says the *Dabistan* (p. 2):—

"Having the heart in the body full of Thy remembrance, the novice, as well as the Adept, in *contemplation*
"Becomes a supreme king of beatitude, and the throne of the kingdom of gladness.
"Whatever road I took, it joined the street which leads to Thee;
"The desire to know Thy being is also the life of the meditators;
"He who found that there is nothing but Thee has found the *final* knowledge;
"The Mobed is the teacher of Thy truth, and the world a school."

But this Mobed was not a mere errand-runner, or droner of Gâthâs perfunctorily without understanding a word he was saying, but a real Mobed. So high an ideal of human perfectibility had he to live up to, Cambyses is said to have commanded the execution of a priest who had allowed himself to be bribed, and had his skin stretched over the chair in which his son and successor sat in his judicial capacity. (*Hist. Magic.* I., 2.) "Mobed" is derived from Mogbed—from the Persian *Mog*, and means a true priest. Ennemoser truly says that the renowned wisdom of the Magi in Persia, Media, and the neighbouring countries, "contained also the secret teachings of philosophy and the sciences, which were only communicated to priests, who were regarded as mediators between God and man, and as such, and *on account of their knowledge*, were highly respected."—(*Ibid.*) The priests of a people are exactly what the people require them to be. Remember that, friends, and blame yourselves only for the state of religion among you. You have just what you are entitled to. If you yourselves were more pure, more spiritual-minded, more religous, your priesthood would be so. You are merchants, not idolaters, but—as Professor Monier Williams pithily remarks in the *Nineteenth Century* (March 1881)—worshippers of the solid rupee. The genuine Parsi, he says, "turns with disgust from the hideous idolatry practised by his Hindu fellow-subjects. He offers no homage to blocks of wood and stone, to monstrous many-headed images, grotesque symbols of good luck, or four armed deities of fortune. But he bows down before the silver image which Victoria, the Empress of India, has set up in her Indian dominions."

And this, according to Zoroastrianism, is a crime as great. In his ecstatic vision of the symbolical scenes shown him by the angel Serosh-yazata for the warning and encouragement of his people, Ardâi Virâf, the purest of Magian priests at the court of Ardeshir Bâbagân, saw the pitiable state to which the soul of a covetous money-hoarder is reduced after death. The poor wretch, penniless—since he could take not a *direm* with him—his heart buried with his savagely-loved treasures, his once pure nature corrupted and deformed—moved the Seer to profoundest pity. "I saw it," says he, "creep along in fear and trembling, and presently a wind came sweeping along, loaded with the most pestilential vapours, even as it were from the boundaries of hell . . . In the midst of this wind appeared a form of the most demoniacal appearance . . . " The terrified soul attempts to escape but in vain ; the awful vengeful shape by voice and power roots him to the spot. He enquires in trembling accents who it may be, and is answered, "I am your genius [that is, his spiritual counterpart and now his mastering destiny] and have become thus deformed by your crimes; whilst you were innocent I was handsome. . . . You have laid in no provisions for this long journey ; you were rich, but you did no good with your riches . . . ; and not only did no good yourself, but prevented, by your evil example, those whose inclinations led them to do good ; and you have often mentally said, 'When is the day of judgment ? To me it will never arrive.'" (*Ardâi Virâf Nameh*, by Captain

J. A. Pope, p. 56.) Say it is a vision, if you will, yet nevertheless it mirrors an awful truth. The worship of the silver image of Victoria on the rupee is even more degrading than the Hindu's worship of Ganesha or Hari ; for he, at least, is animated by a pious thought, whereas the greedy money-getter is but defiling himself with the filth of selfishness.

The Parsi community is already half-way along the road to apostacy. Gone is the fiery enthusiasm that made your forefathers give up everything they prized rather than repudiate their faith; that supported them during a whole century in the sterile mountains of Khurâsân or the outlying deserts ; that comforted them in their exile at Sanjân, and gave them hope after the battle with their hereditary enemy Aluf Khân. Formerly, it was Religion first and Rupee last ; now it is Rupee first and everything else after it. See, I, a stranger, point with one finger to your palatial bungalows, your gorgeous equipages, and your ostentatious annual squandering of twelve lakhs of money at festivals ; with the other to the wretched subscriptions of Rs. 16,000 towards the support of the Râhanumai Mazdiyasna Sabha—a good society for the promotion of your religion among your own children, and of Rs. 10,000 to the orthodox Parsi Society of Khetwadi ! The proverb says, "figures cannot lie," and in this instance they do not. If I wanted the best test to apply to your religious zeal, I should look at the sum of your expenditures for vain show and sensual enjoyment, as compared with what you do for the maintenance of your religion in its purity, and to the sort of conduct you tolerate in your priests. That is the mirror that impartial justice holds up before you ; behold your own image, and converse with conscience in your private moments ! What but conscience is personified in the " maid, of divine beauty or fiendish ugliness," according as the soul that approaches the Chinvad bridge was good or bad in life ? (Yasht. XXII.) She

"the well-shapen, strong and tall-formed maid, with the dogs at her sides,
one who *can distinguish* . . . and is of *high understanding.*"
(Vendidâd, Fargard XIX)

You have asked me to tell you about the spirit of your religion. I have only the truth to tell—the exact truth, without fear or favour. And I repeat, you are already half-way towards religious repudiation. You have already set money in the niche of faith; it only remains for you to throw the latter out of doors. For hypocrisy will not last for ever. Men weary of paying even lip-service to a religion they no longer respect. You may deceive yourselves, you cannot deceive that maiden at the bridge. Let three or four more generations of skeptics be passed through the educational mint of the college ; and let the teaching of your religion be neglected as it now is ; and the time will have come when it will be only the occasional brave heart that will dare call himself a Mazdiasnian. Let that stand as a prophecy if you choose: it *is* one, and it is based upon the experience of the human race. A black page will it be indeed, in the record of human events, when the last vestiges of the once splendid faith of Zarathustra shall be blotted from it, the last spark of the heavenly fire that shone from the Chaldean watch-towers of the sages be extinguished. And the more so, when that last extinction shall be caused, not by the sword of tyranny, nor by the crafty scheming of civil administrators, but by the beastly worldliness of its own hereditary custodians ; those to whom the lighted torch had been handed down through the ages, and who dropped it into the quenching black waters of Materialism.

Time fails me to enter into detailed explanation of the Zoroastrian symbols as perhaps I might—though I certainly am not able to do the subject full justice. The *sûdra* and *kûsti* with which you invest your children at the age of six years and three months have, of course, a magical significance. They pass through the hands of the Dastur, who, as we have seen, was formerly an Initiate, and he imparted to them magnetic properties which converted them into talismans against evil influences. After that a set formula of prayers and incantations is regularly prescribed for the whole life. The wearer's thoughts are directed towards the talismanic objects constantly, and when faith is present his or her will-power, or magnetic aura, is at such times infused into them. This is the secret of all talismans; the object worn, whatever it may be, need have no innate protective property, for that can be given to any rag, or stone, or bit of paper, by an Adept. Those of you who have read the Christian Bible will remember that from the body of Paul, the Apostle, "were brought unto the sick handkerchiefs or aprons, and the diseases departed from them, and *the evil spirits went out of them.*"—(Acts XIX., 12.) In the Ahuramazda-Yasht of the Khordeh-Avesta (25), it is written " by day and night, standing or sitting, sitting or standing, girt with the Aiwyâonhana (*kûsti*) or drawing off the Aiwyâonhana,

> "Going forwards out of the house, going forwards out of the confideracy, going forwards out of the region, coming into a region,
> "Such a man the points of the Drukhs-souled, proceeding from Aêshma, will not injure in that day or that night, not the slings, not the arrows, not knives, not clubs; the missiles will not penetrate (and) he be injured."

—(Haug's *Avesta*, p. 24, Khordeh-Avesta, Eng. Ed. of 1864).

Similar protective talismans are given by every Adept to each new pupil.

The use of Nirang for libations and ablutions is a survival of very ancient—probably pre-Irânian—mythic conceptions. There is nothing in the fluid itself of a disinfectant or purificatory character, but a magical property is given to it by ceremonial magical formulas, as a glass of common water may be converted into a valuable medicine by a mesmerizer by his holding it in his left hand and making circular passes over it with his right. The subject is treated in Darmesteter's Introduction to the Vendidâd. (lxxxviii.) " The storm floods that cleanse the sky of the dark fiends in it were described in a class of myths as the urine of a gigantic animal in the heavens. As the floods from the bull above drive away the fiend from the god, so they do from man here below, they make him 'free from the death-demon' (frânasu), and the death fiend flees away hell-wards, pursued by the fiend-smiting spell : ' Perish thou, O Drug . . . never more to give over to Death the living world of the good spirit !' " It may be that there is a more valid reason for the use of Nirang, but I have not yet discovered it. That an occult property *is* imparted to the fluid by the ceremonial is clear, since, if it be exposed to certain influences not in themselves putrefactive it will speedily become putrid ; while, on the other hand, it may be kept for years in a fresh condition without the admixture of antiseptic substances, and notwithstanding its occasional exposure to the air, if certain ceremonial rules be followed (of course, I have this from Parsi friends and not from my own observation : I would not express an unqualified opinion before investigating the subject). I recommend some Parsi chemist to analyse specimens of different ages, especially to determine the relative quantities of nitrogenous constituents.

When Professor Monier Williams vents his Oxonian scorn upon the ceremonies of the Parsis, he thereby only provokes the pity of such as have looked deeper than he into the meaning of ancient symbolism. "Here and there," says he, " lofty conceptions of the Deity, deep philosophical thoughts, and a pure morality are discoverable in the Avestâ like green spots in the desert ; *but they are more than neutralised by the silly puerilities and degrading superstitious ideas* which crop up as plentifully in its pages as thorns and thistles in a wilderness of sand."—(*Nineteenth Century*, Jan. 1881, p. 176.) Mr. Joseph Cook, the other day, in this hall, said the same. The good portions of the Vedas were so few as compared with the trashy residuum, that he likened them to the fabled jewel in the head of a filthy toad ! It is really very kind of these white Pandits to admit that there is anything whatever except rottenness and puerility in the old religions. Give each a statue !

In what has been said I have, you must remember, been speaking from the standpoint of a Parsi. I have tried to sink my personality and my personal religious preferences for the moment, and put myself in your place. That is the cardinal policy of the Theosophical Society. It has itself no sectarian basis, but its motto' is the Universal Brotherhood of man. It was organized to light the long-buried truths of not one, but all the world's Archaic religions. Its members are of all respectable castes, all faiths and races. It has many intelligent Parsis among them. For their sake and that of their co-religionists this lecture has been given. I have tried most earnestly to induce one of them or some other Parsi to come forward, and show you that no religion has profounder truths, deeper spiritual truths, concealed under its familiar mask, than yours. That I am the incompetent, though willing, spokesman for the ancient Yozdâthraigar is your fault, not mine. If I have spoken truth, if I have suggested new thoughts, if I have given any encouragement to the pious or pleasure to the learned, my reward is ample.

"Yathâ Ahû vairyô" : "The riches of Vohumanô shall be given to him who works in this world for Mazda . . ." is the promise of the Avesta.—(Fargard XXI.) Bear it in mind, ye Mazdiasnian, and remember the maiden and her dogs by the Chinvad bridge. I say this especially to my Parsi brothers in our Society, for I have the right to speak to them as an elder to his junior. As Parsis they have a paramount duty to their co-religionists, who are retrograding morally for want of the pure light. As Theosophists their interest embraces all their fellow-men of whatever creed. For we read in one of the most valuable of all books for the thoughtful Parsi—the *Dabistán or School of Manners :*

"The world is a book full of knowledge and of justice,
The binder of which book is destiny, and the binding the beginning and the end;
"The future of it is the law, and the leaves are the religious persuasions. . ."

For three years we have been preaching this idea of mutual toleration and Universal Brotherhood here in Bombay. Some have listened, but more have turned the deaf ear. Nay, they have done worse—they have spread lies and calumnies about us, until we were made to appear to you in false light. But the tide is turning at last, and public sympathy is slowly setting in our favour. It has been a dark night for us; it is now sunrise. If you can see a good motive behind us, and an honest purpose to do good by spreading truth, will you not join us, as you have other societies, and help to make us strong? We can perhaps be of service in aiding you to learn something more than you know about the spirit of Zoroastrianism. As I said before there are many important secrets to be extracted from ancient MSS. in Armenia. Perhaps they may be got at if you will join together and send some thoroughly competent Parsi scholars to make the search, in coöperation with the Tiflis Archæological Society. See how the Christians have organised a Palestine Exploration Society to search for anything in the shape of proof that can be found to corroborate their Bible. For years they have kept engineers and archæologists at work. Is your religion less important to you? Or do you mean to sit on your guineas until the last old MSS. has been burned to kindle Armenian fires, or torn to wrap medicines and sweets in, as I have seen Bibles utilised in India and Ceylon by heathen Borûs? One of our members (see *Theosophist*, July 1881,) went over the most important ground a few months ago. At the monastery of Soorb Ovanness in Armenia there were in 1877 three superannuated priests: now there remains but one. The "library of books and old manuscripts heaped up as waste paper in every corner of the pillar-cells, tempting no Kurd, are scattered over the rooms." And he says that, "For the consideration of a dagger and a few silver *abazes* I got several precious manuscripts from him"—the old priest. Now does not this suggest to you that through the friendly intermediation of our Society, and the help of Madame Blavatsky, you may be able to secure exceptional advantages in the matter of archæological and philological research connected with Zoroastrianism? We do not ask you to join us for our benefit, but for your own. I have thrown out the idea; act upon it or not as you choose. Beaten with Parsi children's shoes ought the Parsi to be who next gives a gaudy nautch or wedding *tamâshâ* unless he has previously subscribed as liberally as his means allow towards a fund for the promotion of his religion.

I told you in commencing that this subject of the spirit of Zoroastrianism is limitless. In consulting my authorities I have been perplexed to choose from the abundance of material, rather than troubled by any lack of it. There are a few more facts that I would like to mention before closing.

Abul Pharaj, in the *Book of Dynasties* (p. 54), states that Zarathust taught the Persians the manifestation of the *Wisdom* (the Lord's Anointed Son, or Logos, the Persian "Honovar"). This is the living manifested word of Deific Wisdom. He predicted that a Virgin should conceive immaculately, and that at the birth of that future messenger a six-pointed star would appear, and shine at noonday. In its centre would appear the figure of a Virgin. This six-pointed star you see engraved on the seal of the Theosophical Society. In the Kabalah the Virgin is the Astral Light or Âkâsha, and the six-pointed star the emblem of the macrocosm. The Logos, or Sosiosh to be born, means the secret knowledge or science which reveals the "Wisdom of God." Into the hand of the Prophet Messenger Zarathushtra were delivered many gifts. When filling the censer with *fire from the sacred altar*, as the Mobed did in ancient days, the act was symbolical of *imparting to the worshippers*, the knowledge of divine truth. In the *Gîtâ*, Krishna informs Arjuna that God is in the fire of the altar. "I am the Fire ; I am the sacrifice." The Flamens, or Etruscan priests, were so called because they were supposed to be illuminated by the *tongues of Fire* (Holy Ghost) and the Christians took the hint—(*Acts*, II). The scarlet robe of the Roman Catholic cardinal symbolizes the heavenly Fire. In an ancient Irish MSS. Zarathust is called *Airgiod-Lamh* or he of the Golden Hand—the hand which received and scattered celestical Fire—(Ousley's *Oriental Collections*, I., 303). He is also called Mogh Nuadhat, the Magus of the New Ordinance, or dispensation. Zarathushtra was one of the first reformers who taught to the people a portion of that which he had learned at his initiation, *viz.*, the six periods or *gâhambârs* in the successive evolution of the world. The first is *Maedyozarem*, that in which the heavenly canopy was formed ; the second, *Maedyoshahem*, in which the collected moisture formed the steamy clouds from which the waters were finally precipitated ; the third, *Paeti-shahem*, when the earth became consolidated out of primeval cosmic atoms ; the fourth, *Iyathrem*, in which earth gave birth to vegetation ; the fifth *Maediyarem*, when the latter slowly evoluted into animal life ; the sixth, *Hamespithamaedem*, when the lower animals culminated in man. The seventh period—to come at the end of a certain cycle—is prefigured in the promised coming of the Persian Messiah, seated on a horse ; *i. e.*, the sun of our solar system will be extinguished and the " Pralaya " will begin. In the Christian *Apocalypse* of St. John you will find the Persian symbolical prophecy closely copied ; and the Aryan Hindu awaits the coming of his Kalanki Avatâr when the celestial White Horse will come in the heavens, bestridden by Vishnu. The horses of the sun figure in all other religions.

There exists among the Persian Parsis a volume older than the present Zoroastrian writings. Its title is *Javidân Khirad*, or Eternal Wisdom. It is a work on the practical philosophy of Magic, with natural explanations. Hyde mentions it in his preface to the *Religo Veterum Persarum*. The four Zoroastrian *Ages* are the four races of men—the Black, the Russet, the Yellow, the White. The four castes of Manu are alleged to have typified this, and the Chinese show the same idea in their four orders of priests clothed in black, red, yellow, and white robes. St. John sees these same colours in the symbolic horses of his Revelation. Speaking of Zoroaster, whom he admits to have possessed all the sciences and philosophy then known in the world, the Rev. Oliver gives an account of the cave-temple of which so much is said in Zoroastrian literature. " Zoroaster," he writes, " retired to a *circular* cave or grotto in the mountains of Bokhara, which he ornamented with a profusion of symbolical and astronomical decorations, consecrating it to Methr-Az. . . . Here the sun was represented by a splendid gem . . . in a conspicuous part of the roof . . . and the four ages of the world were represented by so many gloves of gold, silver, brass, and iron.— (*History of Initiation*, p. 9.)

And now, gentlemen — orthodox and heterodox — leaders among the Parsi community — a word with you on practical matters before we part. In three days more I shall leave Bombay on a long journey and the accidents of travel, to which we are all liable, may prevent my ever addressing you again. I pray you, therefore, to listen to what a sincere friend has to say : a friend who is none the less one in that he never asked you for a pice of your money for himself and never will.

I have lived among you for three years. During this whole time I have been associating on terms of confidential intimacy with some of your most intelligent young men. I have admitted them, and in some cases their wives with them, into our Society. Thus I have perhaps had exceptional opportunities to learn the real state of your people and religion. I find both in sore need of an organized, unselfish and persistent effort among yourselves. Your people look up to you as their best advisers, the Mobeds respect your influence and court your favour. You have it in your power to do a world of good. Will you do it ? You now spend annually from twelve to fifteen lakhs of rupees upon stupid *tamáshás*—that do not belong to your own religion at all ; that give you no real pleasure ; that crush many poorer than you to the very ground with debt ; that defile your own natures with disgusting pride and conceit; that encourage intemperate habits in the young ; and that weaken pious inclinations. The burden upon the community is so sore, and common-sense of your best men so revolts at them, that years ago you would have returned to the simpler pleasures of your forefathers, but that you lacked the moral courage to combine. A reform like this is never to be effected alone; the leaders must combine. Take two of the fifteen lakhs you now worse than waste and put it aside as a Fund for the promotion of the Mazdiasnian Religion, and see what you might do for your children and children's children. Do not tell me you cannot afford to create such a fund, when the whole world knows that you are ready to give thousands to every object suggested by a European for the benefit or flattery of some one of his race, and even to rear statues to those who are not the friends of your religion. "Charity begins at home;" give, then, first for your own people, and of your remaining surplus to outside objects.

There is a fatal inactivity growing apace among you. Not only are you not the religionists you once were, you are not the old-time merchants. You are being elbowed out of commerce, and it is not very uncommon to see your sons going from door to door in search of employment at salaries of from fifty to seventy-five rupees per month, with their pockets full of matriculation papers or F.E.A. and B.A. diplomas. And instead of your being, as in the olden time, the kings of Indian trade and commerce, you are jostled by successful Bhattias, Borahs, Maimans and Khojahs who have accumulated fortunes. You are making no proper effort to impart a practical knowledge of your religious principles and tenets to the educated rising generation; hence very naturally they are largely becoming skeptics and infidels. They do not as yet actually despise it *en masse*—the time for that has not quite arrived. But on account of your neglect to show them its sublimity and make them deeply respect it, they have reached the stage of indifference. One needed step would be to have your prayer-books translated into the vernacular and English, with footnotes to explain the text, and especially, commentaries to show the reconciliation of Mazdiasnian philosophy with modern science. It is worse than useless—it is highly injurious to one's faith—to chatter off prayers in an unknown tongue, encouraging the hypocrisy of pretending to be pious while one has not the food at hand for a single pious thought. I have watched both priests and *behedin* at their prayers, morning and evening, and seen more that were not attending to the business in hand than that were.

If you wish to revive your religion, you should, besides organising the exploring expeditions and archæological surveys I previously spoke of, also rear a class of Parsi preachers who would be able to expound it thoroughly, and maintain it against all critics and enemies. These men should be highly educated, and versed in Sanskrit, Zend, Pahalvi, Persian, and English. Some should know German and French—like my honoured friend, Mr. Kama. With Western literature they should be familiar. Some should be taught oratory, so as to expound in a popular style the sacred theme. It might also be well to found travelling scholarships, as the Europeans have, to be given to especially meritorious students.

A stricter moral example should be set by you to your youth, who have, as I said above, fallen in too many cases into evil ways. They do not regard truth, nor show as much respect to elders as formerly.

As your understanding of the spirit of your religion has decreased, you have been growing more and more superstitious; essentials are neglected, and non-essentials given an exaggerated consequence.

Finally, and chiefly, the priestly class needs a thorough reformation. There are more than you need to perform the offices of religion and the profession; being overcrowded, their influence is continually decreasing, and they have come, as a Parsi gentleman once remarked to me, to be looked upon as licensed beggars—a state of things which must certainly grieve your really learned Dasturs more than any one else.

The foregoing thoughts are submitted to you with great deference and in the hope that they will be pardoned in view of the kindly interest which prompts them. Before embodying them in this discourse I have taken the counsel of one of my most respectable Parsi friends; so that you may regard them as in fact the views of one of your own community.

And now I ask you, as a final word, if the crisis has not arrived when every man of you is called upon, by all he holds sacred, to be up and doing. Shall the voice of Chaldean Fathers, which whispers to you across the ages, be heard in vain? Shall the example of Zarathust and others be forgotten? Must the memory of your hero-forefathers be dishonoured? Shall there never more arise among you a Dastur Nairyosang Dhaval to draw down the celestial flame from the azure vault upon your temple-altar? Is the favour of Ahura-Mazda no longer a boon precious enough to strive for and to deserve? The Hindu pilgrims to the temple-shrine of Jotir Math at Badrinath affirm that some, more favoured than the rest, have sometimes seen far up amid the snow and ice of Mount Dhavalagiri—a Himâlayan peak—the venerable figures of Mahâtmâs—perhaps of Rishis—who keep their watch and ward over the fallen Aryan faith, and wait the time for its resuscitation. So too—our travelling Brother in Armenia writes—there is a cave up near the crest of Allah-Dag,* where at each setting of the sun, appears at the cave's mouth a stately figure holding a book of records in his hands. The people say that this is Mathan, last of the great Magian priests; whose body died some sixteen centuries ago. His anxious shade watches from thence the fate of Zoroaster's faith. And shall he stand in vain? Is he to see that faith die out for want of spiritual refreshment? Ye sons of Sohrab and of Rustam, rouse! Awake ere it is too late! The hour is here; where are the MEN?

---

* A mountain chain of Great Armenia. For particulars of the legend here described see *Theosophist*, Vol. II., p. 213.

ZOROASTRIANISM IN THE LIGHT OF OCCULT PHILOSOPHY.

THE following letter having been sent to us from a Parsi gentleman, we publish the paragraphs containing his queries *seriatim* as in the original, but separating them with a view of making our answer more comprehensible. This arrangement, we hope, will always simplify the work, and help the reader to a far clearer understanding of both the questions asked and the answers given, than it would, had we published the letter without any break whatever, or answered the queries as usually done, by referring the readers to foot-notes.

> Will you or any of your contributors tell me whether Zoroastrianism, regarded from the stand-point of Occult philosophy, is in itself monotheism, pantheism, polytheism or atheism? I have not been able to ascertain it from the learned lecture of Colonel Olcott on the "Spirit of Zoroastrianism."

The answer depends upon how the question is put. If we are asked Zoroastrianism—loosely and indifferently referred to as Magianism, Mazdaism, Fire-worship and Parsiism, then we answer —" it is all that which you say." It is "monotheism, pantheism, polytheism," and even—"atheism," when placed in contradistinction to modern theism—its respective qualifications depending upon the epoch named. Thus, if we had to describe broadly the origin of this religion from the stand-point, and upon the authority of the Occult teachings, we would call it by its original, primitive name, that of Magianism. Locating its first development in those vast regions which would have to be described as the whole area between the Persian Gulf and the Sea of Okhotsk in its length, and that which stretches through the unexplored deserts between Altai and the Himâlayan mountains in its breadth, we would place it back at an epoch, undreamt of by modern science and, therefore, rejected by all but the most speculative and daring anthropologists. We have no right to give out in this journal

the correct number of years, or rather of ages upon ages, since
—according to the doctrines of the Secret Science—the first
seeds of Magianism were sown by the hand of the BEING to
whose duty it falls to rear, nurse and guide the tottering steps
of the renascent human races, that awake anew to life on every
planet in its turn, after its periodical " obscuration." It goes
as far back as the days of our local *Manvantara*, so that seeds
sown among the first " root-race " began sprouting in its infant
brain, grew up and commencing to bear fruit towards the
latter part of the second race, developed fully during the third*
into what is known among Occultists as the " Tree of Knowledge" and the " Tree of Life"—the real meaning of both having been, later on, so sadly disfigured and misinterpreted by
both Zoroastrians and Christians. But we can inform our correspondent of the following : Magianism, in the days of its full
maturity and practice,† and long ages before the first of the 12
great religions, its direct off-shoots—mentioned and feebly
described by Mohsan Fani in the *Dabistan*,—ever saw light;
and even much anterior to the appearance to the first devotees
of the religion of Hushang, which, according to Sir W. Jones,
" was long anterior to that of Zerathusht (see *Asiat. Res.*, vol.
ii, pp. 48—49), the Prophet of the modern Parsis—that religion, as we can undeniably prove, was " ATHEISM." At any
rate, it would be so regarded now, by those who call Kapila and
Spinoza, Buddha and our Mahâtmas, Brihaspati (of the Char-
vâk) and the modern Adwaitees, all alike, *nâstikas* or atheists.
Assuredly no doctrine about a *personal* God, a gigantic man

---

* One who has studied *The Fragments of Occult Truth* knows that our present race is the *fifth*, and that we have two more to pass through before we reach our end—on this planet.—*Ed., Theosophist.*

† "Throughout the Middle Ages nothing was known of Mazdeanism, but the name of his founder, who from a Magus was converted into a Magician, a master of the hidden sciences," says James Darmestetor, who knows as much as exoteric science will permit him of the former : but being wholly ignorant of *esoteric* sciences, knows nothing of the latter at all and therefore blunders greatly. One could not be a *Magha*, a Magus-priest, without being, at the same time, what is now known under the vulgar term of "Magician." But of this later on.—*Ed., Theosophist.*

and no more—(though a number of so-called *divine beings* were and are still recognised)—was ever taught by the true Magi.* Hence Zoroaster—the *seventh* prophet (according to the *Desatir*, whose compilers mixed up and confused the 14 "Zara-Ishtars,† the high priests and Initiates of the Chaldean worship or Magian Hierophants—the 13th)—would be regarded as an *atheist* in the modern sense of the word. All the Orientalists, with Haug at their head, agree to say that in the oldest, or the

---

* Let it not be understood that we here speak of the "Magi" in general, whether we view them as one of the Medean tribes (?) as some Orientalists (Darmesteter for one) relying upon a vague statement of Herodotus believe, or a Sacerdotal caste like the Brahmans—as we maintain. We refer but to their Initiates. The origin of the Brahmans and Magi in the night of time is one, the secret doctrine teaches us. First they were a hierarchy of Adepts, of men profoundly versed in physical and spiritual sciences and occult knowledge, of various nationalities, all celibates, and enlarging their numbers by the transmission of their knowledge to voluntary neophytes. Then when their numbers became too large to be contained in the "Airyânûm-vaejô," the Adepts scattered far and wide, and we can trace them establishing other hierarchies on the model of the first in every part of the globe, each hierarchy increasing, and finally becoming so large, as to have to restrict admission; "the half-adepts" going back to the world, marrying and laying the first foundation of "left-hand" science or sorcery, the misuse of the Holy Knowledge. In the third stage, the numbers of the *True ones* became with every age more limited and secret, the admissions being beset now with new difficulties. We begin to see the origin of the Temple Mysteries. The hierarchy divides into two parts. The chosen few, the hierophants,—the *imperium in imperio*—remaining celibates, the *exoteric* priests make of marriage a law, an attempt to perpetuate adepts by hereditary descent, and fail sadly in it. Thus we find Brahmans and Magi, Egyptian priests and Roman hierarchs and Augurs enjoining life and inventing religious clauses to prove its necessity. No need repeating and reminding the reader of that which is left to his own knowledge of history, and his intuitions. In our day we find the descendants, the heirs to the old wisdom, scattered all over the globe in small isolated and unknown communities, whose objects are misunderstood, and whose origin has been forgotten; and only two religions, the result of the teaching of those priests and hierophants of old. The latter are found in the sorry remains called respectively—Brahmans and Dasturs or Mobeds. But there is still the nucleus left, albeit it be so strenuously denied, of the heirs of the primitive Magi, of the Vedic *Magha* and the Greek *Magos*—the priests and gods of old, the last of whom manifested openly and defiantly during the Christian era in the person of Appolonius of Tyana.—*Ed., Theosophist.*

† See *Isis Unveiled*, Vol. II., pp. 1289.

second part of the *Yaçna*, nothing is said or fixed of the doctrine regarding God, nor of any theology.

The lecture has elucidated many obscurities and absurdities in the Avesta, from the stand-point of Occult philosophy. But they are so few that the youths whom the Colonel took to task have, I am convinced, become no wiser. Can any one tell me whether the Colonel meant that in order to understand their religion, the Parsi youths should study Yogism and Occultism?

Our President never meant that they should *practise* "Yogism." All that he urged upon them was, that before they scoffed at their own religion, of which they knew so little, and became either modern agnostics or out-and-out corporealists, they should study Zoroastrianism as a philosophy, and in the light of esoteric sciences—which alone could teach them the truth by giving the correct version of the meaning of the various emblems and symbolisms.

The learned Colonel said the Parsis are the heirs of the Chaldean lore, and that the Chaldean and the Hebrew Kabalah would throw considerable light on the meaning of the Avasta. Can any one tell me where and in what language these books are to be found, and whether these works are not also so much allegorical as to require the aid of Occult philosophy to understand their true meaning?

The lecturer stated a fact. More even than the Brahmans, are the Parsis heirs to Chaldean wisdom, since they are the direct, though the latest, off-shoots of Aryan Magianism. The Occultists are very little concerned with that apparent difficulty that the Magian "Chaldees" with all their Priests and Initiates, whether of the Medes, the Scythians, or the Babylonians are regarded by the Orientalists as of Semitic origin, while the ancient Irânians are Aryans. The classification of those nations into Turanians, Akkadians, Semites and what not, is at best arbitrary. The word "Chaldean" does not refer merely to a native or an inhabitant of Chaldea, but to "Chaldeism," the oldest science of astrology and occultism. And in that sense the Zoroastrians are the true heirs to Chaldean wisdom, "the light which shineth in darkness," though (modern) "darkness comprehended it not," and the Parsis themselves know nothing of it now. The Hebrew

Kabalah is but the loud echo of the Chaldean ; an echo which passing through the corridors of Time picked up in its transit all kinds of alien sounds that got mixed up with the original key-notes struck beyond the epochs known to the present profane generations ; and thus it reached the later student of Hebrew lore as a confused and somewhat distorted voice. Yet, there is much to learn in it, for him who has the patience and the perseverance required, since first of all he would have to learn the *Gemantria, Notaricon* and *Themura*.* When speaking of the Kabalah, the lecturer meant by it, the *universal*, not any special esoteric system, already adapted to a later exoteric creed as is at present the Jewish secret science. The word "Kabalah" is derived from a Hebrew root meaning reception of knowledge ; and practically speaking it refers to all the old systems handed down by oral transmission, and is very nearly allied to the Sanskrit "Smriti" and "Shruti," and the Chaldaic "Zend."† There would be little use for the Parsi or Hindu beginner to study only the Hebrew or even the Chaldean Kabalah, since those works upon them which are now extant are written either in Hebrew or Latin. But there would be a great deal of truth unearthed were both to apply themselves to the study of the identical knowledge veiled under the exoteric symbolisms of both the Zend-Avastâ and the Brahmanical books. And this they can do by forming themselves into a small society of intelligent earnest students of symbolism, especially the Zend and Sanskrit scholars.

---

* The Jewish methods of examining the Scriptures for their hidden meaning. —*Ed.*, *Theosophist.*

† Of course, as found out by the Orientalists, the word "Zend" does not apply to any language whether dead or living, and never belonged to any of the languages or dialects of ancient Persia. (See *Farhang-i-Jehangiri*, the Persian dictionary). It means, as in one sense correctly stated, "a commentary or explanation," but it also means that which the Orientalists do not seem to have any idea about, *viz.*, the "rendering of the esoteric sentences," the veil used to conceal the correct meaning of the *Zen-d-zar* texts, the sacerdotal language in use among the Initiates of Archaic India. Found now in several undecipherable inscriptions it is still used and studied unto this day in the secret communities of the Eastern Adepts, and called by them—according to the locality—*Zend-zar* and *Brahma* or *Deva-Bhashya.*—*Ed.*, *Theosophist.*

They could get the esoteric meanings and the names of the works needed from some advanced chelas of our Society.

<small>The Colonel recommends the translating of prayer. Does he mean that the translation of prayers in their present state will better enlighten the youths? If not, then does he imply that the meaning of the whole Zend-Avasta can be made intelligible and philosophical by the aid of a thorough Occultist?</small>

It is precisely what he meant. By a correct translation or rather a correct explanation of their liturgical prayers, and a preliminary knowledge of the *true* meaning of even a few of the most important symbolisms—generally those that appear the meaningless and absurd in the sight of the modern Zend scholars, as the dog, *e. g.*, which plays such an important part in Parsi ceremonies*—the "Parsi youths" would acquire thereby the key to the true philosophy that underlies their "wretched superstitions and myths," as they are called by the

---

<small>* Compare the so-called "*Akkadian* formulæ of exorcism" of the earliest periods known to the Orientalists to which the collection of charms and amulets belong—(in truth very *late* periods)—with most of the injunctions found in the *Vendidâd* (Fargard XIII) concerning the dog. It seems almost incredible that even the dullest among the Zend scholars should not perceive that verse 163, for instance (same Fargard) which says, "For no house could subsist on the earth *made by Ahura*, (in this case the "house"—not the earth—made by Ahura) but for those two dogs of mine, the shepherd's dog and the house dog "—cannot refer really to chess animals. The commentary made in it (*Saddar* 31, *Hyde* 35) is absurd and ridiculous. It is not, as it says, that "not a single head of cattle would remain in existence but for the dogs,"—but that all humanity, endowed as it is with the highest intellect among the intelligences of the animal kingdom, would, under the leadership of Aṅramainyus, mutually destroy themselves physically and spiritually, but for the presence of the "dogs"—the two highest spiritual principles. The dog Vaṅhapara, (the hedge hog, says the commentator) "the good creature that from midnight (our time of ignorance) till the sun is up (spiritual enlightenment), goes and kills thousands of the creatures, the evil spirit," (Farg. XIII. 1) is our spiritual conscience. He who "kills it" (stifles its voice within himself) shall not find his way over the Chinvad bridge (leading to paradise). Then compare these symbolisms with those of the Akkadian talismans. Even as translated by G. Smith, distorted as they are, still the *seven* dogs described—as the "blue," the "yellow," the "spotted," &c., can be shown to have all of them reference to the same seven human principles as classified by Occultism. The whole collection of the "formulæ of exorcism," so called, of the Akkadians, is full of references to the 7 evil and the 7 good spirits, which are our principles in their dual aspect.—*Ed., Theosophist.*</small>

missionaries who would fain force upon the world their own instead.

Prayer is repugnant to the principles of atheists. How then does the learned Colonel reconcile his advice to the Parsis to throw better heart into their prayers? Does he also mean that Occult philosophy will justify the prayers in Zend Avasta, offered to the sun, the moon, almost all the supposed pure things of the creation? If he thinks that the fixing of attention upon such objects is conducive to being freed from worldly desires and thoughts, does he think also that these views or prayers will be believed in, or acted upon, by the present generation?

Colonel Olcott was never an atheist " to our knowledge," but an esoteric Buddhist, rejecting a *personal* God. Nor was *genuine* prayer—*i. e.*, the exercise of one's intense will over events (commonly brought about by blind chance) to determine their direction—ever repugnant to him. Even prayers, as commonly understood, are not "repugnant" in his sight, but simply useless, when not absurd and ridiculous as in the case of prayers to either stop or bring about rain, etc. By "prayer" he means—WILL, the desire or command *magnetically expressed* that such-and-such a thing beneficent to ourselves or others should come to pass. The sun, the moon and the stars in the Avasta are all emblematical representations—the sun, especially—the latter being the concrete and most appropriate emblem of the one universal life-giving principle, while the stars are part and parcel of the Occult sciences.

But since not every one knows in our day " the science of the stars," nor are there many Zend scholars, the best course to be pursued is to make at least a beginning by having the "prayers" translated. The lecturer, as far as we are aware, did not mean to advise any one to believe in, or "act upon," the *modern* prayers in their present liturgic exoteric form. But it is just because they are now muttered parrot-like, remaining incomprehensible to the great majority, that they have to be either correctly rendered, or, bringing on finally indifference and disgust, that they have to be abandoned very soon to utter oblivion. The word "prayer" received its modern significance of a supplication to a Supreme or some inferior divine being, only when its once widely known and real esoteric meaning had already become clouded with an exoteric veil; after which it soon disappeared enshrouded beneath the impenetrable shell of a badly digested anthropomorphism. The Magian knew not of any *Supreme* "personal" individuality. He recognized but Ahura—the "lord"—the 7th Principle* in man,—and "prayed," *i. e.*, made efforts during the hours of meditation, to assimilate with, and merge, his other principles—that are dependent on the physical body and ever under the sway of Aṅra-Mainyus (or matter)— into the only pure, holy and *eternal* principle in him, his divine monad. To whom else could he pray? Who was "Ormazd" if not the chief *Spenta-Mainyus*, the monad, our own god-principle in us? How can Parsis consider him now in the light of the "one Supreme God" independent of man, since even in the sorry remnants of the sacred books of Mazdayasnism there is enough to show that he was never so considered. They are full of his shortcomings, lack of power (during his dependent individuality in connection with man), and his frequent failings. He is addressed as the "maker of the *material* world" in every question put to him by Zarathushtra. He invokes Vâyu (the Holy Ghost of the Mazdeans), "the god-conqueror of light (or true knowledge and spiritual enlightenment), the smiter of the fiends (passions) all made of light,"† for help against Aṅra-Mainyus; and at the birth of Zarathustra he entreats Ardvi-Sura Anâhita‡ that the newly

---

* The seven principles are:—According to Zoroastrianism (*vide* Yasna, Ha 55)—1 Tanu; 2 Uétâna; 3 Kaherpa; 4 Tavishi; 5 Baodhang; 6 Urvan; 7 Farohar. According to esoteric Buddhism—1 Rupa=Body; 2 Pran or Jiva= Vitality; 3 Linga Sharira=Astral Body; 4 Kâma Rupa=Animal Soul; 5 Manas =Human Soul; 6 Buddhi=Spiritual Soul; 7 Atma=Spirit.—*Comp.*

† Yast. XV., 3.

‡ Begging the pardon of our European Sankritists and Zend scholars we would ask them to tell, if they know, who was the Mazdean goddess Ardvi-Sura Anâhita? We maintain, and can prove what we say, that the said personage implored by Ahura, and Sarasvati (the Brahminical goddess of Secret or Occult wisdom,) are identical. Where is the philosophy of the Supreme God, "the omnipotent and omniscient-ALL," seeking for the help of his own creature?— *Ed., Theosophist.*

born should not abandon, but stand by him in his eternal struggles with Ahriman.

The offers made by Ahura-Mazda to Yima (the first man) to receive instruction from him *are rejected* (Farg. II—17). Why ? "Because," as he answers, "I was not born, I was not taught to be the preacher and the bearer of the law." No, he was not born, the Occult Science tells us, for from whom could he have been born since he was *the first man* (let the modern anthropologists and physiologists explain if they can). But he was *evoluted from a pre-existing form*, and as such had no need as yet of the laws and teachings of his 7th Principle. The "Supreme" and the "Almighty" remains satisfied ! He makes him only promise that he will take care of his creatures and make them happy, which promise is fulfilled by "the son of Vivanhao." Does not this show that Ahura-Mazda is something which can be explained and defined, only by the Occult Doctrine ? And wisely does it explain to us that Ahura is our own inner, truly *personal* God, and that he is our Spiritual light and the "Creator of the material world"— *i.e.*, the architect and shaper of the microcosm—*Man*, when the latter knew how to resist Aṅra-Mainyus, or Kâma,—lust or material desires—by relying on him who overshadows him, the Ahura-Mazda or Spiritual Essence. The latter invokes "Vâyu," who, in the Mazdean occult sense, is the *Universal*, as he is the *Individual*, light of man. Hence his prayer to "Vâyu" that Zarathustra, the being who will teach truth to his followers, should side with him, Ahura, and help to fight Ahriman, without which help even "He" (our 7th Principle) is powerless to save man *from himself*; for Ahriman is the allegorical representation of the lower human principles, as Ahura-Mazda is that of the higher. But Zarathustra accepts and worships Ahura-Mazda in the *Vendidâd* and elsewhere, because this prophet in the generic sense of the name is the representative of the latter portion of the *Second* race. And now let the Parsi mathematicians calculate how long ago lived the *first* Zara-Ishtar, or Zoroaster ; and let them study the *real* Mazdaism, not the later excrescences with which it became overgrown throughout the cycles of the ages and races. Which of the Zarathustras was the real law-giver of the Chaldean Mazdaism? Surely not he to whom Ahura-Mazda says: "The fair Yima. O holy Zarathushtra, he was the first mortal *before thee*, with whom I, Ahura-Mazda, did converse, whom I taught the law of Ahura, *the law of Zarathushtra.*" (Farg. II, 2.) Teaching the law of Zarathushtra to the same Zarathushtra, and ages before that Zarathushtra was born, reminds one of Moses made to narrate in *his* "Pentateuch" his own death and burial. In the *Vendidâd*, if Ahura is "the Creator of the *material world*," *i.e.*, the microcosm man, Yima is the real creator of the earth. There, he is shown master of Spenta Ârmaiti, the genius of the earth, and he, by the power of his innate *untaught* light and knowledge, simply for the absence of Aṅra-Mainyus—who comes later on—forces "the earth to grow larger and to bear flocks and herds and men *at his will and wish.*" (Farg. II, 11.) Ahura-Mazda is also the Father of Tistriya, the *rain-bestowing* god (the 6th Principle), that fructifies the parched soil of the 5th and 4th, and helps them to bear good fruit through their own exertions, *i.e.*, by tasting of Haoma, the tree of eternal life, through spiritual enlightenment. Finally and undeniably Ahura-Mazda being called the chief and father of the six "*Ameshâ Spentas*"— or of the six principles of which he is the seventh—the question is settled. He is "Ahura" or rather Asura—the "living spirit in man," the first of whose 20 different names he gives as *Ahmi*, "I am." It was to impress upon his audience the full importance of the recognition of, and reliance upon, (hence that of addressing *it* in "prayer") this one God from whom proceed and in whom are centred *Humate*, *hukhte* and *hvarshte*,* the sublime condensation of all human and social law, that Colonel Olcott recommended to the "Parsi youths," the study of *their* prayers.

Will the learned Colonel be so kind as to say whether in his opinion it does not appear that the Zend-avasta represents the genuine *dictates* of Zoroaster, or

---

* Purity of thought, purity of word, purity of action.

that it contains extreme mutilation and additions made before it was written and after it was written?

We think we can, for the Colonel's opinions are ours, having studied under the same Master and knowing that he shares in the same views, namely, that the Zend-avasta represents now only the general system, the dead letters, so to say, of the dictates of Zoroaster. If the Orientalists agree that the bulk of the Avasta is pre-Sassanian, nevertheless, they do not, nor can they, fix a definite period for its origin.

As well expressed by Darmesteter, the Parsi "sacred books are the ruins of a religion." The Avasta revised and translated into Pahlavi by Ardeshir Bâbagân is not the Avasta of modern Parsiism, with its numberless interpolations and arbitrary commentaries that lasted until the last days of the Sassanian dynasty ; nor was the Avasta of Ardeshir identical with that which was brought out and given to Gushtâsp by Zara-Ishtar (the 13th prophet of the *Desatir*) ; nor that of the latter quite the same as the original Zend, although even this one was but the *exoteric version* of the Zen-Zara doctrines. As shown by Burnouf, the Pahlavi version is found nearly in every case to wander strangely from the true meaning of the original (?) Zend text, while that "true meaning" wandered (or shall we say—was veiled ?) as greatly from the esoteric text. This, for the good reason that the Zend text is simply a secret *code* of certain words and expressions agreed upon by the original compilers, and the key to which is but with the Initiates. The Western scholars may say: "the key to Avasta is not Pahlavi, but the Vedas ;" but the Occultist's answer is—"aye ; but the key to the Vedas is the Secret Doctrine." The former assert correctly enough that "the Vedas come from the same soucrce as the Avasta ;" the students of Occultism ask—" Do you know even the A, B, C, of that source ?"

. . . .

The first Zara-Ishtar was a Median, born in Rae, say the Greeks, who place the epoch in which he flourished 5,000 or 6,000 years before the Trojan war ; while according to the teachings of the Secret Doctrine this "first" was the "last" or *Seventh* Zarathustra (the 13th of the *Desatir*)—though he was followed by one more *Zuruastara* or *Suryâchâria* (later, owing to a natural change of language transformed into Zaryaster and again into Zarathushtra,) who lived in the days of the first Gushtâsp (not the father of Darius though, as imagined by some scholars).* The latter is very improperly called "the founder" of modern Monotheistic Parsiism, for besides being only a revivalist and the exponent of the modern philosophy, he was the last to make a desperate attempt at the restoration of pure Magianism. He is known to have gone from Shiz to the Mount Zebilan in the cave, whither proceeded the Initiates of the Magi ; and upon emerging from it to have returned with the Zend-Avasta re-translated once more and commented upon by himself. This original commentary, it is claimed, exists till now among other old works in the secret libraries. But its copies—now in the possession of the profane world—bear as much resemblance to it as the Christianity of to-day to that of its Founder. And now, if we are asked, as we have been repeatedly, if there are indeed men in whose power it is to give the correct version of true Zoroastrianism, then why do not they do so ? we answer, " because—very few will believe it in *this* our age." Instead of benefiting men they would but hurt the devotees of those truths. And as to giving to the world more information about the locality known as Aiaryanâm-Vaêgo, we need point out but to the sentence in Fargard I, in which we find Ahura-Mazda saying to Spitama "the most benevolent," that he had made every land—even

---

* It is now an exploded theory that showed King Vistaspa, or Gustasp, as identical with the father of Darius, hence as flourshing 600 B. C. Vistaspa was the last of the line of the Kaianian princes who ruled in Bactriana ; and Bactriana was conquered by the Assyrians 1200 B. C. Our earlier Zend scholars are guilty of more than one such gross mistakes. Thus Hystaspes is made in History *to crush the Magi, and reintroduce the pure religion of Zoroaster,* as though those were two distinct religions ; and at the same time an inscription is found on the tomb of Darius or Darayavush, stating that he (the crusher of Magianism !) was himself " teacher and hierophant of magic," or Magianism ! (See *Isis Unveiled*, Vol. II, pp. 141-2).

though it had no charms whatever in it—dear to its dwellers, since otherwise the "whole living world would have invaded the Airyanâm-Vaêgo" (v. 2).* Hence unable to satisfy entirely our readers, we can say but very little. If our opinion in any way can help our correspondent, we are ready to share it with and say, that Zend scholars and Orientalists notwithstanding, it is our belief that not only have the Persian theologians of the latter portions of the Sassanian dynasty disfigured entirely their sacred books, but that owing to the presence of the pharisaical element, and the Rabbis during the pre-Christian as well as post-Christian periods in Persia and Babylonia, they have borrowed from the Jews at least as much as the latter have borrowed from them. If the sacred books of the Parsis owe their angelology and other speculations to the Babylonians, the modern Avasta Commentaries owe the Jews undeniably their anthropomorphic creator, as well as their crude notions about Heaven and Hell.

The learned Colonel will be doing a great favor to the Parsis if he will consent to say what he thinks of the following from the "History of the Conflict between Science and Religion," by W. Draper:—

"Persia, as is the case with all empires of long duration, had passed through many changes of religion. She had followed the Monotheism of Zoroaster; had then accepted Dualism, and exchanged that for Magianism. At the time;

---

* Why do we find Zoroaster in the *Bundahish* offering a sacrifice in "Irân Vej"—distorted name for Airyanâm-Vaejo, and where or what was this country? Though some Orientalists call it "no real country," and others identify it with the basin of the Aras, the latter has nothing to do with Airyanâm Vaejo. The last Zarathust may have chosen, and he has so chosen, the banks of the Aras for the cradle of his newly *reborn* religion; only that cradle received a child reborn and suckled elsewhere, namely, in Airyanâm Vaejo (the true "seed of the Aryas," who were then all that was noble and true) which place is identical with the *Shamballah* of the Hindus and the Arhats, a place now regarded also as mythical. In Fargard II. Ahura-Mazda calls together "a meeting of the celestial gods," and Yima, the first man "of the excellent mortals," in the Airyanâm Vaejo—"*in the far-off lands of the rising sun*," says the *Book of Numbers* of the Chaldees, written on the Euphrates. Those of the Parsis who have ears, let them hear, and draw their inferences; and, perchance it may be also found that the Brahmans who came from the North to India bringing with them all the learning of secret wisdom, came from a place still more northward than lake Mansarovar.—*Ed.*, *Theosophist*.

of Macedonian expedition, she recognized one Universal Intelligence, the Creator, Preserver and Governor of all things, the most holy essence of truth, the giver of all good. He was not to be represented by any image or any graven form." (Page 15.)

Colonel Olcott would probably answer that Professor Draper was right with regard to the many phases through which the great religion of Persia—if we have to call it thus—had passed. But Draper mentions by name only Monotheism, Dualism, Magianism—a kind of refined Visishtadwaitism—and Fire or element-worship, whereas he might have enumerated the gradual changes by the dozen. Moreover, he begins his enumeration at the wrong end. If Monotheism has ever been the religion of the Parsis at any time, it is so now, not then, namely, in the Zoroaster period.

The Zend Avasta, with some exceptions, contains nothing essentially different from what the Vedas contain. The gods, the rites, the ceremonies, the modes of prayers, and the prayers themselves are but a reflex of the Vedas. Surely, then, when Zoroaster dissented from the Brahmans, it could not be merely to adopt the same pantheism or polytheism in a different language. The teaching of Zoroaster must necessarily be something quite different. Some may say he dissented from the idol-worship of the Brahmans; but I think history can prove that the *Brahmans* were idolators before *they left Ariana.* Does it not rather appear that the Magians who followed Zoroastrianism, copied everything from their close neighbours the Brahmans and muddled it up with the current and easily reliable name of Zoroaster, forgetting, perhaps under the sway of altered popular superstitions of the age, the true teaching of Zoroaster. The learned Colonel or yourself, or any of your contributors, whose learning is, I may say without flattery, very enviable, will be doing a great service to the Parsis, if he will kindly say what he thinks the true teaching of Zoroaster was.

Enough is said, we believe, in our preceding statements to show what we honestly think of " the true teaching of Zoroaster." It is only in such rare non-liturgical fragments as the *Hâdokht Nosk*, for instance, that the *true* teachings of Zarathushtra Spitama, or those of primitive Magianism, may be yet found ; and even these have to be read as a sacred code to which a key has to be applied. Thus, every word in the tenets given in the *Hâdokht* and relating to the fate of our soul after death, has its occult meaning. It is not correct to say even of the later versions of the Zend-Avasta that its gods, prayers and rites are all "but a reflex of the Vedas." Neither the Brahmans nor the Zoroastrians have copied one from the other. With the exception of the word *Zeruana* in its later meaning of "Boundless" *time*, instead of the "Boundless" Spirit, the "One Eternity," explained in the sense of the Brahmanical *chakkra* or endless circle, there is nothing borrowed form the Vedas. Both the Vedas and the Zend-Avasta, originating from the same school, have naturally the same symbols only—very differently explained, still—having the same esoteric significance. Professor Max Müller, speaking of the Parsis, calls them "the disinherited sons of Manu"; and, declares elsewhere, that the Zoroastrians and their ancestors started from India during the Vaidik period, "which can be proved as distinctly as that the inhabitants of Massilia started from Greece." We certainly do not mean to question the hypothesis, though as he gives it, it is still but a personal opinion. The Zoroastrians have, undoubtedly, been "settled in India before they immigrated into Persia," as they have ages later, returned again to Aryavarta, when they got indeed "under the sway of altered popular superstitions and forgot the teachings of Zoroaster." But this theory cuts both ways. For it neither proves that they have not entered India together and at the same time as the first Brahmans who came to it from the far north; nor that the latter had not been "settled" in Persia, Media, Babylonia and elsewhere before they immigrated into the land of the Seven Rivers. Between Zoroaster, the primeval institutor of "Sun"-*worship*, and Zaratushtra, the principal expounder of the occult properties and transcendental powers of the divine (Promethean) Fire, there lies the abyss of ages. The latter was one of the earliest hierophants, one of the first *Athravans* (priests, or teachers of "fire"), while the Zoroaster of "Gushtâsp" was living some 4,000 years B. C. Indeed, Bunsen places Zoroaster at Baktria and the emigration of the Baktrians to the Indus at 3784 B. C. And this Zoroaster taught, not what he had learned "from," but with the Brahmans, *i. e.* at Airyanâm Vaêgo, since what is identical with Brahmanical symbology is found but in the earlier Vedas, not in any of the later Commentaries, that it may be even said of the Vedas themselves, that though compiled in the land of the Seven Rivers, they existed ages before in the North. Thus if any one is to be blamed for getting under "the sway of altered popular superstitions" of the Brahmans, it is not the Zoroastrians of that age, but indeed Hystaspes who, after visiting "the Brahmans of Upper India," as Ammianus tells us, and having been instructed by them, infused their later rites and ideas into the already disfigured Magian worship.

Hargrave Jennings, a mystic, has eulogised fire as being the best symbol of worship, but he says nowhere that the fire symbol directly worshipped in its own name as one of the created elements, as is done in Zend-Avasta, is in any way defensible. The learned Colonel, in his lecture on the Spirit of Zoroastrianism, defends fire-worshippers, but does he really understand them as offering direct prayer as above stated? Fire-worship is borrowed from the Vedas.

We think not. Fire-worship, or rather reverence for fire, was in the remote ages, universal. Fire and water are the elements in which, as Occult Science teaches, the active and passive productive power of the universe are respectively centred. Says Hippocrates : (*Divite* I—4) "All living creatures . . . . animals and men originate from the two Principles differing in potency, but agreeing in purpose. I mean Fire and Water . . . . Father fire gives life to all things, but Mother water nourishes them." Has our friend, who seems to show such an evident scorn for the emblems of his own religion, ever studied those of other people ? Has he ever been told, that there never was a religion but paid reverence to the Sun and Fire as the fittest emblems of *Life*, hence—of the life-giving principle; nay, that there is not, even at present, one single creed on our globe (including Christianity) but has preserved this reverence in its ritualism, though the emblems with time have been changed and disfigured? The only essential difference between the modern Parsi Mobeds and the Christian Clergy lies in this : the devotees of the former being profoundly attached to their old religion,— though they may have forgotten its origin,—have honestly left exoteric Zoroastrianism standing before the jury of the world, who judges on mere appearances—*unveiled* in its apparent nakedness; while Christian theologians, less unsophisticated, kept perpetually modifying Christianity in exact proportions as science advances and the world became more enlightened, until finally their religion now stands under a thick, withal very insecure, mask. All the religions, from the old Vaidic, the Zoroastrian and the Jewish creeds down to modern Christianity, the illegitimate and repudiated progeny of the last, sprang from archaic *Magianism*, or the Religion based upon the knowledge of Occult nature, called sometimes Sabaism—the " worship " (?) of the sun, moon and stars.

We invite our correspondent, if he wants to trace in the Ritualism of modern Christian theology the old Fire-worship, to read *The Rosicrucians*, by Hargrave Jennings, with more attention than he had hitherto done. Fire is the essence of all active power in nature. Fire and water are the elements to which all organized and animated beings owe their existence on our Earth ; at any rate, the sun is the only visible and undeniable Creator and Regenerator of life.

—*The Theosophist*, Vol. IV., p. 224, *et seq.*

THE SCRIPTURES.

AS REPRESENTED BY DR. MARTIN HAUG, PH.D., AND BRIEFED BY A "PARSI THEOSOPHIST."

THE religious writings of the Parsis are known by the name of Zend Avasta. They should more properly be designated Avasta-o-Zend. Avasta means the text, and Zend means the commentary. When in the course of ages, the original text or Avasta became unintelligible, owing to the language in which it was written ceasing to be the vernacular of the people, commentaries were written to explain it. And, similarly, when the language of the commentaries also ceased to be the vernacular, further Zend or the commentary of the first Zend was written. And now the words Avasta and Zend, which meant the text and the commentary, are appropriated as the names of the *languages* in which the text and the first commentary were written. The language of the later commentary is known under the name of the Pahlavi language. Avasta-o-Zend, therefore, means the writings in the Avasta and Zend languages. The religious writings, as they originally existed in the combined Avasta and Zend languages, were very voluminous.

Pliny reports on the authority of Hermippus, the Greek philosopher, that Zoroaster composed two millions of verses; and an Arabic historian, Abu Jaffer Attavari, assures us that Zoroaster's writings comprised twelve thousand parchments.

These writings consisted of twenty-one parts or Nosks. The names and the contents of these Nosks, as translated by Dr. Haug, are given below :—

Names and contents of the twenty-one Nosks.

1. *Setudtar or Setud Yashts* (Zend *çtuiti*—praise, worship) comprised thirty-three chapters, containing the praise and worship of *Yazatas* or angels.

2. *Setudgar*, twenty-two chapters, containing prayers and instructions to men about good actions, chiefly those called *jâdungoi*, *i. e.*, to induce another to assist a fellowman.

3. *Vahista Manthra*, twenty-two chapters, treating of abstinence, piety, religion, qualities of Zoroaster, &c.

4. *Bagha*, twenty-one chapters, containing an explanation of the religious duties, the orders and commandments of God, and obedience of men, how to guard against hell and reach heaven.

5. *Dâmdât*, thirty-two chapters, containing the knowledge of this and that world, the future life, qualities of their inhabitants, the revelations of God, concerning heaven, earth, water, trees, fire, men and beasts; the resurrection of the dead and the passing of the *chinvad* (the way to heaven).

6. *Nadar*, thirty-five chapters, containing astronomy, geography, astrology, translated into Arabic, under the name *Yuntal* and known to the Persians by the name *of Fawamazjan*.

7. *Pajam*, twenty-two chapters, treating of what food is allowed or prohibited, of the reward to be obtained in the other world for keeping six *Gahambârs* and the *Farvardagân*.

8. *Ratushtai*, fifty chapters (at the time of Alexander the Great, only thirteen were extant), treating of the different *ratus* or heads in the creation, such as kings, high priests, ministers, and giving statements as to what species are Ahuramazd's and what Ahriman's; there was besides a geographical section in it.

9. *Barish*, sixty chapters (thirteen of which were only extant at the time of Alexander the Great), containing the code of laws for kings, governors, &c., workmanship of various kinds, the sin of lying.

10. *Kashsrov*, sixty chapters (at Alexander's time fifteen only were extant), treating of metaphysics, natural philosophy, divinity, &c.,

11. *Vistâsp Nosk*, sixty chapters (at Alexander's time only

ten were extant), on the reign of Gustasp and his conversion to the religion and its propagation by him through the world.

12. *Khasht*, twenty-two chapters, divided into six parts; *first*, on the nature of the divine being, the Zoroastrian faith, the duties enjoined by it; *secondly*, on obedience due to the king; *thirdly*, on the reward for good actions in the other world, and how to be saved from hell; *fourthly*, on the structure of the world, agriculture, botany, &c., *fifthly*, on the four classes of which a nation consists, *viz.*, rulers, warriors, agriculturists traders and workmen (the contents of the sixth division are left out).

13. *Sfend*, sixty chapters, on the 'miracles' of Zoroaster and *Gâhambârs*, &c.

14. *Jirasht*, twenty-two chapters, on the human life, from the birth and its end up to the day of resurrection, on the causes of man's birth, why some are born in wealth, others in poverty.

15. *Baghan Yasht*, seventeen chapters, containing the praise of high angels like men.

16. *Nayârum*, fifty-four chapters, code of law, stating what is allowed and what prohibited.

17. *Asparum*, sixty-four chapters, on medicine, astronomy, midwifery, &c.

18. *Dvasrujad*, sixty-five chapters, on the marriages between the nearest relatives (called *khvetukdah*,) zoology, and treatment of animals.

19. *Askârum*, fifty-two chapters, treating of the civil and criminal law; of the boundaries of the country, of the resurrection.

20. *Vendidâd*, twenty-two chapters, on the removal of uncleanliness of every description from which great defects arise in the world.

21. *Hâdokht*, thirty chapters, on the creation, its wonders, structure, &c.

All the Nosks are not at present in the possession of the

Parsis. Most, or rather the largest portion, of these writings has been destroyed, and it is the belief of the Zoroastrians that they were destroyed by Alexander at the time of his invasion and conquest of Persia. This opinion is confirmed by the accounts given by classical writers. "We find," says Dr. Haug, "from Diodorus and Curtius that Alexander really did burn the citadel at Persepolis, in a drunken frolic, at the instigation of the Athenian courtesan Thais, and in revenge for the destruction of Greek temples by Xerxes." With the destruction of the palace must have been destroyed the sacred books kept in the Royal archives. During the 550 years of Macedonian and Parthian supremacy which followed Alexander's conquest, it is said that Zoroastrianism had fallen into neglect, and as a natural consequence much of the Zoroastrian literature was lost during this period. Whatever may have been the cause, this is the fact that, at the Sassanian period when the revival of the Zoroastrian religion took place, the largest bulk of the sacred writings was gone and only a very small portion, and that, too, except the Vendidâd, in a fragmentary state, was left. These fragments, the learned men of the Sassanian period put together according to their understanding to make something like a consistent whole, and, to explain them, wrote commentaries in Pahlavi, which was the vernacular of the time. The portions thus preserved and brought together and now extant with the Parsis, are Yaçna (Izeshne), Visparatu (Visparad), Vendidâd, Yashts, Hadokht, Vistâsp Nosk, Afringan, Niayish, Gah, some miscellaneous fragments and the Sirozah (thirty days) or calendar.

The common opinion of the Zoroastrians ascribed all the above-named portions, as well as the twenty-one Nosks in their entirety, to the authorship of Zoroaster. Modern philology has, however, now established beyond doubt, by means of the difference in language, and, where the language is the same, by the difference in style, that these writings were the productions of different persons and brought into existence at different times.

Thus the language, in which the writings exist, has become the indicator of the periods of their composition and of their authorship. According to this test, the oldest of the writings now in existence are the five Gáthás,* which were embodied in the "Yaçna," and which, with the exception of some few passages, are ascribed to Zarthustra himself.

Some portion of the remaining "Yaçna" contains the prayers very well-known to Zoroastrians, *viz.*, "Yatha-Ahuvayirio," "Ashem-Vohu," and "Yañhe-Hátám." These small prayers are declared to have been even older than the Gáthás themselves.

After the Gáthás, the next in the order of antiquity are the following pieces, *viz.*, "Vendidâd," "Yaçna" (excepting the Gáthás and three older prayers), more particularly called "Izeshne," "Hadokht," "Visparad," "Yashts," "Afringan," "Nyaish," "Gah," "Siroza;" other fragments follow, which are collected together under the name of "Khordeh Avasta," and are meant to be recited as daily prayers. These are composed by selecting and putting together, as seemed best to the Dasturs (or high priests) of the Sassanian period, passages from the writings preserved to them. In all the writings, whether Avasta or Zend, the religion taught by Zoroaster is called, at all the various places, by the name of the "Mazdiasn" religion, and the professors of it are called the "Mazdiasnians," from "Mazda," the Most Wise, and "yaçna," to worship.

Mr. K. R. Kama, who is the best authority on this subject in India, shows in his "Life of Zarathustra,"—a work very valuable for its great learning, research and scope—that several times, previous to the advent of Zarathustra, there was preached the religion of one true God, against the prevalent irreligion and polytheism; and the movement at *each* time is mentioned in the Avasta, under the name of

---

* The names of these Gáthás are (1) Gáthá Ahunavaiti, (2) Gáthá Ustvaiti, (3) Gáthá Spento-mainyush, (4) Gáthá Vohu-Khshathrem, (5) Gáthá Vahishtoistis. Gáthá means a song, a hymn.

"Mazdiasni Religion." Thus the Mazdiasni religion, *i. e.*, the religion of the one true God—Mazda, the Most Wise—was in existence among the Persians, even before Zarathustra; and he appeared in the character of a reviver or reformer. His teachings, as distinguished from those which preceded him and which he adopted, are known by the name of Mazdiasni-Zarathusti religion. In one prayer where the true believer confesses his faith, he says "Jasa mè avañhé Mazda, Mazdiasno ahmi, Mazdiasno-Zarathustrish," Help me, O Mazda, I am a Mazdiasnian, a Mazdiasnian through Zarathushtra."

Thus, the name Mazdiasni borne by the religion taught by Zarathustra, as well as by the movements which preceded him, indicates that all these teachings were monotheistic, or the religion thus preached at different times, and consummated by Zarathustra, was monotheism.

We thus arrive at the question whether, as the name implies, the religion is really monotheism or dualism, or a worship in which monotheism, dualism and the worship of angels, the sun, moon and stars, fire and water, &c., are confusedly intermingled.

Dr. Haug says, "That Zarathustra's theology was mainly based on monotheism, one may easily ascertain from the Gáthás, chiefly from the second. Zarathustra Spitama's* conception of Ahurmazd as Supreme Being is perfectly identical with the notion of Elohim (God) or Jehovah, which we find in the Books of the Old Testament. Ahurmazd is called by him, the creator of earthly and spiritual life, the Lord of the whole universe at whose hands are all the creatures. He is the light and the source of light, he is the wisdom and intellect," &c.

---

* *Spitama* means the family of Spitama. It is the opinion of some that Zarathustra was the common name applied to high priests, and that, therefore, Zarathustra, who first taught the religion which bears his name, is distinguished in several places in the Avasta, as Zarathustra Spitama, *i. e.*, Zarathustra of the family of Spitama.

Let us see what a direct examination of the Gáthás themselves tells us. Of all the sacred writings, the Gáthás being the portions ascribed to Zarathustra himself, information as to the basis and essence of the Zoroastrian faith ought to be sought in them. The other portions of the sacred writings came into existence some ages afterwards, and if there is any difference between them and what is taught in the Gáthás, the latter certainly are more to be relied upon as revealing the real nature of the faith which Zarathushtra Spitama taught. The language of the Gáthás is most difficult to understand. Unfortunately the great European scholars, notwithstanding all their labours, have not yet been able to give a translation which can be accepted as final and satisfactory. More or less successful efforts have been made to arrive at the true sense of the Gáthás, and the translation of Dr. Haug, recommended by the high authority of his name, may be accepted as the best that is available at present. Every verse of the Gáthás, as given in Dr. Haug's translation, bears unmistakable evidence as to the teachings of Zarathushtra being preëminently monotheistic. A few of these verses are given below.

1. I will now tell you, who are assembled here, the wise sayings of the Most Wise, the praises of the living God, and the songs of the good spirit, the sublime truth which I see arising out of these sacred flames.

2. You shall, therefore, hearken to the Soul of Nature, contemplate the beams of fire with a most pious mind! Every one, both men and women, ought to-day to choose his creed. Ye, offspring of renowned ancestors, awake to agree with us (*i. e.*, to approve of my lore to be delivered to you at this moment.)

9. Thus let us be such as help the life of the future. The wise living spirits are the greatest supporters of it. The prudent man wishes only to be there where wisdom is at home.

11. Therefore perform ye the commandments, which, pro-

nounced by the Wise (God) himself, have been given to mankind; for they are a nuisance and perdition to liars, but prosperity to the believer in the truth; they are the fountain of happiness.

18. When my eyes beheld Thee, the essence of the truth, the Creator of life, who manifests his life in his works, then I knew Thee to be the Primeval Spirit, Thou Wise, so high in the mind as to create the world, and the Father of the Good Mind.

33. 2. Who are opposed in their thoughts, words and actions, to the wicked, and think of the welfare of the creation, their efforts will be crowned with success through the mercy of Ahura-Mazda.

34. 1. Immortality, truth, wealth, health, all these gifts to be granted in consequence of (pious) actions, words and worshipping to those men (who pray here), are plentiful in Thy possession, Ahura-Mazda!

Blessed is he, blessed are all men, to whom the Living Wise God of His Own Command should grant those two everlasting powers (wholesomeness and immortality). For this very good, I beseech Thee, Ahura-Mazda; mayest thou through Thy angel of piety (Armaiti) give me happiness, the good, true things, and the possession of the good mind.

2. I believe Thee to be the Best Being of all, the Source of Light for the world. Everybody shall choose Thee (believe in Thee) as the Source of Light, Thee, Thee, Holiest Spirit, Mazda! Thou createst all good, true things by means of the power of Thy Good Mind at any time, and promisest us (who believe in Thee) a long life.

15. Thus I believed in Thee, Thou Holy One, Thou Living Wise. There he came to me with the good mind. May the greatest happiness brightly blaze out of these flames; may the number of the worshippers of the liar (bad spirit) diminish;

may all those (that are present) address themselves to the Shoshiants.*

8. Him whom I desire to worship and celebrate with my hymns, I beheld just now with my eyes, Him who knows the truth, Him, the living wise as the source of the good mind, the good action and the good word. So let us put down our gifts of praise in the dwelling-place of the heavenly singers.

1. To what country shall I go? Where shall I take my refuge? What country is sheltering the master (Zarathustra) and his companion? None of the servants pays reverence to me, not the wicked rulers of the country. How shall I worship Thee further, Ahura-Mazda?

2. I know that I am helpless, look at me, being amongst few men, for I have few men (I have lost my followers or they have left me); I implore Thee weeping, Thou, Ahura Mazda, who grantest happiness as a friend gives a present to his friend. The good of the mind is thy possession, Thou True.

As regards the so-called dualism of the Zoroastrian doctrines, Dr. Haug writes as follows:—"The opinion, so generally entertained now, that Zarathustra was preaching Dualism, that is to say, the supposition of two original independent spirits, a good and a bad one, utterly distinct from each other, and one counteracting the creation of the other, is owing to a confusion of his philosophy with his theology. Having arrived at the grand idea of the unity and the indivisibility of the Supreme Being, he undertook to solve the great problem which has engaged the attention of so many wise men of

---

* *Shoshiants* is the name given to those who advanced the Mazdiasni religion before Zarathustra, who also is called one of the Shoshiants. Dr. Haug translates this word, as meaning "fire priest" from the root "such" to burn; according to Mr. K. R. Kama, "such" means "to give light," "to enlighten" and Shoshiants were those who enlightened the people in the true religion. That the latter is the right meaning is confirmed by the word "Shoshiants" which is the name given to those whom, according to tradition, the Parsis expect in the future to revive the Mazdiasni religion. For persons with that mission "Shoshiants" is an appropriate name when it means "those who enlighten," and not when it means fire-priests.

antiquity and even of modern times, *viz.*, how are the imperfections discoverable in the world, the various kinds of evils, wickedness and baseness, compatible with the goodness, holiness and justice of God. This great thinker, of so remote an antiquity, solved the difficult question, philosophically, by the supposition of two primeval causes which, though different, were united, and produced the world of the material things as well as that of the spirit; which doctrine may best be learnt from Yas. XXX.

"The one, who produced the reality (gays), is called *Vohu-mano*, 'the good mind,' the other through whom the 'non-reality' (ajyaiti) originated, bears the name *Ako-mano*, 'the naught mind.' All good, true and perfect things which fall under the category of 'reality,' are the productions of the 'good mind,' while all that is bad and delusive belonging to the sphere of 'non-reality' is traced to the 'naught mind.' They are the two moving causes in the Universe, united from beginning, and therefore called 'twins' (*yema*—Sans., *Yaman*). They are spread everywhere in Ahura-Mazda as well as in men.

"These two primeval principles, if supposed to be united in Ahura-Mazda himself, are not called *Vohu-mano* and *Ako-mano*, but *Spento-mainyush*, that is, white or holy spirit, and *Aṅra-mainyush*, *i. e.*, dark spirit. That Aṅra-mainyush is no separate being opposed to Ahura-Mazda is unmistakably to be gathered from Yas. XIX, where Ahura-Mazda is mentioning his two spirits who are inherent in his own nature, and are in other passages (Yas. 57) distinctly called the 'two creators' and 'the two masters' (páyu). And, indeed, we never find 'Aṅra-mainynsh' mentioned as a constant opponent to Ahura-Mazda in the Gáthás, as is the case in later writings. The evil, against which Ahura-Mazda and all good men are fighting, is called *drukhsh*, 'destruction' or 'lie,' which is nothing but a personification of the *Devas*. The same expression for the 'evil' spread in the world, we find in the Persian cuneiform inscriptions, where, moreover, no opponent of Ahura-Mazda, like Aṅra-mainynsh, is ever mentioned. God (Ahura-

Mazda) in the rock records of King Darius, is only one, as Jehovah, in the old Testament, having no adversary whomsoever."

All these attempts at explanation show but more forcibly the difficulty of solving the question, what is Zoroastranism? All the passages, in which Ahura-Mazda, and the two spirits—"Vohu-mano," and "Ako-mano," or "Spento-mainyush" and Aṅra-mainyush"—are spoken of, seem to be fraught with immense mystic meaning. Great learning and labour have been expended in deciphering these ancient writings, but the result of all this has been to show more and more clearly that there is something within and something beyond, which is not caught hold of. All that has as yet been said or written on the subject, has not succeeded in uniting the separate parts into a consistent whole, and what is the essence of Zoroastrianism is yet an unsettled question. It is, indeed, sad if the means of solving this difficulty are lost to the world altogether, and equally sad if the solution is to be deferred long beyond our time.

ZOROASTRIANISM AND THEOSOPHY.

BY KHARSEDJI N. SEERVAI,

Recording Secretary, Theosophical Society [Eastern Division].

JUST as the oldest religious teachings of the Hindus are contained in the Vedas, so the most ancient religious teachings of the Zoroastrians are embodied in the Zend Avasta or, more properly, those portions of the Avasta which are distinguished as the Gâthâs. These portions are ascribed directly to Zarathushtra, or Zoroaster as the Greeks called him, while the other parts of the Avasta were the writings of his disciples and followers. "The relationship," says Dr. Martin Haug, " of the Avasta language to the most ancient Sanskrit, the so-called Vedic dialect, is as close as that of the different dialects of the Greek language (Æolic, Ionic, Doric, or Attic) to each other. The languages of the sacred hymns of the Brâhmans and of those of the Parsis are only the two dialects of the two separate tribes of one and the same nation. As the Ionians, Dorians, Æolians, &c., were different tribes of the Greek nation, whose general name was Hellenes, so the ancient Brâhmans and Parsis were two tribes of the nation which is called *Aryas*, both in the Veda and Zend Avasta."

The close relationship thus seen in language and nationality also existed in respect of religious truths. Pure Vedaism and pure Zoroastrianism are one. Zoroastrianism sprang up as a reformatory revolution against the corruptions and superstitions which had obscured the primitive Vedic truths, and which stood in the place of the pure old religion to serve the purposes of priestcraft and despotism. Zoroaster did in the far off antiquity what the great and saintly Buddha did after him. . . .

Zoroaster was called "the famous in Airyanam Vaêjô," *i. e.*, "the famous in the Aryan home." Exiles from the old Aryan home, ignorant of the old Aryan wisdom, forgetful of the closest relationship, these two branches in course of ages grew more and more separated and estranged from one another. The comparative study of languages and of religions has had to a certain extent the effect of bringing them together. But it is necessary to dive deeper. To the investigation and expounding of the hidden and occult truths which assuredly are treasured in the sacred writings of the Hindus and the Parsis, is left the lot of uniting, into permanent religious concord, the present direct descendants of the oldest human family ; and this great work the Theosophical Society has prescribed to itself, and to a very good extent already accomplished.

The European nations first became acquainted with the contents of the Zoroastrian Scriptures through the French translation of Anquetil Duperron. Sir William Jones could not persuade himself to believe that the writings as represented by the French translation could belong to " the celebrated Zoroaster." Kant was disappointed to find there was no philosophy traceable in these writings. And yet the most learned of the ancient Greeks and the Romans held Zoroaster and his teachings in the highest veneration. Zoroaster as spoken of by them appears as a demi-god, most profound in learning,—the ' bright star' among men, one to whom nature had revealed all her secrets, master of the deepest mystic lore, the head of the Magi—the great magicians. "The great fame," says Dr. Haug, " which Zoroaster enjoyed, even with the ancient Greeks and Romans *who were so proud of their own learning and wisdom*, is a sufficient proof of the high and preëminent position he must once have occupied in the history of the progress of the human mind." The translation of Anquetil Duperron was, however, imperfect and inaccurate. We are now in possession of translations by Burnouf, Speigel, and Haug, which are pronounced to be sufficiently accurate and scientific. But even in these we can hardly find things which could have deserved the high panegyrics bestowed by the Greek and Roman philosophers. What inference then do these facts suggest ? Either that men like Pythagoras, Plato, Aristotle, Hermippus, Plutarch and Pliny, who lived nearer the time of Zoroaster than ourselves, and who studied and wrote so much about the Zoroastrian writings when those writings were almost wholly preserved and well understood in Persia, formed a wrong estimate of Zoroaster and Zoroastrian writings, or that the meaning we at present make of these writings is not correct. The latter seems to be the more reasonable conclusion.

It is said of Plato's writings that there are many parts, the real meaning of which is different from what appears to be. In the Academy he taught the mysteries, the knowledge of which could only be imparted to the Initiates. When he had to write about these mysteries he wrote so as to convey to the vulgar a different and often absurd meaning, the real meaning being intelligible only to the Initiates who possessed the key to the reading. The Egyptian Hierophants hid their mysteries under the hieroglyphics. The Rosicrucians and other mystic philosophers of the middle ages adopted similar device to keep away from the vulgar and the undeserving the great occult and mystic truths of which they were the masters. May not the same be the case with regard to the Zoroastrian writings?

The following passage from Dr. Haug's learned essay is highly suggestive on this point :—

" Zoroaster exhorts his party to respect and revere the Angra, *i. e.*, the Angiras of the Vedic hymns, who formed one of the most ancient and celebrated priestly families of the ancient Aryans, and who seem to have been more closely connected with the ante-Zoroastrian form of the Parsi religion than any other of the later Brahmanical families. These Angiras are often mentioned together with the Atharvâns or fire-priests (which word, in the form *âthrava*, is the general name given to the priest caste in the Zend-Avastâ), and both are regarded in the Vedic literature as the authors of the Atharvaveda which is called the Veda of the Athervángiras, or the Atharvâna, or Angirasa Veda, *i. e.*, the Veda of the

Atharvâna or Angiras. This work was for a long time not acknowledged as a proper Veda by the Brahmans, because its contents, which consist chiefly of spells, charms, curses, mantras for killing enemies, &c., were mostly foreign to the three other Vedas, which alone were originally required for sacrifices. On comparing its contents with some passages in the Yashts and Vendidâd, we discover a great similarity. Although a close connection between the ante-Zoroastrian and the Atharvana and Angirasa religion can hardly be doubted, yet this relationship refers only to *the Magical part, which was believed by the ancient Greeks to be the very substance and nature of the Zoroastrian religion.*"

And a closer view of the rites and ceremonies of the Zoroastrian religion, *e. g.*, the Afringan and more especially the Ijashne (Yaçna) ceremonies, go to confirm that what the ancient Greeks believed was the truth. It is not possible within the space of the present article to describe in detail these ceremonies. A full account of them is given in Dr. Haug's Essays, pages 394, *et seq.* Unless these ceremonies can be accounted for as being for some spiritual or occult purpose, their performance seems to be quite a farce. We know on the authority of the author of the *Dabistân* that Akbar the Great, the celebrated Mogal Emperor of India, was a great enquirer of religious truths. He had assembled in his court the learned men of all the different faiths,—Mahomedans of all sects, Hindus, Jews, Christians, and Zoroastrians. There were frequent public discussions between these doctors, each striving to uphold the superiority of his own faith. And as the result of all these discussions and researches, he formed a new religious sect called Ilâhi, introduced a new era called Ilâhi, and, says Anthony Troyer in his synopsis of the *Dabistân*, " the months were regulated according to the mode of Irân, and fourteen festivals established in concordance with those of Zoroaster's religion. It was to this ancient Persian creed, that he gave the preference, having been instructed in its sacred tenets and practices by a learned fire-worshiper who had joined him, and from books which were sent to him from Persia and Kirman. He received the sacred fire, and committed it to the faithful hands of Abulfazil, his confidential minister : the holy flames of Zardusht blazed again upon the altars of *Aria*, and after a separation of many centuries, Persians and Indians were reunited in a common worship."

Is it possible that a sovereign so wise, and one who had taken such pains to inform himself carefully of the merits of the different faiths, and who had before him each faith mercilessly criticised and analysed by its opponents, could have given his preference to the Zoroastrian religion, if its rites and ceremonies were a farce, or at best were unintelligible, and if its writings had no more meaning than we at present understand,—meaning that the merest school-boy can now-a-days well afford to sneer at ? No ; Zoroastrian religion *is* a mystery. How shall the veil be lifted up to show us what is behind ? We believed not in mysteries, we believed not in occult and spiritual potencies. The era of this disbelief is past. That marvellous work of this century, *Isis Unveiled*, establishes beyond a doubt for every unbiased and unprejudiced thinker that there is a universe with vast powers beyond what we know as the physical. Truths regarding this universe and powers, as men in different times and places came to know, they locked up in mysteries, in order to save them from falling into the hand of the impure and the selfish. Happily what these mysteries guard is not yet lost to the knowledge of men. These truths are known to some mighty few, the great Initiates and Adepts in India and elsewhere. The Theosophical studies have for their aim and object the acquisition of these truths, and the special interest that a Zoroastrian has in these studies and investigations is that they will throw light upon the mystery which enshrouds his own glorious faith, and reveal the teaching of the great Bactrian sage in their true essence.

As an instance illustrating in some small way what is thus possible, we may quote the following verse from Gâthâ Ustavaiti :

"12. And when Thou camest to instruct me, and taughtest me righteousness; then Thou gavest me Thy command not to appear without having received a revelation, before the angel Sraosha, endowed with *the sublime righteousness which may impart your righteous things to the two friction woods* (by means of which the holiest fire, the source of all good things in the creation, is produced) for the benefit (of all things), shall have come to me."

Like almost all the passages in the Gâthâs this passage is very unintelligible, and the portion in italics is especially so. Zoroaster seems to say that he was forbidden to appear on his mission in the public till he had received inspiration and was visited by Sraosha, whose sublime righteousness was to impart righteous things " to the two friction woods." As Dr. Haug explains by the parenthetical clause which he interposes in this verse, the phrase " the two friction woods" is specially mentioned as denoting the means by which fire—the most sacred element in Zoroastrian worship—is produced. But Zoroaster's was not the age in which fire was first discovered by the accidental friction of two pieces of wood, as is supposed to have been the way in which it became known to the savages. The prominence, therefore, with which this mode of producing fire is mentioned, needs some explanation. Besides, how can righteous things be imparted to two pieces of wood by the friction of which fire is produced? And, again, how can the imparting of righteous things to the two pieces of wood furnish Zoroaster with the necessary qualifications to go on his mission? We fail to see our way through these difficulties. Let us see now if the hints given in the article headed " Cross and Fire," in the *Theosophist* for November 1889, do not throw a ray of light on these difficulties. Let us ponder carefully these passages in the article :—

" Perhaps the most widespread and universal among the symbols in the old astronomical systems—which have passed down the stream of time to our century, and have left traces everywhere, in the Christian religion as elsewhere—are the

Cross and Fire—the latter, the emblem of the sun. The ancient Aryans had them both as the symbols of Agni. Whenever the ancient Hindu devotee desired to worship Agni —says E. Burnouf—he arranged two pieces of wood in the form of a cross, and, by a peculiar whirling and friction obtained fire for his sacrifice. As a symbol, it is called *Swastica*, and as an instrument manufactured out of a sacred tree and in possession of every Brahmin, it is known as *Arani*."

" If, then, we find these two—the Cross and the Fire—so closely associated in the esoteric symbolism of nearly every nation, it is because on the combined powers of the two rests the whole plan of the universal laws. In astronomy, physics, chemistry, in the whole range of natural philosophy in short, they always come out as the invisible cause and the visible result ; and only metaphysics and alchemy (metachemistry) can fully and conclusively solve the mysterious meaning."

" The central point, or the great central sun of the Cosmos, as the Kabalists call it, is the Deity. It is the point of intersection between the two great conflicting powers,—the centripetal and centrifugal forces."

" Plato calls the universe a ' blessed god,' which was made in a circle and decussated in the form of the letter X."

" In Masonry the Royal Arch degree retains the cross as the triple Egyptian Tau."

May we not, after reading these passages, conclude that what is meant by " the two friction woods" is the same as that meant by the Hindu *Swastica* or *Arani*, or the *Cross* of the Kabalists, or the Egyptian *Tau* ? As among the Hindus, " the two friction woods " were used to obtain fire for certain ceremonies, and the cross made of " the two woods" was with Zoroaster what *Arani* was with the Brahmin, and as such possessed the efficacies of what may be called a magic wand in the hand of Zoroaster. Understood in this light, it becomes intelligible how the virtues of " the two friction woods" could have furnished Zoroaster with qualifications to go on his mission of a prophet. This reminds us of the analogous case of Moses with his magic rod. The above interpretation —*i. e.*, that the instrument indicated by "the two friction woods" is the same as the *Arani*, in the land of the Brahmin —comes to be most happily confirmed when we find out the word in Zend Avastâ which Dr. Haug translates as the "two friction woods." That word is *Rana*, the dative dual of which is *Ranoibia* : *Rana* in Zend Avasta, and *Arani* in Sanskrit.

Just as *Rana* resembles *Arani*, may we be permitted to suppose that Tâî in the Zoroastrian rites resembles the Tàu ? Tâî are the twigs of a particular sacred tree (now not known) which the Zoroastrian Mobed is required to keep in his hand when performing the most sacred ceremonies of Ijashne and Darûn. And may we say that *Rana* in the hand of Zoroaster, *Arani* in the hand of the Brahmin, and *Tau* among the Egyptians, is preserved in the *Tai* that the Mobed at the present day holds in his hand when performing the sacred ceremonies of his faith ? But the wand in the hand of the Mobed of the present day has lost its virtues, because the key to the mysteries of the Zoroastrian faith is lost. Perhaps there are some even now to whom Zoroastrianism is not a dumb mystery : unknown to the world, they hold in their faithful keeping the sacred trust. We know with better certainty that there are men to whom the Brahminical, Egyptian, and Kabalistic mysteries have given up their secrets. The knowledge of the one elucidates the other, and viewed from this stand-point, what new and sublime meaning the sacred words of the Zend Avastâ may not unfold. The Gâthâs, which are understood to be Zoroaster's own composition or that of his immediate disciples, have hitherto completely baffled the attempts of all scholars to make any consistent meaning out of them. This may no longer be the case if we seek help towards their interpretation, in the right quarters, which have hitherto been sadly neglected.

.*. The mystery of "two friction wood" require yet another key: cannot these two woods be the two higher "principles" in man, by whose "friction" real spiritual Intuition or Divine Inspiration is obtained ?—*Compiler.*

THE SEPTENARY NATURE OF MAN.

BY A PARSI F. T. S.

MANY of the esoteric doctrines given out through the Theosophical Society reveal a spirit akin to that of the older religions of the East, especially the Vedic and the Zendic. Leaving aside the former, I propose to point out by a few instances the close resemblance which the doctrines of the old Zendic Scriptures, as far as they are now preserved, bear to these recent teachings. Any ordinary Parsi, while reciting his daily Niyashes, Gehs and Yashts, provided he yields to the curiosity of looking into the meaning of what he recites, will easily perceive how the same ideas, only clothed in a more intelligible and comprehensive garb, are reflected in these teachings. The description of the septenary constitution of man found in the 55th chapter of the Yaçna, one of the most authoritative books of the Mazdiasnian religion, shows the identity of the doctrines of Avastâ and the esoteric philosophy. Indeed, as a Mazdiasnian, I felt quite ashamed that, having such undeniable and unmistakable evidence before their eyes, the Zoroastrians of the present day should not avail themselves of the opportunity offered of throwing light upon their, now entirely misunderstood and misinterpreted, scriptures by the assistance and under the guidance of the Theosophical Society. If Zend scholars and students of Avastâ would only care to study and search for themselves, they would, perhaps, find to assist them, men who are in the possession of the right and only key to the true esoteric wisdom ; men who would be willing to guide and help them to reach the true and hidden meaning, and to supply them with the missing links that have resulted in such painful gaps as to leave the meaning meaningless, and to create in the mind of the perplexed student doubts that have finally to culminate in a thorough unbelief in his own religion. Who knows but they may find some of their own co-religionists, who, aloof from the world, have to this day preserved the glorious truths of their once mighty religion, and who, hidden in the recesses of solitary mountains and unknown silent caves, are still in possession of, and exercising, mighty powers, the heirloom of the ancient Magi. Our scriptures say that the ancient Mobeds were Yogis, who had the power of making themselves simultaneously visible at different places, even though hundreds of miles apart, also that they could heal the sick and work that which would now appear to us miraculous. All this was considered *facts* but two or three centuries back, as any reader of old books (mostly Persian) is acquainted with or will disbelieve *á priori* unless his mind is irretrievably biassed by modern secular education. The story about the Mobed and Emperor Akbar and of the latter's conversion is a well-known historical fact, requiring no proof.

I will first of all quote side by side the passage referring to the septenary nature of man as I find it in our scriptures and in occultism.

SUB-DIVISIONS OF SEPTENARY MAN.

According to the Occultists.	*According to Yasna (chap. 55, para. 1.)*
1. *Sthula Sharira*—The physical body.	1. *Tanu*—The physical body.
2. *Prâna*—The Vitality.	2. *Ushtâna*—Heat or vitality.
3. *Linga-sharira*—The ethereal double.	3. *Keherpa*—The aërial mould in which the body is cast. (Pers., *Kaleb, Kâlbûd*.)
4. *Kâma*—Desire, sensation, passion, emotion.	4. *Tevishi*—Outgoing energy, desire, emotion, force.
5. *Manas.* { (i) Lower *manas* giving intelligence, reason. (ii) Higher *manas* giving intuition, spiritual knowledge, holding in store the experiences of all lives, and striving to become immortal by uniting with the Spirit.	5. *Urvân*—Soul, manas, the reincarnating Ego, the one that suffers or enjoys. 6. *Bodhâng*—Intelligence, reason.*

---

* *Bodhâng* or *Buddhi* differs in meaning in Buddhistic and Vedic philosophy, in the former it stands as spiritual soul (the 6th of the above classification), and in the latter somewhat similar to lower manas. How it stands in Zoroastrianism is doubtful. According to *Dûva Vispahûmata*, however, all spiritual thoughts, spiritual words, spiritual deeds are done through *Buddhi*.— *Compiler.*

THE SEPTENARY NATURE OF MAN.

According to the Occultists.
6. *Buddhi.* ⎫
7. *Atma.*   ⎬ Monad.
              ⎭

According to Yasna (chap. 55, para. 1.)
7. *Fravashi*—Spirit, the divine principle underlying every atom of the elemental, mineral, vegetable, animal and human Kingdoms.

The above is given in the *Avastâ* as follows :—

    1   2   3   4   5   6
વીસ્પાએા ગએથાઓસ્ય તન્વસ્ય અજદેખીસ્ય ઉસ્તાનાંસ્ય કેહર્પસ્ય
   7   8   9   10   11   12
તેવીષીસ્ય ખઓધરસ્ય ઉર્વાનેમ્ય ફ્રવષીમ્ય પહરીયદહેમહી આયવએધયમહી
 13   14   15   16   17   18   19
આયત દીશ અવએધયમહી ગાથાખ્યૈા સ્પેન્તાખ્યૈા રતુક્ષથાખ્યૈા અષઓનીખ્યૈા.
    12   13   15   14   11
We declare and positively make known this (that) we offer
           1   2   3
(our) entire property (which is) the body (the *self*, consisting
        4   5   6   7   8
of) bones, vital force, aërial form, desire, consciousness,
 9   10   17   18   19
soul and spirit to the prosperous, truth-coherent (and) pure
16
Gâthâs (prayers).

The ordinary Gujarati translation differs from Spiegel's, and this latter differs very slightly from what is here given. Yet in the present translation there has been made no addition to, or omission from, the original wording of the Zend text. The grammatical construction also has been preserved intact. The only difference, therefore, between the current translation and the one here given is that *ours* is in accordance with the modern corrections of philological research, which make it more intelligible, and the idea perfectly clear to the reader.

The words 3, 4 and 5 need no further explanation. They represent the purely physical part of man: matter and that force which keeps this matter in cohesion for a fixed period of time. The sixth word also has come down to us without undergoing any change in the meaning. It is the modern Persian word *Kaleb*, which means a mould, a shape into which a thing is cast, to take a certain form and features

The next word, the seventh, is one about which there is a great difference of opinion. It is by some called strength, durability, *i. e.*, that power which gives tencity to and sustains the nerves. Others explain it as that quality in a man of rank and position which makes him perceive the result of certain events (causes) and thus helps him in being prepared to meet them. This meaning is suggestive, though we translate it as desire with the greatest diffidence. The eighth word is quite clear. That inward feeling which tells a man that he knows this or that, that he has or can do certain things—is preception and consciousness (*Ahankâr*). It is the inner conviction, knowledge and its possession. The ninth word is again one which has retained its meaning and has been in use up to the present day. The reader will at once recognise that it is the origin of the modern word *Ravân*. It is the conscious motor or agent in man. It is that something which depends upon, and is benefited or injured by, the foregoing attributes. We say depends upon, because its progress entirely consists in the development of those attributes. If they are neglected, it becomes weak and degenerating, and disappears. If they ascend on the moral and spiritual scale, it gains strength and vigour and becomes more blended than ever to the Divine Essence—the seventh principle. But how does it become attracted toward its monad? The tenth word answers the question. This is the Divine Essence in man which promises the *urvân* or soul immortality if the latter obeys and follows the dictates of the former. It is the *Atma-Buddhi*, or the monad of the Occultist. It is the underlying essence of all evolution or manifestation. No atom in space is without it. The idea of Fravashi in Zoroastrian philosophy is exactly similar to that of Âtma-Buddhi. There are Fravashis not only of men and animals, but even of gods and Ahura-Mazda.

If, then, the Avastû contains such a passage it must fairly be admitted that its writers knew the whole doctrine concerning spiritual man. We cannot suppose that the ancient Mazdiasnians, the Magi, wrote this short passage, without inferring from it, at the same time, that they were thoroughly conversant with the whole of the occult knowledge about man. And it looks very strange, indeed, that modern Theosophists should now preach to us the very doctrines that *must* have been known and taught thousands of years ago by the Mazdiasnians—the passage is quoted from one of their oldest writings. And since they propound the same ideas, the meaning of which has well nigh been lost even to our most learned Mobeds, they ought to be credited at least with some possession of a knowledge, the key to which has been revealed to them, and lost to us, and which open the door to the meaning of those hitherto inexplicable sentences and doctrines in our old writings, about which we are still, and will go on, groping in the dark, unless we listen to what they have to tell us about them.

—*The Theosophist*, Vol. iv., p. 20.

.*. Our Brother has but to look into the oldest sacred book of China—namely, THE YI KING, or *Book of Changes* (translated by James Legge), written 1200 B. C., to find that same *Septenary* division of man mentioned in that system of Divination. *Zhing*, which is translated correctly enough 'essence,' is the more subtle and pure part of matter—the grosser form of the elementary ether ; *Khi*—or 'spirit' is the breath, still material, but purer than the *zhing*, and is made of the finer and more active form of ether. In the *hwun*, or soul (*animus*) the *Khi* predominates, and the *zhing* (or *zing*) in the *pho* or animal soul. At death the *hwun* (or spiritual soul) wanders away, ascending, and the *pho* (the root of the Tibetan word *Pho-hat*,) descends and is changed into a ghostly shade (the shell). Dr. Medhurst thinks that "the *Kwei Shans*" (See *Theology of the Chinese*, pp. 10-12) are "the expanding and contracting principles of human life"! The *Kwei Shans* are brought about by the dissolution of the human frame—and consist of the expanding and ascending *Shan* which rambles about in space, and of the contracted and shrivelled *Kwei*, which reverts to earth and non-entity. Therefore, the *Kwei* is the physical body ; the *Shan* is the vital principle ; the *Kwei-Shan* the *linga-sariram*, or the vital soul ; *Zhing* the 4th principle or Kama-rupa, the essence of will ; *pho* the animal soul; *Khi* the spiritual soul ; and *Hwun* the pure spirit—the seven principles of occult doctrine !—ED., *Theosophist.*

REFERENCE—For an explicit exposition see " The Seven Principles of Man," by Mrs. Annie Besant.

ZRAVANE AKARNE AND ZRAVANE DREGHO KHADATE;

OR,

BOUNDLESS DURATION AND THE SELF-EMANATING TIME OF THE LONG PERIOD.

"IT is said in the Good Religion, that that which through its progression rejoins its source is Time, and that which leads from the lowest to the highest is the Path of Wisdom. As to Time, it is said that it is in accord with the force of the motion proceeding from its primal source, and it moves in regular succession. The first work of the Creative Power of the Universe began with Time, and the end of such work pertains to the completion of the Limited Time of celestial revolution. The end of Time is in the completion of planetary motion. All have to regenerate themselves by their own efforts in (reaching) Boundless Duration. At the time of the renovation those that are in communion with the Deity will not have to journey again."

Say the Dasturs :*.

"Time was originally unlimited, but subsequently it came to have a limit. When this limit is reached it will again act in Boundlessness. This is explained by saying, that when the planetary bodies reach the end of their course, Time becomes lost in Limitlessness; and when the course of the planets is completed, there is again an effort to bring about a limit in' Boundlessness. The Creative Power is unlimited in Its wondrous Wisdom, and by Its enduring force It exists eternally in Boundless Duration." †

This passage from the Pahlavi *Dinkard*—which is a book written in the early part of the ninth century of the Christian

---

* The High Priests of the Parsis.

† Translated from Dastur Peshotan Sanyana's Gujarâtî rendering of the Pahlavi *Dinkard*, Vol. vi, page 379.

era, by certain Dasturs or High Priests of the Zoroastrian religion in Persia—is in many respects very suggestive.

The *Dinkard* treats in a miscellaneous manner of various doctrines and observances of the Zoroastrians as they were understood by the later Dasturs of the Parsîs.

There was in Persia a doctrine prevalent at one time, that Ahuramazda (the Divine Spirit) and Ahriman (the Power of Evil and Darkness) were born of Zravâne Akarne or Boundless Time. We shall not however take up that moot point in this instance. Zravân in the Avasta language means the "Old One." In the later Persian dialects the word was transformed into Zamân, meaning an age or a cycle.

The old Iranian Zravân was viewed in two aspects: first, as Zravâne Âkarne or Boundless Time, and secondly, as Zravâne Dregho Khadâtahé or the Self-emanating Time of the Long Period.

Whether Time be or be not merely one of the *subjective* intuitive forms of our own intellect, it is certainly one of the limitations of our material consciousness.

According to the above quoted passage, "Limited Time," which is more properly designated a cycle or an age, is nothing else than the period during which a certain planetary revolution continues. The beginning and end of Time is no other than the commencement and the cessation of a planetary course.

"Time," it is said, "was originally unlimited, but subsequently it came to have a limit," and when the end of that limit is reached, "it again acts in Limitlessness and again there is an effort to bring about a limit."

This statement is a general outline of the law of never-ending cycles which all have their succession in Infinite "Duration." As said in the Stanzas of Dzyan* "Time was not, for it lay asleep in the Infinite Bosom of Duration."

---

* An old archaic work no longer accessible, on some of the stanzas of which the monumental work of Madame H. P. Blavatsky, *The Secret Doctrine*, has been founded.

The "Infinite Bosom of Duration" is the Zravâne Âkarne of the Avasta, and "according to the force of motion of the primal source" each time the cycle or "Limited Time" is launched into being. When it ends there is again Unlimitedness, and again there is an effort to bring about a limited period.

The Creative Power that works during a cycle is Ahuramazda, and he is said to exist eternally even in Boundless Duration. "What is it that ever was?" and the answer is given: "The Germ in the Root."

"Boundless Duration" is the "Root," and the "Germ" is Ahuramazda. The Great Breath is said to be ever "coming and going," and this, as the *Dinkard* says, is the "force of the motion proceeding from the primal source."

It is said again:

"That which leads from the lowest to the highest is the Path of Wisdom. All have to regenerate themselves *by their own efforts* in reaching Boundless Duration.

"At the time of the renovation those that are in communion with the Deity will not have to journey again."

All development and progress upwards from the material to the spiritual plane takes place solely by following the "Path of Wisdom," which is the light of the inner and higher intuition. Before the end of the cycle is reached every one must regenerate himself *by his own effort;* no extraneous help or power can be of any avail.

When renovation takes place—that is, when humanity is at the end of its cycle—those who are in communion with the Deity—that is those who have subdued their lower natures and assimilated their lower Ego with the higher—will not be whirled back into the vortex of the lower desires, and will not thus have to "journey again" through the distractions and temptations of material existence.

N. D. K.

—*Oriental Department Paper, London,* Vol. i, No, 4.

THE SUN AS A SYMBOL OF AHURA-MAZDA.

AHURA-MAZDA, the invisible Spiritual Sun, manifests into ZRAVANE AKARNE, the inconceivable Boundless Spirit, which is now translated into Boundless Time, Whose body is the physical sun, the giver of life and light. The Boundless Spirit has been symbolized by a zero or Circle ○, which has no beginning and no end, and Ahura-Mazda, the Germ from which was evolved the whole universe, seen or unseen, by a point in the circle, thus ☉ We are told in the "Secret Doctrine" that, "At the dawn of manifestation, great or small, of a Cosmos, or of a man, there arises a point from which all energy radiates. Once formed it continues until the object for which it arose is accomplished." This condition of things is symbolized by a circle with a central point as shown above, which is also the Astrological sign for the sun. Thus at the root of all things there is this "Boundless Time" which, when it awakes into manifestation, becomes first the Invisible Fire. In fact the Root of all things is Fire; and in our system the abode of the Fires is the Central Sun. The Central Spiritual Sun is taken to mean the Logos, Ahura-Mazda, and this is the usual meaning attached to the 'Central Sun' in Theosophical literature. It is, therefore, a spiritual conception and has nothing to do with the physical sun known to Astronomy, unless such is specially stated. The four (or seven) suns mentioned in the "Secret Doctrine" (ii—p. 250-51, n. e.) are said to be the central bodies of various planes of being, the Central Sun being the highest of the four and belonging to the spiritual side of nature. Suns here clearly refer to the great Hierarchies of Dhyân-Chohans which correspond to the Ameshâspentas of the Mazdeans, the Archangels of the Christians and the Sephiroths of the Jews, of which so much has been written in that monumental work of Madame Blavatsky. This will show the significance why we have adopted this symbol for Ahura-Mazda. We have also seen that behind and beyond Ahura-Mazda is the Boundless Time, "Zaravâne-Akarne."

"Stepping out of the Circle of Infinity, that no man comprehendeth, Ain-Soph (the Kabalistic synonym for Parabrahm of the Vedantists, the Zravâne-Akarne of the Mazdeans, or for any other 'UNKNOWABLE') becomes 'One,'—the ECHOD, the EKA, the AHU,—then He (or It) is transformed by evolution into the One in many, the Dhyani-Buddhas or the Elohims, or again the Ameshâspentas, his third step being taken into generation of the flesh, or 'Man.'" . . . "The Circle was with every nation the symbol of the Unknown—'Boundless Space,' the abstract garb of an ever-present abstraction—the Incognisable Deity. It represents limitless Time in Eternity. The Zravâne-Akarne is also the 'Boundless Circle of the Unknown Time,' from which Circle issues the radiant light—the Universal SUN, or Ormazd . . . "—(The "Secret Doctrine," Vol. I., p. 139, *n. e.*), which is the Logos, the 'First-Born' and the Sun.

As there seems to be a difference of opinion among the Zoroastrians regarding the idea of Zravâne-Akarne it is necessary to say something on this subject here. It appears that even in Persia the idea of Zravâne-Akarne was not familiar to the masses, and those few who understood the difference between it and the time that we are cognizant of, were called the Zarvânists. Time as we know it by virtue of its relation to our present consciousness, and through our ideas of past, present and future, and which is known in the Avasta as Zravâne-Dregokhadâtahé, is distinct from the Boundless Time, Zravâne-Akarne. The "Secret Doctrine" says :—"'Time' is only an illusion produced by the succession of our states of consciousness as we travel through Eternal Duration, and it does not exist where no consciousness exists in which the illusion can be produced, but 'lies asleep.' The Present is only a mathematical line which divides that part of Eternal Duration which we call the Future, from that part which we call the Past. Nothing on earth has real duration, for nothing remains without change—or the same—for the billionth part of a second; and the sensation we have of the actuality of the division of Time known as the Present, comes from the blurring of the momentary glimpse, or succession of glimpses, of things that our senses give us, as those things pass from the region of ideals, which we call the Future, to the region of memories that we name the Past. In the same way we experience a sensation of Duration in the case of the instantaneous electric spark, by reason of the blurred and continuing impression on the retina. The real person or thing does not consist solely of what is seen at any particular moment, but is composed of the sum of all its various and changing conditions from its appearance in material form to its disappearance from earth. It is these 'sum-totals' that exist from eternity in the Future, and pass by degrees through matter, to exist for eternity in the Past. No one would say that a bar of metal dropped into the sea came into existence as it left the air, and ceased to exist as it entered the water, and that the bar itself consisted only of that cross-section thereof which at any given moment coincided with the mathematical plane that separates, and, at the same time, joins the atmosphere and the ocean. Even so of persons and things, which dropping out of the 'to be' into the 'has been,' out of the Future into the Past-present momentarily to our senses a cross-section, as it were, of their total selves, as they pass through Time and Space (as matter) on their way from one eternity to another: and these two eternities constitute that Duration in which alone anything has true existence, were our senses but able to cognise it." (The "Secret Doctrine," Vol. i., p. 68-69, *n. e.*) Such is the idea we gather of finite and infinite time according to occult philosophy.

The above spiritual ideas may be symbolised by the double interlaced triangles with a point in the centre, and bounded by a circle—thus:

The symbol thus formed represents the Boundless Time, or

Zravâne-Akarne, Ahura-Mazda, and the Ameshâspentas, at one and the same time : the circle representing the first, the point in the middle the second, and the six points of the interlaced triangles the third. This symbol of the highest of Divine Ideas need not be regarded as a degradation of the Sacred ; because, in the words of Carlyle, " Is not a symbol ever, to him who has eyes for it, some dimmer or clearer revelation of the Godlike ; through which all there glimmers something of a Divine Idea." Not so only: in these geometrical figures the students of the ancient Greek philosophy will see the truth of the teaching of their Masters that " God geometrizes"—an occult aphorism easily verified on this plane by those who have eyes to see. Occultists use this symbol to denote the motive power which is the vital soul of all things. It is that hidden force which, during an active Manvautaric period, sends forth creative light, bringing myriads of suns into existence. In its depths are mysteries too great for us to fathom with our finite minds. In its presence is life ; in its essence lies the mind of the ever-concealed Logos [Ahura-Mazda]; and its light—the seven-fold ray [the Ameshâspentas]—illumine our souls, as the light from the visible sun shines upon our bodies. " In the shoreless ocean of space radiates the central spiritual and (*invisible*) sun. The universe is his body, spirit and soul, and after this ideal model are framed ALL THINGS"—(" Isis Unveiled," i, 302). The term is again used to indicate that unseen and unknown point in the heavens toward which all visible suns are gravitating. Occultism and science are at one in showing the whole manifested universe to be in constant motion, and Astronomers find a point or centre in the Milky Way, toward which the mighty suns of our visible Universe are ever being attracted. From this it will be clear that we are not profaning the Divine Sun as the symbol of Ahura-Mazda. These central suns are the immediate causes of the manifestation of their respective systems.

The sun of each system is said to be the reservoir of "the vital electricity that feeds the whole system in which it lives and breathes and has its being; the storehouse of our little cosmos, self-generating its vital fluid and ever receiving as much as it gives out."—("Five Years of Theosophy," p. 165.) This is as accurate a description of the heart of our solar system as could be wished. So the expression may be applied to the centre of that great Being with whom we are in such close connection—the Earth, because each planet is the embodiment of a spiritual entity. Its heart is the Central Sun from which we receive our life-energies, spiritual as well as material. The Heart of Man, too, is the Central Sun, of his being, for it is through the physical heart and the real Heart that come the physical forces and the spiritual powers, the correlation of which makes him man.

From the above our Parsi brethren will be able to see what transcendent and grand ideas underly the symbol of Ahura-Mazda and how the physical sun can be taken as the symbol of the Supreme, and why is it that the Holy Zarathushtra has enjoined on his followers the adoration of the Sun, which is the visible symbol of the invisible Ahura-Mazda, and also why Fire is held in such supreme importance and reverence in their sacred Avastâ.

N. F. B.

—*Theosophic Gleaner*, Vol. vi., No. 11.

AHUNAVAIRYA.

THE second lesson taught to a Zoroastrian child is a short Mâñthra called Ahunavairya. It has been translated into various languages by various scholars. Not two of the translations being similar, I prefer one rendered by Mr. Nowroji Dorabji Khandalavala, for it is, I think, more philosophic than any other. It runs as follows :—

"*As is the law of the Eternal Existence, so [its] Energy, solely through the Harmony of the Perfect Mind ; [this] is the producer of the manifestations of the universe, and [is] to Ahura-Mazda, the Power that gives sustenance to the revolving systems.*"

Commenting upon this Mr. Nowroji says : "In other words, just as the nascent world is about to be called into being, the Supreme Existence, in accordance with its own Will or Law, puts forth its Energy, which, acting in union with the Divine Harmony of the Perfect or Universal Mind, works out all the manifestations of the universe, and, without becoming inactive, remains the Preserving aspect of Ahura-Mazda, sustaining all things in their motion and life, from the minutest atoms to the grandest of systems that course through Infinite Space." "By the action of the manifested Wisdom, or Mahat," in the words of the "Secret Doctrine," "represented by these innumerable centres of spiritual Energy in the Kosmos, the reflection of the Universal Mind, which is Cosmic Ideation and the intellectual Force accompanying such ideation, becomes objectively the Fohat [which is identical in Zoroastrianism with Apâm-Napât]. Fohat, running along the seven principles of AKÂSH, acts upon manifested substance or the One Element, as declared above, and by differentiating it into various centres of Energy, sets in motion the Law of Cosmic Evolution, which, in obedience to the Ideation of the Universal Mind [or Vohumano, as it is called in Zoroastrianism], brings into existence all the various states of being in the manifested Solar System."

All this is contained in the short formula of a couple of lines which has been known by the name of Ahunavairya; but Ahunavairya proper is described in Yaçna 19 as being THE WORD, which was "before the Heavens, before the Water, before the Earth, before the Primeval Cow, before the Trees, before the Fire, son of Ahura-Mazda, before the Holy Man, before the Deamons and vile men, before this world, before every thing good produced by Mazda,—that arises from pure origin."

Compared with the first passage of St. John it has a striking unity. "In the beginning was the Word, and the Word was with God, and the Word was God. The same was in the beginning with God. All things were made by him; and without him was not any thing made that was made. In him was life; and the life was the light of men. And the light shineth in darkness; and the darkness comprehended it not."

What the Word is to the Christians, the Ahunavar is to the Zoroastrians. It is the Sabda-Brahman of the Hindus, the first manifestation of Parabrahman, which they would not call even Íswara for fear of creating confusion. It is the beginning and the end of all.

We are taught that there cannot be an existence unless there is a sound, and wherever there is sound, there must be colour, and colour signifies *rúpa* or form. This is verified by modern science, as will be seen from the "Voice Figures," by Mrs. Watts Hughes. All the *Tattvas* are the modifications of Swara, and the Swara is the root of all sound; it is the substratum of the "melody of the æther" mentioned in the "Oracles of Zoroaster;" it is the spirit within spirit, the "current of the life-wave," the emanation of the ONE LIFE. "*Swara* threw itself into the form of Âkâsh," and thence successively into the forms of Vâyu (Air), Agni (Fire), Âpas (Water), and Prithvi (Earth). " It is the *Swara* that has given form to the first accumulations of the divisions of the universe; the Swara causes evolution and involution; the Swara is God himself, or more properly the Great Power (Maheshwara). The Swara is the manifestation of the impression on matter of that power which in man is known to us as the power which knows itself. It is to be understood that the action of this power never ceases. It is ever at work, and evolution and involution are the very necessity of its unchangeable existence."—(*Sivâgama.*) Thus the universe was produced by Sound, and "the Word was made flesh" in man, according to the Christian Bible. Man is considered the culmination of existence. In him are centred all the *tattvas*, or forces, visible as well as potential. He has again to win his kingdom, which can never be won unless he attains to a state in which he hears the "Voice of the Fire," which has no form.

"It [the Ahunavar or Honover] is the Mediator between the Boundless Incomprehensible Zeroane and the finite being, himself becoming intelligible and revealed in the character of Ahura-Mazda, who has some times manifested himself in a human form in a body resplendent as the Light, at once Spirit and Word; and in Him, rather than in the Zeroane, the attributes which constitute absolute perfection becomes knowable by the mind of man."[*]

Thus is man's ultimate object fulfilled; thus he has attained his ultimate goal.

The power attributed to one who can weild the *mañthra* or speech of Ahunavairya or Honover, is wonderful. Zarathushtra Spitaman was called a Mâñthrân, *i. e.*, a speaker of Mañthra, and one of the earliest names for the sacred scriptures of the Parsis was Mâñthra-spenta. The power of one who can act as the Hotri-priest or Jothi, a corruption of Zend *Zaota*, at the Soma-Yajna or Haom-sacrifice, consists in his possession of full knowledge of the sacred word or speech—Vâch. This Vâch is personified in Sarasvati, which is identical with Ardvisur Anahita in the system of Mazdayasnism, who is the goddess of

---

[*] "Introduction to Hebrew Literature," by Dr. Etheridge.

the Secret Knowledge. " The greatest power of this Vâch or Sacred Speech is developed according to the form which is given to the Mâñthra by the officiating Hotri, and this form consists wholly in the numbers and syllables of the sarcred metre. If pronounced slowly and in a certain rhythm, one effect is produced ; if quickly and with another rhythm, there is a different result."*

The stanza of Ahunavairya contains 21 words, thrice-seven enjoined to be heard, the verb being *srávya*, the same as in Sanskrita, आस्य.

The results achieved by one who can weild this Mâñthra are mentioned in the chapter called Sarosh Yasht Hadokht, where the power is attributed to him, and " whoso utters this spoken word, be it a man or a woman, with very pure mind, with very pure words, with very pure works . . . at every bad hap, as often as one fears a misfortune from the bad, there will not on that day or in that night an oppressor, a tormentor, an afflictor, be seen by him with the eyes—the plague of the numerous thieves marching along will not reach him." But before one can weild the power of this Mâñthra, he must purify himself and become holy.

N. F. B.

—*Theosophic Gleaner*, Vol. iii., No. 11.

---

* *Isis Unveiled*, Vol. ii., p. 409.

THE LUNAR ORB.

IN the sacred Avastâ of the Parsis, the moon is frequently addressed as "*Mah Gao-chithra*," which expression, in accordance with the traditional interpretation of the term, is translated to mean the "Moon that keeps in it the seed of the Bull."

"*Gau*" in the Avastâ means both the "earth" as well as "cow or bull," and "*Geush*," which is another form of the same word in the oldest writing, the Gâthâs, seems to suggest that the word stands either for the earth or the animal creation. "*Taurus*," or the bull in the Zodiac, is a sign of the earth and is a symbol of the seed of life. In the four Kabalistic faces also the bull stands for the element of earth. The expression "*Mah Gao-chithra*" may very appropriately be rendered to mean, "the moon that bears in it the seeds of earthly life."

We may translate the words without much difficulty, but it is not easy to answer why such an epithet was given to the moon. A very crude explanation is very often given that, as the new moon continues during the succeeding few days to present the appearance of the horns of a bull, the ancients, in their simplicity and wild imagery, compared the moon to this particular animal. It is not the external shape of the moon, however, that is referred to by the qualifying expression. A hint appears therein as to the influence, action, and connection of the moon with our terrestrial sphere.

For want of any other source of information on this point, let us turn to "The Secret Doctrine," that marvellous storehouse of suggestive teachings in Religion, Myth, Symbol, and Science.

We learn thence that the moon "plays the largest and most important part as well in the formation of the earth itself as in the peopling thereof with human beings." The moon is the fourth globe in a separate series of seven orbs, and the life-impulse developing after seven Rounds over this Lunar septenary series, gives rise in turn to our terrene series of seven orbs, of which our earth is the fourth and the grossest. The moon in its lunar series of globes stands on the same perceptible and material plane as the earth does in its own series of seven globes, each of these latter spheres being respectively generated by the life-elements and energy that oozes out when each of the corresponding seven orbs of the Lunar series goes into *pralaya* after completing its 7th Round. (The S. D., Vol. i, pp. 179-203, *n. e.*)

The Pitris or Lunar Monads are those which having ended their life cycle on the Lunar chain (which is inferior to the terrestrial chain), have incarnated on this one. There are seven moons as there are seven earths. Six of these in each chain being superphysical, are invisible to the naked eye, while the grossest in each chain (*viz.*, our earth and its satellite, the moon), are alone perceptible to us, occupying as they do the turning point in each septenary circle. As the Lunar Monad therefore passes in its 7th Round over the moon, this orb begins to die and transfer its ' principles' to a ' Laya centre' or a centre whence differentiation commences and our earth slowly comes into being.

The Lunar Monads or Pitris, the ancestors of man, become in reality men themselves by incarnating on our earth. ' Lunar spirits ' have to become ' men' in order that their ' Monads ' may reach a higher plane of activity and self-consciousness.

The statement that the earth is formed out of the ' principles' of the moon, and that Lunar Monads develope into men on earth may appear strange, but it receives unexpected corroboration from the " Avastâ " wherein the word " *Gao-chithra* " taken from still older teachings and traditions has hitherto remained unexplained. The Secret Doctrine fully explains the meaning of the word which in its turn helps to point out that the teaching on this point comes to us from remote Aryan ages.

N. D. K.

—*The Theosophist*, Vol. x, p. 403.

THE IRANIAN OANNËS.

ZOROASTRIAN religious literature is in many parts so fragmentary that it is no easy task to unravel the true signification of various ideas that are merely hinted at in the writings now extant. Many an obscure words is highly suggestive, and an attempt, however feeble, to explain one of these seemingly unimportant allusions, will not prove futile, if it but provoke further research.

Zarathushtra, in the 19th Fargard of the "Vendidâd," is assailed by Añra-Mainyus (Ahriman), the Power of Darkness, and withstands the assaults. He then praises all the Powers of Good; and, among these, he invokes "the Kara fish that lives beneath waters in the bottom of the deep sea." In the Pahlavi Bundahish, which embodies old traditions, it is said that "it was the first day when the tree, they call Gokard (Gokerena), grew in the deep mud, within the wide-formed ocean, and it is necessary as a producer of the renovation of the universe, for they prepare its immortality therefrom. The evil spirit has formed therein a lizard as an opponent, so that it may injure the Hom (the Gokard tree); and, for keeping away that lizard, Ahuramazda has created there ten *Kara fish* which at all times continually circle round the Hom; so that the head of one of those fish is continually towards the lizard. And, together with the lizard, those fish are spiritually fed, that is, no food is necessary for them; and, till the renovation of the universe, they remain in contention."

In the Vendidâd, the word is "Karo masyo." "Masyo," in the Avastâ language, means fish; but the meaning of the word "*Kara*" has not been explained anywhere. The verb "*Kar*," in one of its significations, means, to see, to guard; and the description of the Kara fish, as given in the Bundahish, shows that it continually watches the devouring lizard, and preserves the Gokard tree. The Kara fish, then, is a spiritual principle allegorically represented as the fish, that preserves the white Hom or the allegorical tree of life and immortality.

In the Hari Purana, the God Vishnu is shown as having assumed the form of a fish, with a human head, in order to reclaim the Vedas lost during the deluge. Having enabled Visvamitra to escape with all his tribe in the ark, Vishnu, pitying weak and ignorant humanity, remained with them for some time and gave them instruction. As he was half man and half fish, he used to return to the ocean at every sunset and pass the night there.

The narrative seems to be the original of the story given by the Babylonian Berosus about Oannës, the man-fish, who is no other than Vishnu, the Preserving spirit and the second personage of the Brahminic Trinity. This Deity, having already manifested itself, is still regarded as the future Saviour of Humanity, and is the selected Redeemer who will appear at its *tenth* incarnation or *avatâr*, like the Messiah of the Jews, to lead the blessed onward, and to restore to them primitive Vedas. According to the Secret Doctrine, Messiah is the fifth emanation or potency ; so in the Jewish Kabala, the Gnostic system, and the Buddhistic in which the fifth Buddha (Maitri) will appear at his last advent to save makind before the final destruction of the world.

If Vishnu is represented, in his forthcoming and last appearance, as the tenth *avatâr*, it is only because every unit, held as an androgyne, manifest itself doubly.*

In the 19th Fargard of the Vendidâd (para. 5), Zarathushtra speaks of himself as ruling till Soshyant, the fiend-smiter, " come up to life out of the lake Kasava from the regions of the Dawn." Soshios, the Persian *avatâr* that is to come, appears, from the description given of him, to be a permutation of the tenth *avatâr* of Vishnu. And the ten *Kara fish*, that are spoken of in the Bundahish, may probably be

---

* *Isis Unveiled*, Vol. ii, p. 259.

the ten phases of the preserving spiritual principle that, from time to time, has manifested itself and will manifest itself in the great teachers of the human races.

In a letter* written by a learned Fellow of the Theosophical Society, from the monastery of Soorb Ovaness (Armenia), the writer says that the Armenians, who, until the 4th and even the 7th centuries of the Christian era, Parsis in religion, call themselves Haiks or decendants of King Haig. In the forgotten traditions of these people, we find that they claimed to have remained true to the teachings of Zoroaster. These they had accepted ever since Musarus Oannës or Annedotus—the Heaven or sun-sent (the first Odakoh and Daphos, the manfish)—arising daily from the sea at sunrise to plunge back into it at sunset—taught them the good doctrine, their arts and civilization. That was during the reign of Ammenon the Chaldean, 68 Sari or 244,800 years before the deluge. Since then (as demonstrated by the Assyriologists according to the cylinder records), several other Odakons had ascended from the sea, the last coming during the days of the Chaldean king Ubara-Tutu—"the glow of sunset"—the last but one ·of the Antediluvian kings of Berosus. Each and all these *aquarian teachers* came from his habitat in lands unknown, ascending from the Persian Gulf. If we study the account given of the Annedotus by Appllodorus and then amplify it with the pre-Christian traditions of Armenia, which say that he made them know the seeds of the earth, taught them to worship their mother Earth and their father the Sun, taught mankind the arts of agriculture,—we shall not wonder at discovering that the Chaldean Oannës and Zoroaster are one in their reminiscences. The Chaldean Annedotus was called the "son of the Fish" and the latter was the name of Zarathushtra's mother. It was the Hellenized name of their Zoroaster Annedotus, whom the Greeks called Oannës, that led the old Armenians more easily into accepting Christianity than it otherwise might.

---

* *Theosophist*, Vol. ii, p. 214.

THE IRANIAN OANNES.

According to the Aryan doctrine, the Divine but latent thought in Aditi (the boundless) produces the great Deep or water (primeval chaos) and deposits in it the germ of Universal Life. According to the Bundahish, in the midst of Vourukash or the wide-formed ocean, grows the White Hom, the counteractor of decrepitude, the reviver of the dead and the Immortalizer of the living. This essence of life is subjected to the two opposing principles,—Spenta-Mainyus and Aṅra-Mainyus (spirit and matter), which are respectively typified by the buoyant fish and the grovelling lizard, fighting for supremacy in the great occean of the *Akâsa*. The Kara fish of the Vendidâd is a suggestive allegory for the 6th or Spiritual principle that protects the 5th or personal soul from the fascinations of matter or the lower principles, and leads it on, enabling it to swim in ethereal regions and drink of the juice of the sacred Haoma (pure spirit) to attain to immortality.

The great spiritual teachers of the world, who have had their spiritual sense thoroughly awakened and made potent, are called the Buddhas or enlightened ones ; and, in reference to the above allegory, they are called, in some traditions, sons of the Fish. The name of Zarathushtra's mother, according to the later writings, is Dugdure, which is said to mean the fish ; and this explanation would make Zarathushtra one of the illuminati in whom the spiritual sense shone bright and who thereby helped to generate a great race and teach the right road towards spirituality, or "the highest kind of intellection which takes cognizance of the workings of nature by *direct assimilation* of the mind with her higher principles."

"Oannës the emblem of priestly Esoteric Wisdom ; he comes out from the sea, because the great Deep, the water, typifies also the Secret Doctrine."

N. D. K.

—*The Theosophist* Vol. vi, p. 90.

GAIYOMARD AND ZARATHUSHTRA.

IN the Avastâ, as well as in the "Bundahish," *Geúsh* and *Gaiyahe*, or the Primeval Cow and Gaiyomard, often appear side by side. This Gaiyahe or Gaiyomarethan or Gaiyomard is enveloped in a mystery, although commonly understood as representing the first man on this earth. He is also the Founder of the Aryan race according to the "Farvardin Yasht." The "Bundahish" (ch. iii) says that Ahura-Mazda brought forth a sweat upon Gaiyomard; and formed that sweat into the youthful body of a man of fifteen years, radiant and tall. And, again, it is said that when Gaiyomard issued from the sweat he saw the world dark as night. Gaiyomard issuing from his own sweat is rather puzzling and paradoxical. This reminds us of the Sweat-born race mentioned in the "Secret Doctrine." What this sweat-born race was cannot be here described in the limited space at our disposal, but those who wish to know anything more regarding these mysterious pre-Aryan races, who were not men in the sense now understood by us all, are requested to read the second volume of the "Secret Doctrine," by Madame Blavatsky, which gives as full a description as possible of these pre-historic and pre-Adamic races. Now turning to the next chapter of the "Bundahish" we see there stated that when the Primeval Ox (or Cow) passed away it fell to the right hand, and Gaiyomard afterwards, when he passed away, fell to the left hand. In the fifteenth chapter of the same book we see that Gaiyomard, while passing away, gave forth seed, which was purified by the light of the Sun [the Egg-born Race]; and Neryosang, the Fire, kept charge of two portions, and Spendarmad (the Water or Earth) received one portion, the one active and the other passive nature, one male and the other female. And in "forty years" it grew up with the shape of a one-stemmed plant or tree which in fifteen years more bore fifteen leaves. Matro and Matroyayô, or as they are commonly called, Mashyo-Mashyoï, grew up from the (primordial) earth in such a manner that their arms rested behind on their shoulders and one was joined to the other in such a way that they were both alike. They were changed from the shape of a plant into the shape of man. This is the birth of the Hermaphrodite race mentioned, again, in the "Secret Doctrine." What I want to show definitely here is that Gaiyomard was not a man like ourselves, as he is generally understood to be, but that he was a Lunar god, to prove which I will quote from our own scriptures further on. The above statement is corroborated by Dastur Zad-Sparam, which can be seen from his "Selections." Not only this, but we see something more here regarding Gaiyomard. "When he (Gaiyomard) passed away [not died] eight kinds of minerals of metallic character arose from his various members; they are gold, silver, iron, brass (? copper), tin, lead, mercury, and adamant (an impenetrable stone), and on account of the perfection of gold it is produced from the life and seed."

All these signify human evolution in a nutshell, which will become manifest to deep students of that marvellous work, the "Secret Doctrine."

According to this doctrine the Linga Sharira of man is derived from a certain Hierarchy of Dhyan Chohans or Ameshâspentas presiding over the astral plane generally to which the human astral is correlated. Its planet is Moon which is related to Earth as Parent. Our moon, however, is not "the Sacred Planet" of the Avastâ and of the Mysteries, which is ruled by the Planetary Spirits. Our moon is the representation on this plane of the principle corresponding to the sacred Moon Planet of the higher, *Maunghahem go-chithrem*, the container of the seeds of all *jivas* on earth. From one of the great Hierarchies of Dhyan Chohans, we are taught, proceeded the Sub-Hierarchies of Lunar Spirits which the Hindus call Barhishad Pitris, who were the immediate progenitors of Humanity, *i. e.*, form of humanity on our planetary chain. These Lunar gods, " more closely connected with Earth, became the creative Elohim of form, or the Adam of dust."—(The "Secret Doctrine," Vol. ii, p. 78). Arriving on the first globe of our chain they pass through the various kingdoms, elemental, mineral, vegetable, animal, human. All these are included in our "links of heredity." According to the Secret Doctrine, in the Fourth Round they "ooze out" their astral doubles from the "ape-like" forms which they had evolved in Round III, and it is this subtle, finer, form which serves as the model round which Nature builds physical man."—(Vol. i, p. 203). The Sacred Stanzas of Dzyan says, "the Great Chohans called the Lords of the Moon, of the airy bodies : 'Bring forth men, men of your nature. Give them [to the Jivas or Monads] their forms within. She [the Mother Earth] will build coverings without," [in this case the external bodies].—(S. D., Vol. ii, p. 79.) After having given the Chhaya, the shadowy bodies, which formed the First Root Race, the Lunar gods retire. The Lords of the Moon, after providing with these shadowy bodies to the monads, the material of which is Earth, they depart. "Having projected their shadows and made men of one element, the Progenitors re-ascend to Maha-Loka."—(S. D., Vol. ii, p. 92.)

Let us turn again to the "Bundahish," chapter 24. It is said there, however, that in "the first of the human species, Gaiyomard was produced, brilliant and white, with eyes which looked out for the Great One, Him who was here Zarathush-trotum"—a mystery still more mysterious. Zarathushtrotum, the Chief High Priest, even before the first man Gaiyomard. Zad-Sparam says that Gaiyomard was one-third the height of Zarathust while the "sweat" was produced. If Gaiyomard were the first man, how Zarathushtra comes *before* him ? Granting Zarathushtrotemo, the Chief High Priest mentioned above, to be a title of Ahura-Mazda, we confront another problem about the holy Zarathustra whom Dastur Zad-Sparam holds as higher than Goiyomard. May this name signify only a title or may it be the first or *original* Zarathushtra, as there were said to be about 13 of that name according to the Dabistân. Compare also the "Vendidâd :"—"O Holy Zarathustra! he (the fair Yima) was the first mortal before thee, with whom I, Ahura Mazda, did converse, whom I taught the law of Ahura, *the law of Zarathustra*"—teaching the law of Zarathushtra to the same Zarathushtra! The "Secret Doctrine" hints that by "original" Zoroaster we mean the Ameshâspend called Zarathushtra, the Lord or Ruler of the Vara made by Yima in that land (Airyanam-Vaego). There were several Zarathushtras, or Zertusts, the 'Dabistan' alone enumerating 13, but they were all reïncarnations of the first one. The last Zoroaster was the founder of the fire-temple of Azareksh, and the writer of the works on the primeval sacred Magian religion destroyed by Alexander.—(Vol. ii, p. 5.)

It appears from the foregoing accounts that, just as Gaiyomard appears to be the Lunar ancestor of mankind, the original Zarathustra may be regarded as the first Preceptor of mankind, incarnation of an Ameshâspenta or Dhyani, who is also adored side by side with Gaiyomard in the *Khorshed-Niyayesh*. From the body of Gaiyomard we have inherited not only our ethereal shadows, but various metals also. Any advanced physician will say that man's blood contains iron and his brain the element of copper; and future scientific researches will prove the significance of the occult teaching, that our body contains all sorts of metal. One who knows how to transform his baser nature into the higher one can become a great Alchemist. We cannot go deeper now.

The above ideas are set forth with a view to show the occult meaning of some of the passages in the Avastâ which would never lend themselves to any interpretation except from the occult standpoint. In short, it may be said that the World Scriptures are not to be interpreted by philology alone.

N. F. B.

—*Theosophic Gleaner*, Vol. vi, No. 9.

THE SACRED HAOMA TREE.

> "Zarathushtra asked Ahura-Mazda: 'What is the one recital of the praise of Holiness that is worth a hundred others in greatness, goodness and fairness?'
> "Ahura-Mazda answered: 'It is that one, O holy Zarathushtra! that a man delivers while drinking of the Haoma strained for the sacrifice, at the same time professing good thoughts, good words, and good deeds.'"
>
> YASHT FRAGMENT,
> *Sacred Books of the East*, Vol. xxiii, p. 312.

HAOMA is a religious ceremony performed by the Parsi Mobeds; it corresponds to the Soma-yajna of the Hindus, in which a certain potion is prepared and drunk. Whether this ceremony has been of any advantage, or whether it is necessary to perform it at all, are questions that will not be discussed here. It is intended merely to show that underneath this ceremony there lies a deep philosophical truth, the mystery of which will be manifest to Occultists only. We shall examine this subject from the standpoint first of a philologist, and then of an Occultist.

Professor F. Max Müller, in the *Academy* of October 25, 1884, says :—

"It is well known that both in the Veda and the Avastâ a plant is mentioned, called Soma (*Zend*, Haoma). This plant, when properly squeezed, yielded a juice, which was allowed to ferment; and, when mixed with milk and honey, produced an exhilarating and intoxicating beverage. This Soma juice has the same importance in Veda and Avastâ sacrifices as the juice of the grape had in the worship of Bacchus. The question has often been discussed what kind of plant this Soma could have been. When Soma sacrifices are performed at present, it is confessed that the real Soma can no longer be procured, and that *ci-près*, such as Pûtikâs, etc., must be used instead.

Dr. Haug, who was present at one of these sacrifices and was allowed to taste the juice, had to confess that it was extremely nasty and not at all exhilarating. Even in the earliest liturgical works in the Sûtras and Brâhmanas, the same admission is made, namely, that true Soma is very difficult to be procured, and that substitutes may be used instead. When it was procured, it is said that it was brought by barbarians from the North, and that it had to be bought under very peculiar circumstances."

Notwithstanding Dr. Haug's confession, made after personal experience, and Professor Max Müller's own admission "that true Soma is very difficult to be procured . . . . and that it had to be bought under very peculiar circumstances," he seems to have a faith, and a blind faith too, in the letter of the Oriental Scriptures; and in that faith he appears to have continued his investigations regarding this mysterious Haoma plant. Because, although "all these facts were stated in some papers contributed by Von Roth to the Journal of the German Oriental Society in 1881 and 1883," he still hoped with Von Roth, to point out "how Russian or English emissaries in the northern region of the neutral zone might render useful service if, in their wanderings, they would look out for a plant resembling the Soma-plant." Why? Because, as the Professor says, "wherever that plant grew naturally, it would be safe to place the cradle of the Aryan Race, or, at all events, of the ancestors of the people who, when they had migrated south, spoke either Sanskrit or Zend."

Professor Max Müller, however, believes he knows where the oldest scientific description of the Soma-plant occurs, and refers to his note in the same German Journal (1855), where, he says, "the only botanical description of the Soma-plant which I know at present is found in an extract from the so-called Ayur-Veda quoted in the Dhûrtasvâmi-bhâshyatîkâ." There it is said that "the creeper, called Soma, is dark, sour, without leaves, milky, fleshy on the surface; it destroys phlegm, produces vomiting, and is eaten by goats." This description, according to Sir J. Hooker, points to a Sarcostemma, which alone combines the qualities of sourness and milk; but Professor Max Müller argues that the latter being a native of the Bombay Presidency, militates against the identification, " because the true Soma must be a northern plant, which was replaced in India itself by Pûtikâs or similar substitutes."

In the subsequent numbers of the *Academy* we find several other articles written to prolong the controversy on this subject; but as it is a controversy regarding the etymology, supposed botany and geographical localization of the mysterious plant, it is not important for our present purpose to follow the arguments brought forward. In short, some compared the Soma with a Sarcostemma, others with hops, and others, again, with grapes.

Mr. W. T. Thiselton Dyer, however, quotes Dr. Gubernatis (*Mythologie des Plantes*, II., p. 352) to show that, in his view, this plant was connected with the Moon. This is characteristic of his school of interpretation, which finds a universal solvent for mythology in a few physical phenomena. "I am not, therefore, very hopeful," concluded Dr. Dyer, "that botanical discovery will throw much, if any, further light on the Soma question." He touches here upon the borderland of occult, but, it appears, has no courage to go deeper into the subject.

There might or might not have been a plant in botany bearing that name; but it has very little to do with the mystic Haoma, or Soma tree prescribed in the Avastâ and the Veda. Had these writers, instead of dwelling on stray passages of the Oriental Scriptures, collected all the information available from them, and meditated on the different aspects of the plant, as described in the Shâstras, they would, perhaps, have arrived at a different solution from that which would identify the sacred tree with sarcostemma, grapes, or hops. Because, from the remnants that are left to us of the Avastâ literature, we may find out much more about this "plant" than the solitary elucidation cited above from the Ayur-Veda, which is nothing more than a botanical description; that work being a storehouse of medicine, botany, physiology, and kindred sciences.

Looking to the Avastâ literature, therefore, we find that the fourth, ninth, and tenth chapters of the *Yasna* (*Sacred Books of the East*, vol. xxxi., pp. 213-244) contain the offering, the prayer, and the process of 'preparing the juice' of the Haoma tree.

The ninth chapter, entitled Haoma-yasht, is a dialogue between Haoma and Zarathushtra. Haoma, here personified as pure, 'far from death,' enumerates to Zarathushtra those who had 'prepared' him before the time of Zarathushtra, and the advantages they had gained thereby. Among them the first was Vivañhao.

"A son was born to him, Yima, the bright, possessing a good congregation; the most majestic, who gazes most at the (spiritual) Sun among men."

The second was Âthwya, of whom Thraêtaonô was born, a son with valiant clan.

"Who smote Azi Dahâka, the serpent, who had three jaws, three heads, six eyes, a thousand stratagems."

The third who 'prepared' Haoma before Zarathushtra was Thrita, to whom were born two sons.

"The one a dispenser of the Law and the Path, the other endowed with higher activity, youth, bearer of the Gaêsû, who smote the Serpent Sravara, the poisonous, green, which destroyed horses and men."

The fourth who had 'prepared' Haoma was Pourushaspa.

"Thou wert born to him,—says Haoma to Zarathushtra,— thou holy Zarathushtra, in the dwelling of Pourushaspa, created against the demons, devoted in the belief of Ahûra, the renowned in Airyêna-vaêgo."

Zarathushtra then adores Haoma, the "victorious, *golden*, with moist stalks." Some translate "yellow." Students will bear in mind the symbology of colour.

In the tenth chapter the various attributes of Haoma are given, some in plain words, others very occult, the principal of them being Haoma's power of healing all diseases, the effects of Karma generated in past lives, which being purged away, the soul wins immortality. This seems to be the chief property of the Tree.

Then we come to the Bundahish, an occult work on the Zoroastrian philosophy, wherein Haoma is known by two names: Gôkard (a corruption of "Gaokerena" of the *Vendîdâd*, xx. 17, Ahura-Mazda Yasht, Haptan Yasht and Siroza), White Haoma, and Haoma proper, yellow or golden. It is said of the Gôkard that:

"Amerêdad the archangel, as the vegetation was his own, pounded the plants small and mixed them up with the water which Tîshtar (Tîshtar is the god who presides over rain, Indra or Brihaspati of the Indian exoteric system) seized, and Tîshtar made that water rain down upon the whole earth. . . . From that same germ of plants the tree of all germs was given forth, and grew up in the wide-formed Ocean [Space] from which the germs of all species of plants ever after increased. And near to that tree of all germs the Gôkard tree was produced, to keep away deformed decrepitude; and the full perfection of the world arose therefrom."—(*Sacred Books of the East*, Vol. v, p. 30.)

" . . . It was the first day when the tree they call Gôkard grew in the depth of the mountain within the wide-formed ocean, and it is necessary as a producer of the renovation of the universe, for they prepare their immortality therefrom" (*idem*, p. 65.).

"Of trees the myrtle and date, on which (model), it is said, trees were formed, are worth all the trees of Khvanîras [this earth], except the Gôkard tree, with which they restore the dead" (*idem*, p. 91).

"Near to that tree, the White Haoma, the healing and undefiled, has grown at the source of the water of Arêdvîsûr;

everyone who eats it becomes immortal, and they call it the Gôkard tree, as it is said that Haoma is expelling death: also in the renovation of the universe they prepare its immortality therefrom; and it is the chief of plants" (*idem*, p. 100).

These passages are sufficient to show that the tree has another meaning than the physical one; as the Ocean and "the water of Arêdvîsûr," representing respectively Space or Âkâsha and the Astral Light. The teaching of the Occultists cited further on will throw some light on the above occult passages; although elsewhere, as in the Bundahish also, Haòma is spoken of in various terms, namely, as an angel, a bird,—the symbol of Soul,—as well as a plant or tree. Before we turn to the teaching of the Occultists regarding the mysterious tree, it is necessary to say a few words regarding the modern Haoma ceremonies.

According to the Bhagavad Gîtâ three things are necessary to perfection: Jñâna-yoga, Bhakti-yoga and Karma-yoga. The three should go hand in hand. They are the means of perfection. Jñâna (knowledge) without Bhakti (devotion) or Karma (action with purest motive) is useless, and inversely. Karma comprises ceremonials. The Parsis have preserved their Kriyâ-kânda or ceremonials—at every step we meet with ceremonials and yajnas in the Zoroastrian system—but they appear to have lost the other two Kândas, together with the vast philosophical treasures which have disappeared during their persecution and fall; and if they have any fragments of the other two Kândas, they are few and far between. Hence, while the inhabitants of India, who have, by their conservative nature, preserved all the Kândas, have produced, and are constantly producing, true Yogis, who can teach the Law of Immortality, the Parsis have produced none since the time of Hazrat Âzar Kaivân, the last of the Parsi sages and the author of several mystic books. He had followed, it is said, the Indian system where he could not find Zoroastrian guidance, and hence he was treated as a Hindu by some, although among his disciples there were Christians and

Mohammedans as well. Now the Parsi Mobed or priest, notwithstanding his constant performance of the Haoma ceremony, remains as ignorant of the knowledge of the Law of Immortality as his lay brother. He keeps his eye during the ceremony on the Beresma, the metallic rods which represent the divine twigs of Ahura-Mazda's Tree, and wonders why neither the Ameshâspentas, nor the high and beautiful Haomas, nor even Vohûmano,—good thought—nor his Ratûs,—the offerings made,—help him to become immortal.

Besides the ancient Zarathushtrians who had the knowledge of the mysterious Tree, we see that it was known also,* by different names, to other nations. In the Cuneiform inscriptions, the ideograph *Zi*, which means Jîva or Life, appears in a way which, if put in a vertical position, would resemble a drawing of a flower or tree. The representative of the Mystic Tree of Life, says a writer in the *Platonist* (Vol. iv, p. 117), the Norse Yggdrasil, the Winged Oak of Pherecydes, the Hellenic Tree of Life, the Tibetan Zampun, the Kabalistic Sephirothal Tree, the Tree of Eden, and the Indian Ashvattha, are all one with the 'Holy Tree made by Ahura-Mazda.' The Kosmic Sun-god Dionysos, who is equivalent to the Assyrian Dian-nisi, the 'Judge of Men,' is Dendrites, 'Lord of the Tree,' the same as the 'Chief of the Plants' mentioned in the Bundahish.

This tree is symbolized also in the ceremony performed on the Dasarâ holiday, which falls on the tenth day of the twelfth Hindu month. In the towns of Guzerat on this day the trunk of a certain botanical tree is planted under the ground where people collect; and after reciting certain Mantras and performing a ceremony, the people rush to the tree to secure even a leaf, hoping that it will be transformed into *gold*, and bring them prosperity. They should rather strive to change the real Ashvattha into a golden one within themselves.

The Bhagavad Gîtâ has the following description of the Ashvattha in the beginning of the fifteenth Adhyâya of that sacred book:—

"They say the imperishable Ashvattha is with root above

and branches below, of which the sacred hymns are the leaves. Who knows this, is a knower of Knowledge. Upwards and downwards stretch its branches, expanded by the three Potencies; the sense-objects are its spronts. Downwards, too, its roots are stretched, constraining to action in the world of men. Here neither its form is comprehended, nor its end, nor beginning, nor its support. Having cut, with the firm sword of detachment, this Ashvattha with its deeply-imbedded roots, then should the disciple search out the Supreme whence they who reach it never return again; he is come to that primal Being, whence floweth the never-ending stream of conditioned existence."

Let us see what Occultists say about this Haoma. Simon Magus, an Occultist of Samaria, is considered the first father of the Gnosis posterior to Jesus. Writing on his system, Mr. G. R. S. Mead says :—

"Seeing the importance which the symbolical Tree played in the Simonian system, it may be that there was an esoteric teaching in the school, which pointed out correspondences in the human body for mystical purposes, as has been the custom for long ages in India in the Science of Yoga. In the human body are *at least* two 'Trees,' the nervous and vascular systems. The former has its root above in the cerebrum, the latter has its roots in the heart. Among the trunks and branches run currents of 'nervous ether' and 'life' respectively, and the Science of Yoga teaches its disciples to use both of these forces for mystical purposes. It is highly probable also that the Gnostics taught the same processes to their pupils, as we know for a fact that the Neo-Platonists inculcated like practices. From these considerations, then, it may be supposed that Simon was not so ignorant of the real laws of the circulation of the blood as might otherwise be imagined."

The above description refers to the physico-psychic aspect of the Tree; but the lesson we have to learn from this passage is that, if Simon Magus knew the real laws of the circulation of the blood, why not also the ancient Mazdiasnian and the Indian

Yogis who had praised the same Tree in its higher aspects ages before Simon's time? Madame Blavatsky, in reviewing a book on Zoroastrian philosophy, says:—

"Speaking of the Mystic Trees, the Gôkard, the source of all medicines, is said to grow out of the earth, whereas the White Haoma, 'which will furnish man with immortality at the time of the resurrection, is spoken of as being in the Ocean, or the sea with the wide shores,' esoterically Space. And, we might add, that the one grows with its roots in the earth, the other with its roots in heaven, twin-trees, one the reflection of the other, and both within every man. From all of which we may perceive that perhaps the superstition is not so absurd, for 'the water or sap in the plants circulates like the waters of the earth, or like the blessings which the righteous utter, which come back to themselves,' and as 'blood' is under the same law, therefore it follows that the Mazdean Initiates knew both of the 'circulation of the blood' and, more important still, of the cyclic and Karmic law."—(*Lucifer*, Vol. vii, p. 507.)

In another aspect we find it corresponding to the Moon, one Indian name for which is Soma, the same name by which the Haoma ceremony is known in India. In the oldest systems the Moon is represented as male, and Soma in that respect is treated as the illegitimate son of Budha or Wisdom, "which relates to Occult Knowledge, a wisdom gathered through a thorough acquaintance with lunar mysteries, including those of sexual generation."—(*The Secret Doctrine*, Vol. i, p. 228, note.) "But the real property of the *true* Soma was (and *is*) to make a new *man* of the Initiate, after he is *reborn*, namely, once that he begins to live in his *astral* body (see 'The Elixir of Life'), for, his spiritual nature overcoming the physical, he would soon snap it off and part even from that etherealized form. NOTE.—The partaker of *Soma* finds himself both linked to his external body, and yet away from it in his spiritual form. The latter, freed from the former, soars for the time being in the ethereal higher regions, becoming virtually 'as one of the gods,' and yet preserving in his physical brain the memory of what he sees and learns. Plainly speaking, *Soma* is the fruit of the Tree of Knowledge forbidden by the jealous Elohim to Adam and Eve or *Yah-ve*, 'lest Man should become as one of us.'—(*Ibid*, Vol. ii, *pp*. 498-499.)

"The fruits of all those 'Trees,' whether Pippala or Haoma, or yet the more prosaic apple, are the 'plants of life,' in fact and verity. The prototypes of our races were all enclosed in the microcosmic tree, which grew and developed within and under the great mundane macrocosmic tree ; and the mystery is half revealed in the Dirghotamas, where it is said: 'Pippala, the sweet fruit of that tree upon which come spirits who love the science, and where the gods produce all marvels.' As in the Gôkard, among the luxuriant branches of all those mundane trees the 'Serpent' dwells. But while the macrocosmic tree is the Serpent of Eternity and of absolute Wisdom itself, those who dwell in the microcosmic tree are the Serpents of the manifested Wisdom. One is the One and All ; the others are its reflected parts. The 'tree' is man himself, of course, and the serpents dwelling in each the conscious Manas, the connecting link between Spirit and Matter, heaven and earth." (*Ibid*, Vol. ii, p. 97.)

This tree is, then, in its higher aspect, the macrocosm as well as the microcosm, signifying the Kosmic Universe "pictorial representative of the Invisible, for the unseen ultimate Potency is only observable in its operations."

"O Intelligent [Haoma] ! I praise the upset cup in which thy branches remain.

"O Intelligent ! I praise the upright cup in which I squeeze them with all the might of a man."

Thus we read in the beginning of Hâ 10 of the Puçna. The knowledge of the seven plexes in the microcosm or astral man will throw some light on the above short passages. The Arûnopnishad of the Hindus contains an account of these plexuses which they call *chakras*, or centres of force. Principal among these is the one in the brain called *Sahasrâra*. It is said in that book about this *chakra* that—

"20–21. In that Sahasrâra is a golden cup surrounded by bright rays, the abode of happiness."

"29–32. There is a chakram in which the kundalini attains her early youth, uttering a low, deep note; a chakram in which she attains her maturity; a chakram in which she becomes fit to marry; a chakram in which she takes a husband, these and whatever happiness is conferred by her, are all due to Agni, [the Fire]."

Thus it will be seen that to know the mystery of the Sacred Haoma it is necessary to have the knowledge of Gûpta-vidya or the Occult science.

The light of Wisdom and Immortality can be acquired by him who, has the courage to conquer Desire, transforming it into Spiritual Will, which then becomes the Sword of Knowledge; and by him who has the courage to purify himself; because by purity and holiness—the first lesson taught in Zoroastrianism—the way to the Tree of Spiritual Life is gained, and when it is once gained, the " purified life becomes the 'Wings of the Great Bird' on which we mount, to be carried to its Nest, where peace at last is found." He, and he only, can 'prepare' the juice of the Tree of Wisdom, the Para-Haoma of the Zoroastrian, the Amrita of the Vedântin, the Âb-i-Haiât of the Sûfî—and drink it.

NASARVANJI F. BILIMORIA.

—Altered *Lucifer*, Vol. xv, p. 491.

EVOLUTION.

INTRODUCTION.

THERE is hardly a book in Zoroastrianism which would give us any clear and systematic idea about the manifestation of the Universe or cosmogenesis. Almost the whole literature is fragmentary and withal allegorical. I have adopted, therefore, the line laid down in the "Secret Doctrine," the monumental work of Madame Blavatsky, as far as my humble capacity of grasping the most sublime teaching would permit, and, after searching out scattered passages from various works on Zoroastrianism, arranged them here in such a way as to give a consecutive idea to the reader about the formation of the Cosmos from the stand-point of Zoroastrianism.

I cannot enter into the controversy regarding the manifestation of the Universe, whether it was "created" by, or "evolved" out of, Something. The question of "Creation" or "Evolution" I shall leave to the controversialists themselves; and try to show the order of things as I found them in the respective works. To adapt myself with the age, however, I have followed the scientific method of Evolution.

There are two methods of scientific investigation—Inductive and Deductive. The former is a process of ascending from the known to the unknown; while the latter is a process of descending from the unknown to the known. The system adopted here is the Deductive one, as it appeared to me more suitable for our present purpose, and as it is the one adopted by almost all the sages and prophets to explain the origin and evolution of the Universe.

COSMOGONY.

THE DAWN.

We find in the "Dinkard," one of the Zoroastrian books on philosophy, that—

"That which through its progression rejoins its source is

Time, and that which leads from the lowest to the highest is the Path of Wisdom. As to Time, it is said that it is in accord with the force of the motion proceeding from its Primal Source, and it moves in regular succession. The first work of the creative power of the Universe began with Time, and the end of such work pertains to the completion of the Limited Time of celestial revolution. The end of time is in the completion of planetary motion. All have to regenerate themselves by their own efforts in (reaching) Boundless Duration. At the time of the renovation those that are in communion with the deity will not have to journey again."

The Boundless Duration is called Zravâne Akarne, and the Limited Time, Zravâne Dregho Khadâte, viewed in two aspects of Zravân. Time, it is said, "was originally unlimited, but subsequently it came to have a limit," and when the end of that limit is reached, "it again acts in limitlessness and again there is an effort to bring about a limit." Here we can clearly see the Pralaya and the Manvantara of Theosophy acting in slow succession, one after the other. The creative power that works during the great cycle is Ahuramazda, *who is said to exist eternally even in Boundless Duration.* "What is it that ever was?" and the answer in the *Book of Dzyan*, an archaic mystic work now inaccessible, is, "The Germ in the Root." Zravân is the "Rootless Root," Ahuramazda the "Germ," and the "Force of the motion proceeding from the Primal Source" is the Great Breath,* or Eternal Motion.†

The idea of Zravân is supposed by some of the Zoroastrians, as well as European scholars, to be a later invention of the Sassanide period ; but we have this term used in the *Vendidâd* also (Fargard XIX), which, being a pre-Sassanide scripture, we cannot afford to neglect. Some have reason to suppose,

---

* See "Zravâne Akarne and Zravâne Dregho Khadâte," by N. D. K., *Oriental Department Paper*, No. 4, Vol. i, (Eur. Sec.)

† "Never-resting Breaths," they are Dhyan Chohans or Ameshaspentas.—*The Secret Doctrine*, Vol. i, p. 103.

however, that there may be something beyond Ahuramazda in the philosophical sense, but that something they call "Ahûra."* This idea may not be far wrong, if we take Ahûra in the same sense in connection with Zravân, as Brahman (neuter), the Unmanifested Logos, is with Parabrahman, as we shall see presently.

Ahûra is from the root *Ah=to be*; and the Vedic term *Sat* is translated *Be-ness*, *i. e.*, Being as well as Non-Being. "Occult philosophy, viewing the manifested and the unmanifested Kosmos as a UNITY, symbolizes the ideal conception of the former by that 'Golden Egg' [*Hiranya Garbha*] with the two poles in it. It is the positive pole that acts in the manifested world of matter, while the negative is lost in the Unknowable Absoluteness of SAT—'Be-ness.' "—(The *S. D.*, Vol. i, p. 556.†) "SAT is the immutable, the everpresent, changeless and eternal root, from and through which all proceeds."— (*Ibid*, Vol. ii, p. 449.) SAT is used by the Hindu writers, sometimes for Brahman, and sometimes for Parabrahman.

Zravâne Akarne is, therefore, the "Boundless Circle of the Unknown Time," from which issues the radiant Light, the *Universal Sun*, or Ahuramazda, the Logos, the First-born, whose manifested *shadow* is called Ahriman in the Zoroastrian philosophy. The glory of Ahuramazda is too exalted, its light too resplendent for the human intellect or mortal eye to grasp and see. Its primal emanation is eternal light, which, from having been previously concealed in *Darkness*, was called to manifest itself, and thus was formed Ormazda, the King of Life. The "Darkness" is Zravân in the metaphorical sense. "In the sense of objectivity, both light and darkness are illusions—*Mâyâ* ; in this case, it is not Darkness as absence of Light, but as one incomprehensible primordial Principle, which being Absoluteness itself, has for our intellectual perceptions neither form, colour, substantiality, nor

---

* "Mazda—Ahûra-Mazda—Ahûra," by Dastur Jamaspji Minocherji Jamaspasana, Head Priest of the Parsis, Bombay, 1885.

† The references to "The Secret Doctrine" are to the old edition.

anything that could be expressed by words." So says the Secret Doctrine.

One of the difficulties of the students of Zoroastrianism is, that the terminology is not settled: the words *Ahûra-Mazda*, *Mazda*, and *Ahûra* are used at random without any consideration of their philosophical meaning. *Ahû* or *Ahûra* can be taken, however, for SAT or Be-ness as applied in Theosophical literature; *Mazda* for Divine Wisdom; and *Ahûra-Mazda* for the Creative Logos, though these should not be conceived as separate from each other, but ONE. The terms differ merely as aspects of the UNKNOWABLE.

Here we have seen Ahuramazda in union with the "Universal Sun," which is called Hvara in the Khorshed Niyaesh or "prayer" of that Sun. The "prayer" or Mañthra which is recited before the Sun, the visible symbol of the Invisible Spiritual Sun, by the Parsis, is not the "prayer" of a physical planet, but of Hvara, the (Sûrya) Nârâyana of the Hindus, as well as that of the *Yazata** presiding over the sun. Nârâyana is the name of the sun, as well as of Brahman, among the Hindus, and, as H. P. Blavatsky says, "Ishvara stands for that Second, and Nârâyana for the Unmanifested Logos." Various students of Occultism have defined it to the following effect in Theosophical literature :—This Spiritual Central Sun is that hidden force which, during this active period which is called Manvantara, sends forth creative light bringing the myriads of other suns into existence. Deeply buried into it are mysteries too great for us to fathom with our earthly senses. At the dawn of manifestations, whether of a Kosmos or of a man, there arises this Sun from which all energy radiates. "In the shoreless ocean of Space radiates the Central Spiritual and *invisible* Sun : the Universe is his body, spirit and soul, and after this ideal model are framed ALL THINGS"—

---

* In the terminology of the Avasta, the word *Yazata* signifies, like the Sanskrit *Yajata*, "what is worthy of worship, adorable, venerable"; and is applied to Ahùra himself as well as to the Amesha-spentas and other angels.

(*Isis Unveiled*, i., p. 302). In our immediate manifestation which we name the Solar System, the unknown point in the heavens toward which all visible suns are gravitating, is the Central Sun. As there are suns for each plane of being, it is probable that the visible solar body is the central sun of the visible plane. It must be remembered that "central sun" does not mean one limited fixed thing. The relative nature of such expressions may be realized if we consider that, while in Kosmos the Sun and all suns are the *Kâma Rûpa* (creative forms) of Âkâsha, in our Solar System, Sûrya is the Buddhi of Âkâsh [in relation to *Buddhi* it is called Mithra in Zoroastrianism, which can be seen elsewhere], and becomes, when regarded as an entity in his own kingdom, the Seventh Principle. It is self-evident also from a passage of Khorshed Niyaesh that "*He adores Ahûramazda*, he adores the Ameshaspentas, he adores his own soul, he gives satisfaction to all heavenly and earthly Yazatas, *who adore the Sun*, the immortal, shining, with swift *Aspa*." The last word, which is similar to the Sanskrit अस्व, has been always translated as *horse* or *steed*; but if the term can be taken for the *Asvinikumâras*, the "bestowers of human mind," a mystery can be solved explaining why the Sun is called the lord of the "swift horses." We shall say something further on on this subject.

THE AHUNAVAR.

Before we advance further let us see what it is that is the cause of all the manifestations of Life. In reply to a question of the Holy Zarathushtra, Ahuramazda is made to say, in Yaçna 19, that it was AHUNAVAIRYA which was "before the Heavens, before the Water, before the Earth, before the Primeval Cow, before the Trees, before the Fire, the Son of Ahuramazda, before the Holy Man, before the demons and vile men, before this world, before everything good produced by Mazda,—that arises from pure origin." This Ahunavairya, which is commonly called Ahûnavar or Honover, is the Divine Sound, THE WORD of the Christians and the Shabdabrahman of the Hindus. All the *Tattvas* or elements and their forces are the modifications of this Sound; it is the substratum of the heavenly melodies, the spirit within spirit. It throws itself, as it were, into the form of Âkâsh, and thence successively into other forms of Tattvas, such as Vâyu, Agni, Âpas, and Prithvi, not the material Tattvas that we see around us, but their spiritual counterparts. This Ahunavairya is the first manifestation, itself becoming intelligible and revealed in the character of Ahuramazda to a finite being, Ahunavairya being itself one with Ahuramazda.

THE AMESHA-SPENTAS.

Then come the Amesha-spentas. Ahûra-mazda, the Lord of Wisdom, is the synthesis of these Amesha-spentas, the Immortal Benefactors or Blissful Immortals,—the Word and its six highest aspects,—in Mazdayasna religion. These Immortal Benefactors are described in the Zamyad Yasht as "the shining, having efficacious eyes, great, hopeful, imperishable and pure, which are all *seven* of *like mind, like speech*, all *seven doing alike*, which are the creators and destroyers of the creatures of Ahûra-mazda, their Creators and Overseers, their Protectors and Rulers." These few words alone indicate the dual and even triple character—creative, preservative and destroying (regenerating)—of the Amesha-spentas, who, in the Theosophical literature, are called Dhyân-Chohans. These Amesha-spentas, in their highest occult meaning, are called "*Sravah*,"* the souls or spirits of those manifested powers, the term Amesha-spentas being used exoterically in terrestrial combinations and affairs only.† "On the spiritual plane they are the Divine Powers of Ahûra-mazda; but on the astral or psychic plane again they are the 'Builders,' the 'Watchers,' the *Pitars* (fathers), and the first Preceptors of mankind."‡

Now we shall see the order of the first manifestations of the Universe. The *Bundahish* [" Beginning of the Creation" or "Original Creation"] is a work supposed to be the translation,

---

* The *Vendidad*, Fargard xix, 42.
† The " Secret Doctrine," Vol. ii, p. 385. ‡ *Ibid.*, p. 358.

or an epitome of the Dâmdâd Nûsk; one of the twenty-one books into which the whole of the Zoroastrian scriptures were divided, most of which have been lost. According to this :—The first of Ahûra-mazda's creatures of the Universe was Sky, and his Good Thought (Vohuman), by good procedure, produced the Light of the World, along with which was the good religion of the Mazdayasnians. Afterwards arose Ar*d*avahisht, and then Shatvairô, and then Spendarma*d*, and then Horvada*d*, and then Ameroda*d*."*

In the above passage of the *Bundahish* we see clearly enough in Vohuman the Mahat, the third Logos or Universal Mind of Theosophy, together with the highest aspect of Âkâsh, which the translators have taken for the *sky*. Âkâsh is *invisible* sky. The names given above of the Amesha-spentas are Pahlavi. In the Avastâ language they are called Ahûra-mazda, Vohumano, Ashavahishta, Kshathravairya, Spendarmad, Hurvatat, and Ameredaḍ.

The above teaching furnishes us with one further proof that Ahûra-mazda is used not for the second and third Logos only in the Avastâ literature, but for the first or Unmanifested Logos also; nay, it carries Him nearer, if not unites Him with, Parabrahman. According to the "Secret Doctrine," Âkâsh—the highest aspect of it—has emanated from Parabrahman, which we plainly see in the above passage. We are told that "Âkâsh alone is Divine Space," and its only attribute, if "attribute" it can be called, is Divine Sound, the Ahunavar of the Parsis. Sound, however, is not an attribute of Âkâsh, but its correlation. "The æther of the ancients is Universal Fire, as may be seen in the injunctions by Zoroaster and Psellus, respectively. The former said: 'Consult it only when it is without form or figure,' *absque formâ et figurâ*, which means without flames or burning coals."† " Æther is the Âditi

---

* The *Bundahish*, Ch. 1, 25-26.

† The "Secret Doctrine," Vol. i, p. 331. It is referred to in the "Zoroastrian Oracles" thus—" When thou see'st a sacred Fire without form, shining flashingly through the depths of the world, hear the voice of Fire!"

of the Hindus and it is Âkâsh."* With Ahunavar, the Divine Sound, comes Vohûman, the Divine Thought, together with Ashvahishta, the Divine Fire, and Khshathravairya, Spendarmad, Hurvatat and Ameredad, the rest of the Amesha-spentas.

All these are symbolized in the seal adopted by the Theosophical Society. We see in this seal a symbol of Zravan or Zero-an, the Boundless Circle, the Rootless Root; Ahûramazda, the "Germ" in the root, with a point or cross in the centere, and the six other Amesha-spentas in the hexagon.

THE ASWINS OR "HORSES."

These Aswins, or Aswini-Kûmârau, are the most mysterious and occult deities of all. In mythological symbolism they are "the bright harbingers of Ushas, the dawn," [*cf.* Hoshbâm], who are "ever young and handsome, bright, agile, swift as falcons," who "prepare the way for the brilliant dawn to those who have patiently awaited through the night." Yâska, the commentator in the *Nirukta*, thinks that "the Aswins represent the transition from darkness to light," cosmically, and, it is said, metaphysically also. Astronomically they are asterisms. These twins are, in the esoteric philosophy, the *Kumâra-egos*, the "Reïncarnating Principles" in this Manvantara. The night and dawn above represent the Pralaya and the beginning of the Manvantara, respectively. A Pralaya is a period of obscuration or repose—planetary, cosmic or universal,—the opposite of Manvantara, which is a period of manifestation applied to various cycles, especially to the cycle of 4,320,000,000 solar years, which is called 'the Day of Brahmâ' in the Hindu Shâstra, and to the reign of one Manu (or Mankind), 308,448,000 years.

THE FRAVASHIS OR FEROUERS.

Taking Abûra as Absolute Consciousness, then, the principles evolving out of that Consciousness are the Divine Ideas, which in this System are called Fravashis, which play an important part in the system of the holy Zarathushtra. From Ahura-

---

* The "Secret Doctrine," Vol. i, p. 332.

mazda down to gods, man, sky, fire, water, plants, all are endowed with a Fravashi. "Invoke, O Zarathushtra, my Fravashi, who am Ahûra-mazda, the greatest, the best, the fairest, of all beings, the most strong, the most intelligent, and whose soul is the Holy Word" (Manthra-spenta.)* "We praise the Fravashis. . . . For they are the most active of the creatures of both the heavenlies, the good, strong, holy Fravashis of the Pure, who at that time stood on high, when the two Heavenly Ones created the creatures—the Holy Spirit and the Evil."† The Fravashi existed before the evolution of the material world. They were asked by Ahûra-Mazda either to contend in a bodily form with the Dru*g* that the Dru*g* may perish, or that they may remain under the protection of the evil creator. "The Fravashis of men were unanimous, it is said, with the Omniscient Wisdom about their going to the material world, on account of the evil that comes upon them, in the world, from the Dru*g* Ahriman, and their becoming, at last, again unpersecuted by the adversary, perfect and immortal in the future existence for ever and everlasting."‡

The functions of the Fravashis are much speculated upon by various writers, but I cannot now dwell upon the controversy. Let us examine this question, therefore, from the stand-point of the teaching of the Secret Doctrine only, which doctrine appears to be more in consonance with the fundamental principles of the Avastâ literature.

"It is the Logos," says the former work, "who is shown in the mystic symbolism of cosmogony, theogony, and anthropogony, playing two parts in the drama of Creation and Being, *i. e.*, that of the purely human personality and the divine impersonality of the so-called Avatârs, or Divine incarnations, and of the Universal Spirit, called Christos by the Gnostics, and the *Fravashi* (or Ferour) *of Ahûra-mazda* in the Mazdean philosophy. On the lower rungs of theogony the celestial beings of lower hierarchies had each a Fravashi, or a celestial

---

* The *Vendidâd*, Farg. xix, 14. † Yasht, xiii, 75—76.
‡ The *Bundahish*, Ch. ii, 10-11.

'double.' . . . . The Roman Catholic Church shows its usual logic and consistency by accepting as the Ferour of Christ, St. Michael, who was 'his angel guardian,' as *proved* by St. Thomas." We are further told by De Mirville "that the Ferouer is the spiritual potency at once *image, face* and the *guardian* of the soul which finally assimilates the Ferour." It is the *inner* immortal man or that *Ego* which reincarnates ; it existed before its physical body, and survives all such it happens to be clothed in. But, then, what are the Fravashis of the animals, plants and even elements, such as fire, water, &c.? It is the *spiritual counterpart*, we are told, " whether of god, animal, plant, or even element, *i. e.*, the refined and *purer* part of the grosser creation, the soul of the body, whatever the body may happen to be. Therefore does Ahûramazda recommend Zarathushtra to invoke his *Fravashi* and not himself (Ahûramazda); that is to say, the *impersonal* and *true* essence of Deity, one with Zoroaster's own Âtman (or Christos), not the false and ·*personal* appearance."*

Thus the "celestial doubles" were first formed, call them spiritual prototypes or Divine Ideation or what you will.

THE HIERARCHIES OF THE YAZATAS.

We have seen above the twilight of the Dawn, the beginning of the spiritual manifestations. Now we shall see how other deities manifested themselves from the One.

". . . He shines forth as the Sun. He is the blazing Divine Dragon of Wisdom. The Eka is Chatur (*four*) and Chatur takes to itself three, and the union produces the Sapta (*seven*) in whom are the seven which become the Tridasa (*the thrice-ten*), the hosts and the multitudes."†

Commenting on this stanza, H. P. Blavatsky says in a foot-note that "Tri-dasa, or three times ten (30) alludes to the Vedic deities, in round numbers, or more accurately 33—a sacred number. They are the 12 Âdityas, the 8 Vasus, the 11 Rudras,

---

* The " Secret Doctrine," Vol. ii, pp. 478-480.
† The *Stanzas of Dzyan*, iii, 7. The S. D., Vol. i, p. 28.

and 2 Asvins— the twin sons of the Sun and the Sky. This is the root number of the Hindu Pantheon, which enumerates 33 crores or over three-hundred millions of gods and goddesses."

We have in Zoroastrianism likewise 33 Fareshtas or angels, the root-number. Although no mention is made of the thirty-three crore deities in Zoroastrianism, the *Desatir* says that "Of their excellencies and number little is said ; seeing that the angels are *innumerable*," a statement which agrees with the teaching of the Secret Doctrine, which gives us the number as "*over* three-hundred millions of gods and goddesses."

These thirty-three angels are in association with the seven Amesha-spentas or archangels in the following manner :—

AHÛRAMAZDA—Dep-âdar, Dep-meher, Dep-din.

BEHMAN—Mohor, Gôsh, Rám.

ARDIBESHTA—Âdar, Sraosh, Behrâm.

SHAHRIVAR—Khúr (Khúrshed), Meher, Âsmân, Anerân.

ASPENDARMAD—Âvân, Din, Ârda (Arsesvang), Márespand.

KHURDÂD—Tir, Ardâfravash (Fravardin), Govâd.

AMERDÂD—Rasnu, Âstâd, Zamyâd.

Berezad, Hôm, and Daham are independent of the above thirty.

The *Bundahish*, the *Dinkard*, and other books contain some account of the part they play in the universal drama. These angels or Yazatas preside over "everything created that is pure." They were produced "in order to keep watch over the heaven and the earth, the blowing of the winds, the flowing of the waters, the growth of the trees, and the life and nourishment of cattle and men, and also to protect the material worlds against the creation of the murderous demons."[*] One of their functions is to battle constantly against the Dru*g*-nasus, the elementals, who are always endeavouring to destroy the "creation of the Pure."

Out of the above 33, twelve are presiding over heavens,

---

[*] The *Dinkard*, Vol. iii. 125.

whose names are assigned to twelve months of the year among the Parsis. The *Dabistân* counts Bahman or Vohuman, the 11th, the first created being, with Farvardin, the 1st month, and omitting the 12th month Spendarmad, the spirit of the earth, makes the number of spheres 10, the perfect number. It says "from him [Farvardin] was derived Ardibehesht, the Great (2nd) ; along with the sublime soul and body of the empyrean heaven ; from Ardibehesht the Great proceeded Khûrdad the Great (3rd) ; from him Tir the Great (4th) ; from him Murdâd the Great (5th) ; from him Shahrivar the Great (6th) ; from him Mihir the Great (7th) ; from him Abân the Great (8th) ; from him Âzar the Great (9th) ; and from him Dai the Great (10th) ; these are Lords of Heavens, and after Farvardin the Great are accounted as the months as well as the Heavens collectively."

It may be said parenthetically here that the theory advanced by some Materialistic Christian scholars and their Parsi followers, that the Gâthâs alone are written by Zoroaster himself or his immediate disciples, and that the rest of the Avastâ literature in which the various Yazatas are adored is subsequently fabricated to deceive the credulous people by the Mediæval priests, is quite untenable. If we drop the other literature except the Gâthâs, considering it of less importance, for the sake of argument, the whole fabric of the Mazdean Religion would crumble away, and no philosophy whatever would remain in it—the Gâthâs being simply the highest hymns men could have in this world—and where there is no philosophy there is no religion. It is in the ignorance of real Zoroastrian Cosmogony that these Materialistic students have doubted the existence of other Divine Powers, who are adored in the soul-edifying Mâñthraspenta. When I say "Divine Powers" I do not mean that I recommend the sceptics to believe or worship them ; what I mean is that there exist pure Intelligences or conscious entities known by their several names in the Zoroastrian System, and not merely personifications of nature's powers as the students of Avastâ would have us believe, or "blind forces" as modern science would try to explain. Left to the "blind forces" the universe would not have such harmonious manifestation, as we see by subjecting it to the power of Divine Beings, whose existence to our present state of consciousness is what our own appear to the consciousness of a microbe or an infusoria. Even the late Professor Huxley, one of the prominent scientists of this century, confesses that—" Looking at the matter from the most rigidly scientific point of view, the assumption that amidst the myriads of worlds scattered through endless Space, there can be no intelligence, as much greater than man's, as his is greater than a black beetle's ; no beings endowed with powers of influencing the course of nature, as much greater than his, as his is greater than a snail's, *seems to me not merely baseless, but impertinent.*"* If he believes in these Intelligences, he nearly believes in our Yazatas, never mind in a foreign phraseology. Here he is a Zoroastrian, and for the matter of that, a religious man, than one who calls himself a "Zoroastrian" and yet considers that the belief in such Beings is "superstition and folly."

THE STARRY HEAVENS.

Leaving aside the "Battle of the Gods" that took place in the heavens, we shall now see the result, the formation of the planets and the planetary beings. A reciter of the *Vendidâd* invokes "the seven bright Sravah with their sons and their flocks" (Fargard xix, 42). We have seen above that *Sravah* is the esoteric term for the Amesha-spentas, and "their sons and their flocks" refers to the "planetary angels and their sidereal flock of stars and constellations," says our teacher. Thus we see the suns and stars forming themselves by, or from the Amesha-spentas. But how ? "By the action of the manifested Wisdom, or Mahat [Vohuman] represented by these innumerable centres of spiritual energy in the Kosmos. The reflection of the Universal Mind, which is Cosmic Ideation, and the intellectual force accompanying such ideation, become

---

* Prologue to a collection of his " Essays upon some Controverted Questions."

objectively the Fohat [Apâm-Napât]. Fohat running along the seven principles of Âkâsh, acts upon manifested substance or the One Element . . . and by differentiating it into various centres of energy, sets in motion the Law of Cosmic Evolution, which, in obedience to the Ideation of the Universal Mind, brings into existence all the various states of being in the manifested Solar System."*

> "He fixed a great company of inerratic stars,
> Forcing Fire to Fire,
> To be carried by a settlement which hath not error.
> He constituted them six; casting into the midst
> The Fire of the Sun,
> Suspending their disorder in well-ordered zones."
> *The Zoroastrian Oracles.*

THE KARMIC GODS AND ASTROLOGY.

The *Bundahish* contains an account of the formation of the planets, constellation stars, and stars not of the constellations, and mentions the twelve signs of the Zodiac.† It would appear from this that the ancient Iranians were not unaware of astrology, and occult astrology, too. " Seven chieftains of the planets," says the Zoroastrian genesis, "have come unto the seven chieftains of the constellations, as the planet Mercury (Tir) unto Tishtar, the planet Mars (Vâhrâm) unto Haptok-ring, the planet Jupiter (Ahuramazda) unto Vanan*d*, the planet Venus (Anâhi*d*) unto Satavés, the planet Saturn (Kêvân) unto the great one of the middle of the sky; Gôchihar and the thievish Mûshpar, provided with tails, unto the sun and moon and stars. The sun has attached Mûshpar to its own radiance by mutual agreement, so that he may be less able to do harm."‡

All the " original creations" are said to have been committed to the charge of the Zodiacal constellations which are watching the welfare of the world, and every constellation is ordained

---

* The "Secret Doctrine," Vol. i, p. 110.
† The *Bundahish*, Chapter ii.   ‡ *Ibid*, Ch. v, 1-2.

to have "those 6,480 thousand small stars as assistants; and among those constellations four chieftains, appointed on the four sides, are leaders."* These four leaders are—(1) Tishtar, the chieftain of the East; (2) Satavês, the chieftain of the West; (3) Vanan*d*, the chieftain of the South; and (4) Haptôk-ring, the chieftain of the North. These four leaders or chieftains are the four karmic gods of the Zoroastrians, from which it will be seen why Astrology has a bearing on man's Karma. These four gods are commonly called Tir, Anâhi*d*, Vanan*d*, and Beherâm. In the Secret Doctrine these are called the "Mahârâjas," or Lords of Karma. These are respectively named—

(1) Dhritarashtra—the White guardian of the East.
(2) Virudhaka—the Green guardian of the South.
(3) Virupaksha—the Red guardian of the West.
(4) Vaishravan—the Yellow guardian of the North.

"5. Fohat takes five strides (having already taken the first three) and builds a winged wheel at each corner of the square for the four holy ones . . . and their armies *(hosts).*"†

In explaining the above stanza, Madame Blavatsky says :— "These are the 'four Mahârâjas' or great kings of the Dhyân-Chohans, the Devas who preside, each over one of the four cardinal points. They are the regents or angels who rule over the Cosmical Forces of North, South, East and West, forces having each a distinct occult property. These BEINGS are also connected with Karma, as the latter needs physical and material agents to carry out her decrees, such as the four kinds of winds, for instance, professedly admitted by science to have their respective evil and beneficent influences upon the health of mankind and every living thing."‡ In Zoroastrianism, as well as in any other religion, the North and West are considered to have an evil influence

---

* The *Bundahish*, Ch. ii, 5.   † The *Book of Dzyan*, Stanza V. 5.
‡ The *Secret Doctrine*, Vol. i, pp. 122-123.

on mankind. It will be seen from the above that man's Karma has a very close relation with the science of the Stars ; and hence we find in the *Bundahish* also the following names of the twelve signs of the Zodiac :—

1. Varak (the Lamb)
2. Tôrâ (the Bull)
3. Dô-patkar (the Gemini)
4. Kalachang (the Crab)
5. Sher (the Lion)
6. Khûshak (Virgo)

7. Tarâzûk (the Balance)
8. Gazdûm (the Scorpion)
9. Nimasp (the Sagittarius)
10. Vahik or Nahâzik (Capricornus)
11. Dûl (the Waterpot)
12. Mâhik (the Fish).

These are sub-divided into twenty-eight *Nakshatras* or mansions whose names also appear in this book.

Leaving this aside we have to turn now to the *Desatir*, in which it is said that the heavy-moving stars, *i. e.*, the fixed stars, in contradistinction to the planets, are many, and each has an intelligence, a soul, and a body ; "and in like manner every distinct division of the heavens and planets, hath its intelligences and souls." It is said in the first book, "the Book of Prophet the Great Âbâd," that

"The world, like a radiation, is not separate, nor can it be separated, from the sun of the substance of the mighty God.

"The lower world is subject to the sway of the upper world.

"In the beginning of its revolution the sovereignty over this lower world is committed to one of the slow-moving stars ;

"Which governeth it alone for the space of a thousand years ;

"And for other thousands of years each of the heavy moving stars and swift-moving stars becometh its partner, each for one thousand years.

"Last of all the moon becometh its associate, for a thousand years, like all the rest."

Here the time allotted to the sovereignty of a planet, is "one thousand years." If we take the "sovereignty" for "activity," or Manvantara, the *Vishnu Purâna* allows us "one thousand *periods* of four ages," at the end of which every planet, as well as the earth, retires into Pralaya. Here we are not talking of the Mahâ-Pralaya, however, but of a planetary Pralaya.

The moon is at present in a state of such Pralaya, we are told, and her cycle of life has been finished long ago. " When the moon hath been king," says the *Desatir*, "and all have been associates along with it, and its reign, too, is over, one Grand Period is accomplished . . . And in the beginning of the Grand Period, a new order of things commenceth in the lower world. And not indeed the very forms, and knowledge, and events of the Grand Period that hath elapsed, but others precisely similar to them will again be produced." Before we learn about how this lower world was formed from the moon, let us know something about—

THE SACRED LAND—" ARYANAM-VAE*g*O."

We shall now see how the earth was formed and inhabited, according to the *Vendidâd*, a sacred work of the Parsis, which is recited during the performance of certain ceremonies. The *Vendidâd* begins—

" Ahura-mazda spake unto Spitama Zarathushtra, saying :

"' I have made every land dear to its dwellers even though it had no charms whatever in it : had I not made every land dear to its dwellers, even though it had no charms whatever in it, then the whole living world would have invaded the Airyanam-Vae*g*o.

"' The first of the good lands and countries which I, Ahura-mazda, created was the Airyanam-Vae*g*o, by the good river Dâitya.' "

" That which in the *Vendidâd*," says the " Secret Doctrine," "is referred to as Airyanam-Vae*g*o, wherein was born the *original* Zoroaster, is called in the Purânic literature ' Sveta Dwipa,' (white Island),* ' Mount Meru,' the abode of Vishnu, &c., &c., and in the Secret Doctrine is simply named the land of the ' gods,' under their chiefs, the ' spirits of this planet.' " All the Avatârs of Vishnu are said to have come

---

* See Kurma Purâna.

originally from the White Island. According to the Tibetan tradition this Island is the only locality which escapes the fate of the other Dwipas, and "can be destroyed by neither fire nor water, for it is the eternal land," which supports the statement of the 1st chapter of the *Vendidâd*. This Island is the source of the other Dwipas or Keshvaras, and serves as a link between this physical earth and the other higher earths to follow. It is the seat which is protected and presided over by the three sons or rays of Zarthushtra Spitama, according to the Parsis (*Bund.* Ch. xxxii,); and by three ascetic sons of Priyavarta,—Mêdha, Putra, and Agnibahu, according to Vishnu Purâna. The Dâitik river is the river which comes out from Irân Vej, another name of Airyanam-Vae*g*o, and goes out, according to the *Bundahish*, through the hilly country; "The Dâitik river is the chief of streams."* It is running "in the middle of the earth."

Now Zarathushtra is said to have had three sons, who are respectively considered as three fathers and chiefs of the three classes,—priests, warriors, and husbandmen,—creators, protectors and regenerators. As these three sons appear to play no very great part in the Zoroastrian system, it is supposed by some that they "are little more than three sub-divisions of Zarathushtra himself, who was the 'first priest, the first warrior, the first husbandman.'" (Yt. xiii, 88). The holy Zarathushtra is recognized by the *Bundahish* also (Ch. xxxiii,) as a "heavenly priest," and "was by right, the *ratu* in Airyana-Vae*g*o, where he founded the religion by a sacrifice."

THE SEVEN KESHVARAS OR THE "BHÛMI-MANDALA."

Now we shall descend to earth. Nothing has been said in the "Book of the Prophets" about the formation of the Bhûmi-haptaiti, the septempartite earth, although we see the formation and combination of Elements. "Now, speaking of Elements, it is made the standing reproach of the Ancients,

---

* The *Bundahish*, Ch. xxiv, 14.

that they 'supposed their Elements simple and undecomposable.' Once more this is an unwarrantable statement; as, at any rate, their initiated philosophers can hardly come under such an imputation, since it is they who have invented allegories and religious myths from the beginning. Had they been ignorant of the heterogeneity of their Elements they would have had no personifications of Fire, Air, Water, Earth, and Æther; their Cosmic gods and goddesses would never have been blessed with such posterity, with so many sons and daughters, elements born *from* and *within each respective Element*. Alchemy and occult phenomena would have been a delusion and a snare, even in theory, had the Ancients been ignorant of the potentialities and correlative functions and attributes of every element that enters into the composition of Air, Water, Earth, and even *Fire*—the latter a *terra incognita* to this day to modern Science, which is obliged to call it Motion, evolution of light and heat, state of ignition,—defining it by its outward aspects, in short, and remaining ignorant of its nature. But that which modern Science seems to fail to perceive is that, differentiated as may have been those simple chemical atoms—which archaic philosophy called 'the creators of their respective Parents,' fathers, brothers, husbands of their mothers, and those mothers the daughters of their own sons, like Aditi and Daksha. For example—differentiated as these elements were in the beginning, still they were not the compound bodies known to Science, as they are now. Neither Water, Air, Earth (synonym for solids generally) existed in their present form, representing the three states of matter alone recognised by Science; for all these are the productions already recombined by the atmospheres of globes completely formed—even to fire—so that in the first periods of the earth's formation they were something quite *sui generis*. Now that the conditions and laws ruling our solar system are fully developed; and that the atmosphere of our earth, as of every other globe, has become, so to say, a crucible of its own, Occult Science eaches that there is a perpetual exchange taking place in space of molecules, or of atoms rather, correlating, and thus changing their combining equivalents on every planet. Some men of Science, and those among the greatest physicists and chemists, begin to suspect this fact, which has been known for ages to the Occultists. The spectroscope only shows the probable similarity (on external evidence) of terrestrial and sidereal substance; it is unable to go any further, or to show whether atoms gravitate towards one another in the same way and under the same conditions as they are supposed to do on our planet, physically and chemically. The scale of temperature, from the highest degree to the lowest that can be conceived of, may be imagined to be one and the same in and for the whole Universe; nevertheless, its properties, other than those of dissociation and re-association, differ on every planet; and thus atoms enter into new forms of existence, undreamt of, and incognisable to, physical Science. As already expressed in 'Five Years of Theosophy,' the essence of Cometary matter, for instance, 'is totally different from any of the chemical or physical characteristics with which the greatest chemists and physicists of the earth are acquainted' (p. 242). And even that matter, during rapid passage through our atmosphere, undergoes a certain change in its nature. Thus not alone the elements of our planets, but even those of all its sisters in the Solar System, differ as widely from each other in their combinations, as from the cosmic elements beyond our Solar limits."—(S. D., Vol. i, pp. 140-43).

In the Avastâ literature Moon is called "Maoñhem Gaochithrem," *i. e.*, moon which contains the seed of the *gao*. The word *gao* or *gow* in Zend, as well as in Sanskrit, represents earth, life, cow, tongue, &c. Here it stands for the earth and its life. The seed of earth is in the moon. We have seen above that when the activity of a planet is over, or when it goes into *pralaya*, a new order of things goes on a new planet, out of the dead matter of the former one. "The Moon is now," says the "Secret Doctrine," "the cold residual quantity, the shadow dragged after the new body, into which her living powers and 'principles' are transferred. She now is doomed for long ages to be ever pursuing the Earth, to be attracted by and to attract her progeny." Much can be found in the first volume of this book which would throw abundant light on the mystic passages of the Avastâ regarding this subject. We have to divert our attention, now to the *Bundahish* again. The earth is often called " Hafta-Karshvara Zamin" in the Avastâ literature. This term was translated as the "earth of seven continents," and none could understand the occult or septenary nature of the earth till the teaching of the " Secret Doctrine" was ushered into the world, although we have "regions" and "zones" for the word "Karshvara" in the *Bundahish.*

According to this authority there are *thirty-three* kinds of lands, but it describes only seven. Khvaniras is the name of the land on which our physical consciousness is acting at present. It is in the centre, and the other six portions are situated around it. All the seven portions are called Hafta-Karshvara or seven zones or regions. On the East side of the Khvaniras is the Savah, on the West is the Arzah, on the North-East is the Vourûzarshti, on the North-West is the Vourûbarshti, on the South-West is the Fradadhafsha, on the South-East is the Vidadhafsha. According to the *Secret Doctrine* :—

" The belief in the septenary constitution of our 'chain' was the oldest tenet of the early Irânians, who got it from the *first* Zarathushtra. It is time to prove it to those Parsis who have lost the key to the meaning of their Scriptures. In the Avastâ the earth is considered septempartite and tripartite at one and the same time. This is regarded by Dr. Geiger as an *incongruity* for the following reasons, which he calls discrepancies : the Avastâ speaks of the three-thirds of the earth because the Rig-Veda mentions 'three earths.' . . . . . 'Three strata or layers, one lying above the other, are said to be meant by this.'* But he is quite mistaken, as are all exoteric profane translators.

---

* " Civilization of the Eastern Irânians in Ancient Times," p. 129.

The Avastâ has not borrowed the idea from the *Rig-Veda*, but simply repeats the esoteric teaching. The 'three strata or layers' do not refer to our globe alone, but to three layers of the globes of our terrestrial chain—two by two, on each plane, one on the descending, the other on the ascending arc, as shown in the diagram below. Thus, with reference to the six spheres or globes above our earth, the seventh and fourth, it is *septempartite*, while with regard to the planes over our plane—it is *tripartite*. This meaning is borne out and corroborated by the text in the Avastâ and the Vendidâd, and even by the speculations,—a most labourious and unsatisfactory guess-work—of the translators and commentators. It thus follows that the division of the 'earth,' or rather the earth's chain, into seven *Karshvaras* is not in contradiction with the three 'zones,' if this word is read 'planes.' As Geiger remarks, this septenary division is very old—the oldest of all— since the Gâthâs already speak of the 'Sptempartite earth.' (*Bûmi Haptâiti, Yasna,* xxxii., 3.) For, 'according to the Parsi Scriptures, *the seven Karshvaras are to be considered as completely disconnected parts of the earth,*' which they surely are. For, 'between them *there flows the Ocean,* so that it is impossible, as stated in several passages, to pass from one Karshvara to another.'* The 'Ocean' is *space,* of course, for the latter was called 'Waters of Space' before it was known as Ether. Moreover, the word *Karshvara* is consistently rendered by *Dwipa,* and especially *Qaniratha* by Jambu-Dwipa ('Neriosengh, the translator of the Yasna.')† But this fact is not taken into account by the Orientalists, and therefore we find such a learned Zoroastrian and Parsi by birth as the translator of Dr. Geiger's work passing unnoticed and without a word of comment several crude remarks of the former on the 'incongruities' of this kind abounding in the Mazdean Scriptures. One of such 'incongruities' and 'coincidences' concerns the similarity of the Zoroastrian with the Indian

---

* *Cf., e. g.,* Vol. I., 4, of the Pahlavi Translation; Bdh. xxi., 2-3.

† Foot-note by Dârâb Dastur Peshotan Sanjânâ, B. A., the translator of Dr. Wilhelm Geiger's work on the "Civilization of the Eastern Irânians."

EVOLUTION. 131

tenet with regard to the seven *Dwipas* (islands, or continents rather) as met with in the *Puranas*, namely : "The Dwipas form concentric rings, which, separated by the ocean, surround Jambu-Dwipa, which is situated in the centre' (p. 130, vol. i.), and, 'according to the Irânian view, the *Karshvara Qaniratha* is likewise situated in the centre of the rest . . . . . each of them (the other six *Karshvaras*) is a peculiar individual Space, and so they group themselves round (*above*) Qaniratha.' (*ibid.* p. 131). Now *Qaniratha* is not, as believed by Geiger and his translator, 'the country inhabited by the Irânian tribes,' and the other names do not mean 'the adjacent territories of foreign nations in the North, South, West, and East' (p. 132), but our globe or Earth. For that which is meant by the sentence which follows the last quoted, namely, that 'two *Vourubarshti* and *Vouruzarshti* lie in the North ; two, *Vidadhafsha* and *Fradadhafsha*, in the South ; *Savahi* and *Arzahi*, in the East and West,' is simply the very graphic and accurate description of the 'chain' of our planet, the Earth, represented in the Book of Dzyan, thus :

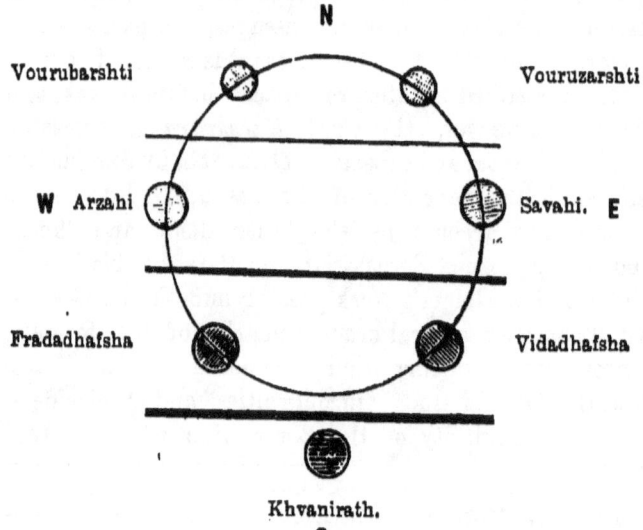

The Mazdean names given above have only to be replaced by those used in the Secret Doctrine to become an orthodox tenet. The "Earth" (our world), therefore, *is* "triparatite," because the chain of the worlds is situated on three different *planes* above our globe; and it is *septempartite* because of the seven globes or spheres which compose the chain [as shown in the diagram above]. Hence the further meaning given in the Vendidâd (xix. 39,) showing that "*Qaniratha* alone is combined with *imat*, 'this' (earth), while all other *Karshvaras* are combined with the world '*avat*,' 'that' or *those*—upper earths." Nothing could be plainer.

As each of our senses being related to each of the physical elements, the ego, encased and united as it is with the physical nature, cannot cognise anything beyond the physical or objective world. To cognise other than physical nature other senses are necessary. These senses are latent in every man, which simply require development, by certain training of body, mind, and soul. History furnishes us with innumerable instances in which men appear to have attained wonderful powers commonly known as miraculous, and to disbelieve the statements of all of them simply because *we* cannot develope them, is simply blind scepticism. If we take the above Karshvaras as simply seven continents on the surface of this solid globe, as hitherto we are told by the orientalists and other students of the Avastâ, the teaching of the Avastâ prove quite inconsistent. Viewed, however, from the stand-point of Occultism we can arrive at a better solution of the teaching of Avastâ-Zend.

These Karshvaras are separated by an occean (ether), and from Vourûbarsht and Vourûzarsht "a lofty mountain grew up, so that it is not possible for any one to go from region to region," without the aid of a mysterious bull named Sarsaok, —a symbol of some occult power. All benefits are to be derived from the Khvaniras, and all the miseries as well are to be found on this physical plane, on account of its superiority. "The good religion of the Mazdiasnians was created in Khvaniras, and afterwards conveyed to the other regions. Sôshyans* is born in Khvaniras, who makes the evil spirit impotent, and causes the resurrection and future existence."† "When the Sun comes out it illumines the regions of Savah, Fradadhafsha, Vidadhafsha, and half of Khvaniras ; when it goes in on the dark side, it illumines the regions of Arzah, Vourûbarsht, Vourûzarsht, and one-half of Khvaniras ; when it is day here, it is night there." The third chapter of the *Bahman Yasht* informs us that when darkness prevails over these seven regions, Mithra calls in Hûshedar, a son or ray of Zarathushtra the Yazata, the restorer of the true religion, and asks him to order Sun, to " move on ! for it is dark" in the seven regions of the earth. "The Sun with the swift Aspa moves on . . . . . and all mankind fully. believe in the good religion of the Mazdayasnians." Each Karshvara has a chief presiding over it : thus the chief of Arzah is Ashâshagahad-ê Hvandchân ; the chief of Savah is Hoazarô-dathhri-hanâ Pareshtyarô ; the chief of Fradadhafsha is Spitoid-ê Ausposinân ; the chief of Vidadhafsha is Airiz-rasp Ausposinân ; the chief of Vonrûbarsht is Huvasp ; the chief of Vourûzarsht is Châkravak ; and Zarathushtra is spiritual chief of the region of the Khvaniras ; " and also of all the religions ; he is the chief of the world of the righteous and it is said that the whole religion was received by them from Zarathushtra."‡

A similar account appears in the "Vishnu Purâna" of the Hindus. Priyavrata is said to be the god presiding over the septenary Earth, who distributed it to his seven sons in the following manner :—"To Agnidhra he gave Jambu-Dwipa ; to Medhâtithi he gave Plaksha-Dwipa ; he installed Vapush-man in the sovereignty of the Sâlomali-Dwipa ; and made Jyotishman King of Kuśa-Dwipa ; he appointed Dyntiman to rule over Krauncha-Dwipa ; Bhavya to reign over Sâka-Dwipa ; and Savola (or Savema) he nominated the monarch

---

* The future Avatâra of the Zoroastrians.
† The *Bundahish*, Ch. xi.   ‡ *Ibid.*, Ch. xxix. 1-2.

of the Dwipa of the Pushkara."—(Amsa ii., Ch. i.) According to this account the last two dwipas are the future subtle globes of our earth-chain, not yet developed.

Although it was impossible to cross the "ocean," the ether, that lies between the globes, nine races proceeded, owing to the increase of the whole fifteen races, on the back of the ox Sarsaok, through the wide ocean, to the other six regions, and stayed there; and six races of men remained on the Khvaniras. These six globes are inhabited, it is said, by "men who, like primitive men, do not eat meat, but live exclusively upon milk." This "milk" of the *Bundahish* cannot be taken as referring to the milk of any animal, but can be taken for the astral fluid, or life-juice, by drinking which Mashyô-Mashyoî, the hermaphrodite, "fell," and separated into sexes, which we shall see further on. It appears that if we know how to ride on the bull Sarsaok, elsewhere called the bull Hadhayôsh, or, acquire psychic power, we can also travel from one Karshvara to the other. Elsewhere it is said that it requires the help of the Yazatas to "cross the sea.' In the reign of Takhmorûp [Tahmuras or Tahmurath of the *Shah-nameh*, the epic poem of the Parsis, the third king of the Peshdâdian or the Primitive Race] men were continually passing and repassing "on the back of the ox," from the Khvaniras to other regions. Looking deeply into Ch. iv, Amśa i, of the "Vishnu Purâna," we find again an identical teaching, which shows that mankind in Sâlmala, Kûsa and Krauncha Dwipas were formerly associating themselves with the celestial Beings; but not on the Plaksha, where mankind became more and more encased into the physical body and lost the power of association with the higher Beings.

ANTHROPOGONY.

THE PRIMEVAL RACES.

Was this first earth uninhabited? "Ahuramazda, through omniscience, knows that Ahriman exists," adds the *Bundahish*, "and that whatever he schemes he infuses with malice and greediness till the end; and because he accomplishes the end by many means. He also produced spiritually the creatures which were necessary for those means, and they remained three thousand years [? periods] in a spiritual state, so that they were *unthinking and unmoving, with intangible bodies.*"*

Commenting upon the fourth stanza, our teacher describes in the "Secret Doctrine" the *Chhâya* Race as the *A-manasas*, who had "neither forms nor mind." These Chhâyas were called "A-manasas" because they were mindless. Pages can be quoted here from the profound work for further elucidation, but as this article is proposed for a mere skeleton the references can be avoided.

The subsequent Race was called "Sweat-born," and in the third chapter of the "Original Creation" it is said that Ahuramazda brought forth a *sweat* upon Gâyômard, "so long as he might recite a *prayer* of one stanza; moreover, Ahuramazda formed that sweat into the youthful body of a man of fifteen years, radiant and tall. When Gâyômard issued from the sweat he saw the world dark as night, and the earth as though not a needle's point remained free from noxious creatures; the celestial sphere was in revolution, and the sun and moon remained in motion; and the world's struggle, owing to the clamour of the Mâzinikân demons, was with the constellations."†

Gâyômard is the first man among the Parsis; but from a description which appears in the same book, he appears to be a Pitar, who, when he disappears (not dies), casts his shadow, and, various kinds of "minerals of a metallic character arise from his various members." An acccount of the evolution at this stage will be found elsewhere (pp. 94-97 *ante*). As we have derived our body from the shadow of Gâyômard, it also contains metallic properties known to the real Alchemists only. The physicists know, however, only one metal, *viz.*, iron, the

---

* Ch. i, 8.
† The *Bundahish*, Ch. iii., 19-20; Selections of Ervad Zâd-Sparam, Ch. i, 8-10; also *ante*, pp. 94-97.

particles of which they find in human blood; but it can be inferred from this very fact that other "principles" have other metallic properties, too; and it is he who transfers the base metals within himself into *gold* becomes a true Alchemist. The "prayer" alluded to above is the Mañthra S'akti, the power of Divine Sound, in which are included the Ichchâ (Creative), Jnân (Preservative), and Kriyâ (Regenerative) Shaktîs.

"Who was the first man before myself," asked Zarathushtra according to the Vendidâd, "with whom thou, Ahuramazda, did converse, whom thou didst teach the law of Ahura, the law of Zarathushtra?" "The Fair Yima," answered Ahuramazda, "the great Shepherd, O Holy Zarathushtra, he was the first mortal before thee, Zarathushtra, with whom I, Ahuramazda, did converse, whom I taught the law of Ahura, the law of Zarathushtra."

"Yima, the so-called 'first man' in the Vendidâd, as much as his twin-brother Yama, the son of Vaivasvata Manu, belongs to two epochs of the Universal History. He is the Progenitor of the Second human Race, hence the personification of the shadows of the Pitris, and the Father of the *post-diluvian* Humanity. The Magi said 'Yima,' as we say '*man*' when speaking of the mankind. The 'fair Yima,' the first mortal who converses with *Ahura-Mazda, is the first 'man' who dies* or disappears, not the first who is born. The 'Son of Vivañhat' was, like the son of Vaivasvata, the symbolical man, who stood in the Secret Doctrine as the representative of the *first three races* and the collective progenitor thereof. Of these Races the first two never died, but only vanished, absorbed in their progeny, and the third Race knew death only towards its close, after the separation of the sexes and its 'Fall' into generation; *i. e.*, Death came only after man had become a *physical* creature. This is plainly alluded to in the Second Fargard of the Vendidâd. Yima refuses to become the bearer of the law of Ahura-Mazda, saying 'I was not born, I was not taught to be the preacher and the bearer of Thy law.' And then Ahura-Mazda asks him to make his men increase and 'watch over his world'—(see Fargards 3 and 4).

" He refused to become the priest of Ahura-Mazda, because he is his *own Priest and Sacrificer*, but he accepts the second proposal. He is made to answer :—

"' Yes !—yes, I will rule and watch over Thy world. There shall, while I am king, neither cold wind, nor hot wind, *neither disease nor death.*'

"Then Ahura-Mazda brings him a golden ring and a poniard, the emblems of sovereignty ; and under the sway of Yima—

"' 300 winters (*i. e.*, 300 periods or cycles) passed away, and the earth was replenished with flocks and herds, with men and dogs, and birds and with red blazing fires, &c.'

"' Replenished,' mark well, that is to say, all this had been on the earth before ; and thus is proven the knowledge of the doctrine about the successive destruction of the world and its life cycles. Once the ' 300 winters' were over, Ahura-Mazda warns Yima that the earth is becoming too full and men have nowhere to live. Then Yima steps forward, with the help of Spenta-Armaiti (the female genius, or spirit of the Earth), makes that earth *stretch out and become* larger by one-third, after which ' new herds and flocks and men' appear upon it. Ahura-Mazda warns him again and Yima makes the earth by the same magic power to *become larger* by the two-thirds. ' Nine hundred winters' *pass* away and Yima has to perform the ceremony *for the third time.* The whole of this is allegorical. The three processes of *stretching* the earth refer to the three successive continents and races, issuing one after and from the other. After the *third* time, Ahura-Mazda warns Yima in an assembly of ' celestial gods and excellent mortals' that upon the material world the fatal winters are going to fall, and all life will perish. This is the old Mazdean symbolism for the ' flood' and the coming cataclysm to Atlantis which sweeps away every Race in its turn. Like Vaivasvata Manu and Noah, Yima makes a *vara* (an enclosure, an ark) under God's direction, and brings thither the seed of every living creature, animals and ' fires.'

"It is of this 'earth' or new continent that Zarathushtra became the Law-giver and Ruler. This was the Fourth Race in its beginning, after the men of the Third Race began to die out. Till then, as said above, there had been no regular death, but only a transformation, for *men had no personality as yet*. They had Monads—breaths of the One Breath, and is *impersonal* as the source from which they proceeded. They had bodies, or rather shadows of bodies, which were sinless, hence *Karmaless*. Therefore, as there was no *Kâma-lôka*—least of all Nirvana or even Devachan for the 'souls' of men who had no *personal* egos, there could be no intermediate periods between the incarnations. Like the Phœnix primordial man resurrected out of his old into a new body. Each time, and with each new generation, man became more solid, more *physically* perfect, agreeably with the evolutionary law which is the *Law of Nature*. Death came with the complete physical organism, and with death came moral decay."—(*The Secret Doctrine*, Vol. ii, pp. 607-10, *old edn.*)

The early Second Root-Race was *A*-sexual, that is, they had no sex, although they were called the Fathers of the later Second Root-Race, who were also called Sweat-born. How could the Chhâyas, the "Sons of Fire," procreate the Second Race, since they were ethereal, *A*-sexual, and even devoid as yet of the Vehicle of Desire or Kâma-Rûpa, which evolved only in the Third Race ? They evolved the Second Race unconsciously, it is stated, as do some plants.

"The astral form," the "Secret Doctrine" teaches, "clothing the Monad, was surrounded, as it still is, by its egg-shaped *Aura* which here corresponds to the substance of the germ cell or *ovum*. The astral form itself is the nucleus, now as then, instinct with the principle of life. When the season of reproduction arrives, the *sub*-astral 'extrudes' a miniature of itself from the egg of surrounding Aura. This germ grows and feeds on the Aura till it becomes fully developed, when it gradually separates from its parent carrying with it its own sphere of Aura ; just as we see living cells reproducing their like by growth and subsequent division into two."

As each Root-Race was sub-divided into seven, each had seven stages of evolution racially. The process of reproduction had seven stages also in each race, each covering æons of time. Thus although the sub-races of the Second Race were born at first by the process described above, the last to appear began gradually, *pari passu*, with the evolution of the human body, to be formed otherwise, details of which can be found in the "Secret Doctrine."

THE DIVINE HERMAPHRODITE.

We shall now enter into the region of the Divine Hermaphrodite. It appears from the *Bundahish* that Mâshya and Mâshyôi, commonly called by the Parsis Mashyo-Mashiâni, "first grew up from the earth" (primordial substance), and that "both of them changed from the shape of a plant into the shape of man, and the breath went spiritually into them, which is the soul," which was created "before the body."

At the end of forty periods Mâshya-Mâshyôi sprung up in the shape of a Rivas-plant and were joined together from the middle in such a manner that "it was not clear which was the male and which the female, and which was the one with the glory (soul) which Ahura-mazda has created."* The pair were happy, until and as far as they knew and believed that everything and all prosperity whose origin and effect are from the manifestations of righteousness, are evolved from Ahura-mazda. Subsequently, however, "antagonism rushed into their minds, and their minds were thoroughly corrupted, and they exclaimed that the evil spirit created the water and earth, plants and animals, and the other things as aforesaid." They remained without food and water—there was no necessity of them—for a period, and then "they came to a white-haired goat, and milked the milk from the udder with their mouths." Just as Adam evolved Eve out of his own rib, and eating the forbidden fruit of the Tree of Life, fell into generation, so Mâshya fell into generation, after evolving Mâshyôi, by drinking the

---

* "Selections of Herbûd Zâd-sparam," Ch. x, 4.

"milk," the life-juice. The idea of separation arose owing to their descending towards comparatively denser matter, "which brought unnatural malice between themselves; they tore their hair and cheeks, by which the demons were pleased, and asked them to worship demons, which the pair did." At this they both became so "dry-backed" that—while in "fifty winters they had no desire for intercourse, and even if they had intercourse they would have no children—the source of desire arose, first in Mâshya and then in Mâshyôi. . . . . From them was born in nine months a pair, male and female." This pair were, it is said, "devoured," one by the mother and one by the father, owing to their "tenderness," and "Ahura-mazda took tenderness for offspring away from them, so that one may nourish a child, and the child may remain." Change the meaning of the words "devoured" and "tenderness" into *absorbed* and *spiritual nature* and you have a more reasonable meaning for the sentence than the one given by the translators. It shows the absorption of the first progeny into their parent. The latter portion of the passage shows clearly the gradual materializing of the bodies, the "tenderness," the spiritual nature, being taken away from them by Ahura-mazda.

Seven is the order in nature. everywhere, and seven pairs arose from one pair, male and female, "each was a brother and sister-wife, and from every one of them, in fifty years, *children* were born, and they themselves died in an hundred years." Siâmak, male, and Nashâk or Vashâk, female, were one of the pairs, from whom another pair was born, whose names were Fravâk, male, and Fravâkain, female. Fifteen pairs were born of these, every single pair of whom afterwards became a race; and from them arose the constant flow of the generation of the world.* Out of the fifteen sub-races nine proceeded to live on the other six Karshvarts, the other globes of the earth-chain, on the back of the myste-

---

* The *Bundahish*, Ch. xv, 25-26.

rious ox Sarsaok, as we have already seen, and six stayed on the Karshvara Khvaniras, our earth.

It appears that there was another "tree" or "plant" similar to the one called Rivas-plant which was transformed into Mâshya-Mashyôi. The fruit of this nameless tree* was another race, which subsequently produced ten sub-races of monsters, "the breast-eared, the breast-eyed, the one-legged, those also who have wings like a bat, those of the forest with tails, and who have hair on the body."† This might appear to some an imaginary fairy-tale ; but while we see even now, in this matter-of-fact age, some monster births like the hairy family, the Siamese twins, &c., and Professor Crookes giving us assurance of the absence of *Calcic phosphate*, as far as bone is concerned, in the first vibration of matter, it is more reasonable to suppose the existence of various shapes of deformity, from our stand-point, in a Race that existed in the hoary past.

The genealogical tree of our Pitar, Gâyomard, then, can thus be traced :—

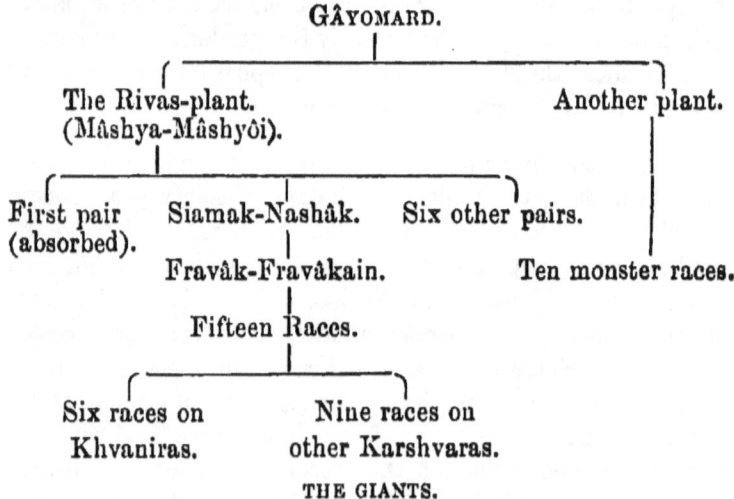

THE GIANTS.

Now we have to descend into the subsequent races, an account of which can be seen in the *Shah-Nameh*, the epic

---

* *Ibid.*, xv, 5. † *Ibid.*, Ch. xv, 31.

poem of Ferdousi, the celebrated Mahomedan Poet of Persia, who was at heart a Zoroastrian. It has no connection with the Zoroastrian religion, nor with the philosophy, although it is considered a traditional and historical account of the Parsis, mostly loved by a class of people for its poetical and legendary beauty. According to this work, Siamak, the son of Gâyômard, was murdered by his giant brother, and then came Husheng, "the prudent and the wise," whose dynasty "re-discovered metals and precious stones, which had been concealed by the devas and giants in the bowels of the earth ; how to make brass-work, to cut canals, and improve agriculture." This divine-king is credited with writing a book called "Javidan-i-Kherad" (Eternal Wisdom), a portion only of which is still in existence with the Parsis.* Husheng had a twelve-legged horse, a progeny of a female hippopotamus and a crocodile. Husheng defeated any giant who opposed him whenever he mounted on this mysterious horse. Notwithstanding the impregnable power attained by this wise adept, he was killed by the giants, who threw an enormous rock at him from the great mountain Damavend. Then came Tahmuras, the Devabandh, the giant-binder. Just as Husheng had a mysterious horse, Tahmuras had a mysterious bird, called Simorgh-Anké. The bird was a "religious" one, and so old that it had seen twelve cycles of 7,000 years each. Multiplying this number by the 12 cycles we have the esoteric figure of 840,000 years, a figure which might assist the future Parsi student of esoteric science in arriving at the age when the Peshdadian or Primordial Race existed. Then came Jamsheed, who reigned 700 years, after which he believed himself immortal, and in pride demanded divine honours from the race. Karma punished him by driving him out of his position. He then wandered for 100 years, when Azidahâk or Zouhak usurped him, who was under the influence of Iblish, and had two serpents on his shoulder for which everyday two men had to be slaughtered in order that their brains might afford food of the serpents. Zouhak was vanquished by Faridun and

---

* A review of this book appears in the *Theo-ophist*, Vol. iii, pp. 80-81.

made a prisoner in the mountain Damavend. Faridun who had three sons, Selim, Tûr and Erach, divided his kingdom among them, and retired into the caves. Erach was killed by his two brothers, and was succeeded by his son, Minochehr, who in his turn was succeeded by some others up to Kaikobad, who established a new dynasty. Up to this time we see the giants, who are called in the Shahnameh as Devas or demons, harassing the good subject of the kings. Even the great Rustom, the hero of the epic, was troubled by the Safid Deva.

It thus appears that Zoroastrianism, is nothing if not mostly allegorical. Even this "Shahnameh" is not without its allegories and mysteries. We have seen in our former account that there are several Karshvaras or globes in connection with the earth, more ethereal and invisible to the naked eye, surrounded by Âkâsh which is called "ocean" in the scriptures, and can be crossed by him only who can ride on a certain mysterious ox. The wandering tribes of Persia believe, even now, that there is, far beyond the snow-capped summits of Caucasus, "*a great continent now concealed from all.* That it is reached by those who can secure the services of the twelve-legged progeny of the crocodile and the female hippopotamus, whose legs become at will *twelve wings*; or by those who have the patience to wait for the good pleasure of *Simorgh-Anké*, who promised that before she died, she would reveal the hidden continent to all, and make it once more visible and within easy reach, by means of a bridge, which the Ocean Devs will build between that portion of the 'dry island' and its several parts. This relates, of course, to the Seventh Race, Simorgh being the Manvantric cycle." Thus we see one of the mysteries of the Shahnameh revealed by the "Secret Doctrine."

It will be clearly seen from the above that the Shahnameh contains, among other soul-stirring episodes, an account of the pre-Aryan or Atlantean Races. Passing over these we approach nearer the Aryan Race, the earlier portion of which, although physical, was more spiritual than what we are at present, which can be seen from the account of the Kaianian and other Sub-races in the Parsi legends.

An exhaustive elucidation is required to unriddle the allegorical and mystic teaching of the Zoroastrian scriptures. But this cannot be done here with the limited space at our disposal and we are therefore compelled to close our subject here although the explanation offered here may appear to many of our readers imperfect.

NASARVANJI F. BILIMORIA.

Theosophist, Vol. xvi, Nos. 1-3.

THE PHILOSOPHY.

"THE PHILOSOPHY OF THE MAZDAYASNIAN RELIGION*"
A REVIEW.

WE are glad to notice that the translator of Dr. Casartelli's dissertation, *La Philosophie religieuse du Mazdéisme sous les Sassanides*, whereby he gained his *Doctorat* at Louvain University in 1884, has added some corrective notes to his excellent translation of the Doctor's treatise. Dr. L. C. Casartelli, who is also a Catholic priest, throughout his work labours under the strange delusion that Mazdeism is largely indebted to Judaism and Christianity for all that is best in it. Whenever he makes a confident statement on this point, his Parsi translator is immediately busy with a refutation, supported either by texts from the Avastâ and other ancient writings, or by quotations from Western scholars who hold opinions exactly the reverse of those of the Louvain graduate. There are also many other points on which the translator picks up the author and corrects his translation of Pahlavi texts or misconceptions of the philosophy. We, however, think that there still remains much to be done, especially in the latter direction, and shall endeavour to point out one or two misconceptions which an elementary knowledge of symbology should have easily avoided. In spite of these blemishes, however, much remains that will be of great interest to the student of Esotericism and of support to the argument of Theosophy as to the unity of all religions.

In the outset but scant justice is done to the primal spiritual postulate of the Mazdean system, that " Boundless Time," *Zravane Akarana*, which connotes the *Parabrahm* of the Vedantin and the *Ain Soph* of the Kabbalah, the Absoluteness;

---

* The Philosophy of the Mazdayasnian Religion under the Sassanides, translated from the French of L. C. Casartelli by Firoz Jamaspji Dastur Jamaspji Asa. Bombay: Jehangir Bejanji Karani, 17 and 18, Parsi Bazaar, 1889.

while on the contrary the Dualism of the religion is unduly accentuated. This draws from the translator a long note beginning with the paragraph :—

"It is a well-known fact, and it is proved by many distinguished *savants*, both European and Zoroastrian, that the leading feature of the theology of the original or Zoroastrian Mazdeism, as contained in the Avastâ and especially in the Gâthâs, was strictly based on Monotheism . . ."

—a view by the way, which has been strongly defended even in the Occident by Dr. West and others.

In describing the Wisdom Doctrine, which is the common property of all Eastern religions and to be found in the Avastâ equally with the rest, Dr. Casartelli follows Spiegel in his effort to set down its *origin* to the credit of the West, and quotes largely from the Sapiential Books of the Old Testament. If there is one thing that is certain, it is that the Wisdom-religion and the Sophia-mythus have always come by the way of the East. However, it is not to be supposed that a man will ever find the root of the tree of the World Religions by keeping his eyes fixed on some particular branch or branchlet.

The frequent recurrence of the number 7 in the Mazdean System is remarkable. For instance we read of 7 continents ; 7 days of creation ; 7 great mountains, the principal off-shoots of Albûrz, the Mazdean Meru ; 7 metals produced from the limbs of the *first man*, *Gâyômart* ; 14 kinds of liquid ; 7 senses, &c. This has, however, escaped the notice of the author. Again in dealing with the *Amesoçpands*,* the *Fravâhars* and *Fravashis*, not the slightest elucidation is offered and the entire puzzlement of the scholars on the subject is frankly admitted. The Amshaspends are esoterically the 7 Primordial Emanations, or Logoi, of their synthesis *Adhara-*

---

* It is to be regretted that the French transliteration has been retained throughout.

mazda who "dwells in the eternal or endless light in the place of Aûharmazd" and which is "clearly distinguished from the created light of the world" (p. 26). The Ferouers or Fravashis are the Reïncarnating *Egos* of Humanity and are said to be *equal in number* to the Drûjs or Demons (p. 93).* At the end of the world each Warrior-Fravashi combats and overcomes his twin-demon. All of which is perfectly clear to the student of Esotericism, who will also see the same idea underlying the mystery of *Ahariman*, the syzygy of Ahuramazda, and the synthesis of the Demons, who are identical with the *Asuras* of the Purânas. Speaking of the Mazdean Satan, Dr. Casartelli writes :—" If he deprives a man of his wife, his children, his whole terrestrial wealth, nay even his life, he does not consider it as a great misfortune ; but if he succeeds in carrying off his soul and in ruining it, he considers it indeed a great wrong that he has done him" (p. 64). So that perhaps after all the devil is not so black as he is painted.

Very far from the truth is our learned Pahlavi Scholar in his remarks on the frequent allusions to rain in the Mazdean scriptures and the reverence with which it was regarded by the followers of the Avastâ doctrines. Of course the reason of this reverence must be attributed to natural causes. It was simply because the populace was largely engaged in agricultural pursuits ! But then what can you think of a superstition which actually believed that the seeds of all things came down in the rain ! ! Such is the tone of the Doctor's remarks. Perhaps such an explanation may satisfy the limited comprehension of a solar-mythologist ; it will not however content the student of occult symbology. Rain and Water correspond to the ether of space and to the *astral* ocean that surrounds the earth. This contains the types or "seeds" of all that grows on the bosom of our Mother *Bhûmi*. But setting aside occult science, for ignorance of which an orientalist may perhaps be excused, the author might at least have found, even from his own notes, some more reasonable explanation of

---

* Because the Drûjs are the *lesser* "Mapasos."

the peculiar reverence for rain which obtained in the Sassanian cosmology.

In the category of the 14 kinds of Water, called by the "general name of *Mayâ*" (p. 114), we read of the "Water in plants," of "Animal seed," "blood," &c. We may compare this with the different kinds of Fire, of which "five . . . are known," these were "diffused through the six *substances*, that is to say, the works of the six periods of creation" (p. 116), which, together with the seventh creation, the "day of rest," complete the 7 mystic Fires. The 5 correspond to the 5 known elements, the remaining 2 being still latent, like the senses. These are given as follows :—

"(1) The fire *Berezi-savang* shines near the Lord, Aûharmazd. It seems to be a spiritual fire which is incorporated in the various forms of material fire, especially like three souls in the three sacred fires. . . .

"(2) The fire *Vôhû-fryân* dwells in the bodies of men and animals and feeds upon water and solid food.

"(3) The fire *Urvâzist* is the fire which is found in plants. It feeds upon water and has no other food.

"(4) The fire *Vâzist* is the lightning which dwells in the clouds . . . This fire has no need either of food or drink.

"(5) The fire *Cpênist* is the common fire of the world which consumes food but not water.

"The fire *Vâhrâm*, the sacred fire of the Mazdayasnian altar, is associated with the fire last mentioned. As we have seen, this fire is rather an incarnation of the celestial fire. It has three bodies or principal centres . . . The three souls of the celestial fire lodge in these three corporeal fires, all of which form the entire body of the fire *Vahrâm*."

Again, speaking of the Mystic Trees, the *Gôkard*, the source of all medicines, is said to grow out of the earth, whereas the *White Hôm*, "which will furnish man with immortality at the time of the resurrection, is spoken of as being in the ocean, or the sea with the wide shores," esoterically *Space*. And, we might add, that the one grows with its roots in the earth, the other with its roots in heaven, twin-trees, one the reflection of the other and both within every man. From all of which we may perceive that perhaps the superstition is not so absurd, for : " the water or sap in the plants circulates like the waters of the earth, or like the blessings which the righteous utter, or which come back to themselves " (p. 119), and as "blood" is under the same law, therefore it follows that the Mazdean Initiates knew both of the " circulation of the blood" and, more important still, of the cyclic and karmic law.

Those who have read Berosus and of the " Monsters terrible and bad" of the stanzas of the *Book of Dzyan*, will find some interesting items in corroboration of the existence of intermediate and monstrous types in the first arc of primordial evolution. We read of gigantic three-legged asses, of tree-fishes and ox-fishes, &c., &c. But more interesting still to the student of the *Secret Doctrine* is the description of the Mazdayasnian anthropogenesis.

" The human race is not only descended from the primeval man, Gâyômart, *from whom the metals are also derived*, but it has also passed through a *vegetable existence* before being constituted in its present state.

" Man was in fact the work of the sixth epoch of the creation. Aûharmazd formed Gâyômart, a solitary male being, from the earth. He was *white, brilliant-looking as the sun*. He had three characteristics, *viz.*, life, speech and mortality. The *first two* were communicated to him by Aûharmazd, the last is owing to the influence of Aharman. The whole of mankind has inherited these characteristics by its descent from Gâyômart.

" He and the primeval ox were the only living beings on the earth during the first 3,000* years. Both of them lived

---

* Three Rounds. Here " man" stands for the future physical man and the " primeval Ox" or Bull, for the ever developing potential nature.

in peace and happiness till the commencement of the millenium of the constellation of *Libra*.* Then Aharman attacked and overwhelmed them with evils during 30 years†, and at length put them to death. Gâyômart, while succumbing under the blows of his adversary, predicted that mankind would be born of him. Then he *bequeathed his body*‡ very justly to Aharman. . .

"Gâyômart while dying dropped his seed, which was purified by the *light of the sun*§. Two-thirds of it were absorbed by the earth. Forty years after, it produced two human beings under the form of a plant, having only one stem, 15 leaves, and 15 years of age. These two beings, Màshya and Mùshyôi (otherwise Matrô and Matrôyâô), were *united together at the middle*‖, in such a manner that it was impossible to know which was the male and which the female. It was not either known if they possessed reason. Then they passed from the vegetable form to the human one; the reasoning faculty . . . which is the soul, spiritually entered into them.¶

"We give below the comments of Windischmann on this curious legend :—**

"'The plant with a single stem is the type of the unique origin of the two sexes, or of their original inseparableness. The stem is aged fifteen years, for this is the perfect age assigned to Gâyômart himself. It has fifteen leaves, for an equal number of human races inhabited the *Kêshvars*.†† The plant appeared for forty years, for that is the normal age of

---

* Symbolizes separation of sexes.
† *Sandhyas* among the Hindus. This signifies the third Root Race of the Fourth Round.
‡ Chhaya.
§ The Egg-born.
‖ Hermaphrodite.
¶ Separation of sexes; incarnation of Manasaputra.
** Windischmann, *Zor. Stud.*, pp. 214, 215.
†† Continents.

generation in the *Var*.* Mâshya and Mâshyôî were twins, like Yama and Yamî in the *Vedas*, like Yima and his sister in the *Bûndahesh*, which derives its information from more ancient sources.'

"Another plant was formed resembling this one : it produced ten races of monstrous and fabulous men, as the Cynocephalus, wigned men, men having tails and others ; but all of them were the issues of the seed of Gâyômart. Those 'of the forests having tails and hairy bodies'† are undoubtedly the great quadrumana, like the gorilla of Africa (?). Besides other cases of relationship between men and some inferior animals were admitted. The Pahlavi version of the *Vendidâd* also asserts that 'all that which appertains to the monkey (*Kâpik*) is precisely like (that which appertains to) man. Elsewhere the monkey, bear and negro are grouped together as *degraded human races, issued from the intercourse between men and evil spirits*‡—devs, drûjs and pariks" (pp. 129-131).

Further on we are told that Mâshya and Mâshyôî, when they first obtained their soul, "covered their bodies with *grass* (giyâh), and had no need of food but drank only water"; afterwards they killed a sheep, and having discovered *fire by friction*, they roasted it. "On this very occasion they covered themselves with *garments of skin*"§. All of which is a plain simple statement of fact to the student of scientific mythology.||

Page 145 gives us an interesting piece of information and another proof of one of the contentions of the esoteric doctrine, for we read : "The age of reason has no fixed limit ; it

---

* The "Ark."
† The "Race of crooked red-hair covered monsters going on all fours." (S. D. ii, 19.)
‡ Animals.
§ This refers to the gradual consolidation of the bodies of primitive men, and to the incarnation of the Flames, or *Mânasaputra*, the reincarnating Egos.
|| N. B.—The Italics are our own.

varies between 7 and 8 years, for before this age 'sin does not take root,'" or as we should say individual Karma does not operate.

Under the heading *Khvêtûkdaç*, the author tries his best to convict the Mazdean scriptures of sanctioning incest! This pious libel brings his translator down upon him in an excellent note, where he conclusively proves that the meaning of the avastâic term *quaetvadatha* cannot even by the most elaborate imagination of prejudice be twisted into any such meaning. It simply means "a giving of oneself, a giving in relationship, self-dedication, devotion." As an epithet of the Mazdayasnian religion, it means "bearing relationship with God" and as an attribute generally means "devout." In other words, it is descriptive of spiritual *Yoga* and occult powers. But what can you expect of the religious mind of the West, which believes literally in the 700 wives and 300 concubines of King Solomon! The same charitable accusation is brought against Ardâ-i Viraf, the most holy of all the Dasturs, who restored the Mazdayasnian traditions to their original purity. This most holy man is said to have had his *seven sisters* to wife, whereas the meaning is, that the Dastur had achieved complete mastery over his seven "principles." O Shades of holy ascetics, into what evil times have the narratives of your great deeds fallen!

Space will not permit us to make more than mention of the wonderful world mountain Albûrz that surrounds the whole earth and is pierced with 360 openings, and of the mundane egg; of the two Maidens that meet the Soul at death, the personifications of his good and evil deeds, and of the *Chinvaḍ Bridge* which unites this world with that beyond the grave and is situated on the "peak of judgment," which is in the middle of the World and a part of the Albûrz; of the Heavens and the Hells, of which latter Virâf says *the worst is on the earth*, and of the end of the World. Under the last heading we read:—

"At last comes the millenium of Soshyâns, the last prophet.

During this epoch the appetite will gradually diminish and men will desist at first from eating meat and lastly they will live upon water. . . . .

"All this regeneration will be accomplished under the direction of the prophet Soshyâns, who will have assistants, certain men and women who have been preserved from death in the mystical regions, like that of Aîrân Vêj, the reminiscence of the primitive country of the Aryas, which has become a sort of *officina gentium* for the last ages. This country seems to be in *Khvaniraç*, on the shores of the ocean. It contains the *Var* or the enclosure formed and governed by Yim; it is under the earth and is one of the abodes of these immortals."

Which is simply a reference to the "imperishable land" and the "race which never dies" of the *Secret Doctrine*.

Finally we would ask the author : (*a*) how, if, as he says, the Mazdayasnian religious writers were most strongly opposed to Christianity, Judaism and Manichæism, they could at the same time owe the most spiritual portions of their system to the two former religions : and (*b*) If he cannot escape from the horns of this dilemma, is he prepared to endorse the statement where he says :—" Among all other non-Christian religions, the Mazdayasnian religion can justly boast of having the soundest, the highest and the most reasonable system of ethics." (*c*) If so, what was the source of this religion, if not the one stream of initiation that has ever watered the earth ?

.*. Although the above is a review of a book, it was considered indispensable here, as it throws some light on various allegorical and mystic points, written as it was by H. P. Blavatsky, the renown Ocultist.—*Compiler*.

PHILOSOPHY AND ETHICS OF THE ZOROASTERS.

> "God is the ground of all existence, and theology is the highest Philosophy."—*Aristotle.*

SIR WILLIAM JONES, in his sixth anniversary discourse as President of the Asiatic Society in Bengal, February 19th, 1789, making the Ancient Persians his theme, and citing the *Dabistân* for his authority, describes the primeval religion of Irân as identical with what Sir Isaac Newton declared to be the oldest of all religions: "A firm belief that one Supreme God made the world by his power and continually governed it by his providence; a pious fear, love, and adoration of Him; a due reverence for parents and aged persons; a fraternal affection for the whole human species, and a compassionate tenderness even for the brute creation."

A faith so simple and pure is profound and ethical enough for the most exacting moralist, as well as the most philosophic schoolman. It leaves little more to be said by way of explanation or supplement. There is a saying that the learned have the same religion, but never tell what it is. We may feel very certain, however, that this brief formula affords us the solution. Yet we have no occasion to suppose that any unworthy motive inspires their silence, or even undue carefulness to refrain from bestowing treasures upon those who know not the value. Rather is it the reason of Timaios, the Lokrian, as given by Platô: "To discover the Creator and Father of this universe, as well as his work, is arduous; and having discovered Him it is impossible to reveal Him to the many." The apocalypse may be made only to those who understand with the heart, as well as perceive with the other senses.

Other writers have tried to show us that a simple faith, like this described by Mohsan Fâni, was characteristic of the Aryan tribes of Upper Asia. Michelet would make us believe that there were no castes, no mages, no kings, among the archaic Persians; the father of each household was mage and king to all belonging to it; the fire on the family altar-hearth received their homage as being the symbol of the life-imparting spirit; the domestic animal was beloved and magnanimously treated according to its rank; the man revered himself as necessary to the universal existence.

When their theology was first devised goodness was the cardinal principle. The Wise One, leader of the heavenly host, carries on the conflict of ages against the Dark Intelligence, not to hurt but to save his adversary. The battles are all without bloodshed or cruel violence. Every act that beautified the earth, that extended the field of usefulness, that wrought the suppression of hatred and the predominance of goodness, was a conquest.

"Let every one this day, both man and woman, choose his faith," cries the great Zoroaster, standing before the altar. "In the beginning there were two—the Good and the Base in thought, word and deed. Choose one of these two; be good, not base. You cannot belong to both. You must choose the originator of the worst actions, or the true holy Spirit. Some may choose the worst allotment; others adore the Most High by means of faithful action."

"The clear moral note, prominent through the whole cycle of Zoroastrian religion," says Miss Frances Power Cobbe, "has here been struck. The 'choice of Scipio' was offered to the old Irânians by their prophet three thousand years ago, even as it is offered to us to-day. 'Choose one of the two spirits. Be good, not base.'"

A religion like this is personal and not public, a subjective living rather than an instituted mode of worship. No wonder that this noble faith, so ancient that we only guess its antiquity, maintained its life through all the centuries, passing the barriers of race and creed, to permeate all the later world-religions. We find its features in them all, its name and utterances translated into their numerous dialects, yet possessing the essential flavour of this primitive origin.

. . . . .

We need only to change the reading to the Persian designation of the Supreme Being, and this would be a very exact outlining of the original Zoroastrian doctrine. Every hymn chanted in the Parsi worship and every prayer is an acknowledgment of the Divine goodness and justice personified in Ahura-Mazda.

It has been remarked that the whole religion of the *Avastâ* revolved around the person of Zoroaster. The Supreme One speaks only to him out of the midst of the fire, and commands him to teach the pure doctrine to the Irânian people. We find in this a memorable revelation like that of Moses. The Sacred Law of Ahura-Mazda inculcated the obligation to truth in speech and action, the superior merit of industry, and goodness transcending all. Words so divine could not be ascribed to a man speaking from his own understanding. The Irânian sage is therefore always represented as uttering only oracles given to him by the Divine Being, and the collection, of which we now possess but fragmentary remains, is named the *Avastâ*, or Revealed Wisdom.

. . . . .

The endeavour has been made to show a Buddhistic influence in the origin of the Mazdean religion. The historian, Ammianus Marcellinus, has preserved an account of a journey into Upper India by Hystaspes, the father of Darius, and his discourses with the Brachmanes, a sect of philosophers. "He was instructed by their teaching," says this writer, "in the knowledge of the motions of the universe and of the heavenly bodies, and in pure religious rites ; and, so far as he was able to collect these, he transfused a certain portion into the creed of the Mages." This account is a garbled relic of an older tradition. Gustasp or Vistaspa, an ancient king of Baktria, celebrated in the *Avastâ* as first promulgating the Mazdean religion in his dominions, was doubtless the personage denoted. The story indicates the great confusion of opinion existing in regard to the matter. Doctor Haug, however, forcibly repudiates the notion, and fortifies his denial by a translation of the *Fravardin-Yasht*, in which the first Zoroaster is described as "that ingenious man who spoke such good words, who was the promulgator of wisdom, who was born before Gautama had a revelation."

It is apparent, however, that early Buddhism was also of remote antiquity. Its tenets embrace the Sankhyan philosophy ascribed to Kapila ; and they can be traced, Mr. Brian Hodgson declares, into far ages and realms. Indeed the Jaina sect was older than Gautama and its last great teacher Vardhamâna was his preceptor. The disciple became more distinguished than his master, and established a system of propagandism which has had nowhere a parallel in history.

Opinion is curiously divided in regard to Zoroaster. The accounts given of him in the *Avastâ* are many times apparently allegorical. The dispute relates to his actual existence, to the age and country in which he lived, and the source of the Mazdean doctrine. Modern scholars assign him a period somewhat exceeding thirty centuries ago; but Aristotle and others date him back six thousand years before their own time. He is called a Baktrian, and yet is represented as a native of Rhaga, in Media, and even to have flourished at Babylon. His name is given in numerous forms and meaning. We commonly write it as Zoro-Aster, which would seem to denote the son or rather priest of the goddess Istar. Tradition has likewise set him forth as the inventor of the Magian rites, and also as an investigator of the origin of the universe and an observer of the planetary revolutions. Another account represents him in a contest with Nin or Ninip, the divine representative of the early Semitic religion; the one employing the philosophic knowledge of the Far East, and the other the Mystic learning of the Chaldæans.

Clement of Alexandria seeks to identify Zoroaster with Eros, the son of Arminios, whom Plato describes in the Tenth Book of *The Republic* as having been slain in battle, but as reviving again after some days, and giving an account of the destinies of certain noble souls as he had himself witnessed the allotment. This was probably a current tale among the later Persians. The Parsis have a book entitled *The Revelations of Ardâi-Virâf,* which was probably written at the time of the restoration of the Persian monarchy in the third century. It is a detailed account of scenes in heaven and hell as beheld by Ardâi-Viraf during the visit of a week, which his soul—leaving his body for that length of time—paid to those regions.

Ammianus Marcellinus has also given an opinion as from the great philosopher. "Plato, that greatest authority upon famous doctrines, states that the Magian religion, known by the mystic name of *Machagistia, is the most uncorrupted form of worship in things divine;* to the philosophy of which, in primitive ages, Zoroaster the Baktrian made many additions, drawn from the Mysteries of the Chaldæans." This account appears to have been inspired from some attempt to identify that form of Parsiism in which the Magian system had become interblended, with the older mystic worship of Assyria and other countries. It is entirely invalidated, however, by the inscriptions of Darius at Behistun. These utterly denounce Magism as false, apparently ignore the existence even of Añramainyus, the Evil Intelligence, and simply acknowledge Ahura-Mazda. This would seem to indicate that no fusion or amalgamation of worships had as yet taken place.

. . . .

This conflict of the remote ages was at its height when the movement began, which should permanently change the usages and the traditions of the Irânian people. The name of the man who carried it forward to success, is utterly lost in the mists of archaic time. We do not know the century or even the millennium in which he was born. He is characterised in the *Yasna* as "famous in the Aryan Home-Country," where both Hindus and Irânians had their first abodes. "The few philosophic ideas which may be discovered in his sayings," says Dr. Haug, "show that he was a great and deep thinker, who stood above his contemporaries, and even the most enlightened men of many subsequent centuries."

The Sacred Writings always speak of him as possessing rare spiritual endowments, and living in intimate communion with divine natures. His utterances have been denominated Magic, but only in the sense of a Wisdom-religion. He never ceased to denounce the arts of sorcery and the incantations employed in the rites of the Dæva-worshippers. At that time the latter consisted of wandering Aryan tribes addicted to freebooting, and having no permanent residence. They worshipped the gods and *pitris* or ancestral spirits, regarding Indra and Varuna as superior divinities. The Irânians had discarded these, but themselves paid homage to the *Ahuras* or spirits of the eternal world.

The first Zoroaster began his reformation by introducing Mazda, the Supremely Wise, as the chief Ahura, the "primeval spirit," the Creator of the Universe, the "loving Father," "God who is the One that always was, is and will be." In the original Zoroastrian doctrine the seven archangels or Amshaspands are not enumerated. Ahura-Mazda is the source of both the Light and Dark Intelligences. "In his wisdom," says the *Yasna*, "he produced the Good and the Negative Mind. . . . Thou art He, O Mazda, in whom the last cause of both these is hidden."

There is in every one, Zoroaster declared, a good and holy will, a *positive* will of righteousness. The reflection of this good mind is its *negative* evil mind, the lower nature following its instincts and incapable of choosing aright. Sôkratês in *Theaitetos*, has expounded the problem of Evil after a similar manner. The earlier Mazdeans thus included the Positive and Negative principles in their concept of the Divine Nature, and did not thereby impair their perception of the Divine Goodness. It was natural, however, to speak of these attributes as personal essences, and this doubtless led the latter Zoroasters to treat of them as so many distinct beings.

We therefore do not find the sevenfold group of Ameshaspentas at this earlier period of Irânian development,[*] but only modes of Divine operation. Indeed, after they had been promulgated at a later period, but two or three of them seem to have progressed beyond the simple personification of qualities. In an ancient hymn we find several of them enumerated according to this idea. " He gives us by his most holy spirits the *good mind* which springs from good thoughts, words and actions—also *fullness, long-life, prosperity and understanding.*" In like manner, the evil spirits or dævas were chiefly regarded as moral qualities or conditions, though mentioned as individuated existences. They have their origin in the errant thoughts of men. "These bad men," says the *Yasna*, " produce the dævas by their pernicious thoughts." The upright, on the other hand, destroy them by good action.

Always before the mind like a beautiful and sublime prospect was the vision of the Life Eternal. A spiritual and invisible world preceded and remained about this visible and material world as its origin, prototype, and upholding energy. Innumerable myriads of spiritual essences were distributed through the universe. These were the Frohars or Fravashis, the ideal or typical forms of all living things, in heaven and earth. In the earlier periods they were designated as psychic beings, and venerated as ancestral and guardian spirits. "This doctrine," says Professor Tielé, " recurring in one shape or another among all nations of antiquity, received among the Irânians a special development, and in a higher form was adapted into the Zarathustrian system from the very beginning."

---

[*] This is one of the blunders of the Western translators of the Avastâ. The Ameshaspentas are there even in the most ancient Gâthâs, but they are transformed into abstract qualifications as will be seen in a subsequent paragraph in talicized words.—*Compiler.*

Through the Frohars, says the hymn, the Divine Being upholds the sky, supports the earth, and keeps pure and vivific the waters of preëxistent life. They are the energies in all things, and each of them led by Mithras, is associated in its time and order with a human body. Everything, therefore, which is created or will be created, has its Frohar, which contains the cause and reason of its existence. They are stationed everywhere to keep the universe in order and protect it against all the potencies of evil. Thus they are allied to everything in nature; they are ancestral spirits and guardian angels, attracting all human beings to the right and seeking to avert from them every deadly peril. They are the immortal souls, living before our birth as human beings and surviving after death. Thus, in the Mazdean philosophy, the eternal world is an ocean of living intelligences, a milky sea of very life, from which all mortals are generated, sustained and afforded purification from evil.

The human soul coming into this world of time and sense, has always its guardian, its own law or spiritual essence, in the invisible region. In fact, it is never really separated. When its term of existence in this world is over, it abides for three days and nights around the body from which it has withdrawn, and then sets out on its journey. It meets its spiritual counterpart in the form of a beautiful maiden, and is conducted over the Bridge of Judgment to the celestial paradises and into the Everlasting Light. Conversely to this, the wicked soul remains three days at the head of the corpse inhaling the hateful odour of the charnel and then goes forth into scenes of an opposite character, entering finally into the presence of the Evil One in the world of Darkness, there to abide till the final redemption and restitution.* It is predicted in the *Zamyad-Yasht* that the Good Spirit will overcome the Evil Intelligence and deprive him of his dominion.

The Zoroastrian teachings were essentially ethical, and

---

* This account is preserved in a fragment of the *Hadokht-Nosk*, one of the twenty-one lost books, and also in the *Minokhird*, or Book of Wisdom.

inculcate, with pious earnestness, veneration for the pure law. By this is denoted homage to the Supreme Being, to good spirits, the guardians and benefactors, and especially to the personal protector of the worshipper. Prayer was the hearty renouncing of evil and complete harmony with the Divine mind. "To attain to prayer," says the *Yasna*, "is to attain to a perfect conscience. The good seed of prayer is virtuous conscience, virtuous thoughts, and virtuous deeds." It is recorded that Zoroaster enquired of Ahura-Mazda: "What form of invocation expresses every good thing? He replied: "The prayer Ashem."* Zoroaster asked again: "What prayer equals in greatness, goodness and fitness all things beneath the heaven, the starry universe and all things pure?" The Holy One responded: "That one, O Spitaman Zarathushtra, in which all evil thoughts, words and works are renounced."

Every Mazdean was required to follow a useful calling. The most meritorious was the subduing and tilling of the soil. The man must marry, but only a single wife; and by preference she should be of kindred blood. It was impious to foul a stream of water. It was a cardinal doctrine of the Zoroastrian religion that individual worthiness is not the gain and advantage solely of the one possessing it, but an addition to the whole power and volume of goodness in the universe.

The *Ahuna-Vairya*, the prayer of prayers, delineates the most perfect completeness of the philosophic life. It adds to the total renunciation, the entire affiliation of the soul with the Divine.

Grecian writers state that Zoroaster wrote many books. This is doubtless incorrect; for such men seldom write. Iamblichos has told us that the priests of Egypt ascribed all their books upon Science and Wisdom to Hermês. This ancient practice of ascribing works to distinguished personages

---

* The *Ashem-Vohu*:

"Purity is the highest good;
Happy he whose purity is most complete."

renders it impossible to know the real author by the name on the book. The primitive writings of the Irânians have the title of *Avastâ* or Wisdom. Appended to the *Nosks* was a *Zend* or Commentary; much of which was finally wrought into the text. The sacred literature of many different peoples and ancient faiths has thus been corrupted.

The authorship of the *Avastâ* will be better comprehended when we bear in mind that the designation *Zarathushtra* was a title of rank, belonging to the spiritual lords of the Irânian peoples. Every high priest was styled the *Zarathustrotema*, or chief Zarathushtra, and was considered as the successor of the great Spitama, and so inheriting his spirit and authority. He was superior in rank to the head of the family, the chief of the village, the lord of the tribe, and the ruler of the province. What he uttered and wrote might therefore be included in the Sacred Writings under the name of the great Sage himself. The *Avastâ*, as we now have it, is therefore the remains of a compilation made during many centuries which had been destroyed and scattered under the Macedonian rulers and partially collected again in a more or less corrupted form in the third century. The *Gâthâs* or hymns and the older *Yasna* are the most genuine.

. . . .

Herodotos has declared that no nation adopted foreign customs so readily as the Persians. Perhaps we should attribute many of the changes made by their kings to this versatility of disposition. While Darius and Xerxes acknowledged only Ahura-Mazda and the "pure religion," Artaxerxes Mnemôn proclaimed the worship of Mithras and Anahid ; the one the personified fountain of living spirit from whom flowed the currents of life to the universe, and the other the chief of spirits and director of the ever-active fructifying energies of nature. Babylon was doubtless the mother of this new cultus. It was carried into Asia Minor and flourished there for centuries as an arcane religion. After the conquest of Pontos and the pirate empire by Pompey, it was introduced into the

Roman metropolis, "where," says the Rev. C. W. King, "it became so popular, as with the earlier-imported Serapis-worship, to have entirely usurped the place of the ancient Hellenic and Italian divinities. In fact," he further declares, "during the second and third centuries of the Empire, Serapis and Mithras may be said to have become the sole objects of worship even in the remote corners of the Roman world. It was the theology of Zoroaster in its origin, but greatly simplified, so as to assimilate it to the previously-existing systems of the West. Under this form it took the name of Mithras, who in the Zoroastrian creed is not the Supreme Being Ormuzd, but the chief of the subordinate power. Mithras is the Zend title of the Sun, the peculiar domain of this Spirit, and hence he was admitted by the Greeks as their former Phœbus and Hyperiôn. In the same character he was identified with Dionysus and Liber, or Phanaces the Sun-god of the Asiatics and his Mysteries replaced the ancient Dionysia. How important the Mithraica had become in the second century appears from the fact recorded by Lampridius, that Commodus the Emperor condescended to be initiated into them. With their penances and tests of the courage of the candidate for admission they have been maintained by a constant transition through the secret societies of the Middle Ages and the Rosicrucians, down the modern faint reflex of the latter, the Freemasons."

It may be remarked in this connection that reference to the Mithraic rites abound in the Book of *Revelation*. The rewards of those that overcome are generally like those of the successful candidates in the secret rites. The fiery dragon with seven heads and ten horns or rays of light forming a halo around them was a simulacrum of the seven-headed Serpent of Akkad and Assyria, which the Zoroastrian believers were destined to destroy. There appears to have been but little difference between the several religions in the earlier centuries of our era. Augustin of Hippo quoted the assertion of the Mithraic priests that their divinity "himself was Christian." The copper coins of Constantine bore the symbol and acknowledgment—the "image and superscription"—of the Unconquered Sun, the *Comes* or soldier; and everybody knows that the 25th of December was from time immemorial celebrated as the Birthday of Mithras. Chrysostom, speaking of the appointing of Christmas at the same time, thus explains the reason: "It was so fixed at Rome in order that while the heathen were busied at their profane ceremonies, the Christians might perform their holy rites undisturbed."

Indeed, as Mr. King remarks, "there is very good reason to believe, that as in the East the worship of Serapis was at first combined with Christianity, and gradually merged into it with an entire change of name, not substance, carrying with it many of its ancient notions and rites; so, in the West, a similar influence was exerted by the Mithraic religion." Afterward the arbitrary decree of Theodosius I, prohibited the further observance of the worship, and the Roman pontiffs in their turn denounced it as sorcery and actual compact with the powers of Evil. Yet it continued for many centuries among the *pagans*, or country-people.

In another direction the Zoroastrian influence accomplished nobler results. Even before the conquest of Babylon, the dominion of Persia had been extended from India to the Hellespont. There appeared from this very time a new energy in speculative thinking. Wherever the Zoroastrian doctrine was introduced philosophy began a career. The Ionic and other schools dated from this historic period.

The criticism has sometimes been made that there was little of a philosophic nature in the Zoroastrian literature. We are not required to be so nice in our distinctions. The *Avastâ* is everywhere ethical, and like all ancient writings, essentially religious. All philosophy takes religious veneration for its starting-point. We are free, likewise, to define religion, as Cicero did, to be a profounder reading of the truth. But it was held anciently to include the entire domain of knowledge. Even here, the *Avastâ* was not deficient. The *Nosks* treated of religion, morals, civil government, political economy, medicine, botany, astronomy, and other sciences. The students of the Zoroastrian lore were therefore proficient scholars. Dêmokritos, of Abdera, who was educated by Persians and professed their religion, was distinguished as a physician and philosopher. He became no less advanced in later years in the Egyptian learning, which he endeavoured to show was similar to the Wisdom of the East.

It is stated, that Thalês, the founder of the Ionian philosophy, spent much time in Egypt and was admitted to familiar converse with the priests of Memphis. Yet his utterances are clearly Zoroastrian. Water, he declared, is the first principle of things : and God is the Intelligence that formed all things out of water. "God is the most ancient," said he, "for he had no genesis : the universe is the most beautiful, because it is the workmanship of God." He taught also that spiritual essences, intelligent and immortal, like the Frohars of the *Avastâ*, pervaded the universe. Anaximenês represented the first principle as æther or divine air possessing consciousness that animated all things. All souls were of the divine substance and the body was evolved therefrom. Pythagoras elaborated the system that bears his name. He had been instructed by the Egyptian priests ; yet his doctrines were essentially Zoroastrian. His biographers declared that he learned them of the sage Zaratas at Babylon. He established the first school of philosophy at Samos, and then at Krotôn, in Italy, with the peculiar characteristics of a secret brotherhood.

Hêrakleitos denominated the elemental principle FIRE ; which, however, was a spiritual and intellectual essence, and not a gross corporeal flame. From it all things emanate and into it they return. This is evidently the cardinal principle of fire-worship as inculcated by the Zoroastrians. The light of Ahura-Mazda, says the hymn, is *hidden* under all that shines. Hêrakleitos also taught that the soul possesses the power to cognise the real truth, while the senses can only perceive that which is variable and particular. The living on earth is a dying from the life of the eternal world, and death is a returning thither. Two other Ionians, Xenophanês and Parmenidês, inculcated the identity of "real being" with thought and knowledge. The perceiving of truth is by intellection; the knowledge obtained by the senses is only apparent. They also taught the existence of two principles, Light and Darkness, the former of which was the essential fire, positive, real, and intellectual ; the other cold, negative, and a limitation of the other. After all these great thinkers had fulfilled their mission, Plato rose and placed the cope-stone on their work. He gathered up all that had been taught by those before him, both Ionian and Oriental, including the under-meanings of the Mysteries, and presented it in a new form and rendering. The Dialectic of Plato has been the text-book of scholars in the Western World, as the Dialogues of Zoroaster with Ahura-Mazda constituted the sacred literature of the Wise Men of the Far East.

A melancholy interest hangs about the later history of the Mazdean religion. The fine gold became dim. The centuries of Parthian rule enabled the Magians to realise the dream of Gomata and make themselves the exponents of the Zoroastrian; and when the restoration took place, the change had been made permanent. For centuries their influence penetrated far into the Christian world. The armies of Mohammed, however, arrested its triumphal progress, and overthrew it in its own native seats. Persecution and massacres have reduced the numbers of the adherents to a few thousands, living in Kirman and Bombay. Yet the leaven of truth which it carries has sufficed to preserve it from utter extinction, and it bids fair to continue for centuries.

This grand religious system has been little known and studied. Its magnitude and influence has been underrated. Yet ages have proved unequal to the effort for its overthrow. It has survived the torch of Alexander and the cimeter of the Moslem. Millions upon millions have been put to death for their adhesion to the "pure religion;" yet wherever it survives it is manifest as the wisdom justified by her children. The moral virtues, truth, chastity, industry and universal beneficence, which are found inculcated in the earliest fragments of the *Avastâ*, and which were characteristic of the Persians of the age of Cyrus, are even now the peculiarities of this remarkable people. "No nation deserves better," says Miss Cobbe, "that we should regard their religion with respect, and examine its sacred literature with interest, than the 120,000 Parsis of India—the remnant of the once imperial race of Cyrus and Darius."

Enough, that the ethics and philosophy of Mazdean religion have been wholesome in their influence and a potent leaven to promote the fermentation of thought. Even to our own day we know and felt it. " So much is there in this old creed of Persia in harmony with our popular belief to-day," Miss Cobbe remarks, " that we inevitably learn to regard it with a sort of hereditary interest, as a step in the pedigree of thought much more direct in our mental ancestry than the actual faith of our Odin-worshipping ancestors according to the flesh."

This conviction is founded on a firm ground-work. Zoroastrianism has mingled with the deepest thoughts of the centuries, purifying wherever it was present. The current from that fountain has flowed for thousands of years, fertilising as it went. Everywhere, in whatever form it has appeared, it had always the same idea foremost, the overcoming of evil with good, the triumph of right over wrong.

ALEXANDER WILDER.

—*Journal of the American " Akadêmê,"* November 1885, *extracted from "Theosophical Siftings,"* Vol. vii, No. 10.

THE ETHICAL SYSTEM OF ZOROASTER.

WHILE studying the sacred books of the "Fire-worshippers," as they have been most erroneously styled, I have many times felt impelled to render mental homage to the magnificent system of ethics therein laid down. It is, I know, a common assertion, that ethics must necessarily be the same in all true religions, and as far as fundamentals are concerned, this would seem to be so, but it is rarely that one meets with such an eminently practical whilst highly philosophical presentation of ethical truths as is afforded us in the Zoroastrian Scriptures; for not only are the ethics themselves of the highest grandeur, but the philosophic explanation given with them is so clear and unmistakable, that conviction of their essential truth must follow and fasten on the student from the very first.

Now I believe that all ethics to be of any value must be founded upon the unassailable rock of Divinity. They must bear, so to speak, "the guinea-stamp" clearly and readably impressed in their substance; they must carry the image and superscription of the Divine, to pass as current coin which all can honour; and I hope to be able to shew that the ethical teachings of Zoroaster fulfil these demands to the fullest extent.

The ultimate conception of Zoroaster was the Unity of God—a Unity which to him could only be looked upon as Goodness, and this Divine Unity is at the root of his ethical teachings.

It will be necessary here that I should attempt to shew you what was meant by the One God, as Zoroastrianism has generally been looked upon as a Dualism. That this was not always the fact is abundantly apparent from a cursory examination of the sacred books. God, or, as Zoroaster styled him, Ahura-Mazda, is never looked upon as *a* God, in the sense of personality; on the contrary, He is "The All-Being" on the manifested plane of being. He is thus the same as the "Logos" of St. John—the Word which was in the beginning with God and which *was* God. He is the first born out of Boundless Time (Zeroana), but not therefore limited by time, but had existed in Eternity in Boundless Time. As Unity he is All. We have, therefore, under the foundation of Zoroastrian ethics the conception of a Divine Unity, whose only attribute is Goodness.

But such a conception is, to ordinary man, necessarily incomprehensible. He perceives in nature and himself a duality which ever appears as two opposing forces—good and evil, light and darkness, life and death—and immediately there arises in his mind the idea of a principle of evil warring against the God of Goodness; not necessarily coëternal, for he may grasp the idea that at the end of all things Goodness will be supreme and the spirit of evil have perished; but for man, this duality must have existed from the beginning of all things—that is, from the beginning of manifestation. In this lies the dualism which is so apparent on the surface of Zoroaster's teachings.

In one of the first of his recorded orations he proclaimed: "In the beginning there were a pair of twins—two spirits, each active; these are the good and the base, in thought, word and deed"; but not only does he never appear to dogmatise as to the independent existence of these two principles, but he endeavours to explain the true nature of the duality, and the sum of his explanation seems to be that these two principles inhere in *our* conception of the nature of the one God: the one principle being constructive, the other destructive; one creates, moulds and fashions; the other decomposes and disintegrates; but only thereby coöperating in creation by providing, so to speak, fresh raw material for creative energy to set in form, and these two forces are set in operation by the One Reality as ministers for the maintenance of the Universe.

But it must be apparent to you that these two principles

have their birth only in the mind of man (in itself a duality), who, unable to understand the All-Being, postulates this dual aspect of the One Reality to explain to himself the various phenomena of nature.

Descending then from the conception of the All-Goodness, the Teacher recognises that man is somehow separated therefrom; knowing good only by reason of the action of evil, he is limited by a duality and regarded as a free agent moving between these two poles, may elect to unite himself with the one or the other. Zoroaster therefore, having, as I have pointed out, acknowledged the duality, as far as man is concerned, goes on—" Choose one of these two spirits! Be good, not base;" and from what follows may be drawn the inference that choosing, you shall either be coöperators with Goodness in manifestation, thereby gaining immortality, or pass to the ranks of those who destroy and who must ultimately perish.

Now man, recognising himself as a centre of consciousness moving between two poles, partaking more or less of the nature of both, may be looked upon as a trinity, being thus the reflex of God on earth, and just as what we may term Divine Ideation (for want of a better phrase) is revealed to man by means of the duality in nature, so the *thought* of man is revealed by *word* and *act*; not by one or the other, but by both, and then only in so far as these can represent the thought.

Man, therefore, being a trinity in his nature, from whichever standpoint we regard him, whether as Body, Soul and Spirit—Bad, Good or Indifferent, as may please us, hangs, like a spark from the Divine, between Heaven and Hell, and any system of ethics by which he is to regulate his behaviour must directly deal with this threefold nature, and here the alphabet of Zoroastrian ethics begins.

Having made the choice for Good, how is the man to attain to the goal? By Good Thought, Good Word and Good Deed.

Bearing in mind what I have previously said with regard

to the revelation of the Divine and the human, you will, I think, perceive that the code here formulated in such simplicity, is founded upon the ultimate conceptions of Divinity which can be realised by man. I need hardly point out to you that "Good Thought" (which, by the way, is the title of one of the Ameshaspentas or seven archangels of Ahura-Mazda) corresponds to what I have called "Divine Ideation," Universal Mind, the Logos or Word, which was in the beginning with God and which was God; and that "Good Word" corresponds, in its highest aspect, to one pole of that thought, whilst "Good Deed" represents the other pole (this in world celestial). Word and act, as I have before stated, are the vehicles whereby thought becomes manifest; hence the beginning, middle and end of Zoroastrian ethics are to be found in these three.

Zoroaster recognises man as a free agent—that is, he is free to move between two poles, which are the ultimates of his conception, and he therefore appeals to his hearers asking them to choose between the good and the base—" Be servants of Ahura, not of Ahuriman!" and since the aim of his teaching is to secure the union of all men with the Supreme, who is all Good, the method of attainment must be by the ordering of every thought, word and deed according to the highest conception of good which man form.

Thus every man, whatever his condition, is able to lay hold of these methods of action, and fixing his ideal where he may, act systematically towards its attainment, being certain all the while that though his ideal be a poor one, yet he has all possibilities beyond it, and he is all the time progressing to a higher stage of development.

I have heard many earnest Christians say, "Well, the Heaven of theology seems but a poor place after all. So much rest, so much joy, so much spiritual knowledge, and so on, together with a draught of Lethe (forgetfulness as to 'our brothers gone astray'), but always falling short of the highest," and I have sometimes answered in the words of Swinburne—" and if higher than Heaven be the reach of the soul, shall not Heaven bow down?" Others have said that "to be one with Christ can alone satisfy them"; yet when I asked whether they mean in sorrow or in joy, it is generally in the latter that their ideal stands. As good old Thomas à Kempis has said—"All desire to rejoice with Him; few are willing to endure anything for Him or with Him."

Still these ideals are worth striving for, if only on attainment we are to find them empty of satisfaction. They may be likened to the jutting crags which front the mountain side; attaining one we have a wider sweep of vision and soon espy a higher crag to scale, while yet the peak is hid in clouds. And the triple talismanic gem which Zoroaster offers to his disciples is alike effective on the plane of airy height. It is not alone for use by those who sense the soul of things and swim the deeps of Spirit, but for him who has not learned to swim and paddles near the water's brim; who lives his life in one small village, so to speak, knowing naught of the life of "The Great Beyond"; he whose day begins and ends in manual toil; whose mind is bent on driving true the furrow, sowing, harvesting that he may eat and live—a blameless happy life. Helping nature he coöperates with Nature's Lord, and the earth and man are better for his being.

And it was probably to a simple pastoral people that Zoroaster's message was delivered—a people moving among their flocks and herds, tilling the soil and living largely agricultural lives; and we find that special instructions were given them as to the care of the earth, and to till the soil was almost a religious duty. It was certainly looked upon as a most meritorious occupation.

To such a people, then, Zoroaster's teaching of Good—Good—Good, otherwise purity in all respects, must necessarily demand an outward manifestation, and this we find to be the case, for just as the thought, word and act must be pure, so must the vehicles of these be kept untainted; accordingly we have in the teachings a sanitary code which it would be difficult to improve upon, even in these days of asserted cleanliness and improved sanitation.

The Teacher evidently grasped the stern facts of the modes of life before him, and whilst endeavouring to raise his fellows mentally and spiritually, would not neglect their physical environment. It has been claimed very often in the present day, as in the past, that man is largely a slave to his environment, and whilst this is to some extent true, yet the grand exceptions of men and women rising out of the vilest social conditions to pinnacles of mankind's estimation and regard, prove that the slavery is no reality, but a mirage which the ever-rising sun of intellect and virtue may dispel at any moment. Still we find there are those amongst us who are hampered in their upward climb by dirt and squalor engendered by our present modes of congested life in large cities; and it is asserted by many very earnest people, that before you can expect a higher morality to obtain amongst our "submerged tenth" you must provide them with better environment. I believe this to be a reasonable statement, though I do not hold that environment necessarily rules the moral sense; yet on the old doctrine of *mens sana in corpore sana* there does seem to be a reasonableness in their demand for better physical conditions, if we would reap higher moral results. You see, the things of sense weave a veil before the Thinker which tends to obscure his vision; and since in the elementary stages of moral culture, we are bound to work by means of these *present* senses, it does appear to me that it will be easier for us to conceive and realise the higher ideals out of the senses which are "The Builders" on this lower plane of consciousness, if the things of sense are of a nobler type—as it is easier for the mind of the devotee to raise itself in aspiration to the Divine, when the temple is swept and garnished, than when the altar itself is befouled and all around speaks of discord—hell.

Now if we would train a baby intellect we do not start with metaphysics, but by means of toys and games, of simple songs and pictured forms we seek to draw the intellect out from its hiding place by gradual and easy stages. So, Zoroaster has milk for babes and stronger meat for those whose growth demands it. Every man, woman and child is thought to be pure, clean and wholesome within and without; and every act of purity is God's good work, however small it be. The earth man walks on, the house he inhabits, the clothes that cover him, the food he eats, the water he drinks or washes in, all are to be kept pure, and many are the laws laid down for the preservation of this sacred purity. Vowed to the Good and Pure, he must, in every act hold purity before him, thus being a helper of Ahura in the manifestation of His Goodness. That the primitive instructions of the Master have been overlaid with much which to us seems childish or superstitious, may be the case, but that it has had a definite and, physically speaking, good effect upon the race is unquestionable. Samuel Laing states that the Parsi, who, as you are probably aware, are the modern representatives of the ancient Zoroastrians, have the lowest death-rate of any of the many races which inhabit Bombay, shewing incontestibly their greater vitality and care for human life. And when it is added that the Parsis are renowned the world over for their probity, high morality, intellectuality and benevolence, it does seem as though the body of teaching contained in the Avastâ was indeed a priceless treasure.

A disciple of Zoroaster was then taught to seek only after the good, the true and the beautiful. All his life was to be attuned to these; the senses were to be kept pure by operating on things of purity, and when the man communed with his soul it was through these three qualities that he learned to know his God. Tradition tells of altars raised on rocky heights whence the eye might roam over a glad bright world bathed in the light of God's angel, the sun; telling the heart the all was good, and if, in after ages, men with eyes less spiritual could not see beyond the symbol, and lifted up their prayers and praises to that minister of God filled with love and simple adoration for the glorious gifts of light and life, of strength and beauty, are we the ones to carp and sneer ; we professing Christians who lately bent the knee to dead-men's bones, or bought a pardon with a gilded shrine?

But the lowliest follower of Zoroaster knew even then, as he knows to-day, that the sun which men have given him for a God, is but a symbol of Ahura, and fire is the sun's representative on earth. Thus though the Parsi may turn sunwards or to the fire upon the altar, in contemplative worship, it is only that he may by these pure symbols be enabled to understand to some slight extent the glory lying far beyond them.

We are all children of the sun in the sense that we draw our light, our food, and clothing from him, but more preëminently because he reveals himself to us as the giver of life—that is, earthly life, and surely there can be no fitter emblem of the One Life than the sun whose rays reach the limits of the universe, and are echoed back from myriad worlds, and which live in all that lives and die not, though their form may change. Animal, plant and stone alike were sunbeams once. I know of no grander symbol save the sign of Love Eternal —Witoba crucified in space, the Christos on the tree.

Purity in thought, word and deed is then the standard whereby the life is to be measured, and it may be of interest to very briefly run over the list of sins which are held up to reprobation.

It must be remembered that in Zoroastrian philosophy sin differs somewhat from our Western conception. Sin with the orthodox Christian may exist independent of man, as an Evil Principle who may use man as a vehicle for the manifestation of himself. Now with the Zoroastrian it is rather the attitude of man himself to The Universal Law which produces sin. A moment's consideration will shew that evil is the result of the imperfect manifestation of that One Law, which itself is perfect Unity, but which man makes twofold as it conflicts or agrees with his desires.

The code includes the following greater sins: murder in all

its forms,—whether by violence, poison or otherwise—adultery, unnatural sins, giving false weight or measure, lying and cheating by word of mouth or in act, breach of promise, slander, stealing, misappropriation of monies or property belonging to those who work for us, receiving bribes, removing land-marks, and many others connected with these. There is also a code dealing more particularly with the mental and psychic man than with the physical, which includes egotism and selfishness of all kinds, envy and want of charity, laziness, and neglect of parental and other home duties.

One point of doctrine in regard to sin is worthy of note—that every crime committed renders the criminal liable to a double penalty—one in this world and the other in the next world; yet while it appears that the penalty in this world cannot be done away with, it is curious to find that a system of atonements crops up in the Pahlavi translations, and the commentary mentions three forms of atonement—one by money, one by the whip (these for this world) and the third by repentance, of which the outward manifestation is the recitation of a certain formula (Patit). This latter only applies to the other world, and no amount of repentance rids one of the penalty to be paid in this world. I am inclined to think, with regard to these atonements, that they do not form any part of Zoroaster's teaching, but were the garnishings of priestcraft, overlaid upon the original teachings to which they seem foreign in spirit. As, however, it was customary in many cases of grave sin to hold over the earthly penalty, which meant death by stripes or decapitation, until old age, it is evident that repentance was not considered to consist in the recitation of any particular formula, but in a turning away from a certain course and by endeavouring to live a better life to, so to speak, put a credit item against the debit account in the world to come.

Now whilst the formula of the Patit or renunciation of sin has to be made in strict form to the priest, that priest is only the instrument which appoints the means of atonement on the *physical* plane there is no remission of sins by reason of priestly authority, for it is distinctly taught in the Shayastla Shayast that such remission is only obtainable by the due performance of the atonement and the effectual determination to avoid any repetition of the sin; in other words, the atonement is only to be achieved by ceasing to sin.

And now a word as to the interior life of the Zoroastrian—I mean the soul life—as apart from that of the man of physical action and social environment. How is the man to approach the inner shrine, having by means of his threefold key gained admittance to the temple? The key he must retain in his possession; for by it alone can other doors be opened; but in order to draw near to Ahura he needs also a guide.*

Now in the teachings we find constant references to Yazatas or angels, and Fravashis—these latter more particularly appearing as the guardian spirits of men; but the greatest of these appears to be the Sarosh, and I must ask your indulgence while I endeavour to shew what I think is meant by Sarosh.

In Yasna 57 we find Sarosh described as a Yazata or angel; beautiful, victorious, having magical weapons; the protector and guardian, the guide through whom man may approach Ahura. He is likewise compared to a flame; is styled the "mediator between Ahura and man." Particularly during sleep is he our protector. The word Sarosh, says Mr. Bilimoria, is derived from the root "S'ru" to hear, and this throws a further light on the nature of this guardian angel, for all the attributes given to him and all we are told of his combats with demons, are those of "The Christos," "The Word" of St. John, the "Higher Ego" of theosophy. He is "The Shining and Resplendent One," and the same as the Augoeides of the Neo-Platonists.

Recognising, then, as his true guide along spiritual paths, his own Higher Ego, the aspirant withdraws himself from

---

* "Give me, O Fire, son of Ahura Mazda! [One] who can instruct me what is best for me now and forevermore, concerning the best life of the Pure, Brilliant, All-glorious!"—*Yasna*, Hâ 62.

objects of sense, and with ears closed to the noise of the world, eyes blind to earthly things, listens for "The Voice of the Fire " to speak in his heart ; endeavouring with the eyes of soul to see "The Master" he as yet knows not, yet feels is present. Those of you who have read that most instructive chapter on "The Higher Manas," in Annie Besant's No. 1 Manual, will, I think, appreciate the mental attitude of the devotee.

The devotee is to endeavour to rise himself into communion with his Higher Ego, who is alone the way, the truth and the life for him ; but this can only be done by means of the practice of the three virtues on the mental and soul planes, and, says Mr. Bilimoria, in the article already quoted from, " before Sarosh can manifest in us, the mind has to be trained in a certain way and we have to purge ourselves of all sins, evil thoughts, evil words and evil deeds ; bodily and psychic,—earthly and heavenly."

From the foregoing, I think you will now be in a position to form a just estimate of the ethical value of what has been called "The Excellent Religion"—excellent in its simple grandeur ; appealing not alone to the intellectual giant, but also to the untutored shepherd—a religion which has played no small part in the mighty past and whose echoes still linger among us to-day. If I had the time and you the patience to listen to me, I could point to its footprints down the ages in this or that religion or philosophy, and in every case the feet which have brought the message of "Purity, Purity," have left the world the better for their passage.

It was the fashion years ago to ask "Can any good thing come out of Nazareth ? " when the teachings of what were called Pagan religions were brought forward to our notice, but there is a broader and more open mind to-day, and men are more ready to give credit where credit is due. The once despised Fire-worshippers are spoken of and looked upon as a race whose record is clear and clean ; whose lives are models for many who have hitherto considered themselves as the salt of the earth. Their sacred books are being compared with those of Christianity; articles dealing with this comparative study are to be found in our leading reviews; theological bug-bears are having a flood of light thrown on them by the process, and true religion receiving fresh strength.

All this is but natural, for there is nothing in the Zoroastrian teachings which will debase, for it is alone the true, the good and the beautiful which are their highest ideals, and these are no fixed points of man's imagination, but find their ultimate only in "the One which is All."

They who saw in fire and sun the ministers of God's good will, made no image of the Imageless, and here the followers of Zoroaster stand out as an example to all ages, not less to us with our "masters of painting"—profaning the majesty of Divinity by representing "The Eternal" as a venerable man of severe countenance, seated on pillows of clouds!—can we dare to say the Parsi has ever fallen so low?

Let me conclude by quoting Tom Moore's well-known lines which well represent the idea hidden behind what we, in our arrogance of intellect, have styled "the worship of the Powers of Nature."

> Thou art, O God! the life and light
> Of all this wondrous world we see;
> Its glow by day, its smile by night
> Are but reflections caught from Thee.
> Where'er we turn, Thy glories shine
> And all things fair and bright are Thine.
> When day, with farewell beam delays,
> Among the opening clouds of even;
> And we can almost think we gaze
> Through golden vistas into heaven;
> Those hues, that make the sun's decline
> So soft, so radiant, Lord, are Thine.
> When night, with wings of starry gloom
> O'ershadows all the earth and skies,
> Like some dark, beautious bird, whose plume
> Is sparking with unnumbered eyes:—
> That sacred gloom, those fires divine,
> So grand, so countless, Lord! are Thine.

When youthful spring around us breathes,
Thy spirit warms her fragrant sigh ;
And every flower the summer wreathes,
Is born beneath that kindling eye.
Where'er we turn Thy glories shine,
And all things fair and bright are Thine."

BAKER HUDSON.

—*The Theosophist*, Vol. xvii, No. 7.

GOD, MAN AND MEDIATOR.

INTRODUCTORY.

BEFORE commencing a consideration of the teachings of the Zoroastrian system, it may be well for us to devote a few moments to the history of the people called Irânian, who became followers of Zoroaster, and to see how this Sage's doctrines became modified. I shall collect, chiefly from Monier Williams, the materials for this purpose.

The Irânians were an offshoot of what is called the Aryan Stock, but the designation "Irânian" ought not, strictly, to be applied to them until after their migration into Persia, it being a term derived from Erân or Irân, the name given to Ancient Persia. For purposes of distinction I will designate the people who afterwards passed into Persia as Irâno-Aryans, and that branch, which passed southwards into the Panjab and contiguous regions, the Indo-Aryans.

Now there was a time, says Monier Williams, at least 2.000 B.C., when these two peoples lived as fellow-countrymen along with, possibly, the ancestors of Englishmen and of the principal European nations, in some central region of Asia, possibly the Hindu-Kush usually known as the Pamirs. They spoke the same language, worshipped the same gods, obeyed the same laws and were called by the same name "Arya"—excellent or noble. The climate was cold and ungenial though capable of producing a hardy race, partly nomad in their habits, partly agricultural, who very soon multiplied beyond the capacity of the soil to support the entire population. Migration became a necessity. A part descended into Hindustan, others occupied the Highlands north of Cabul, or, following the course of the Oxus, settled in what was afterwards called Bactria, and these latter were the ancestors of the Irâno-Aryans.

Now when the Indo-Aryans settled in the valley of the Indus, and the Irâno-Aryans in that of the Oxus, their language, customs, ideas and religion must have been nearly identical; and here I would point out that the time of the separation of these races seems to me to have been much more remote than the 3,800 years Monier Williams gives as a minimum ; for most Oriental scholars are agreed that in all probability the Rig-Veda is at least 4,000 years old; and, as pointed out by Mr. Laing,* the divergence between its form of Sanskrit and the Gâthâ dialect of the Zend in which the oldest Zoroastrian books are written, is quite as great as that between kindred European languages, such as Greek and Latin; and further, the divergence in religious expression is also very early ; as in the Hindu and all other races of the Aryan stock the word used for Gods and good spirits is taken from the root "Div"— to shine. Thus Deva in Sanskrit, Zeus and Theos in Greek, Deus in Latin, Tius in German, Dia in Erse, Dew in Cymric— all meaning "the Bright One;" but in the Iranian the word has the opposite sense, corresponding to Devil or Evil One.

At the time of their settlement, then, whenever that was, these races were probably identical in habits, customs and religion, but no sooner did they begin their new life in their adopted countries than differences began to be developed.

As I intend to merely deal with the religious part of the subject I shall confine my remarks thereto, leaving to the philologist the interesting questions of speech modification.

Turning to the earliest Aryan designation for Divine Beings and comparing some of the names still in use among both Irâno-Aryans and Indo-Aryans, we find that the generic name for gods was Devas and special names were given to the Sun, Fire and Air, such as Mitra (melting), Âthar (piercing) and Vâyu or Vâta (blowing), while the earliest name for the all-investing Deity of Heaven was either Dyaus (the Luminous One) or Varuna (the All-Invester) or Asura (the Breather or Blower). In India, Asura-Varuna became Brahmâ (the Expander), though the worship of the Devas, as manifested by the Sun, Fire and Air, was also encouraged amongst the masses.

---

* "A Modern Zoroastrian."

In Bactria, however, where the people lived chiefly an agricultural life on a less productive soil than their brethren in India, the worship of Devas was more persistent, though their homage was also given to The One Eternal, All-Pervading Spirit of Heaven, or, as they called him, Ahura ; but in course of time the gap between the races widened, shewing strongly where the Irâno-Aryans were in close contact with more idolatrous races and also hastened by their quarrels and controversies with their Indian brothers. The latter having formed a caste of warriors generally came off best in these engagements and it was observed that before going into battle they invoked the aid of the Devas. "What was more natural," says Monier Williams, "than that feelings of hatred for some of these Devas should spring up in the hearts of the Irâno-Aryans." To them the word became synonymous with Demon, and similarly the word Asura, which was cherished by the Irâno-Aryans, acquired a similar reversal and, concludes the author, "it is certain that the quarrels of the two peoples formed the historic basis of the legendary accounts of constant warfare between Gods and Demons—Devas and Asuras—which abound in Sanskrit Literature."

At such a time, when under the clouds of superstition, and loss of faith, and with gods and demons of their own creating, came Zoroaster's message, bidding them fix their faith on The One Living God—Ahura—from that time to be known as Ahura-Mazda (The Great and Wise Ahura).

I do not propose to consider whether Zoroaster was a mythical personage or not, but shall accept the name as applying to the Teacher, or Teachers if need be, who revolutionised the thought of the nation. There is considerable variation as to the date of this religious revival, the figures ranging among various authors between 500 and 8,200 B. C.*

It is first to be noted that, like Jesus, Buddha and other

---

* Eudoxus and Aristotle say 6,000 before Plato or about 8,200 years ago. Berosus makes Zoroaster a King of Babylon 2,200 B.C. Bunsen says 3,000 B.C. Haug says at least 1,000 B.C.

great teachers, Zoroaster is said to have proclaimed himself as a reformer, not the bringer of a *new* religion, and that his mission was to abolish Deva-worship and idolatry as fatal to body and soul, and to spread the truth of beliefs in one God. He meant, however, to deal respectfully with the ancient creed; he was no vandal. He was to perpetuate the adoration of Fire (Âthar), the son of Ahura, that is, his first-born or primal manifestation, as the symbol of the Deity. He was to perpetuate even some of the names of the Devas, such as Mitra and Airyaman—only, they were no longer to be worshipped as gods, but to be looked upon merely as angels. In such connection it is interesting to recall the words of Jesus: "Think not that I am come to destroy the law or the Prophets—I come not to destroy, but to fulfill."

So came Zoroaster as a purifier; one more, I believe, of that Immortal Band who, say the Hindus, arise whenever faith begins to get weak in the world. Zoroaster came then as a reformer, and we should remember that the science of comparative theology is demonstrating to-day that what is called a false religion is the result, not of its fundamental doctrines, but of the perversions and exaggerations of those doctrines.

There is a story in the Books of the Parsis which states that the Reformer called his countrymen together before the Sacred Fire and thus addressed them :—

"I will now tell you, who are here assembled, the wise sayings of Mazda, the praises of Ahura, the sublime truth which I see arising out of these sacred flames.

"Contemplate the beams of fire with a pious mind: every one, both men and women, ought to-day to choose between the Deva and the Ahura religion.

"In the beginning, there was a pair of twins, two spirits, each active; these are the good and the base, in thought, word and deed. Choose one of these two spirits! Be good, not base.

"And these two spirits created : one—the reality, the other the non-reality. To the liar existence will become bad, whilst the believer in the True God enjoys prosperity.

"Thus, let us be such as keep the life of the future. The *wise living spirits* are the greatest supporters of it. The prudent man wishes only to be there where wisdom is at home."

The 12th Chapter of the Yaçna gives the early form of the Zoroastrian creed, of which the following is the principal portion :—

"I join in putting an end to the worship of Devas. I profess myself a believer in Mazda the Omniscient, as taught by Zarathushtra, I am a follower of the law of Ahura. All the universe I attribute to the Wise and Good Ahura-Mazda, the Pure, the Majestic. Everything is His, the earth and the starry firmament. I denounce sorcery and all other evil knowledge. I denounce false gods and those believing in them, with sincerity of thought, word and deed. Thus Ahura-Mazda has taught Zarathushtra in the several conferences that took place between them."

Ahura-Mazda was then the Creator—matter was created (made manifest) by him and was neither identical with Him nor an emanation from Him. He is to be regarded as the sole source of Life, Light, Goodness, Wisdom and Creative Power; He is, therefore, I think, the same as Brahmâ, the Universal Logos.

And here we must linger a while to consider what Zoroaster thought and taught with regard to this Supreme Spirit, as herein lies the key to the apparent dualism of the Parsis.

Zoroaster apparently believed in the constant conflict of evil with good, in the manifested world, but so far as is provable from that part of the Avastâ assignable to him, he never formulated any precise dogma of an eternal independent existence of two opposing good and evil principles, though he did attempt an explanation of the origin of evil which afterwards developed into dualism. This explanation was:—That the two opposites, but not on that account really opposing principles or forces, which he calls twins, were eternal in God's nature and were set in action by him as his appointed mode of maintaining the continuity of the Universe,—the one being constructive the other destructive. One created, moulded and fashioned, the other decomposed and disintegrated, but only to coöperate in the act of creation by providing, so to speak, fresh raw material for creative energy. There could be no life without death, no existence without non-existence, no light without darkness, no reality without unreality, no truth without falsehood, not good without evil.

Now here, it seems to me, we have an exact parallel with the Indian Vishnu, or rather with the Triad of which Vishnu, is the front face. Brahmâ-Prajâpati, the creative constructor, and Shiva, the Destroyer or Disintegrator, revealed as Vishnu the All-Pervader; which latter is also one of the titles of Ahura.

The creative force was to be looked upon as Ahura-Mazda's beneficent spirit or Spento-Mainyus; the destructive or differentiating agency was his malificent spirit or Aṅra-Mainyus, which name was afterwards corrupted into Ahriman. The two principles were only to be looked upon as conflicting in name; they were in reality mutually helpful and coöperative and essential to cosmic being. The only antagonism was between the resulting good and evil, reality and unreality; truth and falsehood *brought about by the free agent man*, who could assist or disturb the processes of Nature, retard or hasten the operation of the laws of creation and destruction according to his own free will and election.*

This was the philosophical attempt at explanation offered by Zoroaster to account for the apparently opposing forces in nature; and his teaching of the essential Unity is re-echoed by Isaiah (chapter 45, verses 6 and 7): "I am the Lord and there is none else. I form the light, and create darkness; I make peace and create evil : I the Lord do all these things."

---

* This may cast a light upon a matter of much trouble to Christians, who often puzzle why they should pray to their Father in Heaven, "Lead us not into temptation," I believe, and Madame Blavatsky says in the Secret Doctrine it is addressed to the terrible spirit of duality in man himself.

With the migration of the disciples of Zoroaster into Persia, however, we find modifications appearing, possibly due to the exoteric form of Magism which appears to have been, for the masses, the worship of the personified forces of Nature, of the Sun, Moon and Elements and the hosts of Heaven. I need hardly say that we who have had the advantage of reading the work of H. P. Blavatsky, dealing with the symbology of all theologies, are probably little inclined to look upon the Magians as blindly pantheistical, Western Orientalists notwithstanding. Whatever may be our opinion, however, it is certain that Zoroaster's teachings and those of Magism not only touched hands on many points, but actually blended to some extent, but every now and again we hear of reformers springing up to preach the old doctrine, and, as we are informed in a carved inscription, Darius the King claims to have made a text of the Divine Law (Avastâ) with a commentary and translation. He concludes "It was written and I sealed it and then the ancient book was restored by me in all nations," &c.

With the decline of the Persian Empire came another falling off in religions matters and at the time of Alexander the Great the Avastâ was nearly stamped out and it is alleged that he even tried to destroy all the sacred writings.

About 225 A. D., however, a great revival set in,—the scattered fragments of the Avastâ were collected, Pahlavi translations were made for the people who could no longer understand the Avastâ language.

. . . . .

It was after the migration into Persia that the dualism so pronounced afterwards began to make itself felt, and Zoroaster's undefined dualistic ideas became crystallised, so to say, into absolute dualism. The Spento-Mainyus (constructive energy) became another name for Ahura-Mazda or the Good Principle, whilst Aūra-Mainyus (the disintegrating energy) was looked upon as another self-existent, independent spirit of evil. Hence Ahura-Mazda, or, in Persian, Ormazd, and Ahriman were looked upon as two antagonistic principles wholly unconnected and always warring one against the other.

These two principles were further looked upon as septenary in their manifestation, hence we have them creating the upper and lower worlds of Archangels and Archdemons. The Upper world consisted of Ormazd and 6 Archangels (Amesha-Spentas), Ormazd being the seventh or synthesis of the whole; from the Archangels we have the creation of Angels and all downwards. Here it is well to remember that the Indo-Irânian God Asura* is frequently stated to be sevenfold* and is said to rule in his sevenfold nature over seven worlds; which worlds, says Darmesteter, in his translation of the Avastâ, "became in Persia the seven Karshvaras (regions) of the earth, *only one of which is accessible to man*, the one on which we live, namely, Khaniratha," which, concludes the Professor, "amounts to saying there are seven earths"; "Khaniratha," he explains, "is also divided into seven climes" and presumably the other six also.

Here appears an echo of the teachings of the Secret Doctrine. It may be of passing interest to give the translations of the names of the Amesha-Spentas which are " Good Thought," *i. e.*, divine thought, that which is "the Word" in man, Excellent Holiness, Perfect Sovereignty, Divine Poetry, Health and Immortality. These Amesha-Spentas are constantly invoked in their sevenfold unity as the friends and saviours of man. Moreover the seven were not regarded as separate units but a unity ; for we find an invocation in Yast 19, verse 16, " I invoke the glory of the Amesha-Spentas, who all seven have one and the same thinking, one and the same speaking, one and the same doing, one and the same Father and Lord— Ahura-Mazda."

Now the seven of the upper world projected, as it were, (says Darmesteter) out of themselves as many Demons, who either in their being of functions were, most of them, hardly

---

* In the Rig-veda primarily the "Asura" is used in good sense.

more than dim inverted images of the very gods they were to oppose and whom they followed throughout all their successive evolutions. Thus we have the formation of the lower world and its hierarchies—"*Demon est Deus inversus*"!

These seven, therefore, are the Avastâ counterparts of the Biblical "Seven of the Presence" and in their differentiated form appear as attributes, Ministers or Archangels of "That" which is their unification. They are, in their manifestations as Ahura-Mazda, the equivalent of Brahmâ, the Universal Logos. From the Amesha-Spentas emanate the Yazatas or secondary Angels styled in their totality "Sraosh" and in the later system Sraosh is looked upon as the synthesis of the whole; Ahura-Mazda being considered superior to all—Sraosh being his emanation.

Among the angels are those looked upon as Fravashis or Guardian Angels, as opposed to the evil spirits also attendant on Man. The attendant spirits of Man are, moreover, held to be of *four* kinds, so says the Favardin Yast:—1st, Those of departed heroes; 2nd, Those of future heroes; 3rd, *Those of Living Men*; and 4th, Those of all deceased persons. I would particularly ask you to make a note of the 3rd class—those of living men.

The formation of man as given in the Bundahish and in the Selections of Zâd-Sparam is highly esoteric and, though space at present precludes my dealing with it, I would certainly advise all students of the Secret Doctrine to make themselves acquainted with it. Very briefly, man is of the seed of Gayomard, the first created or primordial man—as I take it, the Adam-kadmon of the Kabalists (this tentatively—I have not had opportunity for research herein). This seed is thoroughly purified by the motion of the light of the Sun and two portions are given to the Angel Neryosang (the equivalent of Gabriel—?) and the third portion to the spirit of the Earth. This seed in 40 years grew up as the one-stemmed Rivas plant, whence come Matrô and Matroyâo, who are together male and female in one; afterwards they separated and became of opposite sexes. Thereafter they are looked upon as fallen, as is the case in the story of Genesis.

Now man, according to his deeds, belongs either to Ahura-Mazda or to Ahriman, while Heaven and Hell appear to be chiefly looked upon as mental states, dominated by either the principle of good or that of evil. In Yasna 30 it is said, "the two spirits came together at the first and determined how life at the last shall be ordered, for the wicked—the worst life (Hell); for the holy—the best mind" (Heaven); and it was further emphasised that man must be his own deliverer and Saviour as Yasna 46 says, "and this, which is such a life as your own—O ye Vile, your own deeds have brought you. Cursed by their souls and selves, for ever in the house of lives their bodies rest."

The Hindu God Yama appears in the Avastâ as Yima, who is styled the first king, the founder of civilization; and the best of mortals, after death, gather with him in Heaven (Mahâ-Loka?) awaiting the day on which they shall descend to repeople the earth when sin and death are conquered by Saoshyant.

Now a word about this latter. He is the Divine Messiah, of the seed of Zarathust. He is the Avatâr who is to come and at his coming he is "to lead captivity captive and have the keys of Death and of Hell"—to use the Apocalyptic phrase. He is to come at the end of this dispensation, or, as we may say, at the close of the Manvantara, and *a virgin* shall miraculously conceive and bear him. He shall free the world from death and decay, when *the dead shall rise* and immortality commence.

That the belief in the coming of a Messiah or Avatâr in the fulness of time is no new doctrine, is apparent since in Yasht 19 we read "Astavatereta (who is the same as Saoshyant, though the latter is a generic name, both however signifying "Saviour of the Restoration,") will arise from the waters of Kasava, a friend of Ahura-Mazda, a son of Vispatanarvi, the all-conquering, knowing the victorious knowledge which will make the world progress unto perfection."

Again, in Yasht 13, we learn "that 9,999 Fravashis of the faithful watch over the seed of Zarathushtra" whence the Saviour shall come. Now by implication it seems to me that Saoshyant is but another title for " The Son of Man," for, in the case of Saoshyant, he is to be of the seed of Zarathushtra, which is taken by the angel Neryosangh and the angel of the Earth to have in charge until the time is fulfilled. This is exactly what happened at the creation of man who is of the seed of Gayomard, the first created or primordial one, the same angels being connected with its preservation.

It is curious that in Christian Soteriology, Gabriel should be the annunciator, the bringer of good tidings, as in the Zoroastrian scheme.

Now as Zarathushtra is man, and the Son of Man of the seed of Gayomard—so is Saoshyant man of the seed of Zarathushtra. The internal meaning of this should be now apparent, for he that is to come is the Christ Spirit which shall be born in the latter days, immaculately conceived in the Soul of Man.

So do we touch hands with the ages ; and the thought of to-day has its roots in the past, its blooms in the future, and its fruit in enternity.

With regard to the dualism of the Parsis of to-day, Professor Darmesteter* says, " Some forty years ago, when the Reverend Doctor Wilson was engaged in his controversy with the Parsis, some of his opponents repelled the charge of dualism by denying to Ahriman any real existence and making him a symbolical personification of the bad instincts in Man, and this idea," he adds, " cannot be ascribed to any man or time, for there are some faint signs of it at the time when the old religion flourished." Max Müller says, "There is no trace of dualism in the earlier books"*; it is but the worship of the Logos, the Deity manifested in the world, the

---

* "Theosophy or Psychological Religion."

Word which in the beginning was, which was with God and which was God.

Of course the unconscious dualism lying *perdu* in this conception has given rise to the doctrine of Karma, not, however, called by the Indo-Aryan name, nevertheless Karma is a fundamental idea in Zoroastrianism which states that "there is a law in nature, and there is a war in nature. There is a God who fixed that never failing Law and on whom it rests for ever," and the workings of this Law are manifest in the war. The Law, as is Karma, is One that makes for righteousness, but in its connection with man appears as a duality—in one aspect beneficent, in the other punitive. Further, it is apparent from the philosophy as a whole that it is predicated that, though at present there appears this dual manifestation, yet Ahura will slowly bring everything under his unquestioned supremacy, all others, either gods or demons, being not only subservient but in actuality his creatures. This is made particularly clear in that part of the theogony relating to the emanation of the Archangels and their shadows, the Demons.

Whilst, therefore, we find in Zoroastrianism even in the early books an unconscious dualism, yet this duality is founded on Absolute Monotheism.

What then are we to say of Zoroastrianism ? It appears to me a very magnificent teaching. The belief in One Eternal Being to whom all is to be ascribed. In whom we live, and move and have our being ; who is our Father and our Brother ; nay, by the incarnation of his "Good Thought" (Vohu-Mano) our very "Self,"—the ladder on which we rise to Him being the good deeds of our life. Simple, yet grand in its very simplicity—small wonder is there that the people who still hold to this ancient revelation of Divinity are known for their probity, their gentleness, and kindness of heart the world over. We, in our Western home of *civilization*, may well take a lesson from this noble creed which is no stranger to our ears, though mayhap it has not yet touched the chords of our hearts, for is it not the teaching of Him who was despised and rejected of men : is it not the first and last word of Paul ; and is there a human heart in which it cannot find an echo to spur the soul to a higher and nobler life ?

Having to deal with a great mass of theology and theogony, it was impossible to go far beneath the surface, and anything more than the less esoteric matters could not receive due consideration in such a review.

Let us now dive a little below the surface in considering what we may term the "soul" of the religion of the " Fire-worshippers." I do not promise much, for the subject is difficult, but I wish to point out that if it is difficult thus to comprehend, in some small degree, the soul of a religion, what must the Spirit and real essence be ?

I shall divide my examination into three heads, " God," " Man" and " Mediation, " endeavouring to shew the inter-relationships.

GOD.

Now, the Deity of the Zoroastrians, sometimes called, half derisively, " Fire-worshippers," is styled Ahura-Mazda, or in Persian, Ormazd. He is the great Lord, the Lord of High Knowledge, Supreme in Omniscience and Goodness (Bundahish I). He is the King of Life, the First-born out of Boundless Time ; and the term first-born does not mean that he is limited by time, but on the contrary, he has existed from all eternity in Boundless Time, or what the " Secret Doctrine" calls the " Ever-Darkness." The conception is the same as that given in St. John—" In the beginning was the Word (or the Logos—otherwise Ahura-Mazda) and the Word was with God, and the Word was God ; the same was in the beginning with God."

He is the Creator (Yasna I), and, to continue the quotation from St. John, " All things were made by him, and without him was not anything made that was made." He is Lord of Life, "he is the Radiant, the Glorious, the greatest and best, the most firm who sends his joy, creating grace afar, who made us and has fashioned us, who has nourished and protected us, who is the most bountiful Spirit (Yasna I), and St. John says, "In Him was life and the life was the light of men." He is Omniscient (Yasna 31), He is our Law-giver (Yasna 31) and Teacher (*ibid* and Yasna 32), He will establish a kingdom (Yasna 28). It is for the poor (Yasna 34). God is our Friend, Protector, Strengthener and Unchangeable (Yasna 31). He is our Judge (Yasna 42).

As manifested in creation he is then "The Universal Logos," and it is of great interest to observe how the Jews have gathered from the Irânians, possibly through the Medes, at the time of the captivity, the same conception of the "All Being." It is curious in this connection to note that the name "Pharisee" is the equivalent of "Farsee," which, says the Rev. Dr. Mills, is a latter form of Parsi, and the Rev. gentleman goes on to remind us (*Nineteenth Century*, January, 1894), that the Pharisaic faith was largely the foundation of Christianity. The relationship in conception may be carried still further. Although Ahura-Mazda exoterically is Creator, Preserver and Differentiator—a triune Deity as is God in Christian orthodoxy and in Hindu philosophy—he is also seven, as the synthesis of the Archangels or Ameshaspentas, who all emanate from and are collectively Himself. Says Yasht 13: "The Bountiful Immortals who are seven and all of the One thought, and of One word and of One deed; whose thought is the same; whose word is the same and whose deeds are the same, who have one Father and Commander, Ahura-Mazda." The seven Archangels of the Presence, as they are called, we find spoken of in Tobit, chap. 12, and Zechariah, chap. 4, where they are referred to as the eyes of the Lord, which run to and fro through the whole earth.

Again in Revelations (chap. 5), we read of the Seven spirits of God sent forth into all the earth.

Ahura-Mazda, however, is never looked upon as *a* God,— as a personal God, I mean—except in so far as He is personified by our limited conception. He is the All, on the manifested plane of being.

Now Ahura-Mazda is sprung from "Boundless Time," the Ever-Darkness; the Avastâ term being Zeroana-Akerna. This "Boundless Time," the Ever-Darkness, will be familiar to students of the "Secret Doctrine" as symbolising the uttermost conception of Man—the Absolute, at any rate so far as *our* thought is concerned. It is utterly beyond all human comprehension and can only be spoken of in terms of opposites, for it is "The All in All." We speak of It as Boundless Time, yet it is independent of time. The "Secret Doctrine" defines it as "The Ever-Darkness" which is Absolute Light. It is the Self-sustained Container of All, and is alone; nought being, save in It. It is symbolised by the circle having no circumference whose centre is everywhere. It is, as Madame Blavatsky says, "The Abstract Garb of an Ever-Present Abstraction—The Incognisable Deity."

Ahura-Mazda, then, springing from Boundless Time, is the first (Unmanifested) Logos which, as St. John says, "was in the beginning with God, and which was God." But Zoroaster taught that "In the beginning there was a pair of twins" inherent and eternal in the nature of the Deity, which by human minds could only be looked upon as a pair of opposites; so that whilst Ahura-Mazda is to be looked upon primarily as the first Logos, this second conception of the nature of Deity being two-fold is to be looked upon as the second Logos. A similar idea is contained in the Bhagavad Gitâ (chap, 15, slokas 16 to 18): "there are two kinds of beings in the world, the one divisible, the other indivisible. The divisible is all things and creatures, the indivisible is called Kûtastha or He that standeth on high—unaffected. But there is another spirit designated as the Supreme Spirit (Paramâtmâ), which permeates and sustains the three worlds. As I (Krishna, *loquitur*) am above the divisible and also superior to the indivisible, therefore both in the world and in the Vedas am I known as the Supreme Spirit."

The second Logos, in its two-fold aspect, plus its synthesis the first Logos, next appears as a trinity, or the third Logos which may be represented by

ZEROANA AKERNE.

AHURA-MAZDA   AHRIMAN

and this triad manifested in the world of matter as The Primal Force and its differentiations become the Universal Manifested Deity, "in whom we live and move and have our being;" and recognising that this "All Being" was merely the manifestation of that which was unmanifest, Zoroaster gives to It the title—Ahura-Mazda, who is thus not only the three Logoi, but the manifestation of The Eternal Triad and The One Eternal.

Whilst, then, the followers of Zoroaster believed in That which is, was, and shall be, the Eternal Incomprehensible Unity of Deity, their worship was reserved for the manifestation of That in the Universe and in the heart of Man,—the Ineffable Essence being beyond comprehension and even expression ; but Its emanation, The Lord of Life and Light, The All-embracing Father of All, He whose children they were, in whose bosom they were as pulses ;—this was the God of the "Fire-worshippers"; this the immediate Jewel of their hearts. Not a personal God in the anthropomorphic sense, yet personified in each loving human heart which made him its shrine.

Thus must it ever be ; each heart which feels within itself the workings of the Divine Guest must needs build up with loving hands an image of The Imageless—only so can we learn, and as the picture fades in the clearer light of the spirit, so do we make another, grander picture, which again must fade in the greater light. Yet is God beyond all these; ever the same, unaffected and changeless and knowing this Verity of Verities, whilst we build we reach at length that point when form no longer rules the soul. Meantime, living in a world of form, it is only by building higher and higher ideals that God comes to be known at last.

MAN.

Having thus briefly considered the nature and attributes of Divinity; let us endeavour in his creature Man to discover the relationship of the human to the Divine.

Man is of the seed of Gayomard (Bundahish, XXIV), who was the first of the human species—but as Gayomard appears in various characters in the Sacred Books, it will be well to consider who he is in reality. From careful reading and collating all the various passage relating to him, I am forced to the conclusion that Gayomard is, like Zoroaster and Yima, a generic term, and I believe I am warranted in this by an examination of the various passages in the light of " The Stanzas of Dzyan," in which we are told that three races of mankind preceded the present fourth race—that the first of these races was " the self-born ;" the second " the sweat-born," or those evolved from the first ethereal race, the first thus becoming their own children, as it were; and thirdly, "the egg-born" who were Androgynous. The fourth or present race being built up by the Earth Spirit upon the Chhâyas, or astral forms of the third race who had passed away. Now Gayomard is the first of the human species, the first man who withstood the attacks of the Demons for the first 3,000 years of the earth (Bundahish, XXXIV), and he *could not pass away* until the end of this period. Now I fancy these 3,000 years are to be read esoterically as the three epochs of the first three races. Then from Gayomard is born "the youthful body of a man of 15 years, radiant and tall." He is born of the sweat of Gayomard and nothing more is said of *him*, but the verse goes on to speak of *Gayomard* issuing from the sweat and seeing the world as dark as night,

&c., and I believe in this story we have the mystery of the 2nd race set forth,—Gayomard being not only the first, but issuing from his own sweat as the second. As to the third race, I have not been able to find anything which exactly agrees with the stanzas as to "the egg-born" except that the next race sprang from the seed of Gayomard, nourished by the spirit of the Earth and the Angel Neryosangh, appears as the one-stemmed *rivas* plant whence grew up Matrô and Matroyâô, who grew in such a manner that they were one joined to the other and both alike, and as may be inferred from the verses, were Hermaphrodite. And these changed from the shape of a plant into the shape of man, and them Ahura-Mazda says, "You are man, you are the ancestry of the world and you are created perfect in devotion" (Bundahish, XV). This perfection in devotion is striking in this connection, as in the stranzas of Dzyan the third race are said to have become the *vâhan* or vehicle of the Lords of Wisdom. After a long period Matrô and Matroyâô become parents, but devour their offspring. Aferwards seven pairs of children were born, each pair male and female, and these people the whole earth and are, I believe, the 4th race. The whole subject is very difficult to a Western, though of intense interest.

Man, therefore, is said to be of the seed of Gayomard preserved by two angels, one of which is the spirit of the Earth. Now, when the first pair grew up as a rivas plant, it is said that a glory came upon them (Zâd-sparam, X). The word translated "Glory" is "Nismo" meaning "Soul," which, states Darmesteter, has been corrupted by the omission of the initial stroke. And Ervad Zâd-sparam, commenting on this, says, "which existed before ?—the glory (soul) or the body," and Ahura-Mazda spoke thus, "The glory (soul) was created by me before; afterwards for him who created, the glory (soul) is given a body so that it may produce activity and its body is created only for activity." "And afterwards, they (Matrô and Matroyâô) changed from the shape of a plant into the shape of man and the glory (soul) went spiritually into them." Now the esoteric doctrine teaches that the Reïncarnating Egos of mankind are the Mânasaputra—"the angels fallen into generation"—the Bene Elohim; and it is interesting to note how the account given in the Bundahish of the descent of the Egos tallies with the teachings of the "Secret Doctrine." In chap. II, verses 9-11, we read of Ahura-Mazda deliberating with the consciousnesses and Guardian Spirits of men, and asking, "Which seems to you the more advantageous when I shall present you to the world? that you shall contended in a bodily form with the fiend (Drûg) and the fiend shall perish and in the end I shall have you prepared again, perfect and immortal, and in the end give you back to the world and you will be wholly immortal, undecaying and undisturbed; or that it be always necessary to provide you protection from the destroyer? Thereupon the Guardian Spirits of men became of the same opinion with the Omniscient Wisdom *about going to the world* on account of the evil that comes upon them, in the world from the fiend, and their becoming at last again unpersecuted by the adversary, perfect and immortal in the future existence, for everlasting."

Thus we have the Fravashi, the Guardian Spirits of men, electing to have bodies in which to fight the adversary, that through the experiences of the flesh they might conquer the fiend in the flesh and thus become the Saviours of Mankind, as is said of the Mânasaputra. In their totality, again, they are the Christ Spirit, which being born in the heart of Man, becomes the Son of Man and the Saviour.

Another allegory as to the soul and I pass on. When Yima, who, I have mentioned as synonymous with Yama—the synthesis of the first three races—is instructed by Ahura-Mazda to make an ark (*vara*) against the time of tribulation, he is given certain directions for his procedure and the instructions conclude with, "And thou shalt make a door and *a window self-shining within.*" Now by this window is meant the soul and the *vara* is man, for when Yima asks how he is to make the *vara*, he is answered, "Crush the earth with a stamp of thy heel, and then knead it with thy hands as the potter does when kneading the potter's clay." This allegory I have quoted as interesting in connection with the formation of Adam by the Elohim given us in Genesis.

Whilst recognising the triune nature of Man the Zoroastrian system does not neglect the seven-fold. As Man is the expression of the Divine on earth, he is not only One and Three but Seven, and in Yasna 55 we find the septenary division. A similar concept occurs in Yasna 26, where, however, the physical body, the astral duplicate and vital force are grouped under one head "Ahum"—existence; then follow four other principles, making a total of five as in the Vedânta system.

Now the whole interest of the scheme lies in the meaning of Fravashi, and in this respect I shall quote from a little book sent to me by a Parsi on which I have already drawn. It is there stated that "In some Mazdean works it is plainly implied that Fravashi is the Inner Immortal Man (or that Ego which reincarnates), that it existed before its physical body and survives all such it happens to be clothed in." Not only was man endowed with the Fravashi, but gods too, and the sky, fire, water and plants. This shews as plainly as can be shewn that the Fravashi is the spiritual counterpart of God, animal, plant or even element, *i.e.*, the refined and purer part of the grosser creation, the soul of the body; whatever the body may happen to be. Therefore does Ahura-Mazda recommend Zarathushtra to invoke His Fravashi and not Himself (Ahura), that is to say, the impersonal and true essence of Deity—one with Zarathushtra's own Âtman (or Christos) and not the false personal appearance.

Here we see the thought runs along the same lines as in the Upanishads and Vedas—proclaming the Unity of the Divine in Man with Divinity itself, and is the same teaching as that of St. Paul when he exclaims, "Know ye not that ye are the temple of God and that the Spirit of God dwelleth in you" (Cor. III., verse 16). This doctrine seems to me most clear—that in essence Man is one with God, that he, in fact, is designed to be the manifestation of God on earth, and in so far as he coördinates his various principles to the Unity of the Divine Guest within the shrine, so will he become the perfect manifestation of the Godhead.

MEDIATOR.

I must now approach the subject of mediation, by which term I mean the means of intercommunication between God and Man and the uplifting of the human to the divine. I will first endeavour to deal with the subject of prayer. According to St. Augustine, " Prayer is the turning of the heart to God," and St. John Damascene defines it as "the elevation or ascent of the soul to God," and I shall take my definition of prayer from the Catholic Catechism, which states that "prayer is the uplifting of the soul to God."

It will be at once recognised that words are merely accessories in prayer ; simple aids to the aspirant, who, living in a world of form, feels bound to formulate his aspirations either mentally or physically. Spoken words or chanted Mantrams are not prayer, but the true prayer comes from the depths of the heart and is the aspiration of the inner Self towards its source. Do not, however, imagine that I would depreciate the utility of giving voice to our aspirations. By no means! The uttered prayer is a very real necessity to millions of our fellow-creatures ; a very real help in times of trouble. " When thou prayest," said the Master, " go into thy chamber," and Origen describes how the early Christian in his prayer closes, as far as may be, the avenues of sense and abstracts himself from earthly things. " He prayeth in a low voice," he continues, "for the heart and not the lungs is powerful with God." So the Fire-worshipper withdrawing his senses from external object and symbols, turns them inward seeking " His Father in secret." " But," it may be urged, " the Fire-worshipper adores the Sun or Fire ?" Let me ask—does the good Catholic adore the image, crucifix, or shrine, before which his prayers ascend or the orthodox Protestant the table at which he kneels at least three times a year? If you consult your prayer book

(of the English Church) you will find a distinct disclaimer of this. Let me go further—does the savage worship the insect he has chosen for his totem and whose life is in his hand when addressing his prayers to it ? Does he not rather use it as a means whereby to reach to some conception of the glorious life of which it is a manifestation. And shall we scorn his childlike methods—nay, let us but be thankful if *our* aids lead us to higher or nobler conceptions. The Parsi may, in contemplative worship, turn towards the Sun or the Fire on the altar, but these are to him but symbols of The True Light of the World, "that lighteth every man that cometh into the world," of "the Divine Fire" which is hid in every human breast. Hear what they say of themselves in their creed. "We believe in The One God, who created the Heavens and the Earth, the Angels, Sun, Moon and Stars, fire, water and all things ; Him we worship, invoke and adore. Our God has neither face nor form, nor fixed place, there is no other like him. We cannot describe his glory nor can our minds comprehend him."

Throughout the scriptures of the Fire-worshippers we find invocations and prayers addressed to Ahura-Mazda or to one of his aspect. For example—in Yasna 28 we read " with hands outstretched I beseech for the first blessing of Thy most Bounteous (or Holy) Spirit ;" also in Yasna 1, " I invoke and I will complete my sacrifice to Ahura-Mazda, the Creator, the Radiant, the Glorious ; the Greatest and the Best; the Most Firm, who sends his Joy creating Grace afar, who made us and has fashioned us, who has nourished and protected us; who is the most Bountiful Spirit."

Invocations are also addressed to "The Immortal Seven"— the Amesha-Spentas, who are the equivalents of our " Seven of the Presence" or the seven faces or aspects of God. Again, " We sacrifice to the redoubted Guardian Spirits of the Bountiful Immortals. . . Who are seven and all of one thought and of one word and of one deed. . . Who have one Father and Commander, Ahura-Mazda." Now we may here fancy that we have worship given to a plurality of gods or archangels; but let us pause and consider. These seven are merely the attributes, so to speak, of the One God, it is only as *we* separate them from him that we personify them. It is as reasonable to charge a Christian with Polytheism as a Zoroastrian, in fact the Athanasian creed is a standing protest against just such an accusation, and "The Godhead of the Father and of the Son and of the Holy Ghost is all one: the glory equal, the majesty coëternal." "As we are compelled by the Christian verity to acknowledge every person (of the Godhead) by himself to be God and Lord—so are we forbidden by the Catholic Religion to say three Gods or three Lords;" and with regard to worship of the Supreme it concludes, "So that in all things, as is aforesaid, the Unity in Trinity and Trinity in Unity is to be worshipped." Now substitute Septenary for Trinity and you have a series of statements to which I think every orthodox Parsi would cheerfully subscribe.

Further, we find invocations addressed to Guardian Angels (Fravashis) and the powers of the four Elements and seven Regions, but only as manifestations of the Power by whose will they are. More particularly, however, would I notice the invocation of Sarosh, for this is used daily by the Parsi and no prayer is considered to be efficacious without beginning with this invocation, just as no Christian concludes his prayer without a similar invocation "through Jesus Christ our Lord." Now Sarosh has been considered as the angel or messenger of God. "In the Avastâ, Sarosh is called a Yazata, a god (elsewhere spoken of as an Etar Angel—which may perhaps be translated the angel of our nativity)." Western scholars, however, translate the word as "Devotion," "Obedience" "Truthfulness," &c. Yasna 57 gives the attributes of Sarosh. He is a Yazata, He is the Protector, He is beautiful, He is victorious, having magical weapons with him. He is the furtherer of the world's advancement, He is holy, He is ever-wakeful. He has never slept since the commencement of the world. It is through his guidance that man hopes to approach Ahura-Mazda, He is the smiter of evil demons, vicious men and vicious women and

Daeva-Druksh, the world-destroying. He is compared to a flame and is said to be in close connection with the one Divine Fire. He it is who protects us at night, He is the offspring of Ahura-Mazda ; *the Son of the Father.* The word Sarosh comes from the root Shru = to hear, and there seems to me to be a connection with Shruti—revelation (or the revealed one). Sarosh is essentially The Word; he is in man that which Theosophists speak of as the Higher Ego whose magical weapons are Will and Intuition. As it is the Higher Ego (or rather the presiding god)* who is, so to speak, the mediator between the lower self in Man and Âtmâ, the overshadowing God, so is Sarosh the guide, the way, the Saviour of the Parsi believer. And what can Sarosh be but the Christ Spirit in the heart, which is the way, the truth and the Life—and what sayeth the Master of Nazareth as to the manifestation of his spirit ? Turn to St. John 14 : " He that hath my commandments and keepeth them; he it is that loveth me, and he that loveth me shall be loved of my Father and I will love him and will manifest myself to him;" and in answer to the question, "How is it that thou wilt manifest thyself unto us and not unto the world ?" the Master replies : "if a man love me he will keep my words and my Father will love him and we will come unto him and make our abode with him." Hear also what a Parsi says of the manifestation of Sarosh. "Before Sarosh can manifest in us we have to train our mind in a certain way and purge ourselves of all sins, evil thoughts, evil words and evil deeds—bodily and psychic, earthly and heavenly." Surely little more need be said to prove that the conceptions are the same, though clothed in garments of varied hue.

Sarosh, then, is the Immortal Ego in Man, the Christ within the Word incarnate. If this be so, then we may look further and see another correspondence with Christian belief. We find in the Zoroastrian books that it is said—at the last, when the

---

* According to the *Zaredastafshâr*, a later Persian work, Saroash is the angel presiding over mankind and "giver of messages from God."—*Compiler.*

world is in the most evil case, will come a saviour, Saoshyant, who will be born of a virgin and having redeemed the world and conquered the evil one, Sosheosh—which I take to be another form of the same name—will appear seated on a white horse and followed by an army of angels also riding white horses. The dead will arise and enter into the Heaven he has prepared, the regenerated earth. Ahriman and his angels will be cast into a lake of molten metal there to be purified, after which all will enjoy unchanging bliss. Compare this with the Revelation of St. John from the 11th verse of the 19th chapter, and I think you will find the correspondence clear.

He who is called Faithful and True comes riding out of the Heavens on a white horse and he is the Word of God. Out of his mouth goeth a sharp sword and the angels who follow him ride on white horses. He conquers the Beast, who is cast into a fiery lake, and the millenium begins, during which Satan is chained. The dead next arise and at length we read of a new heaven and a new earth. We have the same teaching in very similar garb in the Hindu scheme—Vishnu in his tenth incarnation—the Kalki Avatâr who is yet to come, appears, at the end of this cycle (the Kali Yuga), riding on a white horse, armed with a sharp sword, crowned as in the Apochalypse. The wicked he will send to infernal abodes, in which they will be purified and pardoned; even the devils, who rebel against Brahmâ and are hurled into the bottomless pit by Shiva, will eventually enter into bliss. Sarosh is then the Saviour of Man, and his inmost Self, which is one with God: and it is therefore easy to realise that worship is accorded to the Divinity within. In this, I believe, the Zoroastrian, Brahmanical and Christian doctrine is the same—each accords worship to the Incarnate Word of God—the Âtman; Sarosh, Honover, or Christos.

Means of mediation, however, are not confined to prayer nor to the agency of the All-conquering Saviour, Soshiosh. Man himself must become his own Saviour, or the Saviour must be born in the soul of each man before Soshiosh makes his triumphal descent upon earth.

Very instructive is the story of the fight between Zoroaster and the Fiend. And what is it with which he eventually conquers but the Word of God in his heart? And let me impress upon my readers the ever reiterated means of grace of the Parsi religion—" Purity—Purity in Thought, Purity in Word, Purity in Deed." This is the beginning and the end of it—this is the *summum bonum*, this the key-stone of the mighty arch of Parsi Morality. How is it to be obtained? By each and every man passing each thought, word and deed through the fire of Spirit, the true refiner. That is why Fire is taken as the symbol of Spirit, for it is that which purges away the dross and leaves the refined gold.

BAKER HUDSON, F. T. S.

—*The Theosophist*, Vol. xvi, Nos. 7-8.

AN AFTERWORD.

IN order to describe a religion accurately, one ought to have believed in it; and if the meaning of a writer is to be ascertained we should, in our thought, place ourselves in his condition and surroundings. The affectation of critical acumen should be laid entirely aside. We dissipate our powers of discerning aright, when we dwell too much upon verbal technology or external considerations. These requirements are imperative, if we would peruse intelligently the teachings of the Great Apostle of Mazdaism.

When I read and contemplate the oracular utterances of Spitaman Zarathushtra, I am impressed most vividly with their sweetness and purity, and by the familiarity full of reverence which he always exhibits in his intimate communings with the Divine Being. When the mind is thoroughly pervaded with this sensibility, it can be no impossible matter, nor by any means unwarrantable, to eliminate from the *Discourses* whatever is foreign or heterogeneous. Historic and hermeneutic criticism will sanction this proceeding. It should be borne in mind, that it was a practice in former centuries for scribes and teachers to incorporate their own glosses, notions and explanations into the text of great writers; and that few books that were extant before the invention of the art of printing have escaped such tampering.

The Zoroastrian religion is a very exalted monotheism. It was such in its inception; it continued such all through the times when evil and persecution overshadowed its fortunes; it is such now as professed by the Ghebers and Parsis. A fire so perpetual, a light so extensive, an energy so penetrating, can proceed but from the one fountain. True, they are like utterances in the *Rig-Veda*, and the fragments that remain of the lore of the Akkadians, Assyrians and Egyptians. But these remain rather as historic monuments, while Zoroastrism is still a faith that inspires a people to virtue and goodness.

The plurality of good and bad spiritual powers which tainted the vulgar worship with polytheism and idolatry was a pure concept with those who first described them. "The different gods are members of one soul," says Yaska, B. C. 400. "God, though he is one, has yet many names," says Aristotle; "because he is called according to the states into which he always enters anew." To the popular apprehension, the *nomina* became NUMINA. Yet, perhaps this sentiment of multiplicity could not well be avoided. No one term in human speech can express the All of the Divinity. We ourselves behold the One or the Many as we contemplate Godhood from the interior or the external vision.

The seven Amshaspands of Zoroastrian literature were but the one Ahura-Mazda or Living Essence manifested in seven qualities, as Intelligence, Goodness, Truth, Power, Will, Health and Immortality. The *Rig-Veda* declares that "the wise in their hymns, represent under many forms, the spirit who is but one." So, as Mr. Robert Brown ingeniously remarks: "The Ameshaspentas equally resolve themselves, so far as actual objective existence is concerned, into thin air."

The innumerable spiritual essences, the Yazatas, and Frohars, that are treated of in the *Avastá* need embarrass no one. It is hardly rational, when we observe the endless forms and grades of living things in the realm of objective nature, that we should imagine a total blank of all life about the spiritual being. Our plummet may not find a bottom to the Infinite, enabling us to dredge up living substances on the floor of that ocean; yet we are not authorised, therefore, to affirm that there is no God, or to deny that there are intelligent spiritual beings. Our own souls are of this nature, and we are conscious that they, therefore, rule our life and destiny through the power of the Father. We have to look but a step further in order to perceive the Foreworld, of which we, and all the bodied and unbodied souls are denizens alike. By our good disposition and activity we bring the good about us, while evil thought and action evolve the evil.

The "Dualism" of the Parsi philosophy denotes simply and purely the two aspects of the Divine operation—the interior and external, the spiritual and natural, subjective being and objective existence, organisation and dissolution. So far as relates to their respective functions, both are right as well as necessary; but the latter, when it is exalted and esteemed above the former, like Science above Philosophy, thereby becomes perverted and morally evil. It is thus a liar *ab initio* and father of lies.

The essential difference between the nations of the Irânians and their Aryan brethren was social and ethical. The true Mazdean regarded it as his duty to till the soil and live in orderly society. The Parsi Creed, of which that of Islam is a plagiarism, thus describes it:

> "The religion of goodness, truth and justice,
> Bestowed upon his creatures by the Lord
> Is the pure faith which Zarathustra taught."

In the *Ahuna-Vairyo* (the will or law of God) the entire belief and philosophy of the Parsis is given. The latest version of this formula, which I have seen may be given in smoother expression as follows:

> "As is the will of the Eternal One
> So through the Harmony of perfect thought
> His Energy brings forth the visible world,
> And his power sustains the rolling spheres."

Darius Hystaspês appears from the proclamation at Behistun, to have first established Mazdaism as the religion of the Persian dominions. He came to the throne by the overthrow of the Magians, and he confirmed his power by the instituting of the Irânian worship. The decree recites the matter:

> "Says Darius the King:
> 'I have made elsewhere a Book in the Aryan language that formerly did not exist.
> And I have made the text of the Divine Law, (*Avastâ*), and a *Commentary* of the Divine Law, and the Prayer, and the Translation.
> And it was written, and I sealed it.
> And then the Ancient Book was restored by me in all nations. And the nations followed it.'"

Perhaps from this fact the several notions originated that the first Zoroaster was contemporary with Darius, and that Darius himself had been instructed by the Brachmanes (or earlier Hindu sages) and had combined their teachings with Magism. At any rate, it seems to me that to find any sentiment or illustration in the *Avastâ*, that was originally Jewish or Semitic at all, would require the eye of a vulture, the lantern of Diogênes or the ken of an archangel. Nor does human progress appear anywhere in "a straight line of continuous advance." Life is rounded, history is in cycles, and civilisations come and go like the seasons. At the heel of them all is savagery; but everywhere about them is the life eternal.

A. W.

—*Theosophical Siftings*, Vol. vii, No. 10.

ZOROASTRIANISM—CHALDEAN AND GREEK.

THE religion of Zoroaster (Zarathushtra) is probably the oldest form of Spiritual teaching of which we have any record. We may perhaps except the earlier Chinese beliefs which prevailed in the days of the Yellow Emperor, but any other rival for the honors of antiquity would, it is believed, be seriously contested by this hoary religion of the Chaldeans. The teachings to which the name "Zoroastrianism" properly belongs, are to be found in the *Avastâ*, or more properly that part of the *Avastâ* known as the Gâthâs. It is not a system of nature-worship as is commonly supposed, but more properly a Theism, unless we are willing to extend our ideas concerning nature, to embrace the cause as well as the effect, the soul of things equally with the body in which that soul is vested—as I think we should, and have good reason to do.

The age of the Gâthâs is unknown and will, in all probability, remain so. On this point Bleeck says : " In the time of Darius the religion of Zoroaster was already so old that the language in which it was composed differed essentially from that of the Persian monarch." "This difference may be partly due to dialect," he says, " but there is no doubt that the language of the Avastâ is centuries older than that of the cuneiform inscriptions." The date of the Chaldean Zoroaster is said to be 2459 B. C. Kirsher tells us that the name signifies "the image of a star," or again, "the embodied fire," from *tsura*, a figure of image, and *as'tur*, a star. Others, again, derive it otherwise, making of it "the son of a star," " the fixed or firm star," &c. Boetaset says it means "the contemplator of the stars," from *ser*, to contemplate, and *aster*, a star, and would hence make Sabians of all Zoroastrians !

Be the name what it may, we are faced with a yet greater difficulty in our enquiry after the Chaldean sage, inasmuch as from various writers we may collect no less than six Zoroasters. Probably, however, we are right in taking the first of these, for reasons which will be apparent to all. He was a Chaldean, called by Suidas an Assyrian, said to have died by fire from heaven, alluded to by Dion Chrysostom, when he says that "Zoroaster the Persian came to the people out of a fiery mountain"; or perhaps from the fiery zone, which may refer to the fabulous seat of the gods, or to the starry girdle of the ecliptic, or again to the Chaldean Empyreon.

By most accredited writers on this matter, we gather that Zoroaster was held to be a Magus or prophet, a sage who introduced sciences among the Persians, instituted the Fire-magic, founded an order of Magi among the Chaldeans, and otherwise combined in himself the offices of Prophet, Teacher, and Reformer. His date is in dispute. Eudoxus, Aristotle, Pliny, Suidas and others disagree on this point in commenting on Zoroaster. Plato calls him the son of Oromases, *i.e.*, Ahuramazda, a name of the good Principle in nature among the Chaldeans. Of writings attributed to him, we have, besides oracular verses, treatises on Agriculture and Mechanics, on Magic, Astronomy, Psychology, Dreams, &c. It would require an unusual critical faculty, not to speak of a close knowledge of the Avastâ and Pahalavi languages, to give a lecture upon Zoroastrianism, which should take into account only the original doctrine of Zoroaster and excise all that overgrowth which invariably accumulates upon the bed-rock of any great religion in the course of ages. If, however, we take the Gâthâs as embodying the original doctrine, then what we can gather concerning the pure teaching has been formulated in a few words.

The name given by Zoroaster to the God he worshipped is (Ahuramazda) the *Wise One*, the Great Creator. The Deity is said to have six attributes—Goodness, Order, Power, Readiness, Health, and Immortality,* by which we understand that these were qualities conferred upon his worshippers, deity being thus realized in his human subjects. There is no evil principle or spirit called Ahriman, the original of the Jewish

---

* *Vide* foot-note, page 160, *ante.*

Satan, and this evil spirit Zoroaster held to be in the nature of things. Ahriman is described in the Gâthâs as " one of the two original spirits who came together to create life and life's absence", which is of course a reference to the good and evil, light and dark, spiritual and material kingdoms embraced by nature, taking the latter in its widest and truest sense. This theological quality is however resolvable into a unity, of which these two principles are nothing but the reverse *aspects*. Concerning the soul of man and its state after death, the Gâthâs teach that the soul is conditionally immortal. Heaven is a state, in fact holiness itself. Hell is that state into which a wicked soul falls in passing over the Judge's Bridge, Chondor (Chinvaḍ), which extends between Mount Alborj or the Earth, and Heaven. (*Cf.* " Religions of the World.") This fragmentary river of so great a religious system will not however suffice us, and in extending our survey so as to include the religious and philosophical teachings of the four chief sects which have grown up upon the primeval doctrine, we shall have to make some necessary distinctions, in order that the broad field I am about to open up may not carelessly be attributed to any one of these sects exclusively.

The four chief sects of the Zoroastrians then are—

1. The Charetmim or Hartumim—employed in divine and natural speculations. They were not magicians, but such as studied the nature of mental and physical phenomena, under which were comprehended theology, physics, and psychology.

2. The Astpim or Suphim—employed in the religious worship and rites, were wise men who chiefly concerned themselves with the exposition of the mysteries of the Divine nature. They correspond to the Magi of the Persians, their religious teachings being called magic.

3. The Mecheshpim or Revealers—were employed in every kind of divination, running through all degrees from astrology to sorcery.

4. The Chesdim—were the *savants* of the Chaldeans, and were chiefly concerned in astronomy and the philosophy of nature.

The spiritual, rational, psychic and physical principles of man's nature had thus each their separate students and exponents in this early Chaldaic system.

With so much by way of preface, it will now be allowable to make a general review of the doctrines of the Chaldeans.

Their system treats of all orders of being, from the divine and spiritual to the natural and physical. Zoroaster divided all things into three kinds; the *eternal*, which had no beginning and no end; and the *sempiternal*, which had a beginning, but no end; and the *mortal*, which had both beginning and end. The first two belong to theology and include the subject of God, and the gods; of demons and heroes. The third belongs to the subject of physic, and includes all material things which they divide into seven worlds or planes; one empyreal, three etherial and three physical.

The first kind of things are eternal, and in this Zoroaster names only the Supreme God. It is held to be the one principle, fount and origin of all things, and in itself eternally *good*. God, or Ahuramazda, as the Magi called him, in his body resembles *Light*; in his essence, *Truth*. In this way the sun became his visible agent on the physical plane, and was so regarded and respected by the Magi. God is also called *Fire*, and in this aspect he is regarded as under his form of Love, which they conceived under the name of Father, or the "Paternal Fire." Hence springs the institution of Fire-worship among the Mazdeasnians, which subsequently was transmitted to Persia.

God, as the source of the Spiritual Light and Heat, of Luminosity and Fire, is said to have communicated these properties to the First Mind, and through it to all the sempiternal and incorporeal beings, known as Angels, Demons, Light, Flames, &c., which include the souls of men. The second emanation is that of the Supramundane Light, an incorporeal infinite luminosity in which the intelligences reside. The Supramundane Light kindles the first corporeal world which is the Empyrean or Heaven of Fire, and next to the incorporeal light, is the most effulgent and tenuous of bodies. The Empyrean diffuses itself through the Ether, which is emanated from it, and in which the stars and sun are said to be etherial foci or nodes. This means of course that the sun and stars are not bodies in our sense of the word, but centres of force ; and that the æther of space is in its diffused state the plenum ; but in its concreted or vortical state, nothing less than *fire*. From the æther, then, there is a fire which is transmitted to the physical and sub-astral worlds, which it penetrates to its remotest parts, diffusing through it the properties of light and heat, which successively become transformed through the conditioning state of the material differentiation. We have then, the First Mind (our Logos), the Supramundane Light, the empyrean, the etherial world, the astal or solar world, and the physical; as emanations from Zoroaster's first kind of things—God. The second kind of things, or the sempiternal, are the gods and the souls of men. Of these there is a long category thus arranged, the Intelligibles, Minds, Fountains, Principalities, Unzoned Gods, Angels, Zoned Demons and Souls. Over these, the beings of the second or middle order, Zoroaster sets Mithra, the Great Mind or Spiritual Sun. The Intelligibles are such as are only understood, but understand not of themselves ; they seem to correspond to the monads of the Esoteric Philosophy. The Intellects, or Minds, are those which are understood and also undestand; they are also called the Intelligible Intellectuals. The third order, or Intellectuals, are those which understand only. We have then three orders, the Intelligibles, Intelligible Intellectuals, and the Intellectuals. These are the three aspects of the mind. The last of them is the embodied human or rational principle which unites the two superior orders to the inferior worlds, and is capable of understanding both that which is above and that which is beneath. Thus the Chaldean oracles say :—

> Beneath the measureless, the One and good,
> A vast Paternal Depth is understood,
> Of triads three; a higher, lower, mean;
> A Father, Imaged Mind, and Power between.

This lower triad of the imaged mind embraces the triple trinity in itself, and by mankind is called the first, as Zoroaster says. The second order also consists of three trinities. Of these Psellus says : " There are certain powers next to the Paternal Depth consisting of three Triads reflecting the Paternal Mind, and containing the cause of them each singly within itself." " They are intellectual species," says Pletho : " conceived by the Father Mind, and themselves being conception also, and exciting conceptions or notions by unspeakable counsels." Proclus quoting the Zoroastrian Oracle adds : " Hereby the gods declared as well where the subsistence of Ideas is, as who that god is who contains the one fountain of them, as also, after what manner the multitude of them proceeded out of this fountain and how the world was made according to them ; and that they are movers of the systems of the world, and they are essentially intellectual. Others may discover many other profound things by search into these notions ; but for the present let it suffice us to know that the ancients themselves ratify the contemplation of Plato, inasmuch as they term those intellectual causes *Ideas* ; and affirm that they gave pattern to the world, and that they are conceptions of the Father ; and that they go forth to the making of the world, and that they are of all forms, containing the causes of all things divisible ; and that from the fountain's Ideas proceeded other, which by several parts, framed the world and are called swarms of bees, because they beget secondary Ideas."

The passage referred to by Proclus is as follows :

" The king did set before the multiform world an intellectual, incorruptible pattern, the print of whose form he promoted through the world, and accordingly the world was framed ; beautified with all kinds of *Ideas* (*Fravashis*), of which there is one fountain, out of which came rushing forth others undistributed, being broken about the abodes of the world, which through the past excesses, like swarms, are carried round about every way, intellectual motions from the paternal fountain, cropping the flower of fire. In the point of sleepless time, of this primogeneous Idea, the first self-budding fountain of the father budded."

The third order is that of the Cosmogogues, or Cosmic rulers and guides. "Oh ! how the world hath intellectual guides inflexible," says the Oracle, and Psellus remarks concerning them : "The Chaldeans assert powers in the world which they term Cosmogogi (world guides), for that they guide the world by provident motions. These powers, the Oracles call "Sustainers," as sustaining the world. The Oracle says they are *inflexible*, implying their settled power ; *sustaining* denoting their guardianship. These powers they intend only by the *Causes* and the Immobility of the world."

To this third order also belong the Implacable, and these appear to be the guardian powers of the souls of men, causing them to remain unmoved amid the allurements of worldly things.

Among the fountains we have Hecate, the source of angels and demons and of souls and natures. Hecate is esteemed the fountain of the Cosmic generations, her left side being the the fountain of souls, her right that of virtues. From her proceed the two orders of gods or powers called the zoned or continent powers, the virtues ; and the unzoned or incontinent powers called souls. Hence the Chaldeans say, "The fountain of souls is prompt to propagations, but the fountain of virtues contains within the bounds of its own essence, and is as a virgin uncorrupted ; which stability it receives from the Implacables, and is girt with a virgin zone. The souls here spoken of are cosmic animal souls, in the Kâmic principle of nature, called unzoned, because they use their powers without restraint. They are said to have their throne above the visible gods, these latter being the stars and planets, after which follows our own earth, each and all filled with the propagations of the Light and Dark Principles. Of angels, there were two orders recognized by the Chaldeans. The persuasive or seductive, who employed all manner of gentle arts and inducements to lead the souls of men into the paths of virtue, gaining their allegiance by means of such persuasions; and the commanding or reductive angels, who reduced souls to submission and penitence by the power of their commands and inflictions. Beneath there were the demons, both good and bad, employed sometimes as the agents of these two orders of angels, yet having a nature and determination peculiar to themselves. They are simply termed Demons of Light or Good Demons, and Demons of Darkness or Bad Demons, Spenta-Mainyus and Añra-Mainyus.

Next to demons we have the order of Souls, which is the last of the sempiternal beings. Of these there are three kinds. One wholly separate from matter, a celestial intelligence; another inseparable from it, having a substance not subsisting by itself, but dependent on matter, together with which it is subject to mutation, and finally capable of dissolution. This soul is wholly irrational. Between these is a third kind; a rational soul, differing from the celestial soul, inasmuch as it always coëxists with matter; and from the irrational soul, because it is not dependent on matter but matter is dependent on it; and moreover it has its own proper substance potentially subsistent by itself. It is also indivisible, as well as the celestial soul, and performing some works in a manner allied to it, being itself also busied in the knowledge and contemplation of beings, even to the Supreme God, and is therefore incorruptible. Free from the material body, this soul is an immaterial and incorporeal fire, free from all compounded substances, for nothing material or dark is then mixed with it, neither is it then compounded so that it could be separated into the things of which it consists. It has a self-generate and self-animate essence and draws nothing of its substance from another. For (as the "Oracles of Zoroaster" say) "as it is a portion of the Divine fire, and paternal notion, it is an immaterial and self-subsisting form; for such is every divine nature and the soul is a part of it." The fountain causes of souls are the Paternal Mind, and the fountain of souls, called by the Greek commentators, Hecate; *i.e.*, the individual soul, is born from the fountain soul by the will and idea of the Father-mind. The region of souls is called the circumlucid region. The various mansions are either light, dark, or tenebrous. The sublunar regions are called the dark, the lunar, tenebrous, and the supralunar lucid. The circumlucid region therefore is that above the supralunar, and in this region the souls naturally are. From this region, this kind of soul, *i. e.*, the rational soul, is often sent down to earth, upon several occasions, either by reason of the flagging of the wings (as the Chaldeans term the deterioration of the soul from its original perfection, or from its *post-mortem* aspiration) ; or on account of, and in obedience to, the will of the Father-soul, by which we may understand the law of Karma. This rational soul is coëxistent with a vehicle of an etherial nature in which it passes from one state to another, and which, by association of itself, it makes immortal. In the Chaldean system the approximation of an etherial principle is capable of conferring the nature of that principle upon its vehicle, for as an immortal principle, such as the rational soul, needs always a vehicle in which it may eternally exist, it is said to confer immortality upon such vehicle by approximation. This vehicle or mind-body is not inanimation itself, but self-animated like the inferior souls, such as the irrational or animal soul, which is called the image of the rational. Thus by phantasy or imagination, which is the chief faculty of its vehicle, the rational soul is continually joined to it, and by it again and again joined to mortal bodies which it seeks by affinity, the whole being enfolded in the enlivening spirit of the embryo, and thus out-borne into the sphere of the earth.

The irrational or animal soul, (called the Image of the Rational Soul) which is joined to the rational soul by means of its vehicle, is said to have a part, though an inferior one, in the circumlucid region, because, it is said, the soul never lays down the vehicle which is adherent to it. The soul being sent down from the luminous mansion wholly pure and for the purpose of serving the bodies of matter, (*i. e.*, to operate therein for a certain period for the uplifting of the bodies to animate and adorn them, which it does according to its several virtues,) dwells in several zones of the world. If the soul performs its offices well, it goes back after a while into the mansion it came from ; but if badly or indifferently, it goes to the dark or to the tenebrous mansions. The Chaldeans restore the soul after death to its appropriate and true place in the spheres, according to the degree of its purification in all the regions of the world ; and some souls they also conceive to be carried beyond the world.

The Chaldean conception of the world is of a triple order, *viz.*, the Empyreal, the Etherial and the Material. These three are comprised under the name of the Corporeal world. The Empyrean is said to be round in figure, containing the Etherial and Material worlds, itself contained only by the supra-mundane Light. It is conceived to be a solid orb or firmament and is called the fiery world, because it consists of a resplendent fiery substance. The Empyrean is itself immoveable though pervading, by means of the Etherial world, all those moveable bodies which it sustains and comprehends The Etherial world is of three degrees and penetrates through all the material worlds, being the link by which they are united to the Empyrean. In its lowest degree it manifests in the stars or suns. Thus the planetary bodies or material worlds are joined to the Etherial by means of the sun, and through the ether with the Empyrean, the whole being sustained by the supra-mundane light which is the expression of the First Mind. The supra-mundane light will therefore correspond to the Primum Mobile of Aristotle. I must spare you the recital of all that has been written concerning the astrology and astrolatry of the Chaldeans, since special and exhaustive treatment is needed to do them justice, and the limits of this paper are almost touched. Let us now glance at their demonology for which they were once so famous. It is right, however, to remark by way of preface that the magic of the Chaldeans was far more theurgical and teleological than ceremonial, at least among the Zoroastrian Magi.

Later among the Chaldean and Assyrian priesthood, magic

of the baser kind became all too prevalent as we know. "The gods, it is said, give those things that are truly good, to such as are purified by appropriate sacrifices : and they converse also with these, and by their communication, drive away the wickedness and passion which are the qualities of the natural man, and by their brightness, chase from them the dark spirit ; for the evil spirit, when the light of the gods comes in, fly away as shadows do at the light of the sun. The evil spirits are thus not able to molest any longer the man who is thus freed from wickedness, perverseness and passion. But such men as are pernicious and are by reason of the imbecility of their actions and want of power, not able to attain to the gods, and because of certain pollutions, are repelled from them, and associate with evil demons by whose breath they are inspired. These men, moreover, by the fulness of their passions and wickedness, draw, by the affinity betwixt them, the evil spirits to themselves, by whom they are quickly possessed and are thus again excited to iniquity, the one assisting and strengthening ; the other, like a circle whose beginning and end meet."

Iamblichus tells us that the evil magicians among the Chaldeans used also several rites which they conceived to be efficacious in the evocations of these demons. They were drawn out of the earth and air by the use of certain objects and fumigations, and by voices and figures, which they called characters, which were first of all discovered by the Chaldeans, who found out the proper invocative sign of every demon. There were, as we have said, two kinds of Demons, good and evil, allied to the qualities of light and darkness. The latter are the enemies of mankind. They are of many orders, both with regard to their natures and the quality of their bodies, which follow after and correspond to their several natures. They inhabit all the elements, and whereas some such, as those of the fiery or passional element and those of the airy or phantasmal element, draw men away into an unwitting service of them by insidious arts and glamours : others on the contrary make open assault on men's bodies, and either inflict upon them injuries or diseases, or obsess them, and by stirring up evil passions in them, drive such men into all kinds of violence and lawlessness. All these demons are said to be the degraded souls of men, *i. e.*, their mortal souls. The way by which the more subtle of them affect temptations and bring the soul of man to the like state with themselves, is thus described: They affect these things, not by having dominion over us and by carrying us whither they may please, but by suggestions. This they do by applying themselves to the phantasy or imaginative faculty in the soul of man and by whispers of an internal nature suggest and stir up evil affections and passions. It is not impossible they should speak without voice, if it be remembered of what nature the voice and hearing consist. For just as a man that is distant from us must raise the voice to be heard, and one that is nearer and indeed close by needs but to whisper, so one such as a demon, that is within us and united to the animal spirits, has no need of so much as a whisper, but requires but the impulse to speak and is heard by an interior way, as one may know who has at any time given attention to them. This, the Chaldeans say, is the case with souls, which, when out of the body, can discourse with one another without noise. It is owing to the fact that the "demons," as they were called, are able thus to converse with men, to instil their desires into the brain and that without exciting any perceptible emotion beyond the familiar movement of the imaginative faculty, that such desires and promptings come to us as if they were our own property, or of our own generation, and thus do not appear to us as temptations. It consequently happens that often they are not resisted by us in the same way that similar and even identical promptings would be when coming to us from other persons external to ourselves. These demons, the Chaldeans say, are capable of assuming various forms and colours, and by this means they are capable of resuscitating the remembrance of pleasures and of exciting to the repetition of those things from which through the body of man they take delight and draw vitality. These remarks apply more particularly to the aërial demons which have rapport with the imaginative power of man. Others there are which afflict irrational creatures in a manner somewhat similar. They live a precarious life by drawing upon the vitality and animal heat of such irrational creatures, and naturally they have but little themselves, because they are removed so far from the divine nature which is the source of the fire of life. Of this order of obsessing demon, it is said, they delight most in the heat of animals, such as are temperate and mixed with moisture : and especially in that of men which is the best tempered. Into them, whenever possible, they insinuate themselves, and cause infinite disturbances, contracting the skin and causing fevers, by which the principal faculties are distempered. If the obsessing demon be one of the earthy principle, it distorts the obsessed person and speak by him, making use of his memory and faculties, as if they were its own property. But the nebulous demons get privately into the man, and cause catalepsy ; stopping the voice, sometimes relaxing the limbs and causing the appearance of death ; and because it is the coldest of the demons, it causes a complete, though perhaps temporary, inhibition of the faculties by the sudden abstraction of the animal heat which its presence cause.

It was held that the physical effects, such as lethargies, melancholia, fever, &c., might be cured by medicine and others by external applications or treatment ; but the psychic effects, such as enthusiasm, frenzy, raging and obscenity, could not be cured except by evocations and enchantments, and it is remarked as reasonable that that which could prophesy and effect super-normal actions through the body alone ought not to be regarded as the motions of depraved nature alone. They taught also that no demon is in its own nature either male or female, such being only the property of compounded bodies. The bodies of demons being simple and very ductile as the water or the clouds, they are capable not only of altering their proportions, being small or large in response to their desires, but also of assuming the forms of compound bodies by pervading them. They could not, however, permanently assume any of these forms, as by illustration, water poured or escaping from a vessel does not retain the form of that vessel. It was believed that their own language was effected by means of colours which they could infinitely vary, and these variations of their complexions, when taking place within the body of a man obsessed by them, gave rise to innumerable fancies, desires and imaginations. This power, however, is more in the possession of the fiery and aerial demons, than in the nebulous (or aqueous) and earthy. The bodies of demons, they say, are capable of being struck and wounded, because it is not the physical body which feels, but the animal soul which pervades it, and the demon is of the nature of that soul, or as that soul would be apart from its association with the Rational Principle.

Compounded bodies, when cut, do not come together again, but the body of the demon being simple and plastic, is not destroyed by cutting, but comes together again, though at the moment of its being cut it is hurt. Consequently these demons dread the sharp sword, which is sometime used as a defence against them. In this respect the bodies of the demons are like water to which they have already been compared, inasmuch as they can be disturbed, but not severed.

The Chaldeans employed such means as the above, and also conjurations, for preserving themselves against the evil demons; while, on the other hand, they had recourse to invocations, accompanied by suitable fumigations, colors and objects, for attracting the presence of the good demons. The Magi, however, were able to command their presence by means of certain names, which had a compelling influence upon them or to which it was in agreement with their natures to respond. So much then in regard to their demonology. I may add a word or two in conclusion regarding their religious teachings or "Instructions concerning the aim of the soul," as delivered by Pletho in his transcript of, and commentary upon, the Chaldean Oracles :

The soul of man is spoken of as a beam generated from the

Universal Soul by the Deity which they call the Father-Light. Thus it is said : "*It behoves thee to hasten to the Light, and to the beams of the Father ; from whence was sent thee to a soul, clothed with much mind.*" This soul is endowed with mind, thereby becoming rational and capable of aspiring to, and of understanding the parent mind, while on the other hand by its union with the body it is capable of corruption. "*For the Father of gods and men,* says the Oracle, *placed the mind in the soul and in the body he established you. For all divine things are incorporeal; but bodies are bound in them for your sakes, by reason of the corporeal nature in which you are concentrated . . . And though you see this soul released, yet the father sends another to make up the number ; and these are superlatively blessed above all souls, for they are sent forth from heaven to earth as rich souls which have inexpressible fates, as many of them, O King, as proceeds from thy resplendent self.*"

Concerning devotion it is said :

"*Let the immortal depth of thy soul be predominant: and all thy eyes extended upwards. Stoop not down to the dark world, beneath which lies a fearful depth . . . precipitous and rough, . . , and the winding currents by which many things are swallowed up.*"

"*Seek Paradise. Seek thou the way of the soul, whence and by what order having served the body to the same place from which thou didst proceed, thou may'st rise up again.*"

Very near to the teachings of the *Bhagavad Gítá* and other familiar systems, are the Chaldean teaching with regard to righteous life. "*Drawing through the ladder which hath seven steps, with holy action knit to sacred speech, do not decline ; beneath the precipice of earth is set a throne of dire necessity.*

Enlarge not thou thy destiny . . . O man, the machine of boldest nature, subject not to thy mind the vast measures of the earth ; for the plant of Truth is not among them. Seek thou the measureless, the source of light ; seek thou thine own."

Much more might be quoted to show that the Chaldean

teachings not only have much that is highly spiritual and uplifting in them, equal indeed to some of the finest concepts of later religious systems, but also a deep philosophy which engaged the attention of some of the deepest thinkers of the Greek schools ; and a science of the soul which would even at this day repay attention and study. I have been able only to briefly scan the Theology and Cosmogony of the followers of Zoroaster, and have restricted myself to the Chaldean view of that Sage's doctrines, to the exclusion of the Persian interpretation and the more familiar modern aspect of the same professed by the Parsis. In doing this I have necessarily been the more incomplete through having to rely very largely upon such of the Greek writers as have made this system a subject of special comment. I am satisfied, however, that this is better than accepting the mere husk which is offered to us by modern interpreters who have lost touch with the spirit of those times.

WALTER R. OLD.

—*Theosophist*, Vol. xv, No. 12.

THE "SUN-WORSHIP."

> "He [attaineth the glory of the Sun] who, knowing this adores the sun as Brahma, and grateful shouts soon arise in his behalf and contribute to his gratification—verily they contribute to his gratification."
>
> *Chhándogya Upanishad*, Ch. iii, s. xix.

AMONG the daily or common prayers performed by the religious Parsis is one called "Korshed-niyâesh," which is recited by them in the Avastâ language. They recite this and other prayers without understanding their meaning, in spite of the hard-hearted taunts and bitter reproaches of non-Zoroastrians, as well as their less religious coreligionists. The latter, on this pretext, try to escape from all religious restraints or responsibilities, and regard themselves as the wisest of their community, although now-a-day there are means at their command to understand the meaning of their scriptures. Translations of these, both in English and vernacular, are now easily accessible, but out of sheer indolence and apathy towards religion they care not to look at them, far less study them. Their condition is thus rather pitiable than otherwise, because a man without a religion, or devotional feeling, approaches nearer the animal than to the higher side of his nature. There are now greater facilities for understanding one's scriptures by means of philology, theosophy, and the science of the soul, or Yoga-philosophy, than there were some thirty or forty years ago. Besides this, we are now peacefully settled in India, a country which is the fountain source and motherland of all true spiritual knowledge. Thus the party which has less faith in its religion finds it easy enough to laugh at its more spiritually minded co-religionists, who in simple faith continue to offer prayers to the Sun in the Avastâ language, as their forefathers did, though they themselves have not a leg to stand upon in the position they have taken up in this matter, as will be seen presently.

The religious Parsis perform their common prayers standing either before the sacred Fire or the glorious Sun, the highest symbols of the Supreme that any Saviour of humanity has yet given to the world. I say "common prayers" advisedly, because the true prayer is something else—it is the aspiration of the soul to reach the Supreme source of All—it is the Yoga, the holy union of the soul with Ahura-Mazda. The religious Parsi who recites his common prayer in the Avastâ language in good faith, is accused by a well-known Parsi "Reformer" as "asking God to get him good interest for his money, to provide his son with a suitable berth and his daughter with an eligible husband;" "as if the Creator and Upholder of this vast and magnificent universe had nothing better to do than to devote His time to the affairs of an infinitesimal and insignificant worm like man!" But the god of the Reform party is not a whit better than that of the other. Its exponent, while preaching on a certain occasion, expressed himself that:—"If we want to ask for some gift from God, it is better to ask it after performing a prayer than to ask it at once." This sounds exactly like a fair bargain with a shopkeeper who doles out riches in return for a prayer. And what is a prayer of these "educated" Parsis? Gujerati songs, composed for the occasion, set to modern music. Thus the members of the "Reform" party are in far worse plight themselves than their orthodox brethren. The real Zoroastrian prayer is an offering—a sacrifice—rather than an asking, which will be seen further on when we shall deal with the "Khorshed-niyûesh" proper.

It is difficult to give the true idea of God in words, as it is understood by every individual in proportion to the development of his mental calibre; though the idea has been sufficiently expressed in some of the former articles. We will now enter, therefore, upon an examination of the prayer itself, which is called Khorshed-niyâesh, the prayer of the deity which presides over the Sun, and see whether we can learn something from it. Leaving out the Arabico-Pâzand introduction of this prayer, we notice the following passage:—

"*Obeisance to Thee, Ahura-Mazda threefold, before other*

existence. Obeisance to ye Ameshâspentas, who have ALL LIKE WILL WITH THE SUN. *May this (obeisance) come to Ahura-Mazda, to the Ameshaspentas, to the Fravashis of the Pure, this to Vaiyâm of the Long Period."*

We see in the above passage that the Ameshâspentas, who are called Dhyan-Chohans in the Theosophical literature, are, according to the Zamyâd-yasht, "the shining, having efficacious eyes, great, hopeful, imperishable and pure, which are *all seven of the like mind, like speech, all seven doing alike,* who are the creators and destroyers (or rather regenerators) of the creatures of Ahura-Mazda, their Creators and Watchers, their Protectors and Rulers"—have all "*like wills with the Sun.*" And what Sun could be alluded to here but Ahura-Mazda, the Logos? The Ameshâspentas are identical with, and yet separate from, Ahura-Mazda; in other words, Ahura-Mazda is the synthesis of the Ameshâspentas, and these latter are of one will with Ahura-Mazda, who is called Sun in the above passage. That the Sun stands here for Ahura-Mazda can be seen plainly, and that He is of "three-fold" aspect is also plain enough.

Now, what are the Fravashis referred to in this passage? According to the Avastâ, all existences—whether a god, man, sky, fire, water, plants—have their Fravashis. Much confusion and misconception prevails among the present interpreters of our scriptures as regards the true meaning and function of these Fravashis. According to the latest attempts made to interpret them, they are shown to be "nothing else than the good deeds of animate beings, and good products and properties of the inanimate"* creation; or, in other words, they are merely the effects of visible existence. Columns after columns of a Parsi daily paper are filled with explanations on the basis of this erroneous and misleading hypothesis. In order to have a clear conception of this word we have to turn to Fargard 19, verse

---

* "The Fravashis:" by Aerpat Meherjibhai Palanji Madan: a paper read before the Eighth International Oriental Congress, 1889. The *Bombay Samáchár* has followed this interpetation.

14, of the "Vendidâd," where Ahura-Mazda asks Zarathushtra the Spitama, not to invoke Him but His Fravashi. The passage runs thus:—

"Invoke, O Zarathushtra, my Fravashi, who am Ahura-Mazda, the Greatest, the Best, the Fairest of all Beings, the most Durable, the most Intelligent, and whose soul is the holy Word (Mâthra-Spenta)."

The Theosophical interpretation of the Fravashi is that "it is the *inner* immortal man; . . . that it existed before its physical body, and survives all such it happens to be clothed in. . . . This shows as plainly as can be shown that the Ferour is the 'spiritual counterpart' of each god, animal, plant or even element, *i.e.*, the refined and the *pure* part of the grosser creation, the soul of the body, whatever the body may happen to be. Therefore does Ahura-Mazda recommend Zarathushtra to invoke his *Fravashi* and not Himself [Ahura-Mazda]; that is to say, the *impersonal* true essence of Deity, *one with* Zoroaster's own Âtman (or Christos), not the false and *personal* appearance. This is quite clear."—(The "Secret Doctrine," Vol. II., p. 480.)

Here are two interpretations, to be weighed and judged which of them appears in harmony with the fundamental teachings of the Avastâ. The Fravashis being spiritual prototypes of physical existences, or Divine Ideation, according to the Greek philosophy, they are the *causes*, and not the *effects*—good deeds of men and good properties of things—as explained above. The new-fashioned interpretation of this essentially spiritual idea is obviously opposed to the true spirit of Zoroastrianism, according to which the Fravashis existed even before the condensation of the physical world. The new interpretation, therefore, amounts to nothing short of putting the cart before the horse. We are taught to invoke or adore the Fravashis of the Pure, that is, the essence which is one with God, and not the "good products and properties of the inanimate" things, which would amount to idol-worship, pure and simple. It may be left to any one to decide whether you should bow down, as is enjoined in the Khorshed-niyâesh, to the True Divine Cause which is one with Ahura-Mazda, or to the good deeds of animated beings and good products of inanimate things.

We are required further to make obeisance to Vaiyâm, which is interpreted sometimes as Râm, the Yazata, and sometimes as "Bird of the Long Period," while it is compared sometimes with the Vedic Vâyû. The last interpretation is not very far from the "Bird of the Long Period," if we take Vâyû in its esoteric sense. It gives us a clue to the solution why one should bow down to Vaiyâm. The Vâyû of the Vedas is certainly not the air, or the atmosphere that we breathe, nor that which is the air of the later manifestation, a mixture of gases wherein the atoms have already appeared to exist; but the Vâyû of the Vedas is "the Great Breath of the Supreme," which is essentially Eternal Motion, as is said by Mrs. Besant in "The Building of the Cosmos": "for only when this conception of motion comes in, is any manifestation possible." Thus the distance between Vaiyâm, the "Bird of the Long Period," and Vâyû, the Eternal Motion or "Great Breath," is not great; and Vaiyâm, therefore, being one with the Supreme, the obeisance made to it amounts to the obeisance made to Ahura Mazda Himself.

The subsequent passage teaches us something about the form of prayer alluded to in the beginning of our subject. It should be borne in mind that the original form of Zoroastrian prayers is not a petition or appeal for worldly comforts, or gifts or riches, to an anthropomorphic God, as is sometimes done by some people, but it is the outward form of the inward aspiration of a true devotee who aspires to uplift his soul to become one with the Supreme Source of All. These prayers teach us rather self-sacrifice than self-gratification, as will be seen from the following passage:—

"*I praise the well-thought thoughts, well-spoken words, well-performed deeds. I lay hold on all good thoughts, good words, good deeds. I abandon all evil thoughts, evil words, evil deeds.*

I offer to you, O Ameshâspentas! praise and adoration, with good thoughts, good words, and good deeds, with heavenly mind, the vital strength of my own body."

This passage teaches us self-control, conltrol on thoughts, words and deeds, in which the mind and body are trained in a way to control and subjugate the lower activies of the mind, and this training itself forms, as it were, a sort of sacrifice on the part of the neophyte, hitherto a worldly man. It is self-denial, self-sacrifice. Thus purified by abandoning his selfish thoughts, selfish words and selfish deeds, he offers "the vital strength of his own body" to the Ameshâspentas, whose synthesis is Ahura-Mazda. This offering of one's vitality is true *Jânfeshâni* or *Jân-kurbâni*, which means true devotion.

Then the Parsi "Sun-worshipper" makes

"*Obeisance to Ahura-Mazda; obeisance to the Ahmeshâspentas; obeisance to Mithra of the wide regions; obeisance to the Sun with swift Aspa; obeisance to the Eyes of Ahura-Mazda; obeisance to Geush; obeisance to Gayahi; obeisance to the holy Fravashi of Zarathushtra the Spitama; obeisance to the Pure (heavenly) Existence which was, is, and which is to be.*"

We have said something of Ahura-Mazda and the Ameshâpentas above; now let us take Mithra. It is interesting to note that the Sun and Mithra are inseparable in the daily prayers of the Parsis. One who prays to the Sun must pray to Mithra, as the prayer to the latter immediately follows the former in what is known as the *Meher-niyâesh*. Not only so, but this Meher-niyâesh is almost the same in its composition as the Khorshed-niyâesh, with the difference only of a couple of passages or so. And why? Because just as, according to Theosophy, Âtma is inseparable from Buddhi in microcosm, or Âtma cannot be conceived without Buddhi, the Sun or the Logos is inseparable from his companion, the Mithra. We learn in the Secret Doctrine that Mercury is "identical with the Mazdean Mithra, the genius, or god, established between the Sun and the Moon,* the perpetual companion of 'Sun of Wisdom'" . . . "He is the *Golden coloured* Mercury . . *. . . whom the Hierophants forbade to name . . . It is through the intercession of Mercury that the Emperor Julian prayed to the occult Sun every night, for, as says Vassus, 'all the theologians agree to say that *Mercury and the Sun are one.*'" . . . " He was the most wise of all the gods, which is not to be wondered at, since Mercury is in such close proximity to the Wisdom and Word of God [the *Ahunavairya*] (the Sun), that he was confused with both."—("Idolatry," vol. II., p. 373). And, again, "Man derives his spiritual soul (Buddhi) from the *essence* of the Mânasa-Putra, the Sons of Wisdom, who are the Divine Beings (or Angels) ruling and presiding over the planet Mercury (not a physical planet, but one of those planets which correspond mystically through Buddhi with particular organs, such as eyes, ears, &c.)"

It should be remembered that, just as stated above, the Sun is the occult Central Spiritual Sun, similarly, Mithra or Mercury must also be taken as one of the occult planets and not the physical one known to Astronomy, concerning which something will be said further on. Suffice it to say, however, that we are not far removed from our legitimate purpose of approaching the invisible Sun, the Logos, in making obeisance to Mithra.

We now come to the word Aspa, a term which also possesses a philosophy of its own, like those we have spoken of above. What are these Aspa? They are the "swift horses," say all the translators of the Avastâ, the word being similar to the Sanskrit word अश्व. Some people would have us believe that the number of these horses is seven, and in some of the symbolical representations of the Sun we actually see the *rath*

---

* *Cf. Khorshed Niyâesh* or *Yasht:*—" I praise the friendship which is the best of friendships, *between the Moon and the Sun.*" "Friendship" does not give an exact idea of the word "*Hakhegremcha.*" The Moon of the Avasta also cannot be taken as the physical Moon. "The real Sun and the real Moon are as invisible as real Man," says the "Secret Doctrine," vol. I., p. 179, *o. e.*

or chariot of the Surya-Nârâyan drawn by seven horses. If they are seven in number they might correspond to the Ameshâspentas ; but their number varies, and their significance differs. The Aspa related to the spiritual Sun can be taken safely as the Aswins of the Hindu philosophy, who are sometimes called Kûmâras, or bachelors. Turning to the Vedic philosophy, we see in this term some of the highest gods, the twin-sons of the Sun and Aditi (Space). These Aswins, or Aswinau (dual), or Aswini-Kumâras are the most mysterious and occult gods of all, who have "puzzled the oldest commentators." . . . . . They are "swift as falcons." Esoterically they are the Kumâra-Egos, the reincarnating "principles," says our teacher, H. P. B. The nature and functions of these mysterious beings have been very lucidly and ably described in the "Birth and Evolution of the Soul," by Mrs. Besant, and I cannot do better than offer you some quotations bearing on this subject.

"These mighty Spiritual Intelligences," she says, "had accomplished what we are aiming at now. They are the successful men of past ages, who have developed into perfect men, perfect Intelligences, and now are, so to speak, coöperating in the building of a new race, coöperating in the production of a new humanity. But up to the point at which we are, [*i. e.*, until the form was perfect] they had taken no part in this evolution that had been going on—the physical side, the evolution of form. Now from These is to come a second line, from the Sons of Mind, Lords of Light ; They are called sometimes, Pillars of Light, and so on. These, coming down to the Earth, when the Tabernacles were ready to receive Them, came to give the necessary impulse in order that at this point of junction a new individual might arise, and afforded the active, impelling, positive energy." It is said at the beginning of the "Secret Doctrine" that "some projected a spark," and "some entered the body . . . . Those who entered became Arhats," or Divine Sages. "Those are the great Teachers of Humanity in the earlier days of our Race," it is further stated, "They formed the nurseries of Adepts for the present age ; the Great Teachers who came in order that this infant humanity might be guarded and protected and helped in its earlier stages."

The Zoroastrians will remember that their Scriptures and traditional works contain names of some of These mighty Adepts.*

Until the union was formed between the almost soulless form and the light of the Kumaras there was no Ego, in the proper sense of the term, although there was the animal soul, if we apply that term to the feelings and emotions. But the true Ego, that which is capable of achieving immortality, was not there. "The Ego which is now in each of you was not in existence as Ego, any more than the plant which will develope from a germ if the germ be fertilized, is in existence before that fertilization takes place." Let us take an illustration from the same lecture, from which we have taken the above: "Take one of the lower animals. Next we will come to the domesticated . . . With regard to the wild animal there is the germ of mind, but very little that you can really call mind. Suppose you take an animal and domesticate it, and suppose you domesticate it for generations, you will have handed on in the three bodies of that animal—the physical, the astral, and the kâmic—you will have handed on a very definite heredity ; and if these individuals are domesticated time after time, you will find greater and greater intelligence, as it may be called, evolving. Some qualities are developed in the domesticated animal which we are compelled to say are due to intelligence.† You will develope in it a limited reason ; you will develope in it a limited memory ; you will develope in it a limited judgment. Now, these are qualities of the mind, not qualities of Kâma. How is it that in this lower animal these qualities are developed ? They are deve-

---

* See " The Divine Kings and Adepts of Zoroastrianism," *Theosophist*, July and August 1896.

† It may be remarked here that it is these domesticated animals—*i.e.*, humanized to a certain extent—that are slaughtered for human food in great numbers in every city which we are led to believe is civilized!

loped artificially by the playing upon it of the human intelligence. To that animal, the mind in you to some extent plays the part which the Sons of Mind [the Aswini-Kumâras] play to Humanity; and, thrown out from the comparatively developed Intelligence in man, these rays, these energetic rays of mental influence, vitalize the germ in the Kâma of the animal, and so produce artificially, as it were, an infant mind," which is the mind or human soul which we are now possessed of.

Now, then, you will see that the Aspâ of the *Khorshed-Niyâesh*, the so-called "horses," are our mind-givers, the sons of the Spiritual Sun, Ahura-Mazda. Now it will be easy for you to understand why horse is placed as a symbol of mind in some of the occult works, and you will understand also the mystery of *Aswamedham* ceremony, the horse sacrifice of the Mahâbhârata, in which the horse is let loose in the city of ten gates, this body, before it is sacrificed. But this "horse" or "mind" is not to be understood as the spark projected into us by the Aswini-Kumâras; it is the lower animal mind which existed in us before their contact with us. Yes, it is by sacrificing this "horse," or lower mind, that the object of life is attained; because the "Voice of the Silence" says:—"Having become indifferent to objects of perception the pupil must seek out the *râjâh* of the senses, the Thought-Producer, he who awakes illusion. The mind is the great Slayer of the Real. Let the Disciple slay the Slayer."

Can we support this teaching from Zoroastrianism? Perhaps we can. Open the "Bundahish," and in the very first chapter you will find that, in the beginning Ahura-Mazda " produced spiritually the creatures which were necessary, . . . that they were *unthinking* and unmoving, with intangible bodies." Thus mind was not incarnated into the body in the beginning, it was sent by the Aswinau afterwards.

We come then to the "eyes" of Ahura-Mazda. The sun and moon are stated to be the eyes of Ahura-Mazda, which are also taken as symbols of the heart and mind respectively.

According to the Vedic literature, however, our sun is called *Loka-chakshûh*, the "eye of the world." But the eye of Ahura-Mazda refers to the heart of everything, whether it be an atom, a man or a planet.

Nemo Geûsh, or obeisance to the Primeval Cow, is the point next under consideration. Just as we have seen before, a spiritual truth underlying the symbol of "horse," we shall also see some truth in the symbol of the sacred Cow. *Geùsh* comes from the root *go* or *gow*, which means cow, tongue, earth, life or *jiva*, &c. Happily the modern translators have been trying to interpret the occult terms fairly, and we see that Geûsh has a wider meaning than was formerly attached to it. It means the soul of the universe; it means also *jiva*. Isaac Myer says in the *Path* (March 1887), that "AUM, the sacred word, is the first-born Word or Logos of the Deity, the Memrah of the Jews, the Honover of the Parsis, the origin of the Vedas, which appeared before all things, and the image of Aum is the sacred Cow, which is also a symbol of the universe." Thus, in making obeisance to the "Cow" or *Geúsh*, one makes obeisance to the image of Aum. Gaiyahe or Gayomarathân or Gayomard often appears side by side with Geûsh or the Primeval Cow, in the Avestâ as well as in the "Bundahish," and from the hints thrown here and there about him in this literature, he appears not a man like ourselves, but a lunar man or god. An explanation of this being will be found elsewhere (*vide* ante page 94.)

After making obeisance to the "Existence of the Pure, which was, which is, and which will be," certain formulas relating to certain divisions of time are recited; after which the worshipper enters on the adoration of the Spiritual Sun, and the Existences related to it.

The next passage in the *Niyáesh* runs as follows :—

"*The Immortal Sun, shining, with swift Aspa, we praise. Mithra, possessing wide regions, the truth-speaking, the gatherer, the thousand-eared, well-shaped, with ten-thousand eyes, great, endued with far watching sight, the strong, not sleeping, wakeful, we praise. Mithra, the Lord of all regions, we praise, whom Ahura-Mazda has produced as the most brilliant of the heavenly Yazatas. Therefore come hither, (that is, manifest in us,) Mithra and Ahura the Great. The immortal brilliant Sun, with swift Aspa, we praise."*

In the foregoing passage we do not see anything new to animadvert upon, except that the devotee who prays to the Sun prays also that Mithra, the Yazata who presides over Buddhi, and Ahura may become manifest to him or may be revealed to him from within. He does not ask for any worldly good, but he wills that Ahura the Great may be revealed to him that he may attain thereby that end which is essential to every one.

Proceeding further we find the most occult of the passages in the *Niyâesh* :—

Tistrya with healthful eyes, we praise Thee thrice. Tistrya we praise. The stars pertaining to Tistrya we praise. Tistrya of the shining glory (Khoreh) *we praise. The star Vanant of Mazda we praise. The star Tistrya of the shining glory* (Khoreh) *we praise.*

The Heaven which follows its own law, we praise. The Boundless Time we praise. Time the Ruler of the Long Period we praise. The holy Wind, the well-created, we praise.

The rightest Divine Wisdom of Mazda we praise. The good Mazdayasnian Law we praise. The most acceptable Path we praise. The Golden Tube we praise. The mountain Saokant of Mazda we praise. All holy heavenly Yazatas we praise. All earthly Yazatas we praise. We praise the Heavenly Tree ; we praise our own Fravashi. Come hither (manifest), *O Mazda. The good, strong, holy Fravashis of the Pure we praise. The immortal brilliant Sun, with swift Aspa we praise."*

Superfluously observed, the commencement of this passage will appear as star-worship. But while we have taken the Sun of this prayer as Ahura-Mazda, we must likewise find out what this Tistrya and the stars pertaining to it may mean.

The Tistrya and the Vanant appear to be stars, but they are not the stars that we see. In exoteric religion, Tistrya is considered as the god of rain, corresponding to Indra of the Hindus, and Jupiter Pluvius of the Greeks. An Orthodox Parsi might take objection, however, to the comparison of Tistrya with the Hindu God Indra, on the ground that the latter is scorned at in the Avastâ; but the Indra of the Avastâ does not stand for the god of rain of the Hindus. The term used there may refer to something else. Because if we scorn at Indra, the god of rain of the Hindus, then we scorn at Tistrya, the Yazata or god of rain of the Parsis, which amounts to scorning at Ahura-Mazda Himself, in one sense, as on certain occasions Jupiter, Indra, Bhrihaspati, all stand for Ahura-Mazda, as will be seen from the "Bundahish" and the "Desatir." Just as the word *Buddhi* in the Sanskrit literature bears quite a different meaning, namely, physical intelligence, from what the same word means in the Avastâ and the Buddhistic literature, namely, spiritual wisdom, similarly the word Indra in the Avastâ has quite a different meaning from that given to it in the Vedas. Madame Blavatsky says that "Ahura-Mazda is the Father of Tistrya, the rain-bestowing god (the 6th Principle), that fructifies the parched soil of the 5th and 4th, and helps them to bear good fruit through their own existences, *i. e.*, by tasting of Haoma, the tree of eternal life, through spiritual enlightenment." (*Theosophist*, vol. 4, p. 241, &c). While our personality—the fleeting and evanescent—is related to the astrological stars, our individuality—the eternal Ego—may be related to these two most occult and sacred powers which are called "stars" and invoked here. These stars are centres of various spheres, to whom Hazrat Âzar Kaivân attaches various colours in the "Makâshefât-i-Kaivâni." It is to be remembered that no occultist would reveal occult truth in its naked light, but they generally give out these truths to the masses, in the garb of symbols and allegories. Hazrat Âzar Kaivân is no exception to the rule, as he appears most probably to have used some blinds in regard to colours.

Zravâne Akarnê, the Boundless Time, is then praised. With regard to the Boundless Time, it should be borne in mind, again, that it is not the time as we know it. There is a misunderstanding among the Parsis about the Boundless Time, identifying it with what we know as time. Time as we know it, by its relativity to our present consciousness as Past, Present and Future, is an illusion according to the Secret Doctrine. " Time is only an illusion produced by the succession of our states of consciousness as we travel through eternal duration, and it does not exist where no consciousness exists in which the illusion can be produced, but 'lies asleep.' The present is only a mathematical line which divides that part of eternal duration which we call the future, from that part which we call the past." The modern Parsis confound this time with the Boundless Time, Zravane Akarnê, the inconceivable, 'eternal duration,' and differ from the Theosophical views. But this was understood in a better way by a more philosophical sect of ancient Parsis, whose views agreed with the Theosophical idea, for which they were called the Zarvanists.

Then we praise *Vâtem spentem*, the spiritual Vâyû, about which hints will be thrown out further on, while referring to the channel through which they run.

Razishtâm chishtâm Mazdadâtâm, the wisdom coming from Mazda, the knowledge of true religion, is praised next; then *Daenâm Vanguhim Mazdayasnim*, the Wisdom, the Law, which is true Religion. The word *Daen* or *Din*, commonly means religion, but this religion is not to be taken in its ordinary sense as the masses understand it now : it is the ancient Wisdom-Religion which is so preëminently indicated by Theosophy or *Khodâsanâsi*. It means also the great Law. In the "Vendidad" (Fargard II, 2) Ahura-Mazda is made to say to Zarathushtra the Spitama, that Yima was the "first mortal before thee with whom I, Ahura-Mazda, did converse, to whom I taught the Law of Ahura, the Law of Zarathushtra ;" that is to say, the Law of Zarathustha is the same as the Law of Ahura-Mazda, which was revealed to Zarathushtra. This is the absolute knowledge which is in the Spirit. The Adepts or Initiates who thus acquire the knowledge of the Absolute, time after time, impart a portion of it to mankind in accordance with the growth, mental capacity, and spiritual needs of humanity, in the country and in the age in which they live. In this way have been formed different religions. No religious books, as they are now in our possession, contain absolute knowledge. It is this partial knowledge which has been preserved till now in the scriptures of the various religions of the world. No religion, therefore, however great its literature may be, can possess the absolute knowledge that is in the Spirit. Hazrat Âzar Kaivân also affirms this statement, while he says that at a certain stage in his Yoga training he acquired vast wisdom, the like of which he never learnt in any of the books of the world. In fact the knowledge of the ultimates of things is not to be found in any man-made books, either religious or profane. Every Zoroastrian knows that a greater portion of the religious literature of his forefathers is lost. How can he then boast that he knows *the* Religion ? The man, therefore, who boasts in his self-sufficiency, or self-conceit, after reading a few books of his own religion, that he knows all about his religion, and others do not, lives in a fool's paradise ; because the true basis of every great religion is quite different from what is commonly accepted by the masses. It is necessary, therefore, to study as many scriptures as we can, in order to gain as much knowledge of the Spirit as we possibly can in the present state of human evolution, always bearing in mind the wise words of the "Bhagavad Gîtâ":

"It is best to die in one's own *dharma;* the *dharma* of another is full of dangers."

Now mark the second object of the Theosophical Society: It is "to encourage the study of comparative religion, philosophy and science." It is a known fact, to all students of history, that all the great religions of the world had their rise in the East, nay, their very Founders were all of Oriental extraction. Hence it is that the study of Eastern religious literature has been recommended in the second object of the Society. And the present paper is nothing but an outcome of my humble efforts in this direction. It is, therefore, absolutely necessary to study all the scriptures of the world, side by side, if one wishes to throw any useful light on the scriptures of his own religion. It is for this very reason that every true member of this Society is impelled to the study the literature of other religions, but for the matter of that it is extremely short-sighted on the part of those ignorant of the teachings of Theosophy, to charge its members with being converts to Buddhism, Hinduism or any other *ism* in the world.

The *Niyáesh* further states, "*pathâm khâstâtem yazmaidê*" ; that is, of all the paths, the acceptable one we praise. What is this path which is the most acceptable one? It should be no other path than the one through which we reach nigh unto the Sun. Among the paths, we have the path of daily *Faraziat*, or as a Hindu would call it, the *Nityakarma*, the daily observances; we have the path of reciting Mantras or mantra-japam of the Hindus; then there is the path of pilgrimage to various sacred places; and lastly, there is the path of hearing sacred poems or epics, and holy admonitions from the priests. These are means, no doubt, which may help one, to a certain extent, in preparing for the one true path; but they cannot be called the direct paths to approach the Invisible Central Sun, Ahura-Mazda. Akho, the poet of Gujarat, says:—

" Fifty-three years have passed away in making *tilak* (one of the daily observances of the Hindus) ; the holes of the prayer-beads have worn away; the feet are tired of performing pilgrimages, and yet I have not been able to approach the feet of Hari, the Lord. The ears have almost become deaf through repeated hearing of the sacred epics, and yet." says Akho, "divine knowledge never did dawn on me."

Then what is the path which is the most acceptable or legitimate which would lead us to Ahura? That path is the human heart. Of all the paths, that of the heart is the most acceptable. It is the "Heart Doctrine" which carries us nearer God. It is that Golden Gate, the door from whence divine inspirations come. It is the seat of Faith divine, it is the seat of Love supreme, it is the seat of true devotion or *bhakti*. It is the altar on which all worldly sacrifices are to be made. The Christian Bible truly says that only the pure in heart shall see God. And why? Because it is in the heart that the divine light shines; it is through the heart that the spiritual Sun can be found.

"The way to final freedom is within thy SELF," says the Book of the Golden Precepts; and "Light on the Path" recommends us to "seek out the way. Seek out the way by retreating within. Seek the way by advancing boldly without. Seek it not by any one road exclusively. For each being there may be discovered one road which seems the most desirable. But the way is not found by devotion alone, by religious contemplation alone, by ardent efforts for progress, by self-sacrificing labour, by studious observation of life. Neither, alone, can take the disciple more than one step onwards. All steps are necessary to make up the ladder. The vices of men become steps in the ladder, one by one, as they are surmounted. The virtues of man are steps indeed, necessary—not by any means to be dispensed with. Yet, though they create a fair atmosphere and a happy future, they are useless if they stand alone. The whole nature of man must be used wisely by the one who desires to enter the way. Each man is to himself absolutely the way, the truth, and the life. But he is only so when he sees his whole individuality clearly and, by the force of his awakened spiritual will, recognises his personality as not himself, but that thing which he has with pain created for his own use, and by means of which he purposes, as his growth slowly expands and his intelligence increases, to reach to the life beyond separateness. When he knows that for this his wonderful complex separated life exists, then, indeed, and then only, he is upon the way. Seek it by plunging into the mysterious and glorious depths of your own inmost being. Seek it by testing all experience, by utilizing the senses in order to understand the growth and meaning of individuality, and the beauty and obscurity of those other divine fragments which are struggling side by side with you, and form the race to which you belong. Seek it by study of the laws of being, the laws of nature, the laws of the supernatural ; and seek it by making profound obeisance of the soul to the dim star that burns within. Steadily, as you watch and worship, its light will grow stronger. Then you may know you have found the beginning of the way. And when you have found the end, its light will suddenly become the infinite light."

And a Sufi rightly says :

"I measured intensely, I pondered with heed
(Ah ! fruitless my labor) the Cross and its creed.
To the Pagod I rushed, and the Magian's shrine,
But my eye caught no glimpse of a glory divine.
The reins of research to the Caaba I bent,
Whither hopefully thronging the old and young went ;
Candasai, Herat searched I wistfully through,
Nor above nor beneath came the Loved One to view !
I toiled to the summit, wild, pathless and lone,
Of the globe-girding Kâf, but the Phœnix had flown,
The seventh earth I traversed, seventh heaven explored,
But in neither discerned I the court of the Lord.
I questioned the Pen and the tablet of Fate,
But they whispered not where He pavilions his state.
My vision I strained, but my God-scanning eye
No trace that to Godhead belongs could descry.
But when I my glance turned within my own breast,
Lo! the vainly sought Loved One, the Godhead confessed,
In the whirl of its transport my spirit was tossed
Till each atom of separate being I lost :
And the bright sun of Tanniz madder than me,
Or a wilder, hath never yet seen, nor shall see."

Now we come to the phrase "*Zarenomantem surem yazmaidê.*" Looking at the philological translations of this phrase we do not find any of its sensible meaning. The first two words are translated "dangerous weapon," "golden instrument," "gold-mine," &c. M. Darmesteter, however, cites a footnote on this subject which he calls a "Sanskrit translation" of this and of the phrase that follows, but which appears to be a commentary rather than a translation, and gives us some clue to a better understanding of this obscure phrase, as it was done by a person who may have understood occultism. The note states :—

"On Mount Saokant there is a golden tube coming from the root of the earth; the water that is on the surface of the earth goes up through the hole of that tube to the heavens, and being driven by the wind [*? Vâtem spentem*] spreads everywhere, and thus the dew is produced."

One might naturally ask, what this " golden tube" has to do with the sun-worship. It is by taking this mystic tube in connection with the occult constitution of man that we are mostly concerned. What this "golden tube" is to earth, the channel through which the vital airs run is to microcosm, the man. It is called *Sushumna-nâdi*, which is running right through the spinal cord, and with which all students of the Yoga-vidyâ are so familiar. We find some account of this *nâdi*, or " golden tube," together with the mystical mountain connected with it, the spiritual wind, and the tree of life which is called *Haoma-urvanem*, in one of the sacred books of our Hindu brothers, called "Uttara Gîtâ." Arjuna having forgotten the truth taught to him by Shrî Krishna in his initiation, which we see contained in the "Bhagavad Gîtâ," he was initiated again and taught further truth which we see preserved in the Uttara Gîtâ.

" Like the back-bone of a vînâ, or harp, the long tract of bone, with many joints, that stretches along the trunk up to the head of a human being is called the Meru-Danda (spinal column). There is an aperture or channel hole that passes through this Meru-Danda from the Mûla-Dhâras to the head; through this aperture passes a Nâdi which the Yogîs call the Brahma Nâdi or Sushumnâ.

" Sushumnâ is a fine nerve that passes between Ida and Pingalû ; from this Sushumnâ, all the Jnâna-Nâdis (sensory nerves) take their birth, hence it is called the Jnâna-Nâdi."

[That Nâdi that takes its origin from the Sahasrâra, and growing gradually finer, descends through the canal of the spinal column, is called the Sushumnâ. At first, nine sets of smaller Nâdis spring from it and spread towards the eyes and other organs of sense, etc., afterwards from each joint of the spinal column to which the pairs of ribs are attached, one on either side, and underneath each rib, there are successively stretched thirty-two* sets of Nâdis, with innumerable branchlets covering the whole body like a network ; these produce the sense of touch and perform other necessary work requisite for the up-keep of the Sthûla Sharîra. These Nâdis are so fine in their texture that if 400 of them be collected and tied together, still they cannot be seen by the naked eye ; though so fine, still they are like *pipes*, are hollow, and in this space there exists a certain substance, like oil, in which the Chaitanya reflects ; for this reason the Rishis call the Sushumnâ the parent of all these smaller Nâdis, the Jnâna-Nâdi, and consider it to be just like a *tree* with its innumerable branches covering the whole of the human body, the root, being upwards—at the Sahasrâra—and the branches downwards.]

[As all outward objects that are cognizable by the human senses are reflected in the Sushumnâ Nâdi, therefore the Rishis call this body the "Microcosm." For instance, when you see the sun, moon, or stars, you do not actually go near to them in order to see, but you see them because they are reflected in your Sushumnâ Nâdi. If your mind had the power to go out of your body, in order to see them, then you would be able to see all and everything that lies in the "Royal Road," and in such a case you would know all and every occurrence that takes place in every quarter of this globe, nay, and elsewhere, in this vast universe.]†

---

* The *Kusti*, the sacred thread of the Parsis, has seventy-two warps, each representing a thousand *Nâdis*.

† See article; The Sacred Haoma Tree, *ante* p. 98.

"As various Nâdis have sprung up from the Sushumnâ —the receptacle of the Inner soul of all Jîvas—and are stretched out in all directions of the physical body, therefore it is considered like a huge tree reversed. Tatva-Jnânins alone are able to walk on every branch of this tree by the help of *Prâna-Vâyu*.

"In this human body there exists seventy-two thousand Nadis which admit of sufficient space for entrance into them of Vâyu; the Yogis alone become acquainted with the true nature of these Nâdis by virtue of their Yoga-Karma.

"Having closed up the nine portals of the body, and being acquainted with the source and nature of the Nâdis that stretch up and down the seats of the several organs of sense, the Jîva, rising to the state of superior knowledge with the aid of the Life-Breath, attains Moksha."

It will be seen from the above explanation that the founder of Sun-worship, whoever he may have been, was thoroughly and practically conversant with the science of Yoga—that science which teaches man how to reunite himself to the Supreme Source of which he is a spark. We also see how the mere dead letter interpretations of phrases like those we are now commenting upon, are utterly unintelligible without the aid of mysticism, and how they shine forth in their true sublimity, and in the depth of their spiritual significance when they are seen through the light of occult philosophy.

A few years ago Professor Max Müller, the great Orientalist and Philologist, positively declined to see anything like esoteric or occult significance in the Buddhist, Hindu and other world-scriptures; but latterly has been compelled by advancing studies in the field of Oriental literature to acknowledge that there *is* an esoteric side to the religious scriptures of the world. It is therefore a matter of regret and surprise to see a few of the students and scholars of our scriptures among our own community still clinging to their superficial views as regards the interpretation of our scriptures which they hesitate to handle in any light except that of philology, although a master in that science has seen reason to change his similar views on the subject.

Returning to our subject, we may note that we do not find any clear explanation about the mystic Mount Saokant in the Avastâ literature. But as it occurs after the term "golden tube," in this *Niyâesh*, it can safely be assumed that it signifies certain occult part of earth as well as of human constitution. This mount can be easily identified with Mount Meru of the Hindu scriptures, a mountain which is said to be in the centre of the earth and which is held to be the abode of the holy gods. Compare this with the subsequent phrase in the *Khorshed-Niyâesh*, namely, "All pure heavenly Yazatas we praise ; all earthly Yazatas we praise." The occult teaching places Meru in the very centre of the North Pole, pointing it out as the site of the first continent on our earth after the solidification of the globe. This can be agreed upon by comparing the Sanskrit note given above. We have seen that Meru-Danda is the same as the spinal cord, and as Mount Meru—analogically Mount Saokant—is placed at the North Pole of the earth, we may reasonably seek for this sacred mountain in the human constitution at the very top of the spinal column. In other words, Mount Saokant can be located at the top of the human brain and not in a geographical position, as the bewildered students of the Avastâ literature would have it. To every student of Yoga philosophy a spot at the top of the human brain is known as the Brahmarandhra, and it is the highest of the *chakras* (or occult centre of force), by transferring his consciousness to which the Yogi attains the highest state of spiritual knowledge. There are many such occult or psychic centres in our bodies, as also similar veins and arteries through which the invisible life-currents flow as regularly and systematically as the physical blood through the veins and arteries known to the physiologist ; these occult centres being only discerned in a living state in clairvoyance by a Yogi, and not in a *post mortem* state, after the life has flown away, as is now attempted by the anatomists. This invisible vascular system in our body is metaphorically compared to a tree, and is variously called the Haoma-tree, the Soma-tree, the Aswattha tree, the Tree of Life, &c., in various religious systems. This Tree of Life is spoken of as Haoma-urvânem in the same passage of the Sun worship, and you will now readily perceive why this mystic and sacred tree—which is within man himself or which is man himself—is praised in this *Niyâesh*. It is by drinking para-Haoma, the juice of *this* tree, that the man becomes immortal. I remember to have heard of a Rajah spending thousands of rupees in search of a Soma-tree, which corresponds to this Haoma ; you may have heard also Professor Max Müller and other Orientalists comparing this Haoma or Soma to some botanical plants. We read, sometime ago, of some scientific expedition, sent to Afghanistan, whose leaders were asked, among other things, to search for this plant in that country of hills and rocks ; while the occult teaching points out that the sacred tree is within man himself.

* * * * * *

Subsequently we find some passages which appear to have been applicable to the physical sun ; but as the maxim runs, "as above so below," they can likewise be applied to the spiritual side.

" *When the Sun grows up then it becomes the cause of making the Earth created by Ahura pure, the flowing waters pure, the water of the springs pure, the water of the seas pure, the water of the ponds pure, the pure creation belonging to Spenta-Mainyû is purified.*"

On the physical plane we see that the physical sun is the great purifier : the physical world exists because the physical sun exists. Let the influence of the sun be diminished a little, and the earth is sure to become uninhabitable on account of certain evil prevailing on it. It was most manifest that the sunshine was dim on the occasion of the breaking out of the bubonic plague in Bombay and the surrounding country. The Western scientists are now engaged in investigating the terrestrial influence of the sun upon the life of certain micro-organisms which they call microbes, bacilli, or bacteria. It is said that they are like living dust floating in the atmosphere, and are wafted about from one end of the world to another with extreme rapidity. We are taught that they serve men in some respects as in "breaking up of refuse organic matter, the fertilization of the soil, the production of alcohol, &c.," (if that be useful at all to mankind), yet they are proved very deleterious to him, in that they are the cause of epidemics, plagues, &c., through "their extraordinary power of rapid reproduction." It is estimated that if one bacillus is made to multiply its species without any antagonistic influence, in liquid substances, it will in the course of a day "give rise to a progeny four times as numerous as the whole population of London." The power of their propagation is greater during night or when there is no sunshine. An experiment is recorded which was made by two Germans on the river Isar, near Munich, who sat the whole night on the riverbank determining the number of microbes therein during the night. "At a quarter past six in the evening 160 bacteria were found in about twenty drops of water; but at three and four o'clock in the morning, when the water had therefore been for several hours in darkness, there were more than twice or even three times the number of germs present, indicating that, in the absence of their deadly foe, sun, they had multiplied with great freedom—only, however, as was found when morning approached and day wore on, to be kept once more in subjection and reduced in number."

Here, then, you will find, perhaps, the secret of our grandmother's "superstition," that often warns us not to draw water from a well at night. In this you will find also the secret of religious ablution. When a Parsi or a Brahman performs religious ablution, he takes a handful of water to magnetise or electrify it, as it were, by reciting "Praise be to Ahura-Mazda," if he be a Parsi, and by reciting the Gâetri if he be a

Brahman, and scatters the water over his head. By the spreading of this magnetised or consecrated water the foul Dru*g*as, or elements, which may be hovering over one's body, are scattered away, so to speak, as by a thunderbolt. Thus one of the "superstitions" can be shown to be a scientific truth. But imagine the havoc these insignificant little microbes would perpetrate were they to propagate in the sunlight also, especially if they belonged to that class of microbes which are the germs of cholera or of any such diseases. The scientists affirm that the sunshine is the most efficacious remedy. And it is for this reason that we recognise the truth taught in the subsequent passage in the prayer to the Sun:

" *For if the Sun does not rise then the demons slay all which live in the seven Karshvaras. Not a heavenly Yazata finds out defence nor gains paitishtam* (Sanskrit, *pratishthâ = settlement*) *in the corporeal world.*"

Let us apply this analogy now to the Spiritual Sun. Microbes or bacteria of a still subtler nature can be posited in the higher or subtler state of matter, which, in the Theosophical literature we call, generally, astral matter or Astral Light. In the Avastâ literature we often read of mystic oceans, seas and rivers, which seem to be different states of astral matter, as the spiritual counterpart of water corresponds with the Astral Light. We are taught that there are numerous grades of Dru*g*as and Dru*g*a-nasus, which in the Theosophical literature are called elementals and elementaries, inhabiting the Astral world. These evil ones are said to be in never-ending war with the "creation of the pure," the creation of Ahura-Mazda. We know that the astral plane is the plane of desire, the astral body is the body of desire, and our every thought which has a desire draws an elemental towards it of its own colour and nature, and thus we prolong our destiny and retard our future progress in approaching the Spiritual Sun. But when the inner Sun shines, it likewise destroys all these evil "thieves and robbers," the Yatus and Pairikas,—nay, it dispels the very *death* of man, and makes him immortal. The *Niyâesh* further on says :

"*Who then offers to the Sun, the immortal, shining, with swift Aspa, to withstand the darkness, to withstand the demons who spring from darkness, to oppose thieves and robbers, to oppose the Yâtûs and Pairikas, to oppose the perishable death, he offers to Ahura-Mazda, he offers to the Ameshaspentas, he offers to Haoma-ûrvânem (the Tree of Life), he offers to all heavenly and earthly Yazatas, who offers to the Sun, the immortal, shining, with swift Aspa.*"

NASARVANJI F. BILIMORIA.

—*Theosophist*, vol.

THE "FIRE-WORSHIP."

UNIVERSAL ADORATION OF FIRE.

THE Parsis are sometimes called Fire-worshippers, because they hold fire in higher reverence than any other nation of the world. But the Parsis do not stand alone in their reverence towards this visible symbol of the Divine. Like their brother Adepts of Irân, the ancient Indian Rishis have also installed fire in places of worship. It is quite natural therefore that one should turn to the Vedas to see what has been written therein about this sacred element. Agni—Fire —is there, spoken of as Brahmasvarûpa, *i. e.*, of a form like Brahma. The Rig-Veda is replete with solemn hymns and invocations to Fire ; its very beginning is fire-worship :

"I adore Agni, the most ancient, family priest, the Lord of Yajna, the chief priest, the Hotâr, the source of Light."

The first hymn of the second Mandala is also addressed to Agni, attributing to him all the functions of the sacrificial priests and their assistants :—

"Thine, Agni, is the office of Hotâra, thine the regulated functions of Potas, thine the office of Neshtâra, thou art the Agnidh of the pious ; thine is the function of Prashastara, thou actest as Adhvaryu, thou art the Brahman, and the lord of the house in our abode.

"Thou, Agni, art Indra, the chief of the holy, thou art Vishnu the wide-stepping, the adorable ; thou, oh Brahmanaspati, art the Brahman, the possessor of wealth, thou; oh sustainer, art associated with the ceremonial."—(*R. V.*, ii; 1-1-2.)

In other verses of the same hymn, Agni is identified with Varuna, Mitra, Aryaman, Ansha, Tvashtara, Rudra, Pushan, Savitar, Bhaga,—in fact, with the whole range of Vedic gods—and for the matter of that, the Avastaic Fire can also be identified with the Zoroastrian Yazatas—and it is from the hymns like these that is drawn the belief that the Vedic people worshipped only one Deity under many names. Here, again, it is quite certain that, later on, Agni had a mystical meaning, as the three-fold Self of Fire,—the vital fire in this world, the emotional fire in the middle world, the intuitional fire in the spiritual world. With hymns like this, to Agni, the Lord of Fire, the first eight out of the ten Mandalas of hymns open, to be followed by hymns to Indra, the Lord of Heavens, as will be seen from the following citations :—

"With uprising flame do thou, O son of strength, when praised, give abundant vigour to thy worshippers ; Oh Agni, give brilliant fortune and prosperity to Vishvâmitra and his family,—often have we given lustre to thy form."

" The two sons of Bharat, Devashravas and Devavata, have brilliantly kindled the bright burning Agni ; Oh Agni, look on us with abundant wealth, be for us a bringer of nourishment day by day.

" Ten fingers have engendered the ancient god, the wellborn, beloved of mothers ; Oh Devashravas, praise the Agni of Devavata—the Agni who has become the ruler of beings.

" There I laid down on the most excellent spot on earth, on the place of worship, on a fair day among days ; by the rivers Drishadvati, Apaya, and Sarasvati where Manu's children dwell, shine thou, Agni, brilliantly.

" Agni, the god of all men, like a neighing horse is kindled by the Kushikâs, with their engendering fingers in every age, may this Agni lay wealth on us, with vigour, with horses,— Agni, ever alive among the immortals."

These hymns are evidently mystical and symbolical, " the horses and brilliant wealth" being symbols of spiritual gifts and not worldly affluence.

The Vishnu Purána also speaks of Agni as the " month-born son of Brahma."

Looking to other great religions, we find the early Christians stating " the Lord, thy God, is a consuming fire." Their reference to the "burning bush of Moses" shows them to be as much "fire-worshippers" as any "heathen" venerator of the divine element. The late Bishop Leo Meurin's Writings are replete with ideas showing how even the Christians are one in Fire-worship. We meet at the very inception of the Mosaic religion with the reflection of God, when in the year 1492 before Christ He called Moses and appointed him as His chosen Messenger to king Pharaoh and to the people of Israel. "The Lord appeared to Moses in a Flame of Fire out of the midst of a bush : and he, Moses, saw that the bush was on fire, and was not burnt." We read of ever-burning lamps in Christian sanctuaries, the object and reasons for which will be clearly seen from the following passage :—"The wax candle consumed by its own flame during the holy sacrifice of the Mass, is a representation of what is being repeated on the altar : the holocaust or self-sacrifice on the cross of God, made Man in the virginal womb of Mary. And what else does the Sanctuary Lamp, burning by day and by night in our churches before the Tabernacle, indicate and signify, but the permanent mysterious and real presence of the same incarnate God in the consecrated host kept in the Tabernacle?" The traces of this primeval Aryan worship of Light or Fire are so widespread, various and numerous among the descendants of the Aryan family, that their enumeration and description would fill volumes. Let us cite only a few instances. Among the Greeks we find at Olympia an altar erected to Pan, the Sylvan deity, on which the fire was never allowed to be extinguished. In the temple of Athene Pallas a golden lamp was kept perpetually burning. Xerxes saved the sanctuary of Delos, because of the similarity of its fire-worship with the Zoroastrian. Among the Romans we find at Albalonga the federal altar, from which thirty Latin towns received their sacred fire. The hearth of Vesta at the foot of the Palatine Hill in Rome was the sacred centre for the whole Roman State. And the fire there was also kept perpetually burning by the Vestal Virgins. The eternal fire on it symbolized the perenuity of God's presence, of

Heaven's protection, and of the State's existence. The old Germans had before the statue of their god Thor an ever-burning lamp. The Slavs had in honour of their god Perun, and the Prussians in honour of their Perkun, an everlasting fire which the Crive or sacrificing priest was obliged to maintain with oakwood. The Lithuanians had in Wilna an ever-burning fire, Zincz, and punished the priests with death if they permitted it to go out. The sacred flame in the temple of the Slavic "God of Light," Suantevit, could not be approached by the priests, except whilst keeping back their breath ; a custom reminding us of the *Penom* (*Padân*), the small piece of white cloth which the Parsi Mobeds keep loosely hanging over their mouths while serving the fire, in order to prevent its being polluted by their breath. At Kildare in Ireland a perpetual fire, like that of the Roman Vesta, was maintained in honour of the old pagan *Bridgit*, "the Bright," the Shining ; it was surrounded by a fence, which no man was allowed to approach ; and was not to be blown with the mouth, but only with bellows. Says Dr. Meurin : "With blessed oil the kings, prophets and priests of the Old Testament were anointed : in the New Testament the Promise (*i. e.*, Messiah) Anointed (*i. e.*, Christos) Saviour (*i. e.*, Jesus) is in the highest sense our perpetual High-Priest, Prophet and King. He is present in the Tabernacle not only in His divine nature, in which he is present everywhere, but also in His human nature, however not in its passible, but in its glorious state, hidden under the exterior forms of bread. The ever-burning Lamp before his dwelling-place witnesses and symbolizes his actual presence. Hence, the Church sings with more right than the Synagogue, its prefiguring predecessor."

Even Christian priests themselves show the highest reverence for fire, almost equal to that paid by the Parsis to that Divine Element. Observe what the reverend gentleman has to say on this point :—

"We have before us the sanctuary of the Parsi fire-temple

and the sanctuary of the Christian Church. In both we see a perpetual flame indicating the presence of God: there the Omnipresence of God the Creator, here the Sacramental presence of God the Redeemer. I am unable to express in words the deep and vehement feelings which move my heart, when I kneel in the sanctuary of my Chapel and think of the Parsi fire-temple a few yards off, in which a fire is ever-burning."

The same authority further observes :—

"The Parsis distinguish five fires: the supreme 'Âtar Berezisavo' is the celestial Fire, by way of eminence called 'the Son of Ahura-Mazda.' If this is the third person in the Divine Trias, the doctrine of the Parsis is almost indentical with the original Jewish and with the Christian tenets. The Christians call the Holy Ghost also: '*Fons vivus, ignis, charitas*,' and teach that he proceeds from the Father and the Son, the latter being also called 'Verbum,' the Word, and 'Sapientia,' Wisdom. The Holy Ghost is the Divine Fire of the love that unites the first two persons [principles] of the Holy Trinity. If this spiritual sense be given to 'Fire,' there is enough why the Parsis should be proud of being called Fire-worshippers. In this sense we Christians are real Fire-worshippers. I justly surmise that ' the Son of Ahura-Mazda ' was originally the third of the Zoroastrian and Trias, Ahura being the first and Mazda the second."

Now, the Rosicrucians have also regarded fire in the same light as the Aryans have done. Hermetism is the science of fire, says Eliphas Lévi, the great French mystical writer and occultist. Next to the Parsis, are the Chinese in taking greater care of fire than any other nation of the world at present. A lamp or fire is said to be kept perpetually burning in their houses, whereon they burn incense and other fragrant articles. Passing over the American nations, we find the "savage" of the Western hemisphere proclaiming himself as "born of fire," and herein he seems to have more true and sound philosophy as regards the law of evolution than any modern scientist can boast of, or can hope to expound. Thus we see that fire is held in almost universal reverence by a very large section of humanity, and that both the "savage" and " civilized" unite in adoring this visible effulgent symbol of the Supreme. And

WHY?

Now let us proceed to examine what this general reverence for fire is due to. Is it because the learned Christian theologians of the West inculcate that fire is an instrument of torture—as used by them in the days of the Inquisition —for the punishment of the wicked and impenitent in the state after death, or because the modern scientist teaches that it is the effect of combination : it is heat and light and motion and a correlation of physical and chemical forces in general? This can hardly be the reason for fire commanding the veneration of both the "savage" and the "enlightened." The reason and the true explanation lie in the fact that "fire is the most perfect and unadulterated reflection, in Heaven, as on Earth, of the ONE FLAME"—the all-pervading Deity. "It is Life and Death, the origin and end of every material thing. It is divine 'SUBSTANCE,' " as is taught in the Secret Science. The Rosicrucians who had borrowed all their ideas concerning fire as a mystic and divine element from the " Fire Philosophers," the Magii, or the Persian mystics of yore, defined fire in the most correct way, as can be seen from their writings preserved to us. Much useful and interesting information can be gleaned on this point from " The Rosicrucians," by Hargrave Jennings. Robert Fludd, the famous English Hermetist and the chief of the "Philosophers by Fire," analyses fire into three distinct parts : (1) a visible flame (corresponding to body) ; (2) an invisible astral fire (soul) ; and (3) spiritual essence of fire. He further divides the first into four parts, just as in the case of the septenary division of man's constitution, that is, (1) heat (life), (2) light (mind), (3) electricity (kâmic or molecular powers), and (4) meta-spirit, the synthetic essence or the radical cause of its existence and manifestation. Among the Rosicrucians fire was regarded as the symbol of Deity. It was the source not only of the material atoms, but the container of the spiritual and psychic forces energising them. Broadly analysed, fire, as stated above, is a triple principle, esoterically, a septenary, as are all the rest of the elements. The term "Living Fire" was used by them as a Theurgic term. Its symbol is the sun, certain of whose rays develop the fire of life in a diseased body, impart the knowledge of the future to the sluggish mind, and stimulate to active function a certain psychic and generally dormant faculty in man.

COSMOGENESIS OF FIRE.

I shall now quote a few passages from a standard work on Theosophy to show what part Fire plays in the economy of the Kosmos. These may appear to the average man or to the man of mere intellect without spiritual intuition merely a collection of high-sounding or babbling words. These so-called high-sounding or apparently meaningless passages are not only to be found in the works of all the great saviours and sages of the world, but in almost all literary works which have any pretension to explain the divine mysteries of the Universe or the higher phases in nature and in man. Nay, we may go further and state that the most sublime efforts of the great poets of the world, be they of whatever nationality, are due to their intuitive comprehension, to a certain extent, of these inner workings of nature. It will be seen, therefore, that all the works of these divine sages, mystics and the great poets are not to be discarded simply because they express things which are incomprehensible to our finite mind. Such works are to be approached with the patience and humility of a pure-hearted child, and when we sit down to study earnestly such works with a clean heart and open mind, we are assisted by the very law of nature in understanding their inner hidden meaning, and thus our spiritual intuition is gradually developed, and progress on the divine path assured. It is also true that such passages as I have cited below require exhaustive explanation, but as I have not that capacity and as this paper is too short for that purpose, I have satisfied myself by simply hinting that those who have spiritual intuition will grasp the idea what part these fires play in the universe. With these few words of necessary digression I will now proceed to quote the passages on Fire from the work above referred to, and see how far they assist us in a comprehension of the laws of nature.

"Fire alone is ONE, on the plane of the One Reality ; on that of manifested, hence illusive, being, its particles are fiery lives which live and have their being at the expense of every other life that they consume. . . . From the ONE LIFE, formless and Uncreate, proceeds the Universe of lives. First was manifested from the Deep (*Chaos*) cold luminous fire which formed the curds in Space. . . These fought and a great heat was developed by the encountering and collision, which produced rotation. Then came the first manifested MATE-RIAL—Fire, the hot flames, the wanderers in heaven (comets); heat generates moist vapour ; that forms solid water (?), then dry mist, then liquid mist, watery, that puts out the luminous brightness of the pilgrims (comets ?) and forms solid watery wheels (MATTER globes). Bhûmi (the Earth) appears with six sisters.* These produce by their continuous motion the inferior fire, heat, and an aqueous mist, which yields the third World-Element—WATER ; and from the breath of all (atmospheric) AIR is born. These four are the four lives of the first four periods (Rounds) of Manvantara. The three last will follow."—(The "Secret Doctrine," Vol. i., p. 249-250 *o.e.*).

"Because in the order of cosmic evolution, as taught in the Secret Science, the energy that actuates matter after its first formation into atoms is generated on our plane by cosmic heat ; and because Kosmos, in the sense of dissociated matter, was not before that period." "The first primordial matter, eternal and coëval with space, which has neither a beginning

---

* *Note.*—Bhûmi with her six sisters refer to the seven Karshvaras of the Zoroastrian cosmogony. According to the Vedic teaching there are three earths corresponding to three heavens, and our earth is called Bhûmi. Evidently all thse refer to the earth-chain.

or end, is neither hot nor cold, but is of its own special nature." "This fire is one cosmic element, all-creative force plus *Absolute* Intelligence."

"It (the Web) expands when the breath of fire (the Father) is upon it; it contracts when the breath of the Mother (the root of Matter) touches it. Then the Sons (the Elements with their respective Powers and Intelligences) dissociate and scatter, to return into their Mother's bosom at the end of the Great Day and rebecome one with her. When it (the Web) is cooling it becomes radiant, its Sons expand and contract through their own selves and hearts; they embrace Infinitude."—(Stanza iii—11).

"The expanding of the Universe under the breath of FIRE is very suggestive in the light of the 'Fire-mist' period of which modern science speaks so much, and knows in reality so little. Great heat breaks up the compound elements and resolves the heavenly bodies into their primeval one element," explains the commentary.

From the passages quoted above (which are from the *Stanzas of Dzyan*) we can clearly see the dawn and dissolution of the Universe, in other words, the Manvantaras and the Pralaya.

In Simon Magus, the great Samaritan Gnostic, the Parsis will find a true Zoroastrian. In his philosophy we not only find Vohumano and Ashavahista, but also other Amesha-Spentas —mentioned in the Avastâ—forming the celestial heptarchy. He calls the manifested Deity, Fire—not the physical fire, but that which is "Divine Light and Life and Mind, the Perfect Intellect," which exactly corresponds the attributes of Ahura-Mazda as given in the Avastâ. "The generable cosmos," he says, " was generated from the Ingenerable Fire ; and it commenced to be generated in the following ways. The first six Roots of the Principle of generation (corresponding to the six Amesha-Spentas of the Zoroatrians) which the generated (*sic* Cosmos) took, were from that Fire. And the Roots," he goes on to say, "were generated from the Fire in pairs (dualism in nature)," and he calls these Roots, Mind and Thought, Voice and Name, Reason and Reflection, and in these six Roots there was the whole Boundless Power in potentiality, but not in actuality. "And this Boundless Power is He who has stood, stands, and will stand ; who, if His imaging is perfected while in the six Powers, will be in Essence, Power, Greatness and Completeness, one and the same with the ingenerable and Boundless Power, and not a single whit inferior to that ingenerable, unchangeable and Boundless Power." Here we clearly perceive Boundless Power as the Zarvane-Akarne of the Avastâ.

The above passages require further elucidation, but a paper like this is not the proper place to discuss them in all their bearings, referring as they do to the vast and grand subject of the building of the Universe. Readers who wish to have a better idea on this subject will find enough in the "Secret Doctrine," and they may also profitably consult the series of lectures delivered by Mrs. Besant at the recent (1893) Adyar Convention on the subject of "The Building of the Cosmos."

In the "Oracles of Zoroaster," published in 1593 by the learned Franciscus Patricius, we find various allusions to Fire as an ever-pervading agent throughout cosmic evolution, from its dawn to its dissolution. We select here some of the passages under various heads, where these allusions occur, as they will prove profoundly interesting to all students of occultism :—

"*Monad, Dyad, Triad.*—Where the paternal Monad is, . . . is enlarged, which generates two ; for the Dyad sits by him, and glitters with intellectual sections . . . . . For in the whole world shineth the Triad, over which the Monad rules. This order is the beginning of all section. . . . For thou must conceive that all things serve these three principles [Monad, Dyad, and Triad]. The first course is sacred, but in the middle : another the third aërial, which cherisheth the earth in *Fire :* and fountain of fountains ; and of all fountains ; the matrix containing all things. Thence abundantly springs forth the generation of multifarious matter. Thence extracted a Prester, the flower of glowing *Fire* ; flashing into the cavities of the world : for all things from thence begin to extend downwards their admirable beams.

"*Father, Mind.*—The Father hath snatched away himself; neither hath he shut up his own *Fire* in his intellectual power. For the Father perfected all things, and delivered them over to the second mind, which the whole race of men call the first light begotten of the Father,* for he alone having cropped the flower of the mind from the Father's vigour, for the paternal self-begotten mind, understanding his work, sound in all the *fiery* bond of love, that things might continue for ever.

" *Intelligibles.*—Learn the Intelligible, since it exists beyond the mind, and of the mind which moves the empyreal heaven, for the *Firy* world is the mind of the mind . . . But it behoves not to consider this intelligible with vehemence of intellection, but with the ample *Flame* of the ample mind, which measureth all things except this Intelligible.

"*Ideas.*—But they (ideas) were divided, being by intellectual Fire distributed into other intellectuals : for the king did set before the multiform world an intellectual incorruptible pattern. . . . . .

" Oh how the world hath intellectual guides inflexible ! Because she is the operatrix, because she is the dispensatrix of life-giving *Fire.*"

" For the Father congregated seven firmaments of the world, circumscribing heaven in a round figure. He fixed a great company of in-erratic stars, and he constituted a septenary of erratic animals, placing earth in the middle, and water, in the middle of the earth ; the air above these. He fixed a great company of in-erratic stars, to be carried not by laborious and troublesome tension, but by a settlement which hath no error. He fixed a great company of in-erratic stars, forcing *Fire* to *fire* to be carried by a settlement which hath no error. He consti-

---

* "Fire, son of Ahura-Mazda"—*Avastá.*

tuted them six, casting into the midst the *Fire* of the Sun, suspending their disorder in well-ordered zones."

"*The World.*—The Maker operating by himself framed the world, and there was another bulk of *fire*, by itself operating all things that the body of the world may be perfected, that the world might be manifest and not seem membranous. He framed the whole world of *fire* and water and earth, and all-nourishing ether, the inexpressible and expressible watch-words of the world."

It is said in the "Secret Doctrine," that the Deity, the radical one, is eternal and infinite substance. From It the Arûpa and Rûpa worlds were formed. "From one light seven lights, from each of the seven, seven times seven." We see here seven lights emanating from one light—the one infinite eternal substance.*

In Yasna xvii, Fire is lauded in the following terms:—" Thee, O Fire, son of Ahura-Mazda, the Pure, Lord of Purity, praise we: the Fire Berezi-savo, praise we; the Fire Vohufryana, praise we: the Fire Urvazista, praise we: the Fire Spenista, praise we! The pure King [Fire], the adorable Nairyo-Sañha, praise we! The Fire, the Master over all dwellings, created by Mazda, the Son of Ahura-Mazda, the Pure, Lord of Purity, praise we: together with all Fires!"

Out of the seven fires, five are known, according the Bûndahish, *viz.*, the Fire Berezi-savo, the Fire Vohufryana, the Fire Urvazista, the Fire Vazishta and the Fire Spenista. These five fires correspond to the five known elements, the remaining two being still latent like the two undeveloped senses in man. These five fires were diffused through the six *substances*, that is to say, the works of the six periods, or, as they are called in Zoroastrianism, the six Gahambars, in the successive evolution of the

---

* In the same way the Vedic *Agni* is also described as seven-tongued (*sapta-jihva*) and seven-flamed (*sapta-jvala*). Their names are Káli, Káráli, Mano-Javá, Su-lohitá, Su-dhúmravarná, Ugrá or Sphulinginí, and Pra-diptá, and their esoteric significance denotes the septenary prismatic colours and other septenaries in nature.

world. The six Gahambars are—(1) Maediyozarem, in which the heavenly canopy was formed; (2) Maediyoshahim, in which the collected moisture formed the steamy clouds from which the waters were finally precipitated; (3) Paetishahim, when the earth consolidated itself out of primeval cosmic atoms; (4) Iyâthrem, in which earth gave birth to vegetation; (5) Maediyârem, when the latter slowly evoluted into animal life; and (6) Hamespithmidâm, when the lower animals culminated in man. These periods, it will be observed, describe to a certain extent the cosmic evolution as shown in the passage from the "Secred Doctrine" quoted above. All this will strike perhaps to the most casual reader to be Darwinism pure and simple, but the theory of Darwin does not step beyond the physical evolution of man, and has not a word to say about the monadic.

ANTHROPOGENESIS OF FIRE.

Thus far we have seen what part Fire plays in Cosmogenesis or the building of the Universe; now we shall proceed to examine the part played by it in anthropogenesis or the evolution of man. The human race, says the Bûndahish, is not only descended from the primeval man, Gayomard, from whom the metals are also derived, but it has also passed through a vegetable existence before it evolved into its present condition. This view is further supported by the *Stanzas of Dzyan*, as will be seen from the following passage:—

"The spark hangs from the flame by the finest thread of Fohat. It journeys through the Seven Worlds of Mâyâ. It stops in the first (kingdom) and is a metal and a stone; it passes into the second (kingdom) and behold—a plant; the plant whirls through seven *forms*, and becomes a sacred animal (the first shadow of the physical man). From the combined attributes of these, Manu (*man*), the Thinker, is formed."— (Stanza vii.)

Now let us see what is signified by "Flames" and "Sparks" in this Stanza:—

"Our earth and man," says the commentary, "are the products of three fires—S'uchî, Pavamâna and Pâvaka. These three names answer in Sanskrit to the electric fire, the solar fire and the fire produced by friction. These three fires are spirit, soul and body. In the exoteric accounts they are personified as three sons of Agni Abhimânim, the eldest son of Brahmâ, the Cosmic Logos, by Svahâ, one of Daksha's daughters. In the esoteric sense the 'fire of friction' means the union between Buddhi and Manas, which are thus united or cemented together, the Manas merges partly into, and becomes part of, the Monad ; in the physical it relates to the *creative spark*, or germ, which fructifies and generates the human being. These three 'sons of Agni Abhimânim' were, it is said in the Bhâgavata Purâna, condemned by a curse of Vâsishta, the great Sage, 'to be born over and over again.'" The '*Flames*,' therefore, who are indifferently called Prajâpatis, Pitris, Manus, Rishis, Kumâras, &c., are said to incarnate personally in the Third Root-Race, and thus find themselves "re-born over and over again."

The "*Spark*" mentioned in the above stanza is Jiva, "the Monad in conjunction with Manas, or rather its aroma—that which remains from each personality, when worthy, and hangs from Âtma-Buddhi, the flame, by the thread of life," or Fohat, which corresponds to the Apâm-Napât[*] of the Avasta and the Vedas. This Spark or Jîva, journeying through the seven worlds of Mâyû, alludes to the pilgrimage of the Jîva through the seven globes of the planetary chain, and the seven Rounds, or the forty-nine stations of active existence that are before the Spark or Monad at the beginning of every great life-cycle or Manvantara, which cycle is analogous to Frashokaraitim in the Zoroastrian system.

Again, following the Bûndahish, we find that the three Fires named above—the fires of Spirit, soul and body—correspond in the Zoroastrian scriptures to three Fires—Âdar-Gushaspa, Âdar-Khurdâd or Frohba, and Âdar Meher-Burzin,

---

[*] The word means the "Son of Waters" (of Space, *i. e.*, ether). In the Avasta it stands between the "Fire-yazatas" and the "Water-yazatas."

which all three go to form the whole body of the Fire Vahram or Beharam, and this, together with the terrestrial fire, is the Fire worshipped by the Parsis in their Fire-temples or Âtash-Behram.

Proceeding further the Bûndahish states, "And those breathing souls, *i. e.*, the fires, are lodged in them; a counterpart of the body of man [the astral body] where it forms in the womb of the mother, and soul from the spirit (world) settles with (it), which controls the body while living; when that body dies the body mingles with the earth, and the soul goes back to the Spirit" (xvii. 9). They are also the "priest, warrior and husbandman" combined (Erbud Zâd-Sparam,xi, 8.). The Fire Vahram of the Bûndahish is symbolized by the sacred Fire of the Mazdean altar. It is, so to say, an "incarnation" of the Celestial Fire, identical with the Fire-Self. It cannot be simply the physical fire, seeing that three spiritual fires have emanated from it, *viz.*, the Fire Gushaspa, the Fire Khurdâd, and the Fire Meher-Burzin. These three fires are again symbolized in the three sacred fires of the Parsis, which are the Âtash Behram, Âtash Âdrûn and Âtash Dâdgâh.

Another proof that the physical fire only is not meant when a Parsi prays before it is that when he prays he prays to the "Fire, the Son of Ahura-Mazda," the reflection of the Absolute, which is spiritual, as will be seen from the following passage from Yasna xxxvi (3) :—

"*O Fire! thou [son]* of Ahura-Mazda, most bounteous of His Spirit, thou who art Vazishta, the holiest in all!*

"*O Fire, the Son of Ahura-Mazda! we draw near to Thee with pure mind, with good purity; with deeds and words of good wisdom draw we nigh unto Thee!*"

Here it is also named Vazishta, which is the "electric fire," and the "electric fire" in man is the Âtmic fire,—the Spirit—

---

* In this text the word is *vôi* which is translated in the Pahalvi as *âkâs*, which, if similar to the Sanskrit *âkâsh*, would agree with the esoteric teaching.

a fact confirmed by the "Secret Doctrine" which says, "Man is the product of three fires. The Electric fire—Spirit. The Solar fire—soul. The fire produced by friction—body. Metaphysically the last means the union between Buddhi and Manas ; in the physical it relates to the creative spark of the germ, which fructifies and generates the human being." (Vol. ii, p. 318).

If Âdar Gûshaspa be taken as the "firmamental or electric" fire, corresponding to the Vaidynta of the Vedas, we may also recognise in the Fire Nairyosañha the Vedic Vaishvânara, which is represented to be "equally the prop and navel of the Universe," as that Fire (Nairyosañha) is spoken of in the traditions as the fire "bestowed in the navel of kings," and man is undoubtedly a "king," inasmuch as it is in his power to effectually control and govern his whole kingdom—his lower nature and his higher faculties. Thus Âdar Gûshaspa, with Nairyosañha, seem to sustain human life and support the whole universe, both the macrocosm and the microcosm.

We have spoken of man's threefold division above, *i. e.*, body, soul and spirit ; we shall now proceed to examine him from the stand-point of the sevenfold classification familiar to all students of Theosophy, which are also alluded to in Yasna 55 of the Avastâ. The Seven Principles are correlated to the various fires mentioned above. It is said, "that in the midst of life-winds, *i. e.*, the current of life-forces in man, blazes the Vaishvânara fire sevenfold, for there are seven tongues of the blaze of Vaishvânara—these are the seven officiating priests" : and the priests thus spoken of are the seven principles referred to. Thus in each principle of man we see a fire. Out of these seven we have to deal at present more with the spiritual fire than with any other. The human soul, which comprises *Manas* (mind), *Chitta* (heart), *Buddhi* (intelligence, according to the Hindu classification), and *Ahankâra* (I-amness), is also a fire. This fact has been referred to in the "Zoroastrian Oracles" alluded to above :

"*Soul, Nature.*—For the soul being a bright Fire, by the

power of the Father remains immortal and is mistress of life, and possesseth many complexions of the cavities of the world. The channels being intermixed, she performs the work of Incorruptible Fire. Next the paternal conception *I* dwell; warm, heating all things; for He did put the mind in the soul, the soul in the dull body of us, the Father of gods and men imposed abundantly animating light, fire, ether, worlds."

The "Oracles" teaches that it is in this fire that one should search the truth, in the glorious depth of our inmost Being:—

"Let the immortal depth of thy soul be predominant, but all thy eyes extend upwards. Stoop not down to the dark world, beneath which continually lies a faithless depth, and Hades, dark all over, squalid, delighting in images, unintelligible, precipitous, craggy, a depth: always rolling, always espousing an opacous, idle, breathless body, and the light-hating world and the winding currents, by which many things are swallowed up. Seek Paradise; seek thou the way of the soul, whence or by what order, having served the body at the same place from which thou didst flow, thou mayest rise up again joining action to sacred speech. Stoop not down, for a precipice lies below on the earth, drawing through the ladder which hath seven steps, beneath which is the throne of necessity. Enlarge not thou thy destiny. The soul of man will in a manner clasp God to herself; having nothing mortal she is wholly inebriated from God: for she boasts harmony in which the mortal body exists. If thou extend the fiery mind to the work of piety, thou shalt preserve the flexible body. There is room for the image also in the circumlucid place. Every way to the unfashioned soul stretch the reins of fire. The fire-glowing cogitation hath the first rank. For the immortal approaching to the fire shall have light from God."

"When thou seest a sacred fire without form, shining flashingly through the depths of the world, hear the voice of Fire"—(the Voice of the Silence, the Voice of the Logos, same as the Honovar.) The Yogi has then reached the final goal, the state of Brahman—where, in the words of the Gîtâ, "rests no dread and after attaining which—

"Live where he will,
Die when he may, such passeth from all, plaining,
To blest Nirvâna, with the Gods attaining."

Viewed from any standpoint, it will strike all true students of spiritual science that in establishing Fire as the visible object of worship for the Invisible Infinite Spirit, the renowned prophet of ancient Irán, the Holy Zarathusthra, sought to secure the maximum of good to mankind, and indirectly pointed the way to the *summum bonum* of existence.

THE WORSHIP.

In the Zend Avastâ, by which title the Zoroastrian scriptures are generally known, Fire is a comprehensive term used not merely for the physical fire, but also for that active divine principle in nature which pervades and energises the whole universe. According to Hermès, "The Father of that one only thing [Man] is the Sun; its mother the Moon; the wind carries it in his bosom, and its nurse is the *spirituous* Earth. . . . . and *Spiritual* Fire is its Instructor [Guru]." This Fire is the Higher Self, the Spiritual Ego. It reincarnates under the influence of its lower personal self changing with every re-birth, full of desire to live. It is a law of Nature that on the physical plane, the Spiritual nature remains, as it were, in bondage to the lower. Unless the Ego takes refuge in Mazdam, and merges entirely into the essence thereof, the personal Ego may goad it to the last.

This Fire, the Son of Ahura-Mazda, can be compared favourably with Jivâtmâ of the Hindus, who is the Son of Paramâtmâ: as well as with the metaphysical Christ, the anointed pure spirit of the Gnostics. "The *Jiv-âtmâ* in the Microcosm (man)," says H. P. Blavatsky in a footnote to T. Subba Row's article, "is the same spiritual essence which animates the Macrocosm (universe), the differentiation, or specific difference between the two Jivâtmâs presenting itself but in the two states or conditions of the same or one Force. Hence 'this son of Paramâtmâ' is an eternal correlation of the Father-Cause."* Viewed in this light, let us learn a lesson of life from Yasna lxi or the Âtash Niyaesh, the prayer offered by the Parsis before the Sacred Fire. A part of this prayer runs as follows :—

"*Offering and praise, good nourishment, beneficent nourishment, helpful nourishment, vow I to Thee, Oh Fire, Son of Ahura-Mazda!*

"*To Thee is offering to be made, Thou art to be praised, mayest Thou be provided with offering and praise in the dwellings of man!*

"*Hail to the man who ever worships Thee, holding firewood in the hand, holding Baresma in the hand, holding Jivâm in the hand, holding mortar in the hand!*"

It will be seen from the above passages that in the Avastâ, Fire is emphatically called the "Son of Ahura-Mazda," and rightly so. For what else is there but Fire that inherits in so eminent a degree the divine attributes, the true reflection of its Father,—radiant, pure, all-pervading? Symbolical of all that is holy, adorable and pure, what else but fire, diffused as it is on all the seven planes, could be a fitting emblem for the worship of the Supreme One? It is the divine Seers, the illuminatii alone, who are in a position to estimate at its proper worth the high value of fire as a medium or an object of worship for the masses, knowing as they do the potency of the spiritual power in bestowing on man gifts that ultimately secure his material and spiritual well-being. The "offerings" here esoterically are the self-sacrificing or unselfish actions of man by which the Higher Ego is nourished, a subject on which we shall say something further on. The "dwellings of men" cannot be simply the

---

* It may here be observed in passing that Agni, God of Fire, was the oldest and most revered of gods in India, and that he is regarded as one of the three great deities—Agni, Vâyu, Surya. In fact Agni belonged to the earlier Vedic Trimurti before Vishnu was given a place of honour and before Brahmâ and Shiva were installed in the Hindu Pantheon.

houses made of physical materials, when the term relates to the divine fire. The words Esam, Beresma, Jivâm and the golden mortar in the hands of the priest are symbolical. The symbols used by the sacrificial priest,—and every man is his own priest—are ten in number symbolically representing five physical senses and five spiritual faculties—life, soul, intelligence, consciousness, wisdom.

The subsequent passage, also taken in the same light, will appear a beautiful piece of prayer:—

"*Mayest Those ever obtain the right perfume, the right nourishment, the right augmentation ; mayest Thou be in perfect nourishment, in good nourishment, O Fire, Son of Ahura-Mazda !*"

In the above passage the "good nourishment" of the fire evidently refers to the sweet-scented wood and incense carried to it by the votaries, but taken esoterically it represents Manashni, Gavashni, Kunashni, the pure thoughts, pure words and pure deeds of the votary, the triple principles on which the superb ethics of the Zoroastrian faith are based, which are to be sacrificed to the Spiritual Fire, the Fire-Self. According to the *Bhagavad Gitâ* also, whatever action performed is to be sacrificed to Krishna, the Fire.* Proceeding further the same Niyaesh says :—

"*Mayest Thou burn in this dwelling ; mayest Thou perpetually burn in this dwelling ; mayest Thou be in brightness in this dwelling ; mayest Thou increase in this dwelling, in the Zeruan in which are included the Renovation and the Perfect Renovation of the World.*"

This passage refers to the Immortal Ego which, owing to its essence and nature, is immortal, till the whole eternity with a form or *rûpa*, which is here translated as "dwelling."

---

* "Do thou perform the proper actions, action is superior to inaction. The journey of the body cannot be accomplished by inaction. All actions performed other than as sacrifice unto God make the actor bound by action. Abandon, therefore, all selfish motives and in action perform thy duty for Him alone."—*Bhagvad Gitâ.*

This dwelling, it is stated, prevails during the whole life cycles of the Fourth Round, its resemblance, the personal ego, has to win its immortality.* This dwelling is called the First envelope of the soul by Eliphas Lévy, the great Mystic of France. It can also be compared to the *Kâranopadhi* of the Hindus, "which is the breath really of Âtmâ in Buddhi-Manas, and answers to the Ânandamaya Kosha, the permanent body in which what we call the immortal Triad lives throughout the Manvantara."—(The " Building of the Kosmos," p. 94.) A Zoroastrian implores that the Fire which burns in his "dwelling" may perpetually do so and would not leave him, as such an event is a most deplorable one. So long as there remains a spiritual deed, even a spark, a last potentiality of doing good deeds, it serves as a thread of union to the Lower Manas with its parent, the Fire Divine. But the moment this spark is extinguished, the severance is complete, the light gradually disappears, and the man remains a soul-less one—an animal in human shape. He takes immediate birth after death from Kâma-Loka, a mental state of suffering, and shortly his actual annihilation is completed—a disaster too awful to conceive.

A true "Fire-worshipper" therefore is thus protected by his very action from meeting with such a terrible fate.

Let us go further and see how this spiritual interpretation agrees with the teaching of the Avastâ fundamentally. In the Âtash Niyaesh we come across the following passage:—

"*Give me, Oh Fire, Son of Ahura-Mazda, pure brightness, pure nourishment, pure life ; Perfect Life, Perfect Happiness, Perfect nourishment (illumination); for the soul greatness, wisdom and power of speech, which afterwards grows itself and does not diminished, and then the courage ;*

"*Steadiness, Ever-waking (?) consciousness one-third part of day and night, watchfulness, nourishing, wise offspring, who can*

---

* See The "*Secret Doctrine*," *o. e.*, ii, pp. 566-570; also Subba Row's Notes on the Bhagvat Gitâ, p. 25.

rule on the Karshvaras and assemblies; increasing, enduring, who may advance my house, clan, town, region and religion."

In the above soul-stirring passage the earnest student of psychology will find a fine under-current of the personal experience of the Initiate. It is like a message of hope to humanity; to the faithful devotee it breathes bliss and felicity divine, and offers through spiritual knowledge and purity of life, the salvation he ever yearns after. To man it teaches in hope-inspiring terms his highest destiny—to strive to attain the highest state possible to him. The white, bright path of purity and holiness is pointed out, and the luminous light of spiritual knowledge vouchsafed to him in his earnest attempt to cast off his muddy vesture, to wipe himself clean of all that is earthy, and shine as bright and become as pure as his inner self was when it was first detached from its parent source, Ineffable Effulgence. Here the worshipper asks for brightness and nourishment for his soul, as well as pure life; and knowing as he does that the present life is merely a part of the life eternal, he asks for the Perfect Life, the Eternal Life, wisdom and the power of fluency; in short, all the functions of the Divine Ego. The student of Yoga will see in this short passage the desire of a "Fire-worshipper" in asking from that divine fire which has been vouchsafed to a true disciple, that the very Fire may function in him. The wakefulness, the steadiness, the watchfulness, and all that by which we get strength in the path of Yoga is here depicted, as it were, in a nutshell. Next we come to a passage in which the Fire stands as Instructor, a *Guru* :—

" *Give me, O Fire, Son of Ahura-Mazda, the Teacher who can teach me what is good for me now, and forevermore, concerning the best state of the pure, the shining, very brilliant. May I obtain that [Teacher] in return of purity of long time, goodness and holiness for the soul.*"

True spiritual teacher can never be obtained unless proper time arrives,—unless we deserve that privilege. Before that we must train ourselves in the qualifications required of discipleship. It is useless to go in search of Sâdhus who merely assume robes of ascetics. It is only by becoming pure and following the path marked out for discipleship that one can obtain a Gûru—a Gûrû who might be watching us night and day that we may become like unto himself. And this Gûrû is not to be sought after outside our own selves, but into ourselves, that He may instruct us from within. Who else may be that Gûrû—the great Teacher—the Mahâ-Gûrû, but the Divine Fire itself—the Zaota or Hotri Priest.

From another passage in the Âtash Niyaesh we learn :—

"*With all speaks the Fire, the Son of Áhura-Mazda, for whom he shines throughout the day and the night, and cooks food. From all he desires good nourishment, healthful nourishment, helpful nourishment.*

"*He looks at the hands of all who come to him, and sayeth— what brings the friend to the friend, one who comes hither to the one sits alone.*

"*We praise the holy Fire, the Strong, the Warrior.*"

This is a profoundly significant passage, though to the common eye of flesh meaningless. In an episode of the Chhândogya Upanishad we find identical teaching, where the knowledge attainable through this visible symbol of the divine is clearly inculcated, and how fire can speak to the one who can devotes himself to it, is plainly shown.

The teacher of a Brahmachârin named Upakosala granted leave to all his other pupils to return home, but refused that indulgence to Upakosala while he himself went on a pilgrimage. For twelve years the teacher was absent from his Âshram, and during that time the solitary disciple served the Fire with great devotion and success. When the teacher returned, he at once saw that his faithful disciple had attained to divine illumination during his absence, and he addressed his pupil thus :—"Child, your appearance shines like that of the knower of Brahmâ ; who has given thee instruction ?" "Who will instruct me, Sir ?" humbly replied the devoted disciple, and with bowed head he reverentially pointed at the Fire he had worshipped. "Did it, child, speak unto you ?" enquired the teacher. "Even so," responded the pupil. Then the teacher added, "Child, they have spoken to you about regions : I, too, will speak to you about them : as water attacheth not unto the leaf of the lotus, so doth sin attach not unto him who understands them."

Prophets and sages do not come into the world to teach humanity the mere vulgar art of cooking food. Their mission is divine, and they incarnate in the body to teach the law of Âhura-Madza, to save mankind when wickedness has become too strong for them to resist and when righteousness has declined. They rise from age to age, taking upon themselves the burden of the flesh, moving like ordinary men among the orphan-humanity, succouring the good and thrusting back the wicked.

The *night* alluded to in the passage is the night of embodied existence which we call *death*. The fire cooking the food at night would therefore indicate that the fire, *i. e.*, the Immortal Ego, during the interval between two incarnations, assimilates the aroma of all his unselfish and spiritual actions and aspirations, the "harvest," *i. e.*, our finest spiritual thoughts, our noble and most unselfish deeds, our highest aspirations, our love for spiritual devotion. This "harvest" is the purified essence of our physical, moral and spiritual characteristics, which is carried, after death, by the human soul or Lower Manas (the warrior) to its parent, the Higher Ego, whose direct mediator is the human soul.

Our higher aspirations which are the emanations of the Fire, the Higher Ego, do not come through the brain which is simply a lump of matter, but through the Lower Manas, which is the mediator. If the Lower Manas has no spiritual aspiration or experiences, the memory of all that is good and noble, there is no mental state of Vaheshtem-aūhuim, which can variously be called heaven, devachan, swarga, &c. These harvests are carried from one sphere to another through a bridge, called *Chinvad peretu*, the Jacob's ladder of the

Christians, the Pûl-sarat of the Mahomedans. This bridge is the Antahkaran of man. Compare the Higher Ego to a lamp in a hall, the body with the walls, the Lower Manas with the light of the Higher Ego, and the Antahkaran with the atmosphere through which the light is passing. Our duty is to drive away the mental shadows or sins, and multiply—not children as our priests would have us believe—but brightness, good deeds. The " Friend who comes" is the Lower Ego in his passage to the heavenly state, and the "friend who sits alone" represents the Higher Ego. This passage, read in the light of the following passage from the "Seven Principles of Man," by Annie Besant, will be made quite clear :—

"Soon after the death of the physical body Kâma Manas is set free, and dwells for a while on the astral plane clothed with a body of astral matter. From this all of the Manasic Ray [the coming friend] that is pure and unsoiled gradually disentangles itself and returns to its source [the friend who sits alone], carrying with it such of its life experiences as are of a nature fit for assimilation with the Higher Ego. Manas thus again becomes one, and it remains one during the period which intervenes between two incarnations. The Manasic Ego, united to Âtma-Buddhi, the two highest principles in the human constitution . . . passes into the Devachanic state of consciousness [which the Parsis call "Behasta," a corruption of Vahishtem], resting, as we rest in sleep from the weariness of the life struggle through which it has passed, wrapped in blissful dreams, coloured and peopled by the experiences of the earth-life thus closed. These are carried into the Manasic consciousness by the lower ray withdrawn into its source. They make the Devachanic state a continuation of earth-life, shorn of its sorrows, a completion of the wishes and desires of earth-life so far as those were pure and noble . . . . . the Devachanic period is the time for the assimilation of life experiences [when the Fire "cooks food"], the regaining of equilibrium, ere a new journey is commenced. It is the *night* that succeeds the day of earth-life, the alternatives of the objective manifestation."

"*But if one brings for the same [Fire] Esam, or Baresma bound together in holiness, or the tree Hadhânaepatam spread in holiness, then blesses the Fire (the Son) of Ahura-Muzda,* khshnûto (*contented*), *not dishonoured, satisfied:*—'*May there increase with thee herds of cattle, fullness of men; may it happen according to the wish of thy mind, according to the wish of thy soul. Live thy life as many nights as thou wilt live in happiness.*'

"*This is the blessing of the Fire for him who brings it dry wood, sought for burning, purified with the wish for purity.*"

In the above passage the words Esam, Baresma, and Hadhânaepatam are symbolical, and refer to the inner world. But it might appear rather peculiar to a modern Westernized mind, why the Fire blesses man with "herds of cattle." Cattle is the principal wealth in man's natural condition. Compare the Bhagvad Gitâ, chapter 3: "When in ancient times the lord of creatures had formed mankind and at the same time appointed his worship, he spoke and said: 'With this worship, pray for, increase, and let it be for you Kâmadhuk, the *cow* of plenty, on which ye shall depend for the accomplishment of all your wishes. With this nourish the gods, that the gods may nourish you; thus mutually nourishing ye shall obtain the highest felicity. The gods being nourished by worship with sacrifice will grant you the enjoyment of your wishes. He who enjoyeth what hath been given unto him by them, and offereth not a portion unto them, is even as a thief.'"

As above, so below. We have seen through the whole prayer that the Fire represented in the prayer cannot be taken as the physical fire only, but as divine Fire. But looking at the words "dry wood" one might fall again into the error that it cannot but be the prayer of physical fire, forgetting, however, that the Fire prayed to here is the "son," the reflection of One Infinite Light. The dry-wood, therefore, is the man's pure action, an action without any tinge of personality. Just as a damp wood is harmful to the physical fire, any action saturated with any personal motive is harmful to the Fire divine.

No one has thrown a clear and lucid light on the above passage from the "Âtash Niyaesh," since the Parsis left their motherland of Irân. Here our Parsi brethren may well take a hint of the usefulness of Theosophic study for the interpretation of the scriptures of their grand and sublime religion. We therefore look with the utmost regret at the religions indifference now-a-days prevailing among the small community of the Parsis. We invite them to study the deeper and underlying meaning of their own scriptures with the help of Theosophy, and they will soon see that what at first sight seem to them in the noble fragment of their Avastâ meaningless and unintelligent babbling and jargon, convey in reality the deepest and most profound spiritual truths. To the spiritually-blind the books of divine wisdom are always sealed books, while men of pure heart and humble faith may read them while they run ; in other words, " those that ask shall have, those that desire to read shall read, those that desire to learn shall learn."

NASARVANJI F. BILIMORIA.

MANASHNI—GAVASHNI—KUNASHNI.

A SCIENTIFIC EXPOSITION OF PURITY OF THOUGHTS, WORDS AND DEEDS.

TO every student of the Zoroastrian religion and its scriptures, it will be obvious that the highest importance is given therein to purity of life in Thoughts, Words and Deeds, which ideas are expressed by the words Humata or Manashni, Hukhata or Gavashni, and Hvarshta or Kunashni. Passages in praise of these three sublime concepts will be found scattered in profusion throughout the Avastâ. In fact the entire magnificent fabric of the religion of the High and Holy Zarathushtra rests on these triune ethical concepts of observing absolute purity of life on the physical, mental, moral and spiritual planes. Almost every prayer in the Avastâ begins and ends with the praise of "Ashoi" or purity, as for example:—" Purity is the highest good, is the highest happiness. Happiness is to him who is the purest in purity." Elsewhere it is said—"The man who is pure [holy] is the ruler of the world." In the prayer "Vispa Humata" we see:—

"All good thoughts, good words, good deeds proceed through knowledge;
All evil thoughts, evil words, and evil deeds proceed through ignorance;
All good thoughts, words and deeds lead to Heaven;
All evil thoughts, words and deeds lead to Hell;
All good thoughts, words and deeds end in Heavenly Bliss; so is it manifest to the pure."

A more clear and explicit enunciation of the great law of purity of thoughts, words and deeds cannot be met with elsewhere. In no other religion is it expressed so succinctly, though every great religion worthy of that name expresses the same ideas in a more or less diffused or categorical way. To some, these precepts may appear very commonplace and trite, but if they will give a patient perusal to what follows they will soon find out their mistake, and will see that the question is one of vital importance to every human being, to whatever nationality or creed he may belong.

Our main object in preparing this paper is to demonstrate in the light of modern science, especially to our Parsi brethren, the scientific truths underlying the teachings of the Holy Zarathushtra on this subject, because the tendency of the present generation leads to the rejection or neglect of everything that savours of mere blind faith or dogmatic assertions. The truth of these teachings will not, however, be denied by any sane man who has the least moral sense left in him. In fact most people will be ready to admit them in theory, but will hold them as impossible to practice. Our object, then, is to show that they are not so impracticable as imagined, and that their strict observance is absolutely necessary for one's own happiness as well as for that of those who surround him; from one's own narrow circle of family to the whole human race. This we are not going to prove by mere historical evidence or by religious dogmas, but by experimental evidence furnished by modern science itself; because a scientific or objective proof of the truth of a thing makes a more lasting impression on men's minds than any amount of exhortations, religious or otherwise. For instance, if we were to tell a man who is utterly unacquainted with the property of gunpowder, that nitre, sulphur and charcoal mixed in certain proportions form a dangerous compound possessing terrific destructive power, it is quite probable that he would deride or scoff at the idea; but let him once experience or see the effects of an explosion of gunpowder, and he will be the last man to approach it rashly, far less to handle it carelessly. Similarly, if the mighty potentialities of Thought, which is the very fountain source from which purity of speech and action proceed, for good and evil in one's own interest as well as in the interest of others, are brought home to the minds and hearts of the people by some physical and experimental proofs, they will at once perceive the necessity of keeping their thoughts pure through all the practical affairs of daily life, and once they taste of the true happiness and peace arising from this course of life, they will adhere to it under all circumstances and all risks (if there be any) to their personal selves.

All religious teachings are based on a knowledge of the higher science and higher laws of nature which cannot be investigated by mere physical senses or physical instruments, and about which our modern scientific men are as yet entirely in the dark, with the exception of a very few advanced seekers after truth who have the courage to declare boldly the results of their investigations, which quite upset all the pet theories of orthodox, official science of the day. This higher science and the higher laws of nature were perfectly well-known to all the great and holy Founders of religions, but as the average human mind was incapable of comprehending these higher truths, they were obliged to veil them under allegories and symbology which the Initiated alone could grasp, and leave the bare results of their spiritual knowledge in the form of religious injunctions and dogmas, for the common mass of mankind. Hence it is that modern science which refuses to believe in anything that is beyond the scope of the physical senses, is incapable of apprehending or investigating the higher science which underlies all religious teachings. On the other hand, the present exponents of all the religions in the world are quite ignorant of the true spiritual science on which they are all founded, and want to support their teachings by mere dogmatic assertions, without assigning any valid or reasonable grounds for their acceptance. Hence the constant conflict that we see between the religionists on the one hand and the scientists on the other, or rather between theology and dogmatic official science. True religion and true science can never be in conflict. Because religion is nothing but the reduction of the higher scientific laws of nature to precepts for the guidance of undeveloped humanity. True religion unfolds the mysteries of nature and of man, and asks the latter to abide by the laws of the former in order to accomplish his grand destiny in the scheme of evolution. True science supplies reasons and explanations of these mysteries of nature, either on the objective or the subjective plane, and thus furnishes a satisfactory explanation of all religious teachings as well as of all the phenomena of the objective world ; and thus enforces obedience to them, not on mere blind faith or dogmatic assertions, but by rational, experimental, objective or subjective proofs. Hence it will be seen that religion and science are mutually interdependent, and that neither of them can stand by itself. It is therefore unreasonable to think that if any religious teaching does not fit in with the precepts of modern science it is baseless or superstitious. It only shows that science has not yet sufficiently advanced or developed.

We will now proceed to see what is the basis of thought in nature and in man. Thought is the motive as well as the creative power which brings into objectivity all the phenomena of nature that we see around us ; in fact, all the objects that we see on earth. Thought lies at the bottom of every joy and suffering of man down to every sentient being crawling on this earth. In fact the whole Universe is a thought of God. It was apparently on these considerations that the Holy Sage Zarathushtra inculcated the paramount necessity of the strict practice of purity of thought, words and deeds, the latter two being merely the audible and visible manifestations of the invisible intangible thought. Words and deeds therefore being the manifestations of thought, unless the latter is kept pure the other two cannot be so. Purity of thought is consequently the main object to be attained ; in fact it is the very basis of all Yoga practices. If pure thoughts, or thoughts of love and sympathy for every sentient being, without any distinction whatsoever, however mean and unworthy the object may appear to us, are habitually entertained by one, the words which flow from his lips will be naturally gentle and pleasing, even when they are meant to restrain or reprove an evil-doer, and when thoughts and words are thus harmoniously pure, the deeds done through their instrumentality must of necessity be pure also. Thus we see that everything depends on keeping our thoughts pure. But this purity of thought is not to be exercised exclusively for one's own benefit. It is a holy trust vested in us by the most High for the common good of all and any abuse or breach of this trust is sure to be visited on its perpetrator by condign retribution.

Now we will see what thought can do and undo in the ordinary affairs of life. It is by thought that an architect erects a building, a mechanic evolves mighty engines for human weal or woe, a painter creates beautiful images on blank canvas, and a poet breathes for the images of his soul as if out of nothing. . . .

As an instance of the visible effect of thought we may state that it is a well-established fact in physiognomy and phrenology that the features and cranial developments of men show different lineaments according to the thoughts they habitually cherish, or which are most predominant in their nature; thus showing that thought has the power to mould the solid features of men. In fact the faces of men are a constant revelation, or an open book revealing the innate character of each man, to those who know how to read it. Thus a man who habitually harbours noble and benevolent thoughts will have a benign countenance and a healthy and beautiful body, while one who entertains contrary thoughts—that is, thoughts of anger, hatred, jealousy, malice, &c.,—will have an ugly, repulsive countenance, and a deformed or diseased body as an index to his character Those who wish to have more detailed information on this point will find ample evidence about it in works on Physiognomy and Phrenology. It is a matter, however, which can be verified by any careful observer himself. Of course admitting that there may be exceptions to this general rule which can be explained from other stand-points. The above are some of the commonest visible effects of the working of invisible intangible thoughts. But the invisible effects of thoughts are far more subtle and far-reaching, and are understood and appreciated only by the occultist or the student of Yoga philosophy. A Master of Wisdom has stated :—

" Every thought of man upon being evolved passes into the

inner world and becomes an active entity by associating itself, coalescing we might term it, with an elemental—that is to say, with one of the semi-intelligent forces of the kingdoms (of nature). It survives as an active intelligence—a creature of the mind's begetting—for a longer or shorter period, proportionate with the original intensity of the cerebral action which generated it. Thus a good thought is perpetuated as an active beneficent power, and an evil one as a maleficent demon, and so a man is continually peopling his current in space with a world of his own, crowded with the offspring of his fancies, desires, impulses and passions, a current which re-acts upon any sensitive or nervous organization that comes into contact with it, in proportion to its dynamic intensity."—(*The Occult World*, pp. 89-90.)

From the above passage it will be seen what fearful mischief we must be doing to ourselves as well as to those around us, by the evil thoughts we are thinking while we are in an angry, hateful, jealous or any other evil mood of mind. This is not a mere speculation or theory, but a real fact in nature as will be seen from what follows.

Now to understand the mysterious potency of thought on the objective plane, from a scientific stand-point, we shall have to examine the phenomena of sound—which is the same as word or speech—and its visible effects on the physical plane, because no words or deeds can be brought into manifestation without the agency of thought. If we examine the phenomena or effects of sound on the physical plane, we shall be able to appreciate the attributes and nature of its noumenon or source, which is thought. Modern science accepts the principles of matter and motion as the two factors in the evolution of the universe, without in the least recognising the spiritual forces underlying them. We will not here discuss the latter question, but will proceed with our investigation on strictly scientific grounds. Matter or motion each by itself could not be productive of any result. But when motion begins to act in matter, it generates vibrations, and all vibrations are fundamentally sounds, and therefore all vibrations are changeable or transmutable into sound. The first property generated in cosmic or primordial matter is sound, and it is by the power of sound that the whole universe comes into existence. "This power is Sabda Brahman: it is the force that builds the Kosmos, and it is also the force by which a Yogi brings about all the powers within himself." Without sound there can be no form. Every sound has its own form, every sound generates and builds a form, and again changes (or breaks up) that form into a different form. Thus every sound has "this triple character, that it generates form, that it builds or upholds form, and that it destroys form."— ("The Building of the Kosmos," p. 17, Ind. ed.) This shows that sound lies at the very origin of forms, and that the infinite variety of forms that we see around us, ourselves included, arises out of the variety of sounds. Thus the whole objective universe is continuously resounding with sounds, and he who has developed the clairaudient faculty is capable of discerning these ceaseless sounds in all the kingdoms of nature on this earth, mineral, vegetable, animal and human: and to one who has developed his spiritual faculty, sounds beyond the range of this earth are distinctly audible. Thus the ancient idea of the "music of the spheres" is no idle fancy or mere imagination of the poets, but an actual fact in nature.

The triple potency of sound we have stated above, may be demonstrated by the following physical experiments.* Take an ordinary drum and draw the bow of a violin across the edge of its parchment head. It will be observed that a certain note is given out by the vibrating parchment surface. This note can be made to vary in accordance with the manipulations of the bow across the drum-head. In this case the tones generated can only be heard—nothing is perceived by the eye. But if, on the parchment surface of the

---

* For these experiments see pp. 18, et seq., "The Building of the Kosmos," Ind. ed.

drum, some sand or other light or finely divided stuff such as fine iron filings, or delicate seeds or spores of lycopodium be spread, and then the bow drawn across the drum edge, the sand or other substance will be thrown up in the air, and in falling back on the surface it will not fall evenly over it, but in some definite geometrical figures or forms. So that the sand spread over the parchment was compelled by sound to assume definite geometrical shapes varying in outline as the notes were changed in intensity or pitch by drawing the bow over different parts of the circumference of the drum. When the parchment is made to vibrate in harmony with the sound, geometrical shapes of a far more elaborate character may be produced. Thus we have seen that sound can create forms. Further on we shall see that it can maintain forms as well as destroy them. Similarly, experiments can be made with metallic plates with like results whereby different figures and patterns are produced which are known as Children's figures, a full description of which will be found in Professor Tyndall's "Lectures on Sound." Another experiment for demonstrating the visible effect of the invisible sound may be seen thus :—

Take tuning forks—steel forks of different pitch, which vibrate and give out different notes when struck even gently. The vibrations caused by these forks when struck very gently are perfectly invisible to the naked eye. But it can be arranged by means of reflecting mirrors, so that these vibrations can be passed through a magnifying lens and thrown on a sheet by means of a magic lantern, and in this way the invisible vibrations of the tuning fork may be traced and magnified, and then they are seen to form beautiful geometrical figures. On the sheet on which the image from the magic lantern is thrown, it will be found that every note gives rise to exquisite form, which changes as the notes are changed, so that whenever we are playing any piece of music we form the most exquisite shapes in the ether and the air around us, and those who have developed the clairvoyant faculty can see not only these forms and shapes, but even living, tiny creatures, commonly known as fairies, sprites, etc. Thus we see that that which in modern times is regarded as superstition and fanciful imaginations of the ancients, is really a living fact in nature. Experiments have been made by Mrs. Watts-Hughes, proving that when a succession of notes were sung into a horn-shaped instrument, more elaborate forms were built; forms such as ferns, trees and flowers—all these being generated by the notes of the human voice.—("The Building of the Kosmos," p. 20.) How this result was brought about can be demonstrated by the following experiment. Two pendulums are set swinging in a glass case, each of the pendulums having its own motion. These pendulums are then made to interact with each other, so that friction is produced and the motion of one pendulum modifies the motion of the other : and from these pendulums with their interacting motions—with a pencil attached by means of a lever which can be moved in the resultant-direction obtained from the motions of the two pendulums—most complicated forms are traced on a card put under the point of the pencils; forms like shells of the most elaborate description, geometrical shapes, most perfect in their angles and perfect in their curves. Now, as the vibrations of a note are always in one direction, and as the pendulum motions are simply swinging backwards and forwards, the interferences of the pendulums are really the reproduction of the true vibrations interfering with, or modifying, each other. Thus may be obtained a graphic picture of the modifications which may be caused by vibrations or sounds which are interfering, although each separate one is in one direction, and the result of this interference is this marvellous elaboration of form as stated above. Similarly when light-waves are made to interfere with one another, colour is produced, thus "what we call colour in mother-o'-pearl, is only the result of a very delicate roughness in the surface which makes interference of the light-vibrations with each other."

We have thus proved by actual scientific experiments how the invisible can be made visible, how the power of sound can be made manifest to the eye as well as to the ear, and how it is capable of building up forms. Further, we have seen that the forms so generated assume some one or other regular geometrical shape. When we study outside nature a little more closely than we generally do, we are struck by the strange fact, that everywhere we find geometrical forms. This regularity of shape or form is to be found both in the mineral and vegetable kingdoms. The simplest forms are built on the simplest lines or axes, and the more elaborate the form the more numerous will be the axes on which it is built. In the vegetable kingdom forms are built on the spiral arrangement. This will be easily seen by the examination of a twig of a tree with leaves on it. There is no irregularity in the building up of vegetable forms as would seem at first sight. The most apparently irregular arrangement is only a complicated spiral; for "that which is chaos to the senses is Kosmos to the reason." Plato's dictum thus comes to be true that "God geometrises."

"Not only can sound build, but it can also destroy. Thus the builder of form can destroy the form; and while gentle vibrations build, vehement or violent vibrations tear apart that which the gentle ones have brought together. Inasmuch as no form is solid, but every form consists of molecules with spaces between them, the vibrations of the sound going between the molecules make them vibrate more and more strongly and throw them further and further apart, until the time comes when the attracting force which keeps them together is overcome, and they shoot out and the form becomes disintegrated."—(*Ibid.*, p. 22.) To demonstrate the truth of the above statements the following experiments will be sufficient. Take a glass or tumbler and half fill it with water and find its "fundamental note, which can be done by drawing a bow across its edge and seeing how the water divides. When the fundamental note is found, produce this note near the glass on some instrument from which great intensity and loudness of sound can be obtained." The glass will give out the same note and the water in it will be thrown into vibrations without any apparent contact from outside. As the pitch of the sound is raised higher and higher the water in the glass is thrown into greater and greater agitation, so that a regular tumult of waves is set up in the water, and when the vibrations of the glass which cause all these movements in the water become too great for the glass to stand them, it finally shivers to pieces in every direction by the sheer force of the vibrations caused by the sound.—(*Ibid.*, p. 22.) Similarly, a single note of music 'delivered from the mouth of a master in music' is capable of breaking to pieces an empty glass or tumbler. Another experiment which is given by Professor Tyndall to prove the powerful effects caused by the vibrations of sound is this. Take a glass rod and hold it with one hand at its middle and then rub the upper half gently with some other substance which will produce a gentle sound ; rubbing it more briskly the sound grows intenser, and when the friction is carried to a very high velocity acute sound is generated in the glass rod, until the vibrations thus created are too powerful to preserve the rod in its original shape, and the lower half of the glass rod is shivered into small circular fragments ; thus showing the power of the note which the glass itself had generated.

The potency of rhythmic sound is such that the largest and strongest structures may be made to tumble down and disintegrate under its effect. This is due to the effects of what is known as sympathetic vibrations. It is a well-known fact in acoustics that if one of the wires of a harp be made to vibrate vigorously its movement will call forth sympathetic vibrations in the corresponding strings of any number of harps placed round it, if they are tuned to exactly the same pitch. Thus if any one knows at what rate to start his vibrations, that is, knows the keynote (or the vibratory force which holds it together) of the class of matter he wishes to affect, he will be able by sounding that keynote to call forth an immense number of sympathetic vibrations from the matter or substance against which he is operating. When this is done on the purely physical plane no additional energy is devoloped, but on the subtler or astral plane there is this difference, that the matter dealt with on this plane is in far more active condition, so that, when it is called into action by these sympathetic vibrations, it adds its own living force to the original impulse, which may thus be multiplied a thousandfold, and then by further rhythmic repetition of the original impulse the vibrations may be so intensified that the result is out of all apparent proportion to the cause as regards the tremendous effects of sympathetic vibrations on the physical plane. We may refer our readers to the astounding discoveries made by John Morrell Keely, of Philadelphia, with reference to the potency of Inter-etheric forces.* In fact there is scarcely any limit to the conceivable achievements of this force in the hands of a great Adept who fully knows its possibilities, for the very building of the unievrse, as already observed above, was but the result of the vibrations set up by the spiritual force acting upon primordial matter. Certain classes of mantrams or spells which produce their results not by controlling any elemental or nature-spirit, depend for their efficacy upon this action of sympathetic vibrations. The phenomenon of disintegration is also brought about by the action of extremely rapid vibrations, which overcome the cohesion of the molecules of the object operated upon, as we have seen in the experiments cited above. A still higher rate of vibrations of a somewhat different type will separate these molecules into their constituent atoms. A body reduced by these means to the etheric condition, can be moved by an astral current from one place to another with immense rapidity ; and the moment that the force which has been exerted to put it into that condition is withdrawn, it will be forced by the etheric pressure to resume its original form. It is in this way that objects are sometimes brought almost instantaneously from a great distance at spiritualistic *séances*, and when thus disintegrated they could be passed with perfect ease through any solid substance, such as the wall of a house or the side of a locked box.

---

* *Vide* " Keely and his Discoveries," by Mrs. Bloomfield-Moore.

To show the immense power of vibratory sounds we may quote the following examples :—

It is stated that when the iron bridge at Colebrook Dale was in the course of building, a fiddler came on the spot where the builders were at work and told them that he would fiddle down the bridge. The workmen laughed in scorn and told him to fiddle away to his heart's content. The fiddler, who knew the mighty potency of music or sound, began to play until he struck the key-note of the bridge and under its influence it began to sway so violently that the astonished workmen entreated him to stop.* At one time it was found by the workmen engaged in a mill in America that on certain days they experienced considerable annoyance and hindrance in going on smoothly with their accustomed work, and that on some days the building was so much shaken that pails filled with water would be nearly emptied, while on other days nothing of the sort would happen though the mill was working during all those days as usual. On searching for the cause of these mysterious disturbances it was found that when the machinery was running at a certain rate these phenomena took place. This mysterious disease of the mill was cured by simply making the machinery run at a slower or faster rate so as to put it out of time with the vibrations under which the building was originally constructed. Because all structures, large or small, simple or complex, have a definite note of vibrations, depending on their material, size and shapes, as fixed as the fundamental note of a musical chord ; so that if the vibrations which maintain them in shape are intensified by the creation of similar vibrations within or near them, the form or shape of the building or object is disintegrated and it falls to pieces. It is for this very reason that when crossing a bridge the troops are ordered to stop the music, break step, and open column, lest the measured cadence of condensed masses of men should urge the bridge to vibrate beyond its power of cohesion. Neglect of this rule has led to fearful

---

* *Vide Lucifer*, January 1894, Vol. xiii, page 358.

accidents. The celebrated Engineer Stephenson, the inventor of the steam-engine, has said that there is not so much danger to a bridge when crowded with men and cattle as when men go in marching order over it. It is stated that the bridge at Broughton, near Manchester, gave way beneath the measured tread of only sixty men. A terrible disaster once befell a battalion of French Infantry while crossing the suspension bridge at Angiers, in France. Repeated orders were given the troops to break into sections, but in the hurry of the moment they disregarded the order, and the bridge, which was but twelve years old, and had been repaired recently at considerable cost, fell and almost the whole of the battalion was destroyed in its fall. For this same reason the Swiss muleteers when travelling over the snow-clad mountains of their country are said to tie up the bells of the mules lest by their measured, musical tinklings they might disturb an avalanche or ice-field from its bed and bring it tumbling down upon their heads. A nightingale is said to kill by the power of its notes. (*The Theosophical Gleaner*, Vol. III, page 204.) Examples and experiments proving the mighty and mysterious potencies of sound can be multiplied to any extent. But what we have to gather from these is that everywhere we have proof that sound can create and sound can destroy, according to its character and nature, and not only that, but sound can also preserve what is built up, because without sound there could be no form or shape; in short, without sound nothing can exist on either the objective or the subjective planes. Because "everything is in constant motion; one sort of motion builds up the form, another preserves the form, a third destroys the form, and the destruction of one form is the building up of another. That which is destroyer in one shape is creator in another. In fact nothing is annihilated, nothing is lost, for every death in one sphere is a birth into another."—(The " Building of the Kosmos," page 23.)

Having thus seen the mighty effects produced by sound, or words, on the physical plane, we shall now proceed to examine the subtle and invisible effects exercised by the origin or root of sound, or words, which is on the plane of thought. Because thought, as already observed, is nothing but inaudible sound, and sound is nothing but thought made audible or even visible, and just as the effect of the audible sound can be perceived on the visible plane, so the effect of the invisible sound, in other words, thought, is to be looked for on the invisible plane. We have now to see what this invisible plane is. This plane is known to the occultists as the astral plane or Âkâsh—the ether of modern science, though the latter is the lowest and grossest form of Âkâsh. This plane is also commonly known as the astral light or astral matter. It is on this astral plane or Âkâsh that we can trace the cause of the visible effects of thought on the physical plane, such as the sudden and inexplicable calamities that befall humanity in the form of earthquakes, pestilence, conflagrations, floods, &c. To explain the nature of this astral plane or astral light we cannot do better than quote from that remarkable monograph on this subject, "The Astral Plane," by C. W. Leadbeater, which forms Transaction No. 24 of the London Lodge of the Theosophical Society. "This astral matter or astral essence pervades the kingdoms of nature lying behind the mineral. It is wonderfully sensitive to the most fleeting human thought, responding with inconceivable delicacy in an infinitesimal fraction of a second to a vibration set up in it, even by an entirely unconscious exercise of human will or desire. When any portion of this essence remains for a few moments unaffected by any outside influence (a condition, by the way, which is never realised), it is absolutely without any definite form of its own, though even then its motion is rapid and ceaseless; but on the slightest disturbance, set up perhaps by some passing thought current, it flashes into a bewildering confusion of restless, ever-changing shapes which form, rush about and disappear with the rapidity of bubbles on the surface of boiling water. These evanescent shapes, though generally those of living creatures of some sort, human or otherwise, no more express the existence of separate entities in the essence than do the equally changeful and multiform waves raised in a few moments on a previously smooth lake by a sudden squall. They seem to be mere reflections from the vast storehouse of the astral light, yet they have usually a certain appropriateness to the character of the thought-stream which calls them into existence, though nearly always with some grotesque distortion, some terrifying or unpleasant aspect about them. . . The fact that we are so readily able to influence the elemental or astral kingdoms, at once shows us that we have a responsibility towards them for the manner in which we use that influence ; indeed, when we consider the conditions under which they exist, it is obvious that the effect produced upon them by the thoughts and desires of all intelligent creatures inhabiting the same world with them, must have been calculated upon in the scheme of our system as a factor in their evolution. *In spite of the consistent teaching of all the great religions, the mass of mankind is still utterly regardless of its responsibility on the thought-plane ; if a man can flatter himself that his words and deeds have been harmless to others, he believes he has done all that can be required of him, quite oblivious of the fact that he may for years have been exercising a narrowing and debasing influence on the minds of those about him, and filling surrounding space with the unlovely creations of a sordid mind.*

" The elemental or astral essence which surrounds us on every side is in all its numberless varieties singularly susceptible to the influence of human thought. The action of the mere casual wandering thought upon it, causing it to burst into a cloud of rapidly-moving, evanescent forms, has already been described ; we have now to note how it is affected when the human mind formulates a definite, purposeful thought or wish. The effect produced is of the most striking nature. The thought seizes upon the plastic essence, and moulds it instantly into a living being of appropriate form—a being which, when once thus created, is in no way under the control of its creator, but lives out a life of its own, the length of which is proportionate to the intensity of the thought or wish which called it into existence. It lasts, in fact, just as long as the thought-force holds it together. Most people's thoughts are so feeble and indecisive that the elementals created by them last only a few minutes or a few hours, but an oft-repeated thought or an earnest wish will form an elemental whose existence may extend to many days. Since the ordinary man's thoughts refer very largely to himself, the elementals they form remain hovering about him, and constantly tend to provoke a repetition of the idea they represent, since such repetitions, instead of forming a new elemental, would strengthen the old one and give it a fresh lease of life. A man, therefore, who frequently dwells upon one wish often forms for himself an astral attendant which, constantly fed by fresh thought, may haunt him for years, ever gaining more and more strength and influence over him; and it will be easily seen *that if the desire be an evil one the effect upon his moral nature may be of the most disastrous character.*

"Still more pregnant of result for good or evil are a man's thoughts about other people, for in that case they hover not about the thinker, but about the object of the thought. A kindly thought about any person, or an earnest wish for his good, will form and project towards him a friendly artificial elemental ; if the wish be a definite one, as, for example, that he may recover from some sickness, then the elemental will be a force ever hovering over him to promote his recovery or to ward off any influence that might tend to hinder it. And in doing this it will display what appears like a very considerable amount of intelligence and adaptability, though really it is simply a force acting along the line of least resistance—pressing steadily in one direction all the time, and taking advantage of any channel that it can find, just as the water in a cistern would in a moment find the one open pipe among a dozen closed ones and proceed to empty itself through that. If the wish be merely an indefinite one for his general good, the elemental essence in its wonderful plasticity will respond exactly to that less distinct idea also, and the creature formed will expend its force in the direction of whatever action for the man's advantage comes most readily to hand. Of course in all cases the amount of such force it has to expend, and the length of time that it will live to expend it, depend entirely upon the strength of the original wish or thought which gave it birth ; though it must be remembered that it can be, as it were, fed and strengthened, and its life-period protracted by other good wishes or friendly thoughts projected in the same direction. *Furthermore, it appears to be actuated, like most other beings, by an instinctive desire to prolong its life, and thus reacts on its creator as a force constantly tending to provoke a repetition of the feeling which called it into existence.* It also influences in a similar manner others with whom it comes into contact, though its *rapport* with them is naturally not so perfect.

"*All that has been said as to the effect of good wishes and friendly thoughts is also true, in the opposite direction, of evil wishes and angry thoughts ; and considering the amount of envy, hatred, malice and all uncharitableness that exists in the world, it will be readily understood that among the artificial elementals many terrible creatures are to be seen. A man whose thoughts or desires are spiteful, brutal, sensual, avaricious, moves through the world carrying with him everywhere a pestiferous atmosphere of his own peopled with the loathsome beings he has created to be his companions, and thus is not only in a sadly evil case himself, but is a dangerous nuisance to his fellow-men, subjecting all who have the misfortune to come in contact with him to the risk of moral contagion from the influence of the abominations with which he chooses to surround himself.* A feeling of envious or jealous hatred towards another person will send an evil influence to hover over him and seek for a weak point through which it can operate ; and if the feeling be a persistent one, such a creature may be continuously nourished by it and thereby enabled to protract its undesirable activity for a very long period. *It can, however, produce no effect upon the person towards whom it is directed unless he has himself some tendency which it can foster—some fulcrum for its lever, as it were ; from the aura of a man of pure thought and good life all such influences at once rebound, finding nothing upon which they can fasten, and in that case, by a very curious law, they re-act in all their force upon their original creator.* In him, by unerring law, they find a very congenial sphere of action, and thus the Karma of his evil wish works itself out at once by means of the very entity which he himself has called into existence. It occasionally happens, however, that an artificial elemental of this description is for various reasons unable to expend its force either upon its object or its creator, and in such cases it becomes a kind of wandering demon, readily attracted by any person who indulges feelings similar to that which gave it birth, and equally prepared either to stimulate such feelings in him for the sake of the strength it may gain from them, or to pour out its store of evil influence upon him through any openings which he may offer it. If it is sufficiently powerful to seize upon and inhabit some passing shell it frequently does so, as the possession of such a temporary home enables it to husband its dreadful resources more carefully. In this form it may manifest through a medium and by masquerading as some well-known friend may sometimes obtain an influence over people upon whom it would otherwise have little hold.

" What has been written above will serve to show *how extremely important it is for us to maintain a strict control over our thoughts.* Many a well-meaning man, who is scrupulously careful to do his duty towards his neighbour in word and deed, is apt to consider that his thoughts at least are nobody's business but his own, and so lets them run riot in various directions, *utterly unconscious of the swarms of baleful creatures he is launching upon the world.* To such a man an accurate comprehension of the effect of thought and desire, in producing artificial elementals, would come as a horrifying revelation; on the other hand, it would be the greatest consolation to many devoted and grateful souls who are oppressed with the feeling that they are unable to do anything in return for the kindness lavished upon them by their benefactors. *For friendly thoughts and earnest good wishes are as easily and as effectually formulated by the poorest as by the richest, and it is within the power of almost any man, if he will take the trouble, to maintain what is practically a good angel always at the side of the brother or sister, the friend or the child whom he loves best, no matter in what part of the world he may be.* Many a time a mother's loving thoughts and prayers have formed themselves into an angel guardian for the child, and except in the almost impossible case that the child had in him no instinct responsive to a good influence, have undoubtedly given him assistance and protection. Such guardians may often be seen by a clairvoyant's vision. Even after the death of the mother, when her soul rests in heavenly or devachanic condition, the love which she pours out upon the children she thinks of as surrounding her, will re-act upon the real children still living on this world and will often support the guardian elemental which she created while on earth, until her dear ones themselves pass away in turn. Her love will always be felt by the children in flesh ; and it will manifest in their dreams and often in various events, in providential protections and escapes, for love is a strong shield and is not limited by space or time."

Besides the quality of the astral plane or astral light described above, it has another far more subtle quality, and that is its power of retaining indelibly the impressions of all thoughts, words and deeds originated by men on the physical plane. It is out of this storehouse of impressions that the history not only of this world, but of each human being that has ever existed on it, can be faithfully reproduced by the Adept. Hence it is not only one of the principal agents in the building of the Kosmos or Universe, but an ever-active reporter of what is thought or done by every human being. It is on this account that the Aryans gave it the name of Chitragupta or the Secret Recorder. He is supposed to read the account of every soul's life from a register called Agra-Sandhani, when the soul appears before the Judgment seat after its departure from this world. The meaning of this allegory will be quite plain when read in the light of what has been demonstrated above. The same idea is to be found in the Mazdean or Zoroastrian religion, where the Angel of Light,

Meher Yazata, is represented as weighing the actions of men after their death and allotting them a place either in heaven or hell according to their merits or demerits. Similarly, we find the same idea in the Christian and Mahomedan religions under the form of Recording Angels. Thus we see that this idea of men's thoughts, words and deeds being recorded somewhere, somehow, is common to all great world religions, and that it is founded on an actual fact in nature. Let us demonstrate the subject from the stand-point of modern science.

To explain the phenomena of heat, light, electricity, magnetism, &c., modern science is compelled to assume the existence of an imponderable and invisible medium pervading all space and the interstices of all matter, which they call ether. This ether is nothing else than the astral light or astral plane of which we have been speaking at such length above. But the modern scientists are only aware of its manifested effects on the physical plane, and with a very few exceptions they are entirely in the dark as regards its real nature and occult properties and potencies which are described above. The reason for this lies in the fact that modern science pursues its investigations through the physical senses and physical instruments only, while the domain in which the phenomena of the astral plane lie, can only be approached through the subtler and higher faculties which require to be developed by special training of mind. Those of the Western scientists who have made researches into the nature of Mesmerism, animal magnetism or animal electricity (now called hypnotism), have got some glimpses of the existence of the Astral Plane or Astral Light. This Astral Light has been called by them by various names, such as Od, Odic Force, Odyle or Odylic Force, Magnetic Aura, &c. In the Aryan literature it is known as Tejas or Âkâsh. It should, however, be noted that ether is the grossest form of Âkâsha. The existence of the aura or astral light has been established beyond all doubt by the researches made into this subject by the eminent Austrian Scientist, Baron von Reichenbach (*vide* his "Researches into Animal Magnetism.") Professor Williams describes this aura in the following terms :—

"The aura which pervades the brain and nervous system, though electrical in its nature, is something more than mere electricity. The former seems to be charged with an *intelligence*, so to speak ; a spiritual essence characteristic of itself and clearly distinguished from the latter. Water may be charged with electricity, and but one result can be obtained from it. However, if animal electricity be used, the water partakes of whatever therapeutic virtue the operator desired at the time he charged it."

This aura exerts an influence perceptible or imperceptible on all the material objects which it touches, and especially influences other auras. The human aura* is the most potent among all auras of existing creatures or things, as it carries with it the active living force of human will, in other words, of the soul-power of man. The human aura varies in colours according to the varying tendencies and mental, moral or spiritual development of each man, and according to the quality of the thoughts evolved by him at every movement of his individual existence. Thus the colour of the aura of a very vicious man is entirely black, while that of a high Yogi is of a perfectly white colour. And at intermediate stages it is of a gray, dusky, red, blue, yellow or dusky-white colour according to the degree of progress made towards spirituality. Thus the character as well as the thoughts of any man can be read by a Yogi by looking at his aura. The aura of persons and things is not visible to the ordinary eyes, but only to the trained Yogi or seer or to those who have developed the clairvoyant faculty. As an instance of this fact we may here quote the incident of the interview between Zoroaster and the learned Brahmin, Chandargas, who was sent to Persia by an Indian king to test the spiritual knowledge of the former. Chandargas had prepared certain difficult questions regarding

---

* *Vide* " Human Aura," by A. P. Sinnett; also by A. Marques.

psychology and spiritual philosophy to be solved by Zoroaster. When Chandargas appeared in the court of the Persian king, Zoroaster answered all his questions before he gave expression to them. Thenceforward Chandargas became the disciple of Zoroaster. This phenomenon of reading a man's thought is only explicable from the existence of the astral plane or astral light. This property of the astral light or ether to retain every impression that is made on it by the thoughts, words and deeds of men has been attested by some of the scientific men of the present time. On this point Profressor E. Hitchcock observes :—

"It seems that this photographic influence pervades all nature, nor can we say where it stops. We do not know, but it may print upon the world round us our features as they are modified by various passions, and thus fill nature with daguerreotypes of all our actions. It may be, too, that there are tests by which nature, more skilful than any photographer, can bring out and fix these portraits, so that acuter senses than ours shall see them as upon a canvas."

This view is supported by Professor Babbage who states that "The air (ether) is one vast library, on whose pages are forever written all that man has ever said or woman whispered."

Professor Jevons even goes beyond this and asserts "That every thought, displacing particles of the brain and setting them in motion, scatters them throughout the universe, and thus each particle of the existing matter must be a register of all that has happened."

Professor Draper, in his celebrated work, "The Conflict between Science and Religion," observes on this same point as follows :—

"A shadow never falls upon a wall without leaving thereupon a permanent trace, a trace which might be made visible by resorting to proper processes. Photographic operations are cases in point. The portraits of our friends, or landscape views, may be hidden on the sensitive surface from the eye, but they are ready to make their appearance as soon as proper developers are resorted to. A spectre is concealed on a silver or 'glossy surface until, by our necromancy, we make it come forth into the visible world. Upon the walls of our most private apartments, where we think the eye of intrusion is altogether shut out and our retirement can never be profaned, there exist the vestiges of all our acts, silhouettes of whatever we have done."

Men of science have expressed their beliefs on the invisible effects of thoughts on the ether around us ; and that it is not a mere speculation or theory, but an actual fact in nature, will be clearly seen from what has been stated already regarding the astral light or astral plane and its nature and properties. The pictures of thoughts, words and deeds of men thus preserved in the Âkâsh or astral light can be seen by one who has developed his clairvoyant faculty, in other words, that faculty whereby one is able to see things invisible to the mortal sight. The modern development of the once much-derided science of Mesmerism, now called hypnotism, has brought this fact within the domain of practical demonstration, and we can but refer our readers to the works of that learned writer, Mr. A. P. Sinnett, "On Mesmerism" and the " Rationale of Mesmerism," and to the other works on the same subject.

The science of Psychometry or "soul-measuring," that is, the science whereby one with developed faculty is able to read in a conscious state the thoughts and actions of individuals either in the present, past or future, even past scenes in the history of the world, and also those which are to take place in future, is another branch of the occult science corroborative of what has been said above. On this subject we may refer our readers to the "Manual of Psychometry," by Dr. J. R. Buchanan, and to "The Soul of Things," by Professor W. Denton. The scientific evidences of the occult side and occult laws of nature are now fast accumulating—though these relate only to the borderland between the seen and the unseen—and before the close of this century enough will have been disclosed on this subject to compel men to acknowledge that such things *are*, and that what once was derided as superstition, imposture or imagination, is not really so, but that such things do exist as facts ; that their bigotted opinion on such matters betrays only their own crass ignorance ; that the so-called superstitions have in reality a scientific basis for their existence ; that it requires patient research and broad minded tolerance to bring out the hidden things of nature—whether of light or darkness—within the domain of the real and the practical.

In the light of the information given above we may now profitably understand the following passages from the writings of Madame H. P. Blavatsky and Mrs. Annie Besant. On the tremendous potency of sound the former observes in her " Secret Doctrine" as follows :—

"We say and maintain that sound, for one thing, is a tremendous occult power ; that it is a stupendous force, of which the electricity generated by a million of Niagaras could never counteract the smallest potentiality when directed with occult knowledge. Sound may be produced of such a nature that the pyramid of Cheops could be raised in the air, or that a dying man, nay, one at his last breath, would be revived and filled with new energy and vigour. For sound generates or rather attracts together the elements that produce an *ozone*, the fabrication of which is beyond chemistry, but is within the limit of alchemy. It may even *resurrect* a man or an animal whose astral 'vital body' has not been irreparably separated from the physical body by the severance of the magnetic or odic chord. *As one saved thrice from death* by that power, the writer ought to be credited with personally knowing something about it."—(Vol. i, p. 606.)

Mrs. Besant expresses herself on the potency of sound as follows :—

" By the power we possess of shaping or wielding our thoughts for good or evil we either make or mar the potencies of to-day which are sure to re-act upon us either in this life or some future life. As we think, the thought burning in our brain becomes a living force for good or evil, for a longer or shorter time in the mental atomsphere of the world, in proportion to the vitality and the intensity that are thrown into it by the thinker. If one finds himself unable by the force of circumstances to do good to his fellow creatures on the material plane, he has however within him the power and choice to do far greater good on the thought or mental plane. There is no woman however weak, there is no man however obscure and insignificant, from a worldly standpoint, who has not within him this divine creative force of thought."— (*Theosophic Gleaner*, vol. iii, p. 270). It is by this very creative power of thought that prophets of all ages, yogis, and sages, have been able to perform the so-called miracles of which we read in religious histories. As a man thinks, so he moulds his own destiny, and thoughts from him go out to mould also the thoughts and lives of other men. As he thinks thoughts of love and gentleness the whole reservoir of love in the world is filled to overflowing, and such thoughts are taken up by those who are capable of putting them into execution, and the object aimed at by the original thinker is thus carried out without his taking any visible action in the matter or uttering a single word about it to any body else. Such is the mysterious and creative potency of thought and it can be verified by any one who chooses to take the trouble.

It may further be observed that the words spoken by, as well as the name of, every individual, largely determines his future fate. On this point an eminent French occultist observes as follows :—" When our soul (mind) creates or evokes a thought, the representative sign of that thought is self engraved on the astral fluid, which is the receptacle and, so to say, the mirror of all the manifestations of being. The sign expresses the thing : the thing is the (hidden or occult) virtue of the sign. To pronounce a word is to evoke a thought, and make it present: the magnetic potency of human speech is the commencement of every manifestation in the occult world. To utter a name is not only to define a

Being (an actual entity) but to place it under, and condemn it through, the omission of the word (Verbum), to the influence of one or more occult potencies. Things are for every one of us, that which it (the World) makes them while naming them. The Word (Verbum) or the speech of every man is, quite unconscious to himself, a *blessing* or a *curse*; this is why our present ignorance about the properties and attributes of the *idea*, as well as about the attributes and properties of *matter*, is often fatal to us. Yes, names and words are either *beneficent* or *maleficent* ; they are, in a certain sense, either venemous or health-giving, according to the hidden influences attached by Supreme Wisdom to their elements, that is to say, to the *letters* which compose them, and the *numbers* correlative to these letters." On this passage Madame H. P. Blavatsky makes the following remarks :—" This is strictly true as an esoteric teaching accepted by all the eastern schools of Occultism. In Sanskrit, as also in the Hebrew and all other alphabets, every letter has its occult meaning and its *rationale* : it is a cause and an effect of a preceding cause, and a combination of these very often produces the most magical effect. The vowels, especially, contain the most occult and formidable potencies. The mantras (magical rather than religious invocations, esoterically) are chanted by Brahmins, and so are the rest of the Vedas and other scriptures."—(The " Secret Doctrine," vol. i, p. 121.)

It is for the reasons stated in the preceding passage that the sacred word of the Brahmins (Aum) contains in it every power of generation (*vide* " Patanjali's Yoga Aphorisms"), preservation and destruction when it is correctly chanted or intoned by an adept in the mysteries of sound. This word when incorrectly pronounced or chanted is productive of fearful consequences to the utterer. The careless use of this word was therefore forbidden, and its utterance amidst mixed audiences or where many people are gathered together was strictly prohibited ; " because where mingling and hostile magnetisms are making a confused atmosphere, any great sound—sound of great potency—thrown into it must cause tumult and not harmony. For this reason the word was never to be sounded save when the mind was pure, save when the mind was tranquil; it was never to be used except when the life was noble, because the sound that is working in the harmonious, builds, working in the inharmonious, destroys; and everything that is evil is tumultuous, while everything which is pure is harmonious. For the Great Breath which is purity, goes forth in rhythmical vibrations, and all which is one with that rhythm is essentially pure and therefore harmonious. But when the Great Breath working on matter, finds friction, then it is that impurity is set up, and if a man in his own atmosphere —using that breath which comes out from him, which is the reflection of the Supreme Breath—is impure, that is, inharmonious, then to sound the name of the Supreme under these circumstances is to invite his own destruction, his own disintegration, for he throws the very force of the Divine into disharmony. What then can he do but destroy that which has nothing in common with the divine harmony. This is not only true of the sacred word, but of the mantra that is used to build."—("The Building of the Kosmos," pp. 23-24.) The holy prayers or mantras are chanted when the new-born soul comes forth into this world, so that the sacred harmony may surround it and give it the impulse in the birth hour, which shall send it on towards harmonious development throughout his wordly career. When at the age of seven the spirit is able to work more directly on the physical body, the ceremony of initiation takes place and the child is invested with the sacred thread during again the chanting of a mantra which is to be the key-note of the future life. For this reason *the mantra should come from one who knows the key-note of that life, and is able to give it the sounds which are wanted to keep it harmonious through life.* It is in such ceremonies, which are also to be found in more or less modified forms in the Mazdean and other world religions, that the great preserving power of sound is manifested. " Because whenever that life is in danger the pronouncing of the sound or mantra imparted to him at the ceremony protects him, and whenever his life is threatened by visible or invisible danger the murmur of the muttered mantra comes between it and the danger, makes round it waves of harmony from which every evil thing is thrown back by the force of the vibrations. Any foe visible or invisible threatening that life is driven back in terror and confusion when it touches these vibrations. Every day of that life begins with the utterance of this mantra so that the day passes harmoniously and without any accident to disturb its spiritual state, and it also closes with the repetition of the same mantra, so that in the night the spirit may be made fit to held communion with its Lord and bring down on this plane the wisdom which he so learns from Him, and so carries it on into his every day life. When the span of that life closes on this earthly plane, once again the mantras are chanted for him in the ceremonies which take place after death, so that the sound or vibrations thus created may break the bondage house of the soul, that is, destory the body generated on the other side of death, and thus free that soul in its onwrad flight towards Devaloka or heaven. During his sojourn there he has on longer any need of such mantras because there he lives surrounded in an ocean of harmony which is not mingled with the discord of the earth, and after resting there for a longer or shorter period according to his karmic merits in this life, he again descends on this earth to fulfil his destiny, and so on continues life after life until he learns the lesson of living in perfect harmony with the great Divine Harmony, and then it is that the shackles of the senses and the bondage of the body fall oft from him and he stands in the midst of creation a liberated, glorious and angelic being, one with the Divine Soul, one with the source from whence he came"—"The Building of the Kosmos," pp. 24-25.) Thus we have seen the mighty and mysterious potencies of sound, in other words, words or speech, on all manifested creations, more especially on the life and actions of a man, and we have further seen that harmonious sounds, in other words, peaceful, loving and gentle thoughts and words, are absolutely necessary for fulfilling his destiny in the cycle of his existence from the very commencement of his career on the manifested world up to his final and glorious end when he is united with the Supreme Soul, and becomes one of the active creators in the Universe.

Having so far demonstrated the effects of thoughts and words on the happiness or misery of mankind, we may now, before closing our subject, briefly see some of the effects of human deeds or actions on the physical plane. The struggle made by men in pursuit of money and in each one securing for himself as much comfort and luxury as possible at the cost of his weaker and more helpless brethren, is a fruitful source of all human miseries which cannot be controverted by any one. The hunger of power and dominion is another prolific source of human misery, the evil effects of which have been too obvious in the past historical records of the world and can be clearly seen in the present political and military atmospheres of Europe and other so-called civilized countries of the age, and in the establishments of all sorts of secret societies such as Nihilists, anarchists and the like—trying to subvert all existing order of things and persons. All these human miseries are caused by the evil thought-forms generated by the oppression of the strong over the weak, which thought-forms charge the aura of the world with malicious, revengeful and hateful thought-creations, actual entities which pursue mankind like veritable fiends, as we have demonstrated above, both individually and collectively bringing about disastrous wars, famines, pestilence and all such wholesale visitations which now and again so torment and affect humanity. Yet another pregnant source of human misery is the daily slaughter of millions of dumb helpless animals for food. This cruel butchery of our helpless fellow-creatures is a direct interference with the law of evolution, inasmuch as the development of the souls encased in these forms is thereby considerably retarded and thus the whole current of evolutionary progress is thrown into disharmony and confusion for which man alone is responsible, and for which he has to pay terribly in consequence, in the way of more intense pressure on his life and keener forms of miseries. It may be observed in passing, that the struggle for existence is more accentuated and keenly felt among the Western nations, among whom the daily slaughter of animals is unchecked and universally prevalent, than among the Oriental nations in whom it is not so unchecked. It will be easily perceived that all these human actions are the emanations of selfish and wicked thoughts of men, and that nobody but men themselves are responsible for that terrible miseries they thus bring down upon them. We have thus traced the source of all human miseries, whether visible or invisible, to one main source alone, and that is the *power of human thought*, a power which is divine in its origin, and being so, is omniscient, omnipotent and omnificent. As is well said by a Master of Wisdom, "all that we are is the result of what we have thought: it is founded on our thoughts, it is made up of our thoughts. If a man speaks or acts with an evil thought, pain follows him, as the wheel follows the foot of the ox that draws the carriage."

Enough has here been said on the mighty *Potentiality of Thought*, for human weal and woe, and it is now for each one of our readers to judge for himself how far he should conform his life to this mighty Law of Thought, and thus gather true happiness for himself and for his fellow-beings. Says the "Light of Asia":

> "Such is the Law which moves to Righteousness,
> Which none at last can turn aside or stay;
> The heart of it is Love, the end of it
> Is Peace and Consummation sweet. Obey!"

B. E. UNWALA.

THE MAHATMAS OR ADEPTS.

THE word Mahâtmâ is indiscriminately applied by people to any individual. Alexander, the Macedonian soldier who was most greedy of lands and lives, is even called a Mahâtmâ. For a correct application of this word, therefore, we shall classify religious development of man into various grades. In his preliminary stage man is like an animal, acting only from instinct for physical gratification. Subsequently, however, he feels some perception of latent higher powers in him. These he begins to search at a later stage, but the lower nature being still predominant, does not allow his higher impulses to manifest themselves. By continued efforts and trials an equilibrium having been obtained between these forces, he tries to search for the divine element from which these higher impulses arise, but being still attracted by the lower, he generally fails. On a higher stage, however, he anxiously searches the source of his true nature, but *outside* of himself. Disappointed, because not finding it there, he tries now to seek for the divine light *within* himself, which he succeeds in finding later on ; and finding there he tries to develop his self-consciousness, which grows into Divine Knowledge. During this development, while yet on a lower stage, his inner spiritual senses begin to become active, and thereby he recognizes the presence of other spiritual beings existing on the same plane on which his consciousness works. His will, which is an impersonal force, an aspect of God, then becomes free from every selfish or worldly desire, and controls his thoughts, which then become obedient, and his *word* or sound then becomes so forcible that it could construct or destroy, and then he could well be called a Mahâtmâ, an Adept, an Yogi, or a Holy Man. He thus acquires the Light of Wisdom and Immortality. A passage in Yasna (Hâ 8), which has been repeated in the " Hoshbânm," runs thus :—

"Mayest Thou rule, O Ahura-Mazda ! in Bliss, according to Thy Will: as Thou wilt over the Waters, over the Trees, over all that is of the pure origin.

THE MAHATMAS OR ADEPTS. 313

Make that the Holy man may rule; the unholy may not rule. *May the Holy man rule as he will;* may the unholy not rule as he will. May the unholy disappear, driven away by the creatures of Spentamainyu, may he be conquered, not ruling as he would."

"May the Holy man rule *as he will*," because the Holy man, the Adept, is always ruling in harmony with the Will of Ahura-Mazda, his will being one with the Divine Will. The Holy men of ancient Persia did wonders because they were acting in harmony with the Supreme Will of Ahura-Mazda. They were in communion with Him, because they knew where to find Him. They were searching Him through the right way, in their own hearts. A man who has not found Him in his own heart will never find Him anywhere else in the universe. Let any one examine his own actions and ascertain if they are in harmony with the higher impulses of his heart, and he will find, perhaps without much effort, that his actions are often conflicting with his own utterances; his utterances often conflicting with his own thoughts, and his thoughts always uncontrolled, never in touch with or never controlled by the Divine Will. Thus we are far, far removed from our judicious sphere. But the will of a Mahâtmâ being trained in a way to harmonize with the Will of Ahura-Mazda, he generally lives on a higher plane of Consciousness than we do at present. Before the highest state of consciousness could be reached, however, the Adept has to pass through various grades. We are told that there are about sixty grades of such Adepts. Those of the lower grade are progressing, whilst still attached to their physical bodies, while others of a higher Order, who cannot remain any longer in the earthly decomposing tabernacle, are said to have been making further progress in ethereal bodies imperceptible to our physical senses, and remain for long period encased in such dwellings.

A deep study of any Aryan religion will show to any unprejudiced observer that man is composed of seven " principles"— (1) The physical body; (2) the *Jiva* or vital force; (3) astral body; (4) the Lower Manas; (5) the Higher Manas; (6) Buddhi; and (7) Âtmâ or Spirit, an emanation from the

40

ABSOLUTE—a state rather than a being. The third principle plays an important part here. Usually it is without consciousness, being always connected with the physical body; but it can be made to be the seat of life and consciousness when the latter is withdrawn from the physical body and concentrated in the astral one. A person who has succeeded in doing so can live independent of his physical encasement, and a Mahâtmâ, entirely throwing away this shell, can remain ever after in the ethereal and invisible form. He develops it in himself as he proceeds on the Path. "Having reached the goal and refused its fruition, he remains on Earth, as an Adept; and when he dies, instead of going into Nirvâna, he remains in that glorious body he has woven for himself, *invisible* to uninitiated mankind, to watch over and protect it," says "The Voice of the Silence." How far this teaching agrees with the Avastâ and the Pahlavi literature will be seen presently.

Commonly we understand only one body, the physical shell. But studying the human constitution theosophically, we find that there are other vehicles, too, intervowen into each other. Similarly we find more bodies than one in the Avastâ literature as constituting the human being. The *Keherpam* (Zend) or *Kâlebûd* (Persian) mentioned in the Behram Yasht, Hâ 55 of the Yasna, and Gâthâ Ahunavaiti (7), distinct from *Tanvas*, the physical body, seem to correspond with the astral body of Theosophy, on which the physical body is moulded; and the "dwelling" of the Fire, the son of Ahura-Mazda, supposed to last from Renovation to Renovation in the Boundless Time, (*Atash-niyaesh*), seems to correspond with the first Envelope of the Soul as taught by Eliphas Lévy, the French Mystic. There are thus other bodies than the physical one according to the Avastâ, but it is premature at the present stage of our study to decide which of them corresponds with the Nirmankâyâ of "The Voice of the Silence." The following passage, nevertheless, from Gâthâ Ahunavaiti might appear suggestive :—

"To Him [*i. e.*, to the Holy man] Armaiti approached, and with her came

Sovereign Power, the Good Mind, and Asha (the Righteous Order): and Armaiti gave a *Kcherpam* (form), she abiding and ever-strenuous."

Armaiti stands in the Avastâ generally as the Hindu Sarasvati, the goddess which presides over Divine Knowledge, and those who have studied "The Voice of the Silence" will see in this passage, so profound in its character, if they have sufficient insight, what has been said there about the Hall of Wisdom. Suffice it to say, however, that there are various vehicles or principles through the medium of which the Ego has been working.

For such *Vriddhi* or religious progress, Zoroastrianism has, like all other religions, two sides, one exoteric and the other esoteric, the former is intended for the masses and is called *záhir* or open, the latter for the select few and is called *báten* or concealed. The masses who consider God as something separate from themselves are satisfied with the idea of the so-called Monotheistic form of worship—a worship of an extraneous Being—agreeable to the first few stages of religious progress described above. But souls which are sufficiently advanced to assimilate higher truths would not be satisfied by such an external worship, and would seek therefore something higher. For such, a system is provided in almost every religion which we shall call Advaitism or Monism and the path of its realization *Yoga*, in contradistinction to Ekeshwarvâd or Monotheism. The watchwords on which this teaching is based appear to represent the same idea in all religions, *viz.*, the unity of man with God. Man, that is, *manas*, the real man, has emanated from Ahura-Mazda, and is destined, after fulfilling certain conditions, to be absorbed again into Him, in lifetime, as can be seen from various passages of the Zoroastrian Scriptures. In the Book of Shet Shaikiliv, in the Celestial Desâtir, we see a prayer in the manner following:—

" Thou hast immersed the pure substances in the ocean of Thy effulgences!

"The [inner] eye of purity saw Thee by the lustre of Thy substance!

" Dark and astounded is he who hath seen Thee by the efforts of the Intellect."

But as the Desâtir is not recognized by all the Parsis, except a few, as a book of purely Zoroastrian philosophy, it being a work supposed to be written for the use of esotericists, the citation of various other quotations from this book would be of less avail for the prejudiced and dogmatic. I shall take the liberty, therefore, to call in my aid the Avastâ literature against which no Parsi, however dogmatic, will demur.

"May we see Thee, attain to Thee to Thy oneness, by the best purity, the perfect purity."

Yasna, Hâ 60 (20).

"Him will we serve with praiseworthy prayers, for now is He revealed to the [inner] eye. He who in acts and speech and thoughts knows Purity, he [knows] Ahura-Mazda."

Yasna, Hâ 40 (8).

" Whoso, O Ahura! believe Thee as Lord by their actions, speech and good prayer, whose primitive Protector Thou art, O Ahura-Mazda! they by the glory of their purity at last will *merge in Thee!*"

Gâthâ Vohukhshathrem, Hâ 51 (3).

"Every one is wise through the purity of Armaiti, all that [is] in Thy Kingdom, O Ahura!"

Gâthâ Spentomad, Hâ 49 (5).

" Whoso *unite* swiftly unto the pure Consciousness of the Universal Mind, take their birth in the happy abode of Mazda."

Gâthâ Ahunavaiti, Hâ 30 (10).

These passages are sufficient, I suppose, to establish Advaitism in Zoroastrianism. The fifth name of Ahura-Mazda in the Yasht of that name signifies, however, clearly enough this system to be such, namely, " *Visparohu Mazdadât ashachithra*" (all pure things created by Mazda) is His fifth name, or, in other words, "I am in all things: all things I am."

A marked peculiarity observed in the passage cited above from Gâthâ Ahunavaiti is that, in the text the word for the holy union in Zend is almost similar to, if not identical with, the Sanskrit *yuj,* the root of the word *Yoga,* which may have been common among the Perso-Aryans as well as among the Indo-Aryans of old, as the word *Yozdâthregar* implies, by which name the Parsi Mobed who performs ritual is known even at present, although the word Yoga seems to have been forgotten by the modern Parsis.

A yogi who would attain immortality has to evolve another body, as we have already seen, far superior and of etherial substance, and has to remain in other spheres uncontaminated by the impure and sensual thoughts of ordinary mankind. You might ask, how do they evolve such body? Have they the power to create such body? A moment's consideration would, perhaps, solve the question. How do we, imperfect as we are, build our physical body, from a span's length at our birth to a height of four or five feet at the age of twenty-one? If there is a process manifest in us ever working for the growth of our physical body, analogically . there must be a process, latent though in all of us and active in a holy man, for the growth of a superior dwelling. Thousands of years have passed away since the Holy men mentioned in the Avastâ became Adepts, and such period demands disintegration of the physical structure. The attempts, therefore, to search the Adepts in their physical body, on some secluded parts of this Khvaniras (earth), would be futile and fruitless. These Adepts, when they reach a certain stage, do not belong to any particular religion, as religions are at present known. They are above religion; they belong to no religion, and at the same time they are of all religions. In support of this I shall call in my aid Hazrat Âzar Kaivan, who says in his "Jâm" (the Cup) :—

"I renounced the conducts of every exoteric religion or faith, and acquired the conduct of the ancient Hokmûs [Adepts.]"

He had, it is said, among his disciples not only the Parsis of India and Persia, but Hindus, Christians, and Mahomedans also, as was the case with Zoroaster, who had among his disciples Changargâch, a Hindu, and other Greek philosophers. From this, it would appear that the path or Yoga was open for those who deserved it. This path is not *a* religion as religions are at present understood.

All the religions of the world are, nevertheless, a necessary help towards this path if they are understood in their esoteric light, just as a plank or a rafter is a necessary adjunct to a beginner in the art of swimming. Just as the plank would become unnecessary after acquiring mastery over that art, religion becomes of less importance to a man whose soul becomes free to swim in the internal spiritual region. If every Adept of the White Lodge can be taken as an Aryan,—Theosophically this human race is called Aryan—then they can also be taken as Zoroastrian, as every Zoroastrian is supposed to adore the *khureh* or the "glory" of all the Aryan Holy Ones in the Avastâ.

The idea about the existence of the Mahâtmâs was, however, during the few years of Western civilization lost among the Parsis to such an extent that while it was reännounced in India by the prominent members of the Theosophical Society, the majority of the Parsi community were taken aback, and many of them ridiculed the idea that a man can become a Mahâtmâ or a Mahâtmâ can exist at all amid modern "culture and reason." Few Parsis believed in what the Founders of the Theosophical Society said, and still very few heard them with patience and candour. That every man can become an Adept if he properly understands his position in the universe, is a Theosophical idea; and for the matter of that, every Zoroastrian is in duty bound a Holy man, if he, in his turn, understands his position, his mission, and his religion aright. Every Parsi who recites his Manthra standing before the sacred Fire, is made to ask—

"Give me, O Fire, son of Ahura-Mazda ! [One] who can instruct me what is best for me now and for evermore, concerning the best life of the Holy men [Adepts], brilliant, all-glorious !"

A Parsi asks for a Teacher who can instruct him about the best life of the Holy man. This passage can be interpreted into three different ways :—(*a*) It is true that a Dastur in the modern sense of the word is a teacher for a modern worldly man ; but, as we have seen before, there are stages in human life, in which the advanced soul seeks something higher than a modern Dastur can impart, and wants to lead a higher life than the common herd of mankind could lead. (*b*) In such cases the teacher mentioned in the above passage can be safely taken as an Adept who can instruct the aspirant from *within* concerning the best life of the Holy men. And (*c*) lastly, the Divine Fire, the son of Ahura-Mazda, the Âtmân, becomes one's own Instructor when the aspirant reaches a certain stage.

How can we obtain that Instructor, the Adept, who can impart to us the knowledge desired? It is certain that the principal qualifications requisite for an aspirant are pure religious knowledge, pure devotion and pure actions. It is needless to say that " purity" pervades the whole of the Avastâïc teaching, and to act on this noble principle becomes the duty of every one who aspires to rise above the average humanity.

The true *way* is to follow perseveringly, in the Society, the path shown by the holy Adepts. Let us try to become sinless and pure. It is very easy to talk and preach about purity : we have heard too much of *manashni, gavashni, kunashni*; *humata, hukhta, hvarshta*. By *manashni, gavashni, kunashni* one can approach Ahura-Mazda, says Gâthâ Ushtavaiti " Him will we serve with praiseworthy prayers, for now with the [inner] eye I see Him clearly. He who in works and words of the good Spirit knows Purity, he knows Ahura-Mazda. His praise also will we lay down in Garo-nemana." —(*Yasna XIV, 8.*) But we have not realized Ahura-Mazda, because in action we are far, far below these principles, much less are we trying to understand them. In the first place we do not understand what that is which is to keep pure. Some might say we must keep our *mind* pure ; but let us ask, have we understood what Mind is? We talk, parrot-like, without understanding, and here is our failure. We are not earnest, we do not wish to improve ourselves by the dictates of our heart. The heart is our sun, the mind is our moon, and they are the eyes of Ahura-Mazda. The moon is out of focus at present. We refuse to listen to the voice that comes from within our heart, the Golden Gate. Let us try to open it. Let us find out the way. Instead of clogging the heart by making it subservient to the Lower Mind, let the mind be controlled by the heart. Then through the heart will the light of Mithra shine, the Golden Sun will rise, the door will open—and you are perhaps face to face with your Master!

It is not inconsistent while discussing the subject of the Adepts to know something of the way by which we can find Them out. Each sense of mankind was developed with the manifestation of each element in nature. For example, with the manifestation of Âkâsha we have acquired the faculty of *hearing;* with that of Vâyu we have developed the faculty of *touch*; with Fire, the faculty of *sight;* with Water, the *taste;* and with the manifestation of Earth, we have developed the faculty of *smell*. Besides these five, there is another sense, hazily developed in few persons, and dormant in all of us at present, called the faculty of *Clairvoyance*—a faculty which corresponds to the Astral or ethereal element. The faculty of pure clairvoyance has magnetic connection with the heart, call it the Golden Gate or the *Chinvad-peretu*, the bridge which leads us to the Divine. Special training is necessary to open this Way.

One of the primary steps or rather means of purifying the heart is the idea of nonseparation, a lesson often repeated by every Zoroastrian while performing his *kusti*, several times a day. The *Jasmedvañghe* is a short pledge, according to which every Parsi pledges before his God that he belongs to a religion which is the dispeller of separation and performer of the *Khvetvodathâm*, the holy marriage of soul with Ahura-Mazda.

This is a most important step for an aspirant to a sinless life, and every Parsi who calls himself a Zoroastrian is an aspirant to become an Adept from the time that he is initiated into the mystery of his own religion at the age of seven years. Whoever hath courage to purify himself like unto those Masters of Compassion may see Them even while in the world of woe and suffering. Let us consider the happiness of the world our own happiness, the misery of the world our own misery, and the Divine light will shine into the heart. But the key is lost. *Nil desperandum*, nevertheless. The Theosophical Society gives some hope, and that hope is not that the Society would help you if *you* would remain idle. That hope is to be realized by men *individually* as is said in the *Gâthâ Ahunavaiti*. One of the primary objects of this Society is to form a nucleus of the Universal Brotherhood, and if separation is a curse on mankind according to Zoroastrianism, this Society's advent should not be inimical to the Parsis but a welcome aid. It steps on the Indian sacred soil with greetings and good tidings for all. Let us raise, then, the great standard and proclaim to the world our divine message, " Universal Brotherhood," and let us fill the whole universe with boundless love from that fountain-head, the heart, that the reign of peace and everlasting happiness may come on earth, and the earth would become once more the Garden of Eden.

N. F. BILIMORIA.

—*Theosophic Gleaner*, Vol. v, No. 9.

THE LAST PARSI ADEPT.

"The path by which to Deity we climb,
Is arduous, rough, ineffable, sublime.
And the strong, massy gates, through which we pass
In our just course, are bound with chains of brass."

THE ways by which we arrive at a knowledge of God and of a future life are two; and these are denominated in modern Persian *Istedalâl* and *Mushâhedât* or *Makâshefat*. The first is that knowledge which we derive from our observation and experience of the material universe and the changes we see therein; while the second is the illumination consequent on the practice of great purity and intense contemplation, by which the soul acquires the power of visiting the spiritual world.

Those who follow *Istedalâl* are of two classes;—(1) *Hukmâ Mashayin*, who believe in natural religion without acknowledging the authority of any one prophet, and (2) *Hukmâ Mutkalemin*, who believe in some revealed religion.

Of those who practise *Mushâhedât*, there are three divisions:— (1) the *Hukmâ Elahiyat*, who look upon all prophets and all objects as the light of God; (2) *Hukmâ Ishrâkin*, who do not believe in any one religion, but look upon all religions as true in principle; and (3) the *Sufis*, who outwardly profess the religion that they are born in.

The laws of the ancients, according to which *Mushâhedât* (Yog) is practised, are called *Elm-i-Tasavof*, or *Elm-i-Saluk*, and the student is called *Sâlek*. There are four states in which the Adept sees the glories and secrets of the world of spirit:—*Khâb*, or sleep, (2) *Gaib*, (3) *Masti* or *Moainat*, and (4) *Khale-badan*. Those whose inner self is not altogether powerless, often see real visions in their *Khâb*, or sleep; but when "divine grace is communicated to the holy ascetic from the worlds on high, and the transport arising therefrom locks up external perceptions, it is the state of *Gaib*. *Masti* means that state in which divine grace being communicated without the senses being overpowered, the person is transported for the time being from the world of reality. The state higher than this, called *Khale-badan*, is the power of the soul to quit the body and return to it at pleasure."

"Among the modern Parsis, the chief of the Âbâdian, or Âzur Hoshangian sects was Âzur Kaivân, who resided in Khum for 28 years, and removed in his latter days from the land of Irân to India where, in A. D. 1617, he died at Patna, at the age of eighty-five." He was at the head of the *Ishrakin* philosophers of his time, and, having attained all the four states of *Mushâhedât*, was styled *Zul-ulum* or the Master of Sciences. Leading a pure and holy life, practising austerities from his earliest years, he had developed the powers of the soul to the highest extent. His visions of the empyrean worlds have been portrayed by him in Persian verse, and are still extant in the book called *Jâm-i-Kai-Khoshru*,[*] which contains an admirable commentary on the poem by Khoda Joi, one of his disciples.

He thus begins:—"I purified my body, and leaving aside the observances of every religion or sect, I betook myself to the rules enjoined by the sages of old. Silence, sedentariness, living in a dark and narrow cell, gradual diminution of food and sleep, and constant recitation of the name of God, constituted my discipline, which in time unfolded before my soul's eye the visions of the world on high. In the state of *Khâb*, or sleep, a ghastly form first broke upon my sight, and I was terrified, and invoked the name of God, when the form disappeared, and a glaring fire rose to view and struck me with alarm. It gradually melted away, and in its place appeared a scowling fiery form with its head hanging down the breast and navel, and kept me in agitation. Next there burst upon my sight fires of various hues, and my soul acquir-

---

[*] The present paper is based upon a Gujarati translation of this book, published from the Sir Jamsetjee Jejeebhoy Translation Fund, in 1848; and partly upon the notice of Âzur Kaivan and his disciples, given in the *Dabestân*.

ed the power to swim over the ocean. I saw crystal water, beautiful avenues and grand palaces, with table richly spread, birds singing, and fair men and women moving about. A brilliant splendour played before my breast, and I saw a blue blaze, out of which a sweet scent pervaded on every side. I also saw lights of red, blue and yellow, and various souls, besides dark and variegated lights; and I heard a voice which said 'Who is then here like unto me?'

"I next perceived a light of excellent colour in which I saw numerous veils, good and bad, which might be computed at ten thousand, and a blue light seemed to envelope me, and ten thousand veils of beauteous hues met my gaze. Splendours of ruby-red, of brilliant white, and golden yellow next came across me, and I saw in each ten thousand curtains. Then came to view a form dark and terrific, before which I forgot myself and began to tremble. I heard fearful sounds, and ghastly forms met my sight; but I flinched not, and passing through ten thousand such veils, I saw a splendour of green, but I was unconscious, and next a splendour, boundless and without form, overtook me, and seeing it, I felt as if my existence was wrapped up in it, and I was one and the same with it.

"In the second state, called *Gaib*, I first saw a splendour of green which seemed unlimited, and there a sovereign of noble aspect was sitting on a throne, surrounded by learned and brave personages, with guardsmen all dressed in green. When I offered praise to the king, he did the same in return and seated me beside him. He was an Izad (angel), and I embraced him a hundred thousand times, and each time I did so, methought I became an Izad too, and when I separated I became myself again. Next, I came to other regions—purple, white, yellow, scarlet, blue and azure, in each of which I met the respective kings and, embracing them, became an Izad like them. Thence I came to a joyous place when I met numerous other kings and noblemen whom I embraced, and they were happy to see me. Going further, I came to a vast and lonely desert where I could see nothing for a long time till, at last, a being of benignant and cheerful aspect came before me, and embracing it, I became an Izad. I next came upon a dark form, and onwards I came in the presence of the Almighty, *where I found that nothing of my individuality remained and that, wherever I turned my eye, I saw Myself.* Thus having mounted upwards, step by step, I came back again to this earthly abode with consciousness.

"In the third state of *Masti* or *Hâl*, I first saw a large and prosperous city in which I found myself sitting on a throne, with four sages standing around me. I there heard many sweet sounds and I saw beauteous youths, incomparable viands, and downy beds. A person next came to me and said I was called, and, following him, I found myself in a place where they made me sit on a throne and up it flew and brought me to a place where there were wise and illustrious personages dressed in green, who paid me respect and took me to a palace, where I embraced the king who made me sit beside him. He asked me several things, and I learned wisdom from him. I then went to a place which was all blue, where there were scribes, sages, mathematicians, magicians, astrologers, merchants, physicians, and prophets, who, coming up to me, took me with great respect to the presence of the king, who embraced me, and made me sit down beside him. From him I derived a great part of my knowledge of the mysterious. I next went to other worlds which were white, golden, red, blue, azure, and there I was treated in the same way. Further I went to a vast place where also I derived great profit. Thence I went to a dark world, where God guided me by his splendour, and as I saw Him, He drew me within Himself, and my existence was lost in His. All the future was revealed to me, and I returned the same way I came.

"In *Khale-badan*, the fourth state, I passed to a world where I could see objects in endless variety and all the different cities of the world. There were many men and women there, who showed me a palace where I went and sat as king. I learnt every language, and was taught wisdom by the sages of every country, so that I am able to tell everything regarding their various creeds, languages, customs and observances. Wandering in this world, I returned again to my body, and leaving it again, I learnt all the mysteries of the creation, its beginning, end and aim. Casting aside this body as if it were a garment, I could see all the worlds on high at a single glance. Going to the first heaven, I saw it all, and thence I went to the worlds of Mercury, Venus, Mars, Jupiter, Saturn, to the fixed stars, and lastly, to Falk-Atlas, or the highest Heaven. All the planets and stars shine by their own light except the Moon, and their revolutions cause all the happiness and misery which men experience in this world. When I passed onwards, I came near pure souls and found myself in a congenial atmosphere. If the soul that dwells in man love understanding and justice, it attains to Heaven by its righteousness, and, leaving this earthly body, tastes the fruits of purity, and benefits itself by the association with Intelligences higher than itself, ultimately reaching Heaven. But if a man be impure and unholy, the soul wanders about in misery underneath Heaven, and all the evil acts, committed in this world, surround it with their hideous forms. Sometimes the soul frees itself from this state and joins the spirits and elementaries, or if the man be very wicked, the soul enters the body of one of the brute creation, or that of a vegetable.

"All this I saw myself. Next, out of the souls that were moving around me, I drew one towards myself and united myself with it. Then I reached up to *Sarosh* and there a flash of light came upon me from the splendour of the Supreme. As the radiance increased, my understanding departed, and I found myself an Izad among Izads. God alone existed and there was no sign of my individuality; everything appearing to be but a shadow of myself. From the Angelic Intelligences to the souls I moved about, and from them up to the earth there was nothing but myself. I became acquainted with a thousand mysteries of the Supreme and returned the way I had gone up. I can at will leave my body, and, ascending upwards, stand before the presence of God. I am willing to leave this world wherein I am, as it were, a bird from Heaven. The dignity of the Supreme Lord is too exalted for intercourse with his servants. By his effulgence, intellect becomes illumined as the earth by the sun. Through love He confers bounties upon His servants and raises up the downfallen. None but He can duly praise Himself as He cannot be the object of speech or hearing."

The above is a short abstract of the visions which the great Parsi ascetic has himself described, and those who would like to know more, should read the book itself, which contaiñs an excellent commentary.

"Âzur Kaivân was master of noble demonstrations and subtile distinctions. He mixed little with the people of the world; shunned with horror all public admirers, and seldom gave audience to any but his disciples and searchers after truth; never exposing himself to the public gaze." The author of the *Dabestân* has given a short but interesting account of him and his many disciples, several of whom—as he relates —he personally met and conversed with.

To the ordinary reader the above visions will probably appear to be the product of a disordered or overwrought imagination; let such a one, however, before he dogmatically passes his verdict, read, and, if possible, try to examine the beautiful and wondrous phenomena revealed by mesmerism, which modern science has so grossly neglected. These phenomena conclusively show that in mesmeric sleep or trance, and in ecstasies, distinct states of consciousness are evolved. Dr. Gregory, in his book on "Animal Magnetism," quotes a case of ecstasy, which is worth while reproducing. At page 83, he says:—"In the very remarkable work of M. Cahagnet, already alluded to, there is an account of a most remarkable clairvoyante, who could at pleasure and with the permission and aid of her mesmeriser, pass into the highest stage of ecstasy, in which she described herself as ineffably happy, enjoying converse with the whole spiritual world, and herself so entirely detached from this sublunary scene that she not only had no wish to return to it, but bitterly reproached M. Cahagnet for forcing her back to life. On one occasion, at her urgent request, he allowed her to enjoy that state longer than usual. But he took the precaution of placing another very lucid clairvoyance, a young lad, *en rapport* with her, with strict orders to watch her closely. She seemed at first unconscious, but by degrees her body assumed an alarming aspect, pulseless, cold, and devoid of respiration. The lad who kept his eye (the internal vision of clairvoyance) on her, at last exclaimed, 'She is gone! I see her no longer.' M. Cahagnet then, after much fruitless labour, and not until, as he informs us, he had prayed fervently to be enabled to restore her to life, succeeded in establishing warmth and respiration. The girl on waking overwhelmed him with reproaches for what he had just done, and could not be pacified till he succeeded in convincing her, she being a young woman of pious character and good feeling, that what she desired amounted to suicide, and was a grievous crime, for which he would be held responsible." Numerous other well-authenticated instances could be adduced to prove that "the soul has the capacity of a conscious existence apart from the body; and that it is limited by neither time nor space, being able to visit and return from the farthest localities." But all these instances would be useless to the sceptic, who is not actuated by the spirit of true inquiry. To the humble searcher after truth, however, who, doubting, seeks to gauge the mysteries of Nature, they are invaluable. *Mushâhedât*, or Yog, has been practised in every age and country, in some more so than in other and not always by the practice of rigorous austerities. Self-denial, self-control, and the highest morality form its bases. These are universally preached, but not easily acted upon. No wonder then, that the power of the soul is so little known and "God-knowledge" is a secret.

N. D. KHANDALAVALA.

—*Theosophist*, vol. I, p. 194.

TRANSMIGRATION IN THE AVESTA.

THE doctrine of the transmigration of animal life or the rebirth of men, is so little referred to in the extant writings of the Avestâ, which are incomplete in many ways—a large part of them having been irretrievably lost,—that it is as a surprise that the following passages are found in the Vendidád, the most orthodox of the Zoroastrian books.

"Creator of the material world, Pure One! If a (female) dog that has ceased to *bear*, or a (male) dog whose seed is dried up, happens to die, where does its consciousness (*baodhangh*) go?"

Then answered Ahura-Mazda, "O holy Zarathushtra! it goes into a stream of water, where, from a thousand male, and a thousand female dogs, a pair,—one male and one female—of the *Udra*, that reside in the waters, comes into being."—(Vendidád, Fargard XIII, paras 50, 51.)

Among the ancient Irânians, the greatest care was taken of the dogs, and the most severe punishments were decreed to those who injured, maltreated or starved these animals. The *Udra* or water-dog, (probably the seal, Walrus) was considered of far greater value, even than the dog. This was very likely owing to the belief that the *Udra* was the adversary of the demon *Apaosh* who caused drought and scarcity of rain. According to the Vendidád the person who killed an *Udra*, was to be punished with death, for the killing of this animal was supposed to cause decrease of crops, unhealthiness, and decline of prosperity. The way of avoiding such distress—as mentioned in the Vendidád—was to perform, before a burning fire, with *barsem* spread, and fermenting *Haoma*, the *Ijasne* ceremony for three days and three nights, to the pure soul (damen urvanem) of the *Udra*.

Some scholars try to explain the passage away by saying that it means that the consciousness or intelligence of the

Udra is as great as the intelligence of a thousand dogs, but the statement in the passage as to *transmigration* is unmistakable. The word 'thousand' in the Avestâ, as in other languages, stands for a large number, and we learn that the old Irânians had a very strong and distinct belief that the intelligences of numerous male and female dogs, when they ceased to procreate young ones and died, passed after their death to reservoirs of water and incarnated, a thousand each, into a single *Udra*.

The statement as to the male dog with dried up semen, and the female dog that has ceased to bear young ones, is probably an allusion to a belief that as long as the male or female dog could procreate, its intelligence would incarnate over again in a dog, but when the animal had lived long enough to become semenless, or had ceased to bear any young ones, its function in the body of a dog had been fully performed, and the consciousness transmigrated and become a part of the soul of the *Udra*, a creature supposed to have far greater spiritual energy in it than the dog.

Whether it be true or not that the consciousness of the dog has any connection with the consciousness or soul of the Udra, the fact remains that the ancient Zoroastrians believed in the *transmigration* of the souls of animals.

Mr. Bertram Keightley, in an excellent article on "Animal Reïncarnation," in the July number of *Lucifer*, speaks of the Monadic Essence, informing the animal kingdom in *blocks*. He writes—" Each 'block' of Essence forms the 'common soul,' as it were, of a number of animals of the same kind, each separate animal body of that kind being ensouled by a portion of Essence, temporarily separated from the corresponding block, a portion which, on the death of the animal, pours back into the same block and diffuses throughout its whole mass the experience and development which have been acquired by that particular portion during its quasi-separated life as the 'soul' of the particular animal body in question."

The consciousness of a thousand or a large number of dogs

therefore may form a single block of the incarnating monadic essence, which block may be supposed as a whole to inform a higher animal. The assertion therefore in the Vendidâd that the consciousnesses of a thousand dogs form the soul of an Udra, has some reference to an occult truth and does not appear to be an imaginary statement.

In the above quoted passage from the Vendidâd, not only is transmigration distinctly mentioned, but a veiled allusion is also made to an intricate occult truth. The Vendidâd does not in any way treat of the philosophy of Zoroastrianism, but is a book of religious laws as observed by the highly orthodox Magi, and the clear reference in it to transmigration of consciousness leads us to suppose, that in other books treating of the philosophy of Zoroastrianism there must have been more lucid explanations in greater detail, both of the transmigration of animal consciousness and of the reincarnation of the human ego. The doctrine of reincarnation is a highly complicated one, and we should not be surprised if the remnants of the Zoroastrian sacred writings that we have, and which are all books belonging to the orthodox priesthood, do not refer to reincarnation : there is however nothing in the extant writings against rebirth. Rather there is distinctly and in many places mentioned the doctrine of resurrection in bodily life, the renewed life as it is called, in a harmonious world free from strife. This regenerated life (*Frashem ahum*) is nothing else than the culmination of a series of rebirths, when humanity and the earth itself, during the course of evolution, will have attained a high level of spiritual existence.

N. D. K.

—*Theosophist*, Sept., 1896.

THE CEREMONIES.

> "And I announce and complete (my Yasna) to all those who are Thirty and Three lords of the ritual order, which coming the nearest, are around about Hâvani, and which (as in their festivals) were inculcated by Ahura-Mazda, and were promulgated by Zarathushtra, as the lords of Asha Vahishta, who is Righteousness the Best."
>
> *Yasna I.*, 10.

ALL NATIONS HAVE CEREMONIES.

THERE is no nation on earth without some religious ceremony or other. The Hindus have their Sômayagna and other ceremonies; the Mahomedans have their Fatiah and other ceremonies; the Christians have their Mass, Eucharist and other ceremonies; the Parsis have their Afringân, Yasna and Haoma ceremonies somewhat similar to the Hindus. But Modern Zoroastrianism is highly ceremonial. Every step one meets with some ceremony or other. Ceremonies can be political, social and religious, but the last only are considered sacred on account of their spiritual origin. These ceremonies or rituals have their own particular significance as well as they are the outward expressions of great and eternal spiritual truths. Religious ceremonies are ordained for various purposes, such as to train men in a way to mould their character; to overcome darkness and sloth; to impose a duty to do certain act at a certain time; to substitute self-sacrifice as a duty for self-gratification. Every religious ceremony is a way of training men to lead a true and higher life.

The rites and ceremonies are related to the natural beings, celestial as well as sublunary, and put one in a position to secure their sympathy and their mutual application; as they produce extraordinary results. By this kind of magical rites the Chaldeans are said to have performed many admirable things, not only upon particular persons, but upon the whole countries. R. Maimonides instances the expelling of noxious animals and other evil things out of cities and the driving away of all kinds of harms from plants, the preventing of hail and the destroying of worms so that they may not hurt the agriculture. They are said to have written much in their books concerning these rites, but these books are not available at present to the Parsis. These ceremonies, on account of their being so much effective in their character, were formerly called Magic (White), and the priests who performed them were called Magii. Pliny says that Magic had its beginning in Persia since Zoroaster, but which of the several Zoroasters is a question not easily to be decided.

THE YASNA.

It may be observed that the "prayers" recited in most of the ceremonies of the Parsis are taken from that portion of the Avastâ which is called *Yasna*, a word similar to the Sanskrit word *Yagna*, which means sacrifice or offering. These sacrifices are of various kinds; but they may be broadly divided into two classes, *viz.*, the esoteric and the exoteric. The former is the offering of one's own "principles" or elements, on the altar of God. It is the inward aspiration of the soul to form the holy union with the ABSOLUTE— the *Khretvodatham* as it is called in the Avastâ. The result of this esoteric sacrifice is the attaining of that state in which man obtains the real Knowledge of Self by direct perception. "Sacrifice becomes more than the paying of a debt," says Mrs. Besant: "it becomes a joyful giving of everything the man has to give. The partial sacrifice is the debt that is paid, the perfect sacrifice is the gift of the whole. A man gives himself, with all his activities, with all his powers, no longer paying part of his possessions as a debt, but all of himself as a gift. And when that stage is reached Yoga is accomplished and the lesson of Karmayoga has been learnt." One of the lower forms of this sacrifice is a philanthropic and self-sacrificing work for the good of humanity without hope of reward or fruit thereof. In the exoteric sacrifice, however, external materials are used instead of the inner "principles" or elements—the materials of ceremonies, *jivam, beresma,* &c., of the Parsis symbolically representing in the exoteric what in the esoteric are "principles." In no case, however, any animal sacrifice is to be understood. The phrase *pasúm pachayén* in Avastâ and *pishta paśú yâga* in Sanskrit can esoterically be taken to mean the boiling or killing of our *animal* or lower nature by self-sacrifice or self-denial, and not the cooking or slaying of harmless creatures in the name of religion.

In the Zoroastrian ceremonies the Mâthras recited are of course in the Avastâ language; but most of the religious scriptures of the Parsis have now been translated into English and form part of the well-known series of "The Sacred Books of the East." Any one who wishes to know what these Mâthras are, will see from the translations of the Yasna that they are in the form of invocations and offerings, obeisance, propitiations and praises to

THE AMESHASPENTAS AND THE YAZATAS,

the Conscious Cosmic Agents or the Builders of the Universe. They are the Agents through whom the Universe is evolved, and through whom it is progressing, and will ever progress. One of the functions of some of these hierarchies is, it is taught, to protect the souls of the dead from falling under the influence of the evil entities. Sraosh is one of them. Mithra is another according to the 19th Fargard of the Vendidâd, as also Râm, Rashnu and Âstâd, who approach the *Kerdâr,* the Karma-form, of the dead on the Chinvad bridge.*
Nairiyô-sang is another of such protecting angels and also Vohnmano.

As there are two opinions regarding the existence of such Beings as Ameshaspentas and Yazatas—the religious party believing in the existence of them while the other party disbelieving in them—I suppose it is necessary to go in particulars in this matter.

---

* See note to paragraph 4, Chapter xvii, "Shâyast lâ-shâyast," Sacred Books of the East, vol. V., part I., p. 383.

The latter take the Yazatas as the invention of the priestcraft to prevail upon the laity, and the Ameshaspentas as mere attributes of God, whom we call Ahura-Mazda. They take as their authority the Gâthâs only, which even give us several names of the Yazatas, beside the Ameshaspentas.

"Asha! When shall I behold thee and Vohumano with knowledge?
The place which belongs to Ahura-Mazda, the most beneficent,
The way of which is shown by Sraosh.

* * * * * * *

Give, O Asha! that reward which men desire;
Give thou, O Armaiti, his wish to Vistaspa and thou also to me."

The above passages are taken from Gâthâ Ahunavaiti, in which there appear two Yazatas, Sraosh and Armaiti. By translating these proper nouns into abstract qualities one cannot extricate himself from the responsibility of misrepresenting the whole thing. The Yazatas stand here, as plain as plain could be, the living entities, active and intelligent. If any one find the above passages insufficient to go to prove the existence of these Higher Intelligences or gods, then we may invite his attention to what has been said on the same subject by one of the highest modern scientific authority. The late Professor Huxley than whom there is hardly any higher authority in matters scientific, rising from Agnosticism to Gnosticism, or from Materialism to Metaphysics, says in the Prologue to a Collection of "Essays upon some Controverted Questions:"—

"Looking at the matter from the most rigidly scientific point of view, the assumption that amidst the myriads of worlds scattered through endless space, there can be no Intelligence as much greater than man's, as his is greater than a black-beetle's; no Beings endowed with powers of influencing the course of nature, as much greater than his as his is greater than a snail's seems to me not merely baseless, but impertinent. Without stepping beyond, the analogy of that which is known, it is easy to people the Cosmos with entities in ascending scale until we reach something practically indistinguishable from omnipotence, omnipresence and omniscience. If our intelligence can, in some matters, surely reproduce the past of thousands of years ago and anticipate the future thousands of years hence, it is clearly within the limits of possibility, that some greater intellect even of the same order may be able to mirror the whole past and the whole future; if the Universe is penetrated by a medium of such a nature that a magnetic needle on the Earth answers to a commotion in the Sun, an omnipresent agent is also conceivable; our insignificant knowledge gives us some influence over events, practical omniscience may confer indefinably greater power."

Here the late professor talks of the belief in the existence of "beings endowed with powers of influencing the course of nature," and the functions assigned by the "Dinkard" to the Yazatas are exactly identical to the above. They exist, says the Pahlavi book, "to keep watch over the heaven and the earth, the blowing of the wind, the flowing of the waters, the growth of the trees, and the life and nourishment of cattle and men, and also to protect the material world against the creation of the murderous demons."—(vol. iii, 125). They preside over "everything created that is pure," and constantly battle against the Drugas, the evil elementals, who are always endeavouring to destroy the "creation of the Pure." This view is again supported by another scientist, A. R. Wallace, one of the greatest Evolutionists of our day and the coadjutor of Darwin, who admits the guiding action of "Higher Intelligences" as a "necessary part of the great laws which govern the material universe." From this the Parsis might see the guiding action of their Ameshaspentas and the Yazatas.

The number of Intelligences, according to the "Celestial Desâtir," are innumerable: "The heavy moving stars [i. e., the fixed stars] are many, and each has an Intelligence, a Soul and a Body. And in like manner every distinct division of the heavens and planets hath its Intelligences and Souls. The number of the Intelligences and Souls, and stars and heavens, Mazdâm knows." According to the Avastâ literature. however, these Intelligences, who are there called Ameshaspentas and Yazatas, are divided into seven great Hierarchies, at the head of which is Ahura-Mazda, and each of these Hierarchies has several *hamkârs* or coöperators assigned to it:—

AHURA-MAZDA—Dep-âdar, Dep-meher, Dep-din.
BEHMAN—Mohor, Gosh, Râm.

THE CEREMONIES. 337

ARDIBESHTA—Âdar, Sraosh, Behrâm.
SHAHRIVAR—Khur, Meher, Asmân, Anerân.
SPENDARMAD—Avân, Din, Arda (Arsisvang), Mârespand.
KHURDAD—Tir, Ardâfarvash (Fravardin), Govâd.
AMERDAD—Rasnu, Âstâd, Zamiâd.

The first of these names represent the Ameshaspentas, and the following ones, are those of their coöperators. Berezad, Hom, and Daham are independent of the above 30 and along with them go to form the sacred **33** Divine Agencies. It is interesting to note that this number corresponds to the number of gods given in Aitareya and S'atapatha Brâhmanas, in the Atharva-veda and in the Râmâyana of the Hindus, to the striking coincidence of which Dr. Haug first called attention. These Devatâmandalas of the Hindus are known in Christianity as hierarchies of Angels, Thrones, Dominions and Principalities. This belief in gods is then

COMMON THROUGHOUT ALL THE RELIGIONS OF THE WORLD,

whose Founders were undeniably far superior in wisdom and knowledge to persons who pretend to be reformers of these religious customs. When the "reformers" who pose as religious teachers deny the existence of these minor gods, and say that such beings are merely the outcome of superstition, they only betray their own ignorance, not only of the fundamental spiritual truths, but also of what the most eminent of modern scientists have to say on the subject. The whole root of this contention lies in the word "god" which conventional religious usage has made applicable to the Supreme Source of All. Men have blindly fought and massacred one another for the mere interpretation of words without recognizing the fact that spiritual truths are always the one and the same, call them by what name you will. It is, therefore, of no consequence whatever whether we call these higher Powers in nature by the name of Ameshaspentas and Yazatas, Gods, Devatas, Intelligences or Angels.

If there exist such Beings as the Ameshaspentas and the

43

Yazatas far superior than man; if they are beneficent to mankind; if man is bound down by his actions to depend upon these holy Powers;—is it not wise for him to invoke them; to make obeisance to them, to propitiate them, and to praise them? We have seen some men bowing, propitiating, praising and flattering other men for the purpose of self-interest.; we have seen feasts and fasts created in honour of such men; who were perhaps beneficent to a few and maleficent to many;—is it unwise, then, to sacrifice something in honour of those holy Beings who are beneficent to the whole universe?

Man in his present condition cannot conceive about these Intelligences, just as a crawling insect is incapable of conceiving the intellectual efforts of a Plato or an Aristotle, a Darwin or a Huxley. Yet there are means through which these Intelligences can be influenced. The mediums through which they can be influenced are the various

RELIGIOUS RITES AND CEREMONIES.

Before we know something of these mediums, we shall illustrate here the working of the modern signalling by electric light to facilitate the mental grasp of our subject. A flood of light is thrown on the sky from an electrical apparatus, and its flashes are seen rapidly moving from one direction to another, which can be seen by other persons living far away from the place where the instrument is placed. Here the light plus men's ideas expressed by the movement of the rays of light is thrown on the atmospheric matter which we call sky, the reflection of which can be read and understood by any one who has acquired the knowledge of understanding the significance of the movements of these light rays, however far away he may be from the situation of that light. In the same manner a Mobed (priest)—I mean an adept in the ceremonial rites—while performing ceremonies or rites, utters certain

MANTHRAS,

or formulas of words arranged in a way to produce certain results by the power of their sounds or vibrations when recited in a proper way. These Māthras become, as it were, a medium of communication between man and Higher Intelligences somewhat in the manner described above. The idea of Māthra is so nicely expressed by P. Christian, the learned author of "*Histoire de la Magie*," that it is better to quote him *in extenso* :—

"When our Soul [mind] creates or evokes a thought, the representative sign of that thought is self-engraved upon the astral [ethereal] fluid, which is the receptacle and, so to say, the mirror of all the manifestations of being.

"The sign expresses the thing: the thing is the [hidden or occult] virtue of the sign.

"To pronounce a word is to evoke a thought, and make it present: the magnetic potency of the human speech is the commencement of every manifestation in the Occult World. To utter a Name is not only to define a Being, but to place it under and condemn it through the emission of the Word [Verbum], to the influence of one or more Occult potencies. Things are, for every one of us, that which it [the Word] makes them while naming them. The Word [Verbum] or the speech of every man is, quite unconsciously to himself, a BLESSING or a CURSE; this is why our present ignorance about the properties or attributes of the IDEA as well as about the attributes and properties of MATTER, is often fatal to us.

"Yes, names [and words] are either BENEFICENT or MALEFICENT; they are, in a certain sense, either venomous or health-giving, according to the hidden influences attached by Supreme Wisdom to their elements, that is to say, to the LETTERS which compose them, and the NUMBERS correlative to these letters."

Here my Zoroastrian brothers will see the reason why their religion enjoins them to act upon the principles of pure thoughts, pure words, pure deeds. Moreover, those who have insight to see into spiritual matters will find from the above passages one of the reasons why some of the formulæ of their Māthras are recited certain *number* of times.

Before we come to know how these Māthras or magical sounds become a medium of influence between the Yazatas and men, it is necessary again to take another illustration from the modern physical science.

"One of the marvels of modern science is the conversion of a beam of light into sound. The light ray is thrown through a lens on a glass vessel containing lamp-black, coloured silk, worsted, or other substances. A disk having slits or openings cut in it is made to revolve swiftly in this beam of light so as to cut it up, making alternate flashes of light and shadow. On putting the ear to the glass vessel, strange sounds are heard so long as the flashing beam is falling upon it. Another phase of this remarkable discovery is still more interesting. A beam of sunlight is passed through a prism. The disk is turned, and the coloured light of the solar spectrum is made to break through it. If the ear is placed to the vessel containing the silk, wool or other material, as the coloured lights fall upon it, sounds will be given by different parts of the spectrum, and there will be silence in some other parts. To illustrate. if the vessel contains red worsted and the green light flashes upon it, loud sounds will be heard. Only feeble sounds will be heard if the red and blue rays fall upon it, and other colours make no sound at all. Green silk gives sound best in red light. It is by no means improbable that this discovery foreshadows a new law of harmonies, and Remington's experiments in tone colour may possibly, by this new application of light and sound, result in some practical theory which will give us an entirely new scheme of music. The thing is but in its infancy, but the mere fact that such a discovery has been made cannot but forecast important results."*

Mrs. Besant's article on Sound in the "Building of the Kosmos," Mrs. Watts Hughe's "Voice Figures," Babbit's work on "The Principles of Light and Colour," as well as Professor Tyndall's work "On Sound," will help materially any one

---

* *Invention*, an American Scientific paper.

who wishes to have a knowledge of the power of Sound, either constructive or destructive.

We have thus seen that light when passed through a prism, transforms itself into colours, and is also converted into sound; and in the same manner sounds can be converted into a variety of colours. Colours are produced in the world of ether or *âkâsh* by the vibrations of sounds, which become the

"LANGUAGE OF THE GODS."

One of the Masters says in the "Occult World":—"How could you make yourself understood by, command in fact, those semi-intelligent *forces*, whose means of communication with us are not through spoken words, but *through sounds and colours* in correlation between the *vibrations* of the two." This law stands equally true in relation to man and the higher Intelligences of Nature, as the harmony of colour in human *aura** with the intonation of Mâthras with pure heart becomes, as it were, the language of the holy gods. With every sound and thought the harmony of the colour in the aura is changed; and if the words are arranged in a way to produce sounds which can give discordant vibrations, the colour in the *aura* will not be in harmony agreeable to the Yazatas.

The Zend, Sanskrit and other languages in which the ancient scriptures are written, are considered sacred by the people whom we call orthodox. These orthodox people always oppose

---

* Mesmer was laughed at while he made the announcement about mesmerism or animal magnetism. It was a new discovery to the Western world, although known to the Aryan ages ago. The modern scientists, ashamed to call it by the same name while convinced, rechristened it as hypnotism. Now we hear of Reichenbach's "phosphorescent light," and "luminous emanations," which have "colours" it is said, and "extend from 6 to 8 feet" from every human body. All these lead to the verification of that light which in the Avasta is called *Kharnenghantem* or *Khureh*, and in theosophical literature "aura." A leading article appeared, three days after this paper was read, in the *Times of India* (May 20, 1896,) under the heading "Exteriorization of Sensations," which mainly supports the views expressed here about the aura.

intuitively—although they cannot express their reason—to allow any change in a word or phrase, even so much as an inflection, related to the scriptures in which the Māthras or "prayers" are written; they do not like the "prayers" to be recited in a translation of these. Māthras rendered into a current vernacular. The reason is now not far to seek. It is because by so doing the desired harmony of colours—" the language of the gods"—to be produced on ākāsh, or one of the higher states of ether, by the intonation of the Māthra, becomes discordant, and the object of the holy author who composed the Māthra is thus frustrated. It is for this reason, also, that the so-called "prayers" in vernacular, as well as the translations of the Avasta, are considered fruitless so far as their spiritual and hidden effects are concerned.

Now we come to

THE CONDITIONS

to be observed for the invocation of the holy Yazatas. If a scientist has to create or conserve electricity he has to prepare certain chemicals, and place therein certain metallic plates, which he connects by means of wires in order to bring forth the electricity thus produced. Just in the same manner a priest, who must be a scientist, so to speak, in his own line, *i.e.*, a pure man qualified for the purpose, should collect and arrange things prescribed by the holy Teachers of old in a manner to attract or invite the holy Yazatas. There are things which either attract or repel these Intelligences: things which are attractive to the beneficent agencies might generally be taken as repulsive to the maleficent agencies, which are called Drugas, Druga-nasus, &c., in the Zoroastrian system. In the same manner things towards which the Drugas or evil elementals are attracted are abhorrent to the holy Yazatas. We shall examine with this view the few things which are considered necessary in the Zoroastrian rites. Here first comes

THE FIRE.

No rite can be performed without the presence of Fire, no

sacrifice can be given without the presence of this holy symbol. Much has been said about fire and much more yet remains to be said. But at present we shall satisfy ourselves by simply alluding to the part played by fire in the performance of the *yagnas* or sacrifices. As fire is considered one of the best mediums to drive away the Dru*g*as, &c., while fed with sweet-scented wood and incense, it becomes a powerful means of attracting the beneficent Yazatas. The sacrifices, according to the Old Testament, were offered over fire in the name of God, and, they said, they were accepted by God. because God was in the fire over which the sacrifices were offered. The sacred fire of the Parsis and also of the Hindus is the conscious altar kindled in the essence of God—Fire, the *Brahmasvarûpa*, of God-like form. And as God is Infinite Fire, the Yazatas and others invoked in the Zoroastrian rites are, so to speak, the Flames of One Infinite Fire. We shall quote here a passage or two from the scriptures of our cousins, the Hindus, to show what relation the fire bears with Yagnas and ceremonies. The *Rig-veda* begins with a prayer in which Agni, the fire, is made the lord of all Yagnas :—

"I adore Agni, the most ancient, family priest, the Lord of Yagna, the Chief Priest, Hotâr, the source of Light."

In the S'arbhopanishad it is stated that—

"The fire over which the sacrifice is made, the sacrifice which is made over the fire, and the person making the sacrifice, are all Brahman (God)."

"It is because," says Mrs. Besant, "man has to learn that his body owes a debt to earth and to the Intelligences that guide the processes of Nature by which Earth brings forth her fruits, by which she produces nourishment for man ; as man takes the nourishment for his body, his body owes back, in payment of the debt, the returning to Nature an equivalent for that which has been given it through the instrumentality of those Kosmic Intelligences, those Devas, who guide the forces of the lower world. And so man was taught to pour his sacrifice into the fire. Why ? The phrase that was given as an explanation was: 'Agni is the mouth of the gods,' and people repeat the phrase and never try to understand its meaning, nor to go below the surface of the external name of the Deva to His function in the world. The real meaning of course that underlies the phrase is that all around on every side there are the conscious and sub-conscious workers in Nature in grade after grade, a great Kosmic Deva at the head, as it were, of each division of that vast army, so that below the Deva as a Ruler in fire, in air, in water, in earth, below that particular Deva come a vast number of lower gods who carry on the different and separated activities of the natural forces in the world, the rain, the productive powers of the earth, the fertilising agencies of various sorts. And this first sacrifice is a feeding of these lower agencies, a giving to them of food by fire ; and fire is called 'the mouth of the gods,' because it disintegrates, because it changes and transmutes the solid and fluid things which are placed in it, turns them into vapour, disintegrates into finer materials, and thus passes them on into etheric matter to become the sustenance of those lower grades of elemental lives that carry out the commands of the Kosmic Devas. And in this way a man pays his debt to them, and then in return in the lower regions of the atmosphere the rain falls and the earth produces, and nourishment is given to man. And that was what Shri Krishna meant when he bade man ' Nourish the gods and the gods shall nourish you.' For it is that lower cycle of nourishment, as it were, which man has to learn. At first he accepted it as a religious teaching ; then came the period in which he thought it superstition, knowing not the inner working and seeing only the outer appearances ; and then comes deeper knowledge when Science, which tends first to Materialism, by deeper study rises towards recognition of Spiritual realm. Spiritual Knowledge begins to say in scientific terms what the Rishis said in terms of the spirit, that man may rule and regulate the working of the lower powers of Nature by action that he himself performs and in this way growing knowledge justifies the ancient teaching, justifies to the intellect what the spiritual man sees by direct intuition, by the spiritual sight."

We cannot go deeper at present into this subject as we have yet to examine other things, such as—

THE FLOWERS AND THE FRUITS.

In some of the Zoroastrian rites flowers are considered only necessary, while in others they are arranged in certain definite ways. "The Bûndahish" gives us some knowledge about the relation they bear to the Ameshaspentas and the Yazatas. "Whatever sweet-scented blossom arises at various seasons, through the hand-labour of men, or has a perennial root and blossoms in its season with new shoots and sweet-scented blossoms, as the rose, the narcissus, the jasmine, the dog-rose (nêstarûn), the tulip, the colocynth (kavastik), the pendanus (kêdi), the *k*amba [or *chamba*], the ox-eye (hêri), the crocus, the swallow-wort (zarda), the violet, the kârda, and others of this genus, they call a flower."* This is the description of the flowers that are to be used in a Zoroastrian rite. Further on it is said in the same chapter that every single flower, cultivated as above, is appropriate or sacred to an Ameshaspend. The names of these flowers are given there, as well as the names of other flowers sacred to the other Yazatas.†

Along with other conditions, the flowers as described above, some particular green and dry fruits, especially the pomegranate, the symbol of the universe, the pure water, and the fire blazing with sweet-scented fuel, are the principal things in Zoroastrian rites. The fruits are the offerings or sacrifices to the Yazatas, which, after the ceremony having been done, are considered as consecrated.

OBJECTIONABLE THINGS.

In certain ceremonies, however, occasionally things are offered by some parsis, which are highly objectionable, from the stand-point of Esoteric science, and the ceremony then cannot be called a *Zoroastrian* one. How the custom of

---

* Ch. xxvii. (11)   † *Id.* (24.)

presenting such things crept into the sacred rites, such as the viands prepared out of animal flesh and alcoholic drinks, which directly attract the evil elementals or Dru*g*as, and therefore are considered repulsive to the holy Yazatas, it is difficult to say. Perhaps the cause may be traced to a certain passage in the Yasna, Hâ 11th, which is thus rendered by the translators:—

"The Holy Father Ahura-Mazda has given me, the Haoma a portion to eat, together with the *tongue and the left eye.*"

This mystic passage has been very much misunderstood, not only by the Orientalists, but even by the Parsi Mobeds, the latter, taking it in a superficial way, were till lately in the habit of keeping in their presence the head and some other organs of a slaughtered goat or sheep while performing the Haoma ceremony, transforming one of the most sublime and holy ceremonies into unconscious Black Magic. Wherever such passages occur in the Avastâ they have a purely symbolical or allegorical meaning. Because it is absolutely opposed to the very spirit of the Zoroastrian religion to take the life of any animal, as it enjoins over and over again to take care of and nourish all the Gospandas, cows, goats and other useful animals. In spite of this very obvious fact it is very curious to note that even the Orientalists and other translators of Avastâ have seriously blundered in their interpretation of such passages. Mons. C. D. Harlez has substituted the word "ear" for the words "to eat" in the above passage, in rendering the text word "*hañharené*" which, he said, is traditionally used by the previous Parsi translators of the Avastâ-Zand language. Unfortunately, however, he adds parenthetically other words of his own at the end of the sentence, *viz.*, "of Gospand," *i.e.*, of the cows, goats, &c., which interpretation appears to be a violation of the original intention of the holy author. M. Darmesteter translates the phrase "*la mâchoire avec la langue et l'œil gauche*"—"the jaw with the tongue and the left eye"—(*vide l'Avesta*, vol. 1, p. 110, ed. 1892)—rendering *hañharené* into *jâw*. In the translation of the Avastâ by Spiegel and Bleeck, we find a note on the above passage, in which it is also stated, "that formerly it was not the whole head, but only the left eye and tongue which were offered to Haoma." They thus supported the Druga-worship, which was unconsciously practised by the Parsi Mobeds who have long since lost the key of deciphering the mysteries of the Avastâ literature, forgetting that the spirit—the very essence—of the Zoroastrian religion was emphatically opposed to such worship. This and similar passages, again, are regarded by the advocates of animal food among the Parsi community as Avastaic authority in favour of flesh-eating, although throughout the whole Yasna there are numerous passages enjoining on every Zoroastrian to have compassion for poor helpless Gospandas and to protect them.

The consecration of flesh and alcohol in their sacred ceremonies by the modern Parsis is one of the reasons why my Parsi friends are so backward to-day in their religious matters. It is a matter for serious consideration, as the attraction of the evil agencies are rightly considered injurious to the spiritual progress of mankind. According to the true spirit of Zoroastrianism the use of these articles—blood and wine or flesh and alcohol—is prohibited as will be seen from the following passages from the Yasna:—

" Evil are they who advise the killing of the *gospandas* (goats, sheep, kine, &c.),"—Gâthâ Ahunavaiti (Hâ 32, para. 12).

" All other toxicants go hand with Rapine of the bloody spear, but Haoma's* stirring power goes hand in hand with friendship."—Yasna, Hâ 10 (para. 8).

Some of you may have seen the low-caste people offering sacrifice of the blood of animals and alcohol in their worship

---

* See my article on the Sacred Haoma, in *Lucifer*, Feb. 1895; and also in *The Theosophist*, March 1895. The passage cited here is in its exoteric sense.

of the evil elementals, and if the Parsis want to call themselves better informed in matters religious than these Bhûta-worshippers, they must in right earnest try to prevent this custom. But if they carried out this pernicious custom they must not expect any real improvement in regard to their religion. They should not, therefore, be surprised, that instead of attracting or invoking the beneficent Yazatas in their rites, they verily invite the loathsome Drugas or evil elementals which are harmful both to religion and men; and hence they must wash their hands of all sanctity and holiness, the fundamental principles of the Zoroastrian religion. This custom then can never be called the Zoroastrian custom, and no ceremony which contains such objectionable things can be regarded as sacred ceremonies which are always intended for universal good.

Another condition of the Zoroastrian rites is that the place of worship where these ceremonies take place should be uncontaminated by any impurity, physical as well as ethereal. There is no question about the physical purity of the Parsis. It is for the ethereal purity that a Parsi is so strict in keeping

THE NON-ZOROASTRIANS

out of the sanctuary. It will be remembered that non-Zoroastrians are not allowed to take part in the Zoroastrian rites, nor are they allowed to enter the place of worship. This may at first sight appear selfish or sectarian, looking from the standpoint of Zoroastrianism as an universal religion. But the condition of a sacred rite demands higher purity or sanctity, not on the physical plane only, but on the ethereal and mental plane also. The harmony on the ethereal atmosphere of the place of worship is preëminently necessary. Now suppose if there is a non-Zoroastrian present in an assembly of Zoroastrians in a certain ceremony, outwardly sympathising with them all, but inwardly smiling or ridiculing the whole thing or a part of the ceremony, of course not understanding the truth underlying that ceremony, the harmony on the mental plane of that place of worship is disturbed and thus becoming discordant, the condition of the ceremony is broken and its efficacy is lost. If for this reason the orthodox class resolve to-morrow not to allow even a materialistic Parsi who is not in sympathy with them, to take part in their ceremony, I suppose they would be perfectly justified in doing so. Viewing from this point certain class of Mobeds who do not like to perform ceremony with even other class of Mobeds who differ from them in certain points, are also justified in doing so. Another reason for keeping them off from such ceremonies is their unsympathetic aura, about which there is no time at present to say anything here.

The rites or ceremonies performed in the Zoroastrian places of worship being the sacrifices and invocations, obeisance, propitiations, and praises of the Ameshaspentas and the Yazatas, the Universal Conscious Beneficent Powers, are

BENEFICIAL TO THE WHOLE UNIVERSE,

seen and unseen, and therefore they cannot be held to be for the benefit of the priests alone, much less for the benefit of an individual alone. The man who gets these rites performed gives his share, as it were, in doing abstract good to the universe. If you find these rites and ceremonies, rightly performed, with the object of doing universal good, they deserve your support, as there is nothing selfish or injurious in them. The Ameshaspentas and the Yazatas are not supposed to take care of the living and the dead Parsis only. On referring to the Fravardin-yasht, which is also recited in certain ceremony, you will find that the pure Fravashis or Higher Egos of even the Turanians, who are historically known to be the bitter opponents of the Irânians, are praised along with the other pure Fravashis of all countries and of all ages. This shows that there is no selfishness or sectarianism in Zoroastrian rites, and that they are meant entirely for the universal good.

Now with regard to the benefit derived by the individual who performs the ceremony, it may be observed that the sacrifices, obeisance, propitiations and praises of the Ameshaspentas and the Yazatas form a part of the duty of the worshipper towards the universe, seen and unseen, and they thus become one of the means of his spiritual progress. By constantly practising these rites with an unselfish motive the Mobed becomes more and more conscious of such existences—he feels their existence to be true, and a time comes when by stepping on a certain path he actually realizes their existence and comes in direct communication with them, as will be seen from a passage in the "Dinkard" quoted further on. That path is

THE PATH OF YOGA.

Even men already on that path were not advised to drop the devotion and regard towards these Ameshaspentas and the Yazatas in Zoroastrianism as will be seen from the "Vistaspa-yasht":—

"Converse ye with the Ameshaspentas," said Zarathushtra unto the young king Vistaspa, "and with the devout Sraosh, and Nairyô-sangha, the tall formed, and Âtar; the son of Ahura-Mazda, and the well desired kingly glory.

"Men with lustful deeds address the body; but thou, all the night long, address the heavenly Wisdom; but thou, all night long, call for the Wisdom that will keep thee awake [for evermore]."—(vi—40-41.)

If it were so,—if Zarathushtra the Spitama himself advised a king who was already on the path of Yoga, to endeavour to consciously communicate with the divine Ameshaspentas and the Yazatas—it becomes the duty of every individual who calls himself a Zoroastrian to believe in their existence, to invoke them, to bow to them, to propitiate them, and to praise them not for their own good only, but for the good of the universe. Why? Because, according to the Bhagavad Gitâ, a book which is now universally appreciated, Shri Krishna says:—

"For those who, thinking of Me as identical with all, constantly worship me, I bear the burden of the responsibility of their happiness. And even those also who worship other gods with a firm faith in doing so, involuntary worship Me, too, O son of Kunti, albeit in ignorance. I am he who is the Lord of all sacrifices."

"The Lord of all sacrifices". is Shri Krishna, and according to the first shloka of the first Mandala of the Rig-veda, it is the Agni [Fire] who is the Lord of all sacrifices. Thus we see Agni or Fire in Shri Krishna also.

There may be some Parsis who would object to the above and other quotations as being from non-Zoroastrian books. To such we will refer again to the "Dinkard," to show that truth cannot be monopolised by any one religion, however vast the literature of that religion may be :—

"Be it known that the words of the excellent wisdom of God were communicated *through the Yazatas*[*] to the good learned men of all countries before and after the preaching of the Mazdayasnian Faith in this world. And these learned men of various continents were connected with the truth of this manner that they became acquainted with the precepts and writings of the good religion like the followers of the Mazdayasnian Faith themselves."—(Vol. vii, p. 486.)

CONCLUSION.

It is said in the "Bundahish" that Ahura Mazda Himself performed the spiritual *yasna* ceremony together with the Ameshaspendān (ch. ii, 9), meaning thereby that it is by Yasna, the Great Sacrifice, He became the Cause of the manifestation of the universe. The manifestation of the universe is the result of the Law of Sacrifice on the higher planes. In the same manner we see Soshyans performing Yasna ceremony, with his Assistants (*ibid*, ch. xxx, 25). This Yasna can be taken as the Great Sacrifice or Renunciation of the blessed Immortals, the coöperators of Soshyans, who, renouncing their claim of attaining Nirvâna,—if I may be permitted to use the term,—are waiting on the spiritual planes, till the millennium comes

---

[*] The italicised words were omitted by the English translator, in the "Dinkard," published by Dastur Pesutanji B. Sanjana, however they appear in the Gujarati translation, which is one of the most important points when seen in the light of Theosophy.

and the humanity is perfected, to guide and watch her tottering steps. What these Great Sacrifices and Renunciations may be, it is difficult at present to conceive. However, to renounce a claim that is one's own by right in virtue of attaining it through great suffering and pain, is a Sacrifice true and great.

The Yasna and other ceremonies are thus the outward expressions of spiritual truths, as well as they have their own particular significance. If the ceremonies are a *cause*, they must produce some effect in the universe. No cause remain without its effect; and it is absolutely necessary, therefore, to preserve and perform them with all the purity of our hearts in the manner enjoined. They were handed down to us by the Great Teachers of mankind for the good and welfare of our own as well as that of the whole universe. It is utterly unwise to try to abolish religious ceremonies without understanding their true spiritual import. It is easy enough to destroy a thing or custom, but difficult to create or construct it; and before any one thinks of abolishing ceremonies which have been established æons ago—it was the Treta Yuga, according to the Hindu doctrine, when the Yagnas were instituted—he must pause and think whether he is capable of replacing them by something better and holier. The work of destruction of customs that carry us, gradually though it may be, to the Divine, is the outcome of Ignorance; while that of construction and preservation of them is the result of foresight and true wisdom.

NASARVANJI F. BILIMORIA.

INDEX.

AB-I-HAIAT, 108.
Ablution, 251, 252.
Absolute, Absoluteness, 111, 145, 171, 196.
Abu Jaffer Attavari, 52.
Abulfazil, 67.
Adam and Eve, 96, 107, 139, 200.
Adam-Kadmon, 190.
Adar, Atash, Azar, see Fire.
Adepts, 4, 9, 17, 67, 72, 236, 242, 312, 313, 317.
Adhavaryu, 254.
Aditi, 92, 115, 127.
Aditya, 118.
Advaitism, 315, 316.
Æther, see Ether.
Afringan, 55, 66.
Agni, 85, 108, 114, 254, 255, 265, 267, 272, 343.
Agnibahu, 126.
Agnihotra, 19.
Agrasandhani, 300.
Ahankar, 269.
Ahmi, 44.
Ahriman, 15, 43, 77, 111, 147, 149, 150, 172, 187, 188, 197, 206, 213, 214.
Ahu, Ahura, 42, 43, 80, 101, 111, 112, 116, 159, 172, 175, 184, 187.
Ahuma, 201.
Ahunavairya, Ahunavar, 29, 84, 85, 86, 87, 113, 114, 162, 206, 210, 234, 238.
AHURA-MAZDA, 13, 42, 43, 44, 57, 61, 77, 78, 80, 82, 84, 86, 97, 110, 111, 112, 114, 117, 118, 122, 136, 139, 146, 147, 156, 159, 169, 184, 186, 187, 188, 189, 190, 191, 194, 195, 196, 197, 198, 201, 203, 209, 213, 215, 240, 258, 316, 351.
AIN-SOPH, 80, 145.
Airân Vej, 153.
Airyanam-Vaejo, 37, 46, 49, 63, 97, 101, 125, 126.
Aiwyâonhann, see Kûsti.
Ajyaiti (non-reality), 61.
Akâsha, 14, 15, 20, 29, 84, 85, 103, 113, 114, 115, 122, 143, 295, 301.
Akbar, 66, 67, 72.
Akhad, 164.
Akho (poet), 243.
Akomano, 61, 62.
Alburz mount, 146, 152, 214.

Alchemy, 69, 127, 135, 136.
Alexander, 2, 55, 97, 167.
Amardad Ameshaspenta, 102, 115.
Ameshaspentas, 15, 44, 79, 80, 82, 95, 97, 104, 110, 114, 115, 119, 146, 159, 160, 172, 189, 190, 195, 203, 209, 230, 262, 334, 335, 336, 337, 349.
Ammenon, 92.
Ammianus, 50.
Amrita, 108.
Anahid, 122, 123, 163.
Anandamaya Kosha, 274.
Androgyne, 91, 198.
Angels, 119, 178, 189; fall of—200, 218, 219; guardian—300.
Angiras, Angra, 65, 66.
Animals: monster—149; slaughter of—310, 311; protection of—347.
Anecdotus, 92.
Añra-Mainyush, Añgro-Mainyush, 42, 43, 44, 61, 62, 91, 93, 155, 170, 171, 187, 188, 219.
Ansha, 254.
Antahkaran, 278.
Apâm-Napât, 84, 122, 267.
Apas, 85, 114.
Apash, 329.
Apaya (river), 255.
Apocalypse, 30, 206.
Apollodorus, 92.
Apple tree, 107.
Aquarian Teachers, 92.
Arani, 69, 70.
Archangels, 79, 119, 189.
Arda-i-Viraf, Dastur, 22, 152, 158.
Ardavahista or Ardibeheshta, 115, 119.
Ardeshir Babagan, 22, 45.
Ardvisur Anahita, 42, 86, 102, 103.
Arhat, 10.
Aristotle, 3, 65.
Ark, 151.
Armaiti, 314, 315, 316, 335.
Arunopanishad, 107.
Aryans, Aryas, 63, 65, 69, 94, 99, 143, 182, 210.
Arzahi (Kershvara), 129, 131, 133.
Ascetic, 323.
Ashavahishta, 262.
Ashem-Vohu, 56, 162.
Ashvattha tree, 104, 105, 250.
Aspa, 113, 234, 237.
Aspandarmad, 115.

15

Astâd Yazata, 334.
Astavaterota (Saviour), 191.
Astral—light, 14, 29, 103,—body 106,— man, 107, 138, —plane, 95, 295, — ocean, 147, 216, 252, 298, 299, 300, 301.
Astrology, 122, 221.
Asura, 44, 147, 183, 184, 189.
Aswinikumaras, 113.
Aswins, 116, 119, 235, 237.
Aswamedham Coromony, 237.
Atash—Bohrâm 8, 268, —Adrân, 268, —Dâdgah, 268.
Atharva Veda, 65.
Atheism, 36.
Athravan, 49, 65, 66.
Athwya, 101.
Atlanteans, 143.
Atmâ, Atman, 118, 205, 206, 319.
Atmâ-Buddhi, 74, 267.
Augoeides, 178.
Aum, 238, 307, 308.
Aura, 138, 301, 302, 318, 341.
Avastá, 9, 10, 45, 46, 48, 49, 52, 56, 63, 95, 103, 155, 163, 165, 167, 175, 187, 210, 211, 212, 329.
Avtar, 91, 117, 125, 191.
Ayur Veda, 99, 100, 101.
Azareksh, 97.
Âzar Kaivan, 103, 104, 240, 242, 317, 323, visions of—323, 327.
Azi-Dahák, see Zouhak.

BACHUS, 98.
Bacteria, 251, 252.
Bahman, 120, —Yashta, 133.
Baktria, 3, 182, 184.
Baresma, 18, 104, 272, 273, 279, 329, 334.
Barhishad Pitris, 95.
Battle of the Gods, 120.
Behistun, 158, 210.
Behram 123, see also Atash Behram.
Bolus, tower of, 10.
Be-ness, 111, 112.
Berezad (angel) 119, 337.
Berezi-Savang, see Fire.
Berosus, 3, 91, 92, 149.
Bhagvad Gita, 29, 105, 106, 103, 196, 197, 226, 246, 271, 273, 279, 280, 350, 351.
Bhakti-Yoga, 103.
Bhumi—Haptaiti, 126, 130 —mother 147, 261 —Mandala, 126.
Bird—the great, 108, —of long period, 232.
Birth, ceremony at, 308, 309.
Black Magic, see Magic.
Blissful Immortals, 114.

Blood, circulation of, 105, 149.
Bodhang, 72, 74.
Bo-tree, 10.
Brahmá, 183, 186, —Prajapati, 187,190, 206, mouth-born son of—255.
Brahman, 111, 112.
Brahmans, 37, 47, 48, 49, 63, 98.
Brahmarandhra, 249.
Breaths: never-resting—110, great— 78, 110, 232, 308.
Bridgit (God) 257.
Brihaspati, 102, 240.
Brotherhood, 27.
Bubonic Plague, 251.
Buddha, 16, 63, 91, 93, 106, 184.
Buddhi, 72, 73, 74, 113, 239; union of— with Manas, 267, 269.
Buddhism, 157,—in Zoroastrianism, 156.
Builders, 114, 174, 334.
Bull, 88, 149.
Bundahish, 91, 93, 94, 96, 102, 104, 114, 115, 119, 122, 124, 126, 140, 141, 190.

CASTES, the four, 126.
Caucasus, mount, 143.
Cave of Zoroaster, 30, 31.
Celestial Double, 118.
Ceremonies, 66, 67, 103, 332, 338, 342.
Chakra (the circle), 49, 107, (plexuses), 108, 249.
Chaldean teachings, 215.
Chandargas, 302, 303, 317.
Chaos, 261.
Chatur (four), 118.
Chhaya, 96, 138, 150, 198.
Chemistry, 69.
Cheops, Pyramid of, 305.
Chinvat Perotu or Bridge, 23, 27, 152, 161, 214, 277, 320, 334.
Chitragupta, 300.
Chitta, 269.
Chohans, 96.
Christ, 173, —spirit, 192, 200, 205, 271.
Christianity, 164, 165.
Christmas day, origin of, 165.
Christos, 117, 118, 176, 178, 206.
Circle, 79, 80.
Clairvoyante, 327, 328.
Classes, the four, see Castes.
Colours, 85, 341.
Comets, matter of, 128.
Concealed continent, 143.
Cosmic Gods and Goddesses, 127, —Ideation, 84, 121, —Rulers, 218.
Cosmical Forces, 123.
Cosmogenesis, 109, 125.

INDEX.

Cosmogony, 109, 122.
Cow, Primeval, 85, 88, 94, 238.
Creation, 109, 122, periods of—149, 170, three kinds of—215, 216.
Creative Power, 78.
Crocodile, 142, 143.
Cross and Fire, 68, 69.
Cuneiform inscription, 61, 62, 104, 212.
Cyclic Law, 106, 149.
Cyrus, 168.

DABISTAN, 21, 27, 66, 96, 97, 119, 327.
Daen or Din, 241.
Daham (angel), 119, 337.
Daitya (river), 125, 126.
Daksha, 127.
Damavend (mount), 142, 143.
Dâmdâd Nûsk, 114.
Daphos (Man-fish), 92.
Darius Hystaspes, 3, 4, 46, 62, 168, 188, 210, 211.
Darkness, 111, 116, 196.
Darun, 70.
Darwinism, 266.
Dasara (Hindu holiday), 104.
Dasturs, 1, 8, 33, 56, 76, 77, 111, 318, 319.
Dawn, 109, 110.
Day of Brahma, 116.
Days of month, 119.
Death, origin of—136, 138, state after—278, ceremony at—309.
Deductive method, 109.
Deity, Incognizable, 69, 80, 196.
Dendrites, 104.
Dervishes, 17.
Desatir, 3, 45, 46, 119, 124, 125, 315, 316, 336.
Deva, and Demons, 61, 123, 142, Safid—143, 119, 135, 147, —worship 159, 160, 183, 184, 185, 198, 218, 219, 222, 223, 224.
Devachan (heaven), 138, 277, 278, 309.
Devashravas, 255.
Devatâ, 337.
Devdata, 255.
Dhritarashtra, 123.
Dhyan Chohans, 79, 95, 110, 114, 123, Dhyani, 97, —Buddhas, 80.
Dian-Nisi (Assyrian), 104.
Dinkard, 76, 77, 78, 109, 119, 336, 351,
Directions, the four, 123.
Divine Ideas, 116.
Divine Powers, 120.
Dogs, symbolism of, 40, 329, 330.
Double, the Celestial, 118.
Dragon of Wisdom, 118, fiery—164.
Drashadvati (river), 255.

Drug Ahriman, 117.
Drug-nasus, 119, 147, 252, 342.
Druksh or Druga, 61, 147, 342, 346, 348.
Dualism, 11, 48, 57, 60, 61, 111, 146, 159, 169, 170, 171, 176, 186, 187, 188, 192, 193, 209, 210, 213, 262.
Dugdure, Zoroaster's mother, 93.
Duration, 76, Boundless—110.
Dwipas, 126, 130, 131, 133, 134.
Dyonisius, 104.
Dzyan, book of, see Stanzas of Dzyan.

EARTH, 95, 129, 130, 132, —Chain, 88, 89, 134.
Echod, 80.
Egg-born races, 138, 150, 198, 199.
Egg, mundane, 152,
Ego, 118, higher—178, 179, 277, 278, immortal—273.
Eka, 80, 118.
Elemental essence, 295, 296.
Elementals, 16, 296, 297, 298, 299, 300, 346, 348.
Elements, 126, 127, 128, worship of—203, 204, 212.
Eliphas Lévi, 258.
Elixir of Life, 106.
Elohim, 57, 80, 95, 107, 200.
Esam, 273, 279.
Eshwara, *see* Ishvara.
Esoteric interpretations, 68, 70.
Esoteric Knowledge, 72, 91, 97, 98, 103, 129, 140, 147, 150, 151, 152, 153, 246, 248, 272, 273, 276, 277, 280, 331, 334, 346, 347.
Eternity, 80.
Eternal Land, 126.
Ether, 130, 132, 147.
Eucharist Mass, 332.
Evil, 61, 159, causes of—310, 311.
Evolution, 84, 86, 109, 122, 137.
Exploration Society, 29.

FALL OF ANGELS, 200.
Faraziat (daily prayers) 243.
Faridun, 142, 143.
Ferdousi, 142.
Forouers, *see* Fravashi.
Fire, 11, 12, 13, 14, 29, 49, 67, 68, 79, 166, Sons of—138, Voice of—51, 86, 179, Neryosang—94, Son of—138, five kinds of—148, 265, mystic, —148, 151, —worship, 11, 50, 85, 166, 254, —worshippers, 169, 179, 194, 202 —the Guru, 178, 180, 184, Divine—203, 207, 215, 216, 254, 255 —wor-

ship among different nations, 256, 257, 258, reason for reverence for—259, constitution of—259, 260, cosmogenesis of—260, 261, philosophy of—262, 263, Oracles of Zoroaster on—263, 264, 265, Land of,—in Yasna, 265, anthropogenesis of—266, Adar Gushaspa,—Adar Khurdat or Frohba,—Adar Meher Burzin—267, 268, 269—Son of Ahuramazda—258, 265, 268, 270, 271, 272, prayers to—273, blessings conferred by—275, 279, allegory of cooking food, 277, 279, 318, 342, 343.
Fish, see Kara Fish.
Flood, 137.
Flowers and fruits, offerings of, 345.
Fohat, 84, 122, 123, 266.
Forbidden Fruit, 107.
Forces (centripetal and centrifugal), 69, 110.
Fravashi, 73, 74, 116, 117 118, 146, 147, 160, 161, 166, 178, 190, 192, 200, 201, 204, 209, 217, 230, 231, 239, 349.
Fravardin, 120, —Yashta, 157.
Fradadhafsha (Kershvara), 129, 131, 133.
Freemasons, 164.
Free-will, 172, 187,

GABRIEL, 190, 192.
Gah, 55, 56.
Gahambars, seasonal periods, 30, 265, 266.
Gaiyahe, Gaiyomard or Gaiyomarethan, 94, 95, 96, 97, 135, 141, 142, 146, 149, 150, 190, 192, 198, 199, 238.
Gao-chithra, 89.
Garonemana, heaven, 319.
Gâthâs, 56, 58, 60—quotation from, 70, 120, 146, 163, 212, 213, 335.
Gautama, 157.
Gâyatri, 251.
Germ in the Root, 78, 110.
Geush, 88, 94, 101, 128, 238.
Ghebers, 208.
Giants, 141,
Gnosis, 105.
Gnostic, 91, 105, 117.
Gobi Desert, 4.
Gochihar, 122.
God, 82, 172, 182, 183, 194, 195, 197, 198, 203, 209, —geometrizes 82, union with—172, 182, 316.
Gods and goddesses, 33 crores—119, 120, 204, 337, language of the—341.

Gokard tree, Gokerena, 91, 92, 102, 105, 107, 148.
Golden Egg, 111.
Gospel, St. John's, 85.
Great Breath, see Breath.
Great Renunciation, 352.
Greek, philosophy, 166, —philosophers, 2, 3, 65, —historians, 166.
Greeks, 63, 64, 212.
Guardian angels, four kind of, 190, 204, 334.
Guardians of the four quarters, 123.
Guru, 178, 271, 275, 276, 318, 319.
Gustasp, 3, 45, 46, 49, 50, 156, 157,

HADHANAEPATAM, 279.
Hadhayosh (bull), 134.
Hadokhta Nosk, 48, 161.
Hafta Keshvara Zamin, 126, 129.
Haiks, Haig, 92.
Hamkârs, co-operators with Ameshaspentas, 336, 337.
Haoma, 102, 103, 104, 240, 250, 253, 329,—ceremony, 332, White—148, 105, 106, 107, Para—17, 44, 108, —Yagna 86, 91, 92, 93, 98, 99, 100, 101, —Yashta 101.
Haptan Yashta, 102.
Haptoring, 122, 123.
Hari Purana, 92.
Hazrat Âzar Kaivan, see Âzar Kaivan.
Heart, 83, 243,d 243, 316, 320.
Heaven, 47, 152, 172, 191, 214, 319,
Hecate, 218.
Hell, 22, 47, 152, 172, 191, 214.
Hellenic tree of life 104.
Herakleitos, 166.
Hermaphrodite, 95, 105, 139, 199.
Hermetic philosophy, 258, 259, 271.
Hermippus 2, 52, 65.
Hierarchies, 79, 95, 117, 118, 190, 218, 334 336, 337.
Hieroglyphics 65,
Higher, Ego 205,—Self, 271.
Hippocrates, 50.
Hippopotamus (mysterious) 142, 143.
Hiranya Garbha, 111.
Holy Ghost, 258.
Hom(angel),119,337,-(tree), see Haoma
Honovar, see Ahunavairya.
Hormazd (vide Ahura-Mazda).
Horvdad, 115.
Hoshbam 116, 312, 313.
Hotri, 86, 87, 276.
Humata, Hukhata, Hvrashta, Purity of Thought, Word and Deed, see Manashni, Gavashni, Kunashni.
Hurvatat, 115.

Hushedar, 133.
Husheng, (king) 142.
Hvara, the universal sun, 112.
Hymns, 65.
Hypnotism, *see* Mesmerism.
Hystaspes, *see* Gushtasp.

IAMBLICHUS, 222.
Iblish, 142.
Idá Nâdi, 246.
Ideas, 217.
Ideation, Divine, 171, 172, 231.
Idolatry, 202, 209.
Ijasne, *see* Yasna.
Ilahi Religion, 66.
Immortal Benefactors, 114.
Imperishable Land, 153.
Indo-Aryans, 182, 183.
Indra, 102, 240, 254, 255.
Inductive method, 109.
Initiates, 14, 65, 67, 106.
Inner Immortal Man, 118.
Intelligences, Divine, 120, 121, 209, orders of,—216, 335, 338.
Irân, 182, —Voj, 153, *see* Airyanam Vaejo.
Irânians, 182, 210.
Iráno-Aryans, 182.
Ishwara, 85, 112.
Isis Unveiled, 14, 67.

JAMBU DWIPA, 130, 133, *see* Dwipas.
Jam-i-kaikhosru, 323.
Jamsheed, 142.
Jaina sect, 157.
Javidan-e-Khirad, 30, 142.
Jehova, 57, 62.
Jennings, Hargrave, 11, 50, 51.
Jesus, 17, 184, 257.
Jews, 47, 211.
Jothi, 86, *see* also Zaota.
Jivam, 273, 334.
Jivas, 95, 96, 267.
Jivatma, 271.
Jnâna-Yoga, 103.
Jnán Nadi, 246.
Jupiter, 122.

KABBALLAH, 5, 9, 11, 39, 70, 91.
Kabirim, 5.
Kalanki Avtar, 30.
Kalob, Kalbud (body), 73, 314.
Kali Yuga, *see* Yuga.
Kalki or Kalanki Avatar, 30, 206.
Kâma Rupa, —of the Kosmos, 113, —of Man 138.

Kâma, 72, 74, 236.
Kâmaloka, 138, 274.
Kâmdhuka, 279.
Kâmic principle, 218.
Kaianian, (race,) 144.
Kaikobad, 143.
Kara fish, or Karo Masyo, 91, 92, 93.
Karanopadhi, 274.
Karma, 102, 103,—Yoga, 103, 333.
Karmic—Gods, 123,—Law 106, 123, 149, 152, 193, 102, 129, 132, 133.
Kasava (lake), 91, 191.
Keherpam (body), 72, 314.
Kerdar, 23, 152, 161, 334.
Kershvaras, 126, 129, 130, 131, 132, 140, 141, 143, 150, 189, 261.
Kevan (planet), 122.
Khale-badan 323, 325.
Khetvadath, 5, 6, 152, 320, 333.
Khordad Ameshaspenta, 115.
Khordeh-avasta, 56.
Khorshed Niyayesh, 97, 112, 228, 229, 230.
Khureh, *see* Aura.
Khvanirath, 140, 141, 152, 189.
Kirmari, 67, 167.
Kosmos, 113.
Kriya-Kanda, 103.
Kumara Egos, 116, 267.
Kundalini, 108.
Kushika, 255.
Kûsti, 8, 24, 25, 248, 320.
Kutastha, 196.

LAMPS, over-burning, 256.
Land—of the Gods, 125, thirty-three kinds of—129.
Language of Scriptures, 341, 342.
Laya centre, 89.
Lethe, 172.
Libra, constellation of—150.
Light, eternal—111, 215, supra-mundane— 215, 221, marvels of— 340.
Linga-sharira, 72, 95
Lizard, 91.
Logoi, 146, the three—196, 197.
Logos, 80, Unmanifested— 111, 112, 115, Creative— 112, Third—115, 117, 170, 172, 186, 190, 197, 234, 238, Universal—195, 196 (*infra*).
Loka-Chakshuh (sun), 238.
Lords--of Heaven, 120,--of Karma, 123.
Lunar—chain, 89,—god, 95, —monads, 89, —spirits, 95.

MAGI, Magianism, 1, 3, 4, 7, 10, 12, 36, 37, 46, 48, 51, 158, 167, 188, 210, 213, 259, 333.

INDEX.

Magic, 15, 66, 159, 333, Black—222, 356,—staff wand, 18, 69, 70.
Magnetic Aura, 301.
Magnetism, 10.
Magus, 10, 213.
Mâh Gaochitra, 88, 95.
Maha-Abâd, 124.
Maha Loka, 96, 191.
Maha Pralaya, 124.
Maharajas, the four, 123.
Mahat, 84, 115, 121, 216.
Mahâtmas, 190, 312, 321, 320.
Maheshwar, 86.
Mahomed, 10.
Maitree Buddha, 91.
Makashefat-i-Kaivani, 240.
Man, 83, 86, building of,—96, apo, ancesters of—96, the first—136, the fall of—136 (*vide infra*),—principles of,—42, 97, 201, sinless or karmaless—138, evolution of physical—138—and personality, 138, monster—141, 149, —plant, 150, 151, —and monkey, 151,—a trinity 171, —a free agent, 172, 182, 187, 198, —temple of God, 201, —union with God, 202, 266, —product of three fires, 269, —and his growth, 312, 315, principles of— 334.
Manas, 72, 107, 266, union of—with Budhi, 267, 269, 274, lower— 274, 277, 278, 315.
Manashni, Gavashni, Kunashni, 14, 15, 44, 171, 172, 173, 176, 207, 209, 273, 319, 339.
Manasputras, 150, 151, 200.
Mansarover, 47.
Manthra or Mantra, 19, 66, 84, 86, —spenta, 86, 87, 117, 120, 202, 307, 308.
Manu, 116.
Manvantara, 82, 110, 116, 124, 143, 191, 261, 262, 267, 274.
Mars, 122.
Mashyo-Mashyoi, 94, 95, 134, 139, 140, 150, 151, 190, 199.
Masonry, 69.
Mathan, the last of the Magi, 34.
Mathras or Mantras, 309, 334, 338, 339, 340, 341.
Matro-Matroyayo, *see* Mashyo-Mashyoi.
Matter, states of, 127.
Maunghahem-go-chithram, 95, 128.
Maya, 111, 148.
Mazda—Ahura-Mazda—Ahura, 111, 112, 159.
Mazda, 56, 57.
Mazdaism, 56, 57.

Mazdaism or Mazdeiasni Religion, 115, 146, 153, 167, 210, 351.
Mazdean Initiates, 106, —morals, 162, 167, 168.
Medha, 126.
Mediator, 182, 202.
Meher Niyaish, 233.
Meher Yazata, *see* Mithra.
Memphis, 166.
Mercury, 122, 233, 234.
Meru-danda, 246, 249.
Meru, mount, 125, 146.
Messiah, 91, 191.
Mesmerism, 304, 327, 341.
Metals—creation of 95.
Microbes, 251, 252.
Microcosm, 247.
Milk of white-haired goat, 139.
Milky-way, 82.
Millenium, 150, 152.
Mind, Universal—115, good and evil —159, 172, 216, human—237, 319.
Mithra, 113, 133, 161, 163, 164, birth-day of—165, 185, 216, 233, 238, (*vide infra*),—239, 255, 301, 320, 334.
Mitra, 183.
Mithraic rites, 164, 165.
Mobeds, 1, 7, 8, 18, 21, 22, 29, 70, 72, 98, 103.
Moksha, 9, 248.
Molecules, 127.
Monad, Monads, 74, 89, 96, 138, 267.
Monadic essence, 330, 331.
Moon, 89, 95, Lords of—96, 106, 124, 125, 128, 129, 234, 237.
Monism, 315.
Monotheism, 48, 57, 146, 193, 208, 315.
Montezima, 114.
Months, 120.
Moses, 10, 70, 256.
Motion, Eternal, 110.
Musarus Oannës, 92.
Mushpar, 122.
Mysteries, 5, 12, 15, 37, 65, 67, 70, 95, 106.

NADIS, 246, 247, 248.
Nairyosang Dhaval, 13, 34, 94, 130, 190, 192, 199, 269, 334.
Nakshatras, 124.
Narayan, 112.
Nature-spirits, *see* Elementals.
Nazars, 4.
Neo-Platonist, 105.
Niagaras, 305.
Nirang, 25, 26.
Nirmankayas, 314.

INDEX. 359

Nirukta, 116.
Nirvana, 9, 138, 314, 351.
Nityakarma, 243.
Noah, 137.
Non-reality, 61.
Nosks, 52, 53, 54, 55, 115, 163, 165, 166.
Numbers, 339.

OANNES (Man-fish) 90—93.
Obsession, 223, 224, 225.
Occult physiology, 249.
Occult science, 12, 16.
Ocean (of Space), 102, 103, 130, 143, 147.
Odakoh (Man-fish), 92.
Od, Odic force and Odyle, 301.
Old Testament, 57, 146.
Omar, 2.
OM, *see* AUM.
ONE, 112.
Oracles of Zoroaster, 85, 122, 217, 218, 219, 263, 270.
Ormazd (*vide* Ahura-Mazda).
Ox, the mysterious, 143.

PADAN or PENOM, 257.
Pahalvi, 9, 52, 55.
Pairikas, 252.
Pamirs, 182.
Pantheism, 188, 209.
Para-Haoma, 108.
Parabrahman, 80, 85, 111, 115, 145.
Paramatma, 126.
Parmenides, 167.
Parsis, 32, 49, 53, 167, 175, 193.
Parthians, 167.
Path of Wisdom, 76, 78, 110, spiritual—244.
Patit, 177.
Persians, the Ancient, 154, 155.
Peshdadian race, 142.
Pharisees, 5, 195.
Phœnix, 138.
Physics, 69.
Pingla Nadi, 246.
Pippala tree, 107.
Pitris, 89, 96, 114, 135, 159, 267.
Planes, 130, 132.
Planetary Chain, 128, 129, 130, 131.
Planetary Progenitors, 96.
Planetary spirits, 95, 124, 336.
Planets, sacred, 95, 361.
Plato, 3, 65, 167.
Plotho, 225.
Plexuses, 107.
Pliny, 52, 65.
Poles, 111.

Polytheism, 204.
Pourushaspa, 101.
Prajapatis, 267.
Pralaya, 110, 116, 125, 128, 262.
Prâna, 72.
Prayers, 20, 21, 32, 41, 162, 202, 228, 229, 232.
Preceptors, 114.
Primeval races, *see* Races.
Primum mobile, 221.
Principles of man, *see* Man.
Prithvi, 85, 114.
Priyavarta, 126, 133.
Promethean Fire, 49.
Prometheus, 13.
Psychometry, 304.
Pul-sarat, 278.
Purity, 108, 162, 178, 179, 207, 226, 319, 328.
Pushan, 254.
Putikas (soma), 98, 100.
Putra, 126.
Pyramids, 305.
Pythagoras, 65, 166.

QUANIRATH, 130, 131, 132, (*see* also Khvanirath.)

RABBIS, 47.
Race, the Chhaya or mindless—134, 138, the sweat-born, 134, 138, the second —136, first three—136, fourth—138, a-sexual—138, 139, 140, monster—141, genealogical tree of—141, the giant—141, 142, seventh—143, 150, 151.
Races, of man, 30, 36, pre-historic and adamic—94, 96, first root—96, 134, primeval—134, 138 (*infra*),—first four—of mankind 198.
Râma (Yazata) 332, 234.
Rain, 147.
Rashnu, 334.
Ratu, 104, 126.
Râvana, 74.
Reality, 61.
Recording Angels, 300, 301.
Redeemer, 91, 258.
Reincarnating Egos, 116, 147, 200, 267.
Reincarnation, 220, 329, 330,—in animals, 330, 331.
Religion, 165, growth of—242, 283, 284, exoteric and esoteric—315, 317, 318.
Renovation and Resurrection, 78, 331.
Rig Veda, 129, 130, 254, 183, 208, 209, 343.

INDEX.

Rishis, 10.
Rivas plant, 139, 141, 190, 199.
Rootless Root, 110.
Rosicrucians, 51, 65, 164, 258, 259,
Rounds, 89, 96, 149, 267.
Rudras, 118, 254.
Rupa, 85.
Rustom, 143.

SABAISM, 51, 212.
Sacrifice, 333, 334 —to Gods, 343, 344, 345, the Great— 351, 352,.Law of— 351, 352.
Safid Deva, 143.
Sahasrara (chakra), 108, 247,
Saktis, 136.
Sakya Muni, 10.
Sandya 150.
Sanitation, code of—see Vendidad.
Sankhya philosophy, 157.
Saokant (mount), 239, 246, 249.
Sapta (seven), 118.
Sarasaok (bull), 132, 134, 141.
Sarasvati, 86, 315.
Sarcostemma, 100.
Sarosh Hadokhta Yasta, 87.
Sat, 111, 112.
Satan, *see* Angromainyush and Ahriman.
Saturn, 122.
Satves (planet), 122, 123.
Savah (Kershvara), 129, 131, 132.
Saviour, 91, 200, 201, 205, 206.
Savitar, 254.
Science of the Stars, 124, physical and spiritual,—283, 284, ancient and modern,—16.
Secret Doctrine, The, 45, 46, 88, 93, 95, 106, 107, 109, 128, 261, 262
Secret Recorder, 300.
Selections from Dastur Zad-Sparam, 95.
Senses, 174, growth of the—320.
Sephirothal tree, 104.
Sephiroths, 79.
Septenary—archangels, 189.
Septenary constitution of man 71, 72, 75, 201, 314 —of earth, 129.
Serapis-worship, 163, 164.
Serpent, 107.
Seven (number) 140, 146,—years age 152, 308.
Seven principles of Man, The—75, of kosmos, 113, 269, 313.
Sexes, 150, 191.
Shabda-Brahman, 85, 113, 114, 287.
Shah Nameh, 134, 141, 143.
Shamballah, 47.
Shayast-la-Shayast, 178, 334.

Shiroza, 55, 56, 102,
Shiva, 187, 206.
Simon Magus, 105, 262.
Simorgh-Anke, 142, 143.
Sin, 176, 177.
Sinai, mount, 10.
Solar system, 113.
Solomon, 152.
Soma, 17,—Yagna, 98, 99, 100, 106, 107, 250, 86, 332.
Sons of the Fish, 93.
Sophia mythus, 146.
Sorcery, *see* Magic.
Soshios,   ⎫ 5, 60, 91, 133, 152, 153, 191,
Soshyans,   ⎬ immaculate conception
Soshyant,   ⎭ of,—191, 192, 206, 351.
Soul, creation of the—199, 200, 214, 219, 225, 226, evolution of the—236, 269, 270.
Sound, 85, 86, 113, 115, 286, 287, effects of—287, 289, phenomena of—293, 294, 305, 306, 340, 341.
Space, Divine, 115, 149.
Spendarmad, 94, 115, 120.
Spenta-Armaiti, 44,
Spenta-Mainyus, 42, 61, 93, 155, 187. 188, 219.
Spiritualists, 10.
Sravah (the Ameshaspentas) 114, 121.
Sravara (serpent), 101.
Srosh-yazata, 22, 68, 178, 179, 190. 204, 205, 206, 334.
St. Michael Ferour of Christ, 118.
Stanzas of Dzyan, 77, 96, 110, 131, 149, 198, 262, 266.
Stars, 124, 216.
Sthula Sharira, 72, 73.
Sudra, 24.
Sufi mysticism, 322.
Sufis, 17, 108.
Sun, 50, 51, 69, Spiritual,—79, 82, Central—79, 112, 165, 83, 133, 150, Universal—111, 112, 113, 79, 175, 176, 180, 215, worship,—203, 228, 234, 237, 235, 250, 252.
Surya, 112, 113 —Narayan, 235.
Suryacharya, 46.
Sushumna Nadi, 246, 247.
Sutras, 99.
Sveta Dwipa, 125.
Swara, 85, 86.
Swastika, 69.
Sweat-born, 94, 138.
Sword of Knowledge, 108.
Symbols, 54, 68, 99, 81, 82.

TAHMURAS or TAKHMORUP, 134, 142.

INDEX. 361

Tai, 70.
Talisman, 25.
Tamus, 88.
Tanu, 72, 73.
Tanvas (body), 314.
Tattvas, 85, 86, 113, 114.
Tau, Egyptian, 69, 70.
Tejas, 301.
Ten (number), 120.
Tevishi, 72, 74.
Theism, 212.
Theosophical Society, 64, second object of the—242, 243, 321.
Theosophy, 67, 146, 241, 280.
Thirty-three divine agencies, 337.
Thought, 171, 172, 284, 285, 286, 295, 296,—elementals 296, 297, good 297, evil—298,—control, 299,—as guardian angels 300, (vide infra), opinion of scientists on,—303 photographs of—303, 304, creative power of,—305, 306, 311.
Thrætaona, 101.
Thrita, 101.
Time, 76, 79, 80, 81, 110, 241.
Tir, Tistriya, and Tishtar, 44, 102, 122, 123, 239, 240.
Tree, 102, 125, in human body, 149.
Treta Yuga, see Yuga.
Tridas (thirty), 118.
Trinity, 91, 171, 197, 204, 217, 258.
Tripitikas, 10.
Tur, 143.
Tvashtar, 255.

UDRA (water-dog), 332, 330, 331.
Universal mind, 115, 121, Logos, 190.
Universe, 69, (Plato's definition), 107.
UNKNOWABLE, The, 80, 112.
Upanishads, 201.
Upara-Tatu, Antediluvian King, 92.
Upkosala, 276.
Urvan, 72, 74.
Urvatâd Nara, 126.
Urvazist, see Fire.
Ushas (the Dawn), 116.
Ushidarina, 10.
Ushtana, 72.
Ustavaiti Gâthâ, 67, 68.

VACH, 20, 86, 87.
Vahram (planet), 122.
Vahram, see Fire, also Atash-Behram.
Vaishvanara, 269.
Vaivashvata Manu, see Manu.
Vaivasvata—136, 137, 267, 358.

Vaiyâm, 232.
Vanand or Vanant, (planet), 122, 123, 293, 240.
Vara of Yama, 97, 151, 153, 200.
Varuna, 183, 254.
Vasus, 118.
Vayu, 42, 43, 85, 114, 183, 232, 241.
Vazist, see Fire.
Vedanta, 201.
Vedas, Vedism, 9, 45, 48, 49, 50, 63, 65, 66, 92, 98, 201, 254.
Vemis, 122.
Vendidad, 9, 54, 55, 56, 66, 96, 102, 110, 121, 125, 136, 173, 174, 329, 331.
Vesta, 256, 257.
Vestal Virgins, 13, 256.
Vidadhafsha (Kershvara), 129,131,133.
Virgin, 191.
Virudhaka, Virupaksha, &c., Guardians of the four quarters, 123.
Vishistadwaitism, 48.
Vishnu, 92, 125, 187, 206, 254.
Vishnu Purana, 124, 125, 133.
Vispa Humata (prayer), 281.
Visparad, 55.
Vispatanarvi, 191.
Vistasp, 2, 3, 4, 156, 157, 350.
Vistasp Nosk, 55.
Visvamitra, 92, 255.
Vivañhao or Vivañhat, 43, 101, the son of—136.
Voice Figures, 85, 340.
Voice of the Fire, see Fire.
Voice of the Silence, 244, 314.
Vohufryan, see Fire.
Vohumano, 61, 84, 104, 115, 119, 121, 193, 262, 334.
Vourubarshti (Kershvara), 129, 131, 132, 133.
Vourukash sea, 93.
Vouruzarshti (Kershvara), 129, 131, 132, 133.
Vriddhi (religious progress), 315.

WALRUS, (water dog,) 329, 330.
Wand, Magic, see Magic Wand.
Warrior Fravashis, 147.
Watchers, 114.
Water, 50, 51, 93, 147, 148.
Waters of Space, 130.
White Island, 126, —Lodge, 318.
Winds, four kinds of, 123.
Wine, 347.
Winged Oak of Pherecydes, 104.
Wisdom, 107.
Wisdom-Religion, 146, 241.
Witoba, 176.

46

Word of power, 19, 20, the,—83, 113, 114, 172, made flesh 86, 178, effect of—306, 307, 309, 339.
World periods, 137,—guides, 217, Chaldean divisions of—221.

XENOPHANES, 167.
Xerxes, 55, 256.

YAGNA, 103, 133, 343, 352.
Yama and Yami, 151.
Yama, *See* Yima.
Yanhe Hatam, 56.
Yashka, 116.
Yashta, 55, 56, 66.
Yasna, 18, 55, 56, 66, 70, 71, 101, 107, 329, 332, 333, 343, 351, 352.
Yatha Ahu Vairio, 56.
Yatus, 252.
Yazata, 15, 17, 112, 119, 120, 134, 178, 190, 209, 239, 334, 335, 336, 338, invocation of,—342, 343, 349.
Yggdrasil (tree), 104.
Yima, 43, 44, 47, 96, 101, 136, 137, Yima's *vara*, 137, 153, 191, 198, 200, 241.
Yoga, 9, 105, 152, 315, 316, 328, path of,—350.
Yoga-Vidya (occult science), 108, 246, 275.
Yogi, 10, 14, 105, 106, 229, 312, 317.
Yozdathraigar, 10, 27, 316.
Yuga, Kali, 206, Treta, 352.

ZAD SPARAM, Dastur, 95, 96, Selections of—190.

Zaman, 77.
Zampun (tree), 104.
Zamyad yashta, 114, 161.
Zaota, 86, 276.
Zarathushtrotum, 96, spiritual chief of Khvanirath, 133, 136, 138.
Zarathushtra, ethics of—154, 169, 156, 157, 158, 159, 163, Dialogues of—167, age of—184, mission of—185, a sermon of—185, further, discourses of—192, 208, 208, 212, line of—212, 213—and Chandragas, 302, 303, Greeks and Romans on —64.
Zaratushta, Zaradusht or Zoroaster, 1, 2, 3, 4, 16, 19, 29, 30, 37, 43, 44, 45, 46, 49, 56, 57, 63, 64, Oracles of,—85, Spitaman, 86, 126, 92, 93, 96, 97, 101, Original—125, 126, Son of,—133.
Zaravanist, 80.
Zaredastafshar, 205.
Zend-avesta, see Avesta.
Zenzar, 39, 45, 52, 163.
Zeruana, 49.
Zi, Jiva or Life, 104.
Zodiac, 88, 112, 124.
Zones, 130.
Zoroastrianism, 16, 35, 63, 64, esoteric—11, 63, spread of—165, philosophy of—165 science, 166, 167, 168, Profession of faith in—166, 193, 208, Chaldean and Greek—212, 227,—is non-sectarian, 349.
Zouhak, 101, 142.
Zravan, Zeroane, 77, 86, 113, 111.
Zravane-akarne, 76, 77, 78, 79, 80, 82 110, 111, 170, 145, 194, 196, 197, 241 263.
Zravane Drogho-khadhaté, 76, 77, 80, 110.

ERRATA.

Page	Line	Incorrect	Correct.
1	22	name	home.
3	ft. nt. 11	Indian	an Indian.
4	ft. nt. 3	Heirophant	Hierophant.
6	19, 25	Andishan	Ardeshar.
7	ft. nt. 4	Zeremiah	Jeremiah.
9	15	Koth	Roth.
13	26	thousand	the Thousand.
16	9	bear	hear.
16	13	Hackel	Haeckel.
16	27	Sorveral	Several.
17	13	Darvishes	Dervishes.
18	25	bidding	budding.
25	15	Confideracy	Confederacy.
27	4	to light	to bring to light.
31	33	common sense	the common sense.
35	5	always	at once.
35	15	Zoroastrianism	about Zoroastrianism.
35	16	Parsiism	Parsism.
36	ft. nt. 5	his	its.
37	ft. nt. 34	Appolonius	Apollonius.
45	31	soucrce	source.
46	8	Parsiism	Parsism.
47	5	with	with him.
47	15	owe	owe to.
49	7	form	from.
51	4	advances	advanced.
68	31	1889	1879.
86 ; 87	25 ; 11, 20	weild	wield.
90	4	words	word.
92	24	Appllodorus	Appollodorus.
93	29	Oannës	Oannës is.
96	30	Now Zarathushtra comes	Now comes Zarathushtra.
96	35	ariginal	original.
260	13	merely a	a.
274	31	dinimish	diminish.
278	11	passage	one.

www.ingramcontent.com/pod-product-compliance
Lightning Source LLC
Chambersburg PA
CBHW032025220426
43664CB00006B/366